THE FABER BOOK OF UTOPIAS

THE FABER BOOK OF
UTOPIAS

EDITED BY

John Carey

faber and faber

First published in 1999
by Faber and Faber Limited
3 Queen Square London WCIN 3AU

Phototypeset by Intype, London
Printed in England by Clays Ltd, St Ives plc

A CIP record for this book
is available from the British Library

ISBN 0–571–19785–X (cased)
0–571–19790–6 (pbk)

2 4 6 8 10 9 7 5 3 1

Contents

CONTENTS

[vii]

CONTENTS

Introduction

Utopia means *nowhere* or *no-place*. It has often been taken to mean *good place*, through confusion of its first syllable with the Greek *eu* as in *euphemism* or *eulogy*. As a result of this mix-up, another word *dystopia* has been invented, to mean *bad place*. But, strictly speaking, imaginary good places and imaginary bad places are all utopias, or nowheres. Both are represented in this book. To reject the useful word *dystopia* just because it arose from a misunderstanding would, though, be pedantic and self-defeating, and in the following pages I have used it freely. I have generally reserved *utopia* for imaginary good places or for places which (like the Utopia of Sir Thomas More, who made the word up) resist being classified as either good or bad.

So this is a book of nowheres. But it is not every nowhere that can call itself a utopia. Many imaginary places lie outside utopia's boundaries. To count as a utopia, an imaginary place must be an expression of desire. To count as a dystopia, it must be an expression of fear. As well as being a book of nowheres, then, this is a collection of humanity's desires and fears as recorded over the past two thousand years and more. Because they grow from desire and fear, utopias cry out for our sympathy and attention, however impractical or unlikely they may appear. Anyone who is capable of love must at some time have wanted the world to be a better place, for we all want our loved ones to live free of suffering, injustice and heartbreak. Those who construct utopias build on that universal human longing. What they build may, however, carry within it its own potential for crushing or limiting human life.

This is the dilemma that confronts all utopian projects. They aim at a new world, but must destroy the old. Their imaginative excitement comes from the recognition that everything inside our heads, and much outside, are human constructs and can be changed. But how and what to change is endlessly controversial. For this reason the utopia is the most divisive of literary forms. Its very name generates divisiveness. To some, 'utopian' means 'hopelessly impractical'. Others insist that without the capacity to formulate utopias human progress would be inconceivable. The divisiveness of the form is illustrated, too, by the development of dystopias. For a dystopia is merely a utopia from another point of view. Orwell's Big Brother or the directors of Huxley's Brave New World (pp. 432, 447) are utopians in their own eyes. With many utopias (More's, Swift's, most of H. G. Wells's) you cannot be sure whether their authors regard them as utopias or dystopias. They divide against themselves. Ultimately it is the divisiveness of utopias that ensures their vitality. They reveal intractable divisions within their cultures – and within us. In this introduction I shall try to identify some of these divisions and the topics that engender them.

The first is the human race and its composition. The aim of all utopias, to a greater or lesser extent, is to eliminate real people. Even if it is not a conscious aim, it is an inevitable result of their good intentions. In a utopia real people cannot exist, for the very obvious reason that real people are what constitute the world that we know, and it is that world that every utopia is designed to replace. Though this fact is obvious, it is one that many writers of utopias are reluctant to acknowledge. For if real people cannot live in utopias, then the utopian effort to design an ideal commonwealth in which human beings can lead happier lives is evidently imperilled.

However (and this is the point over which opinion divides) to aim to eliminate real people may not be as bad as it sounds – may not, indeed, be bad at all. When we consider the atrocities that real people have committed within our own century alone, it must occur to us that there are some human types – tyrants, torturers, terrorists – that could, with advantage, disappear. The real people eliminated from utopias generally include such noxious specimens. Readers of this book will notice that visitors to utopias are often informed that criminals of every description have been made obsolete. That has undeniable attractions, however keen we may be on preserving the rich and varied tapestry of human life. It is true that many utopias also exclude lawyers (the Digger, Gerrard Winstanley, recommends that they should be executed – see p. 68). But even this might arouse less widespread indignation than those within the legal profession would like to think.

The people who are admitted to live in utopias differ from real people in certain standard ways. They are often represented as having vanquished selfishness, an achievement that disposes of many of the real world's uglier features. Tommaso Campanella's sun-worshippers (p. 61), almost wholly purged of self-love, are typical in this respect. In Louis-Sébastien Mercier's *The Year 2440*, citizens cheerfully pay far more tax than they need, out of sheer public spirit (p. 158). In the future America of Edward Bellamy's imagination, falsehood is so despised that even criminals refuse to lie to evade punishment (p. 284). It is clear that if these are human beings, then the people we have been living among all our lives belong to some other species.

Writers of utopias deal with this problem in different ways. Some defiantly advertise the fact that their utopians are not real people. Jonathan Swift, for example, substitutes talking horses for people; Ludwig Holberg, talking trees (see pp. 121 and 125). More commonly, the inventors of utopias suggest that, given certain radical adjustments, human beings could be converted into utopians without ceasing to be human. They often argue that the abolition of money or private property would improve the human character out of all recognition. But how people are to be improved enough to give up their money and private property in the first place, so that utopia can begin, remains a difficulty. H. G. Wells's novel *In the Days of the Comet* proposes an astronomical solution. A comet approaches the earth and by some mysterious magnetic means has the effect of making all earth-dwellers good and rational. Wells's book was considered improper and banned from circulating libraries, because rational behaviour, in his view, included free love. In Aldous Huxley's utopia *Island* (p. 447) people with anti-social tendencies simply take two pink pills after meals, and that cures them. The composition of the pills is not disclosed. Newman Watts's *The Man Who Did Not Sin* (p. 419) solves the problem by having Christ return to earth. But that is not an eventuality mortal planners can count on, and if it did happen it might involve unwelcome surprises for virtuous utopians.

The greatest social experiment in human history – Soviet Communism – was itself understood by its founders to be a system that could not accommodate real people and must therefore eliminate them. The 'higher' phase of Communism that will eventually dawn on a grateful world presupposes, Lenin frankly admits, a species of human being quite different from the current model. 'The present ordinary run of people' will not be able to enter the Socialist paradise. They will have been eradicated or transformed. The attentions of an armed workers' militia will aid their transformation, Lenin predicts. But there must also be an inner, spiritual change. People must become unselfish, good-hearted workaholics, labouring with no hope of personal gain (p. 265). Though Lenin – and Marx – ridiculed utopias, it is clear that this vision fits precisely (and, as events have proved, disastrously) into a utopian mould.

Lenin's recipe for turning real people into utopians includes 'swift and severe punishments', and punishment is a subject that inevitably concerns creators of utopias, since the eradication of wrong-doing is one of their prime targets. Tit-for-tat deterrents – burning off the hands of arsonists, castrating rapists, destroying an adulteress's face – have all gained utopian approval in the past and still have their adherents (pp. 120, 174, 501). At the other end of the scale, the ideal England of William Morris's *News from Nowhere* (p. 315) has no legal system or penal code. Where there is no punishment to evade and no law to triumph over, Morris believes, criminals will inevitably feel remorse for what they have done. By that time, of course, their victims may have been irreparably harmed – a consideration Morris chooses not to investigate.

A recurrent utopian worry is that criminals, whatever harm they do, and whether or not they feel remorse, are not responsible for their crimes, so should not be treated as criminals. This view is by no means modern. At the start of the nineteenth century the utopian cotton-mill owner Robert Owen was already insisting that, since character is formed by education and upbringing, it is irrational to suppose that any human being can deserve praise or blame, reward or punishment (p. 193). Oddly enough the irreproachably upright Owen is in perfect agreement here with the Marquis de Sade, whose heroic lechers frequently explain, as they whip or sodomize their victims, that they are in no sense to blame for their perversions, because they are merely following their natural inclinations (p. 168).

Since they reduce criminals to automata, these arguments can be used, however, to justify not leniency but the reverse. If criminals are indeed helplessly programmed to do harm, then perhaps it would be better to destroy them so as to safeguard the non-criminal majority – much as we destroy, if we can, harmful bacteria or malignant tumours. As H. G. Wells robustly proposes, 'People who cannot live happily and freely in the world without spoiling the lives of others are better out of it' (p. 370). The possibility of identifying a 'criminal gene' in certain humans gives this debate topical relevance. As legislation currently stands, it has been pointed out, the 'criminal gene' defence could save a convicted killer in some American states, because he would be held not responsible for his actions. But in other states the virtual certainty that he would kill again would ensure his execution.

To obtain general agreement on which course to follow in such an extremity seems impossible. Some people find the Wellsian approach shocking, others are attracted by its rationality. As we have observed, it is characteristic of utopias that they bring to the surface issues of this kind over which the human race divides, and divides in ways that seem to cut across other divisions such as class, age, gender and education. The existence of these fundamental clashes of opinion in real people is another factor that makes the construction of utopias difficult. For the uniformity requisite in utopias cannot accommodate such basic disagreements. True, some utopias (More's, for example) advertise the fact that they are tolerant of almost all opinions. But on questions such as those raised by the criminal gene and capital punishment, tolerance is of no avail. Action, one way or the other, is required, and whichever way the decision falls it will distress and alienate many people.

Punishing criminals, not punishing criminals, and exterminating criminals have all, then, been proposed as methods for turning people into utopians. Eliminating poverty and introducing universal education were also commonly put forward as reformative measures in the eighteenth and nineteenth centuries. It was assumed that the educated mind would rise above crime, and that no one would steal or kill unless driven to it by dire want. Oscar Wilde is representative of a whole school of utopian thought when he blandly asserts that 'Starvation, and not sin, is the parent of modern crime' (p. 312). Nowadays these arguments seem less convincing. That the greatest criminals are not the very poor is a matter of common observation, and more than a century of free, compulsory, universal education in the British Isles has not seriously diminished the crime-rate. Indeed, the notion that education should be designed to prevent crime meets fierce opposition in our century, as the reception of B. F. Skinner's *Walden Two* in the United States illustrates (p. 426). 'Conditioning' children to behave unselfishly and exercise self-control is held to be an abrogation of personal freedom and a distortion of the child's nature. Such protests express a trust in the innate rightness of the child that is itself deeply utopian.

The method of producing ideal citizens that has been most repeatedly advocated by utopian thinkers is the abolition of the family. Originally expounded by Plato (p. 12), this simple though drastic plan has recommended itself to a wide range of otherwise incompatible social thinkers. The Platonic idea is that the family should be completely obliterated. No child will know its parents, no parents their child. Children will be reared exclusively by state officials, the unfit and weaklings being destroyed. Later utopians sometimes modify this design. In More's Utopia children still live with their natural parents, but if the family grows too large they are sent to live with other, less prolific, families. So, as in Plato, parent–child bonding is discouraged, and the harmful effects of parental indulgence avoided. Feminist utopians have found the Platonic model attractive, partly because it frees mothers from irksome domestic tasks. In Charlotte Perkins Gilman's all-woman utopia, private homes and families have been phased out. Offspring are reared by state-appointed child-psychologists (p. 382).

Historians of child care have suggested that the high rates of infant mortality prevalent in past cultures may have been instrumental in diminishing family-feeling, and consequently making schemes such as Plato's seem less objectionable than they do now. Since parental love was likely to end in heartbreak, it was discouraged, and regarded as socially unacceptable. Accordingly infants were separated from their parents in their early and most vulnerable years, and sent to live with wet-nurses or carers. In the English upper classes, similar social habits have persisted. Children are reared by servants, and sent to boarding school at an early age, following a modified Platonic pattern. These measures tacitly, and no doubt sometimes correctly, accept that the parents are unable to bring up their own children properly. Social service departments in Britain, and some other European countries, are empowered to take children, usually of poor or violent families, into care for the same reason, and this too is an acceptance of the Platonic principle that in the last resort the state, not the mother or father, is qualified to decide what is best for the child. Except in these special cases, though, the Platonic abolition of the family now seems antipathetic to many. On the other hand, the Platonic recommendation that children considered unfit to survive should be killed is now widely accepted in Europe and America, though scientific advance allows the child's life to be terminated before rather than after birth. This might be regarded as a triumph for utopianism. But in fact it is another of the issues that utopianism brings to the fore over which people divide into irreconcilably opposed camps.

So, too, with eugenics. How to beget excellent offspring has always been a prime utopian concern, and it offers, supposing it could be made to work, an absolutely foolproof way of replacing real people with utopians. Plato gave his Rulers the duty of pairing off males and females on eugenic lines (p. 13). Tacitus's admiring account of the Germans added the refinement that intermarriage with foreigners should be avoided, so as to preserve the purity of the race (p. 16). The eugenics movement, headed by Francis Galton in the late nineteenth century, aimed to discourage degenerates and other undesirables from breeding, and to promote parenthood among healthy, intelligent people by tax concessions and maternity benefits. Sterilization of the 'unfit', proposed by H. G. Wells and other utopians, was official policy before the Second World War in Nazi Germany and some American states. Thanks to the Nazis, eugenics became a dirty word for a time after the war. But it is fast regaining ground. The promise that genetic engineering holds out for improving the human race represents the most significant scientific advance since nuclear fission. It at last brings into the sphere of the possible the production of real live utopians, disease-free, super-brainy, super-fit, of the sort that the more imaginative utopian writers have been dreaming about for centuries. Lee M. Silver's prediction (p. 513) that parents able to buy these advantages for their children will go ahead and buy them no matter what legislation is put in their way seems entirely plausible. Silver's further conclusion – that the human race will split into two incompatible species, the Gene-enriched and the impoverished, sub-standard Naturals, is equally hard to avoid. The motive-power in this revolutionary development will be simply parent–child love. That may reconcile some readers to Plato's attempt to root it out, however unappealing they may find his alternative Republic of obligatory orphans.

For the last hundred years or so, the question of eugenics has been inextricably entwined with alarm at population explosion. It was not just that the wrong people were breeding, eugenicists protested. The planet was becoming choked with humanity. Birth control became more or less standard in utopias throughout this period. The methods of enforcing it were often ingenious. John Macmillan Brown's utopians invent an electric sterilizer, armed with which globe-trotting birth-control specialists are able to sterilize the 'morally or physically diseased' world-wide. Though science has not yet caught up with Brown's imagination in this particular, he has proved an accurate prophet in other respects. He foresaw, for example, that medical science would be able to investigate the health of the embryo and alter its development (p. 374) almost a century before this became a practical possibility. Birth control is imposed in Barbara Goodwin's Aleatoria by impregnating the water supply with contraceptive drugs. Women who draw a maternity ticket are given an antidote for a one-year period (p. 497). Seething, overpopulated dystopias, of which H. G. Wells's *When the Sleeper Wakes* (1899) was among the earliest, are the other side of this coin. Wells was alert to the disastrous spread of the human race, and the destruction of animal and plant species and their habitats, long before these developments became a common concern. Other utopian writers learned from him. Their message has been largely ignored, although it was potentially the most important contribution the utopian tradition could have made to human well-being. By 2025 the world's population is set to rise to 8.6 billion. The earth has never sustained such numbers, and whether or how it can, no one knows.

The likely consequences if it cannot – nuclear war, plague, famine – have been amply investigated by dystopians, starting with Wells, who was a specialist in disaster scenarios (p. 371). His personal view, at any rate in 1901, seems to have been that the removal of the populations of Africa and Asia could do much to ease overcrowding. The 'swarms of black and brown, and dirty-white, and yellow people', who cannot keep up with the West's pace of technological advance, 'will have to go'. Quite how his chilling imperative is to be implemented, he does not say. Genocide is the most extreme of utopian methods for eliminating non-utopian types, and has a long history. More's Utopians are in favour of exterminating the Swiss, on the grounds that their savage, warlike disposition makes them unfit to survive (p. 45). Swift's Houyhnhnms, guided by perfect reason, intend to wipe out the Yahoos – that is, the human race (p. 121). Edward Bulwer Lytton's future world-rulers ruthlessly destroy rival peoples with the equivalent of intercontinental ballistic missiles which can travel six hundred miles and reduce a capital city twice the size of London to ashes (p. 260). Bulwer Lytton, writing in 1871, seems to have found this admirable. Needless to say, an alternative utopian tradition regards genocide with horror and revulsion (p. 100). But late-twentieth-century developments in the real world suggest that genocide is gaining ground as a political expedient, and that small areas of the globe will be fought over with increasing ferocity. Utopian writers of Wells's generation would feel that their fears about unchecked population growth had been proved right.

In one class of utopias, consisting of heavens, paradises and after-life elysiums, the elimination of non-utopian types is automatic. No such extremes as eugenics or genocide are needed, for only the perfect are admitted. The problem, rather, is what the perfect are to do with their time. Since all activity implies a want or lack (we walk to get where we want to; eat to appease hunger) activity seems debarred from paradise, where nothing can be wanting. Consequently utopias of this kind tend to be defined by negatives. There will be no sorrow, no night, no sea – or, in the case of Rupert Brooke's fish, no land (p. 380) – no winter, no need to work, no 'sharp and sided hail' (pp. 31, 251). Speculating how the blessed will occupy themselves has produced two brilliant anti-utopias, by Lucian and Julian Barnes (pp. 31, 483). It has also produced, from the religious-minded, much fulsome and ugly invention, culminating in Tertullian's heaven for sadists (p. 34).

Whereas most utopias reform the world, some reform the self. They suggest that if only you were to look at the world, with all its imperfections, in the right way – through the eyes of a saint, or of a mystic – you would be secluded in your personal utopia, irrespective of what was going on outside. You would realize that labouring to put things right on earth was futile, for it is in your mind that the world is transfigured – or is not. Thomas Traherne's ecstatic, childlike vision is a utopia of this kind (p. 76). So is the improved world that every drunk or junkie hopes to enter – Tennyson's Lotos-Eaters for example (p. 222), or Aldous Huxley, awestruck after taking mescaline (p. 448). The past, if lived in intensely enough, can be just such a utopia – insulated, enveloping, heart-achingly beautiful – as the ardent, sentimental memories of Joseph Conrad's Marlow reveal (p. 349). All these solitary utopians are Robinson Crusoes of the mind, inventing islands for themselves to inhabit. By comparison with normal, public-spirited utopians they can seem selfish. Or they can seem wiser. For they implicitly reject the utopian belief that happiness can be achieved through better social arrangements, more efficient machines, or improved labour-saving devices (suppositions akin to our modern belief that schoolchildren will be more intelligent if they have more computers). Back in 1856, when railway trains and the telegraph seemed the last word in modernity, John Ruskin was already ridiculing this simple-minded trust in technology (p. 246). But it is still around, as Michio Kaku's excited anticipation of a world of 'smart' buildings and lavatory-seats proves (p. 508).

Books about utopias tend to stress how they reflect historical developments. The discovery of the New World, the Age of Enlightenment, the French Revolution, the rise of science – all these brought new fashions to utopianism, as readers of this anthology will readily pick up. Less attention has been given to the set of deeply divisive topics that utopias have always tended to circle around, irrespective of period. Some of these – crime and punishment, eugenics, the role of the family – we have touched on already. But four of the most fundamental remain – nature, reason, justice and gender.

With nature, even more than with the others, the problem is that the term itself seems meaningless. That mankind should live in accord with nature, that the natural is better than the unnatural – these are utopian truisms, but they yield no meaning when inspected. Rousseau believes that, in his natural state, man lived alone, ate acorns, and had sex with every woman he came across (p. 129). Tacitus's Germans show that they live according to nature by wearing very few clothes, killing sodomites, and flogging their wives through the village if they commit adultery (p. 16). Montaigne thinks that the natives of Brazil are closer to nature than civilized Frenchmen because they fight all the time, just for the fun of it, and eat their enemies (p. 50). Hobbes asserts that man's life in a natural state is 'solitary, poor, nasty, brutish and short' (p. 71). These differing accounts of what 'natural' man was like seem to have no other basis than the writer's imagination.

Even supposing that dependable knowledge of the life-style of prehistoric man were available, and yielded a single pattern, convincing arguments for imitating it would be hard to construct. In the absence of any such pattern, opinions about what is natural to man amount to little more than wishful thinking. Countless utopians attest that man is by nature good. Voltaire, on the other hand, concludes that just as hawks naturally kill pigeons, so man is by nature 'false, cozening, faithless, ungrateful, thieving, weak, inconstant, mean-spirited, envious, greedy, drunken, miserly, ambitious, bloody, slanderous, debauched, fanatic, hypocritical, and stupid' (p. 149). Who is right? On Voltaire's side it can be said that to discover the nature of any species we observe its habits. Observing hawks, we see that they kill pigeons. Observing pigs, we see that they cannot fly. Observing man, we see that he is capable of being all the things Voltaire says. However, he is also capable of being all their opposites – true, honest, faithful, grateful, and so on. Man, it becomes apparent, has a much wider range of possible behaviours than other creatures, and none of them can be called unnatural, because the nature of a creature is defined by its behaviour. So it is as natural for man to stockpile nuclear weapons or use chemical insecticides as it is for him to protest against both these practices. Given this breadth of application, the words 'natural' and 'unnatural' become useless for praise or blame. Nothing any human being does can be unnatural to human beings. It is probably fair to say that utopian writers have been insufficiently aware of this difficulty. But what is important is that the hopes and ideals to which they give expression compel us to confront the issue.

'Reason', like 'Nature' is a standard persistently invoked by utopian writers. But what constitutes reasonable conduct is difficult to decide. Is it reasonable to believe in a Supreme Being? Some utopian advocates of Reason answer yes, others no. If Reason cannot guide us on such a momentous issue, its usefulness seems limited. More to the point, how can Reason deal with the unreasonable? Charles Fourier's utopia of gratified passions and sexual liberties (p. 208) was created in defiance of Reason and its repressive strictures. Reason, inevitably, can judge it only from a reasonable point of view. But that is obviously inappropriate. From a reasonable point of view passion has no chance. The judgement is over before it can begin, because judge and judged have no common ground. Reason judging passion is like a blind man judging pictures. To fit itself to judge passion adequately, Reason would need to embody passion, which means that it would cease to be Reason. Of course there are utopian writers – Edward Lear, D. H. Lawrence (pp. 253, 399) – who are quite aware of Reason's shortcomings. But too ready a dependence on Reason is a common utopian fault (at any rate from the viewpoint of passion and unreason). Dystopian writers such as Zamyatin and Orwell (pp. 387, 432) recognize this when they identify the suppression of sexual passion as a leading feature of tyrannical utopias.

The issue of Reason leads inevitably to the issue of Justice. To most utopians 'just' and 'reasonable' are virtual synonyms. But from a reading of utopias two different and irreconcilable concepts of justice emerge. Marx's definition of social justice is 'From each according to his ability, to each according to his needs' (p. 265). Many people would consider that entirely reasonable, indeed, right. State welfare systems, which depend on the rich contributing and the poor drawing out, assume the tacit acceptance of some such principle. But why should the rich contribute? Christianity and other major religions enjoin the virtue of charity. But no one is obliged nowadays to adopt a religious faith and, that being so, why should anyone be obliged to obey its ethical teachings? An alternative to the Marxist ideal is, simply, freedom, where everyone enjoys the rewards that his or her abilities win, perhaps with some deduction to pay for efficient policing, which inequalities in wealth will render necessary, but with no obligation to support the poor. The advantages of this arrangement were especially apparent to early-twentieth-century utopians, concerned about a soaring birth-rate and the spectre of massed paupers demanding welfare handouts. John Macmillan Brown, writing in 1903, argues that philanthropy is positively immoral since it encourages the incompetent and unprogressive to breed, and destroys the habit of providence and self-help which alone can raise them from destitution (p. 375). Edward Bellamy foresaw such reasonings, and attempted to counter them. It was mistaken, he objected, to regard some members of society as dependent and others as capable of self-support. In reality all are dependent, since all depend on mankind's past achievements (p. 288). However, it might be asked why, if everyone benefits from mankind's past achievements, the rich should pay more for that benefit than the poor? It is true that they are able to do so, but ability does not constitute an obligation, unless something like Marx's principle is accepted, and it is not easy to find clinching reasons why it should be.

The idea that all citizens should be paid the same for their labour is among the commonest of utopian doctrines. Often money is abolished in utopias, and everyone draws equal rations from the state storehouses. The heroic egalitarian Gracchus Babeuf, later guillotined for his beliefs, defended this system, contending that, if wages were not equalized, the clever and persevering would be 'given a licence to rob and despoil with impunity those less fortunately endowed with natural gifts' (p. 176). That is one way of putting it. But another way is to say that if wages are equalized the lazy will be just as well off as the hard-working, and the incompetent as the highly skilled. Babeuf thought it unfair that a watchmaker should be paid more highly than a ploughman. But Hobbes points out that the 'fair' recompense for any service or product is simply what consumers are prepared to pay for it. The idea that there is some divinely sanctioned fair price, or fair wage, is an illusion. On this issue, most people would probably take up a position somewhere on the wide spectrum between Hobbes and Babeuf, the high earners perhaps inclining towards Hobbes, the low towards Babeuf. But it is another of the utopian topics that reveals deep and irresolvable divisions in popular opinion.

The issue of gender has the air of being a more modern concern than nature, reason and justice, but in fact it has persistently engaged the attention of utopians ever since Plato. In his Republic the female Guardians undergo the same training, physical and mental, as the male. They exercise naked with the men, and fight in war. Though this appears as an elimination of sexual inequality, in fact it simply makes women conform to male standards. The potential contribution of women to the culture is purportedly recognized, but actually cancelled, since they are obliged to behave like men. Some traces of this subordination to masculine standards can be detected even among early feminists. Elizabeth Wolstenholme's theory that women would not menstruate if it were not for man's brutal treatment of women in prehistory (p. 323) betrays a loathing of menstruation ('the noisome habit'), and a desire for the 'wholesomeness and strength' of the male, which would now be considered disgracefully unfeminist. Modern feminist utopias tend to reverse Plato's prejudice, and assimilate men to women. In these utopias maleness is either excluded altogether (as it is from Gilman's Herland, p. 382), or reconstructed so as to eradicate masculinity. In Marge Piercy's *Woman on the Edge of Time*, men have breasts and suckle children (p. 475). The idea that gender-roles are socially constructed, not biologically determined, is usually thought of as an invention of twentieth-century feminism. But in utopian writing it can be traced back for almost two hundred years, as James Lawrence's *The Empire of the Nairs* illustrates (p. 181). Whether, and to what extent, masculinity and femininity are biological or cultural is a matter of ongoing dispute, and is argued over in utopianism too. In contrast with Lawrence, the Victorian philanthropist Walter Besant parades a fervent belief in the superior intelligence, authority and artistic genius of males, and the naturalness of their dominant position in Victorian society (p. 272).

An ultimate conflict in utopian ideals is between human-centred systems and systems that diminish or obliterate mankind. In this anthology these extremes are represented by the physicist John Freeman Dyson and the naturalist Richard Jefferies. Readers may like to test themselves by scanning these two pieces and deciding which future they find more attractive. Dyson envisages mankind spreading through the solar system, and perhaps eventually filling the galaxy with himself and his inventions (p. 468). This is a common scenario in science fiction, often accompanied by destructive warfare against space-aliens. Jefferies, on the other hand, imagines man largely dying out and the world returning to wild and beautiful greenness (p. 276). Like the other issues we have identified, this is profoundly divisive. To the green camp, the space-invader lobby seem puerile, arrogant, and ridiculously unaware of the ultimate, inevitable death of our species. To the space-invaders, the greens seem defeatist and backward. Confrontation between the two sides tends to end in blank incomprehension. At its sharpest the division is between those who assume man's God-given superiority, and those who see him as a blemish on the face of the earth. As the planet grows more overcrowded, and other species become extinct, this conflict can only intensify. If utopias are any indication, it promises to be one of the formative antagonisms of the twenty-first century.

It would be interesting to know whether greens and space-invaders would be found to disagree in predictable ways on other issues besides extra-terrestrial colonization and wildlife conservation. Do these two mind-sets represent a fundamental division in humanity that has opened up at the end of the twentieth century? It seems possible. The question of animal rights, for example, which has been a component of utopian thought since the mid-eighteenth century (see p. 139), is one where the reactions of the two groups would seem relatively easy to anticipate. Greens, it seems a safe bet, would be pro-animal, whereas space-invaders would tend to press the claims of humanity.

More difficult to anticipate would be the positions the two camps would take up on a seemingly unrelated topic such as euthanasia. This is another recurrent utopian measure, recommended as long ago as the sixteenth century (p. 39), and likely to become increasingly popular in the twenty-first. Already a do-it-yourself euthanasia machine has been developed by the Australian euthanasia campaigner Dr Philip Nitschke. It incorporates standard intravenous equipment, controlled via keystrokes on a laptop computer. The machine asks a series of questions, and the patient taps in appropriate replies. In May 1995 euthanasia became legal in Australia's Northern Territory, and four patients used Dr Nitschke's machine to terminate their lives. Since then the Australian National Senate has banned euthanasia. But it seems improbable that the demand for a painless end to life among the very old or terminally ill will be legally controllable. Instructions for building a Nitschke machine were, during the period of legalization, made available on the Internet. How our two groups, space-invaders and greens, would divide on this issue is a matter of speculation, and no doubt (as Anthony Trollope suggests, p. 269) it is a question on which one's opinions change with age. But space-invaders, convinced of the value and importance of human life, might be expected to come out against its premature termination, whereas greens, inclined to regard humanity as an encumbrance, of which the earth could well be rid, might be expected to favour it.

Considerable research and opinion-canvassing in the population at large would be needed to test the two-group hypothesis. But supposing two such opposed mind-sets did indeed prove widespread, then it might become possible, as knowledge of the human brain advances, medically to correct those with the wrong configuration. 'Wrong' in this case would, of course, mean different from the mind-set of the medical authorities. That would be an eminently utopian solution.

There is no shortage of utopias. If you tap 'utopia' into the Bodleian Library's on-line catalogue, it comes up, after prolonged clunking and whirring, with 577 titles. Lyman Tower Sargent's *British and American Utopian Literature, 1516–1985: An Annotated Chronological Bibliography* lists over 3000 items. I have found both these sources invaluable. But many of the works and authors I include appear in neither. Thomas Traherne does not, for example; nor do Tennyson's Lotos-Eaters or Kipling's law-abiding animals or Conrad's seamen or D. H. Lawrence's Etruscans. This means that I have extended the definition of utopia beyond the strictly formal, and I have done so knowingly. For the books and authors I have included seem to me evidently utopian, and if strictly formal definitions cannot include them then strictly formal definitions must be widened. Compiling this anthology has made me realize that utopianism permeates literature and life far beyond the narrow boundaries of bibliographical classification. A survey such as Bernadette Vallely's (p. 500) suggests that we all carry a utopia inside us. Utopia is where we store our hopes of happiness. Before starting this anthology, readers might like to jot down their personal utopia. Then they will be able to compare it with the dreams of humankind.

Holy Snakes

Utopias elude definition. The genre merges, at its edges, into related forms – the imaginary voyage, the earthly or heavenly paradise, the political manifesto or Constitution. But an average, middle-of-the-road utopia will include transit to some other place, remote in space or time or both, where the inhabitants are different from us, perhaps recognizably human, perhaps not, and where something can be learned about how life should be lived. If we take these as the defining factors, then the earliest surviving utopia seems to be 'The Tale of the Shipwrecked Sailor', an Ancient Egyptian poem dating from the early years of the Middle Kingdom (1940–1640 BC).

Ancient Egyptian literature remained unread for three and a half millennia. Hieroglyphs were regarded as impenetrable magic signs. The discovery that they were a practical script, used for a wide range of writings, came only in the 1820s. It now seems that fictional literature emerged in Egypt at the start of the Twelfth Dynasty, with the accession of Amenemhat I, around 1938 BC. It was an élite culture – less than one per cent of the population, it is estimated, could read – and most of its products have vanished. Some thirty-five texts survive, in whole or in part, from the Middle Kingdom. 'The Tale of the Shipwrecked Sailor' is preserved in a single papyrus manuscript, now in St Petersburg. The scribe records his own name (Ameny son of Amenyaa), and adds the abbreviation '(l.p.h.!)' ('May he live, be prosperous, and healthy!'), but the name of the Tale's author is unknown.

The situation in the poem is that a clever 'Follower', or retainer, tries to comfort his master, the 'Count', who is sailing home in despair having, apparently, failed in his mission. The Follower's Tale is meant to cheer him up, because it reveals that even divine beings, such as the gorgeous talking snake the Follower met on the paradise island, may suffer misfortune and can overcome it. Also, the holy snake laughs at worldly riches and splendour, which should hearten the Count in his misfortune. In these respects the Tale recommends stoic endurance and self-control. However the Follower seems to get carried away by his own Tale. Recounting the precious gifts the snake gave him, and the honours he received on his return home, is hardly tactful in the circumstances. In a snarling rejoinder, at the poem's end, the Count rejects the offered comfort and identifies himself as a dead duck (or goose).

The 'Mining Region' the Follower refers to is the Sinai peninsula, so the mysterious island was in the Red Sea. 'Punt', over which the snake claims sovereignty, was a semi-mythical land of riches.

A clever Follower speaks:
'May your heart be well, my Count!
Look, we have reached home,
and the mallet is taken, the mooring post driven in,
and the prow-rope has been thrown on the ground;
praises are given and God is thanked,
every man is embracing his fellow,
and our crew has come back safe,
with no loss to our expedition.
We've reached the very end of Wawat, and passed Biga!
Look, we have arrived in peace!
Our own land, we've reached it!

Listen to me, my Count!
I am free [from] exaggeration.
Wash yourself! Pour water on your hands!
So you may reply when you are addressed,
and speak to the king with self-possession,
and answer without stammering.
A man's utterance saves him.
His speech turns anger away from him.
But you do as you wish!
It is tiresome to speak to you!

I shall tell you something similar,
which happened to me myself:
I had gone to the Mining Region of the sovereign.
I had gone down to the Sea,
in a boat 120 cubits long,
40 cubits broad,
in which there were 120 sailors from the choicest of Egypt.
They looked at the sea, they looked at the land,
and their hearts were stouter than lions'.

[2]

Before it came, they could foretell a gale,
a storm before it existed;
but a gale came up while we were at sea, before we had reached
   land.
The wind rose, and made an endless howling,
and with it a swell of eight cubits.
Only the mast broke it for me.
Then the boat died.
Those in it – not one of them survived.
Then I was given up onto an island
by a wave of the sea.
With my heart as my only companion,
I spent three days alone.
I spent the nights inside
a shelter of wood, and embraced the shadows.
Then I stretched out my legs to learn what I could put in my mouth.

I found figs and grapes there, and every fine vegetable;
and there were sycamore figs there, and also ripened ones,
and melons as if cultivated;
fish were there, and also fowl:
there was nothing which was not in it.
Then I ate my fill, and put aside
what was too much for my arms.
I took a fire drill, made fire,
and made a burnt offering to the Gods.

Then I heard a noise of thunder; I thought it was a wave of the
   sea,
for the trees were splintering,
the earth shaking;
I uncovered my face and found it was a serpent coming.
There were 30 cubits of him.
His beard was bigger than two cubits,
his flesh overlaid with gold,
and his eyebrows of true lapis lazuli.
He was rearing upwards.

He opened his mouth to me, while I was prostrate in front of him.
He said to me, "Who brought you?

Who brought you, young man?
Who brought you?
If you delay in telling me
who brought you to this island,
I will make you know yourself to be ashes,
turned into invisibility!"

"You speak to me, without me hearing.
I am in front of you, and do not know myself."
Then he put me in his mouth,
took me away to his dwelling place,
and laid me down without harming me.
I was safe, with no damage done to me.

He opened his mouth to me, while I was prostrate in front of
    him.
Then he said to me: "Who brought you?
Who brought you, young man?
Who brought you to this island of the sea,
with water on all sides?"
Then I answered this to him, my arms bent in front of him.
I said to him, "It's because I was going down
to the Mining Region on a mission of the sovereign,
in a boat 120 cubits long,
40 cubits broad,
in which there were 120 sailors from the choicest of Egypt.
They looked at the sea, they looked at the land,
and their hearts were stouter than lions'.

Before it came, they could foretell a gale,
a storm before it existed;
each one of them – his heart was stouter,
his arm stronger, than his fellow's.
There was no fool among them.
And a gale came up while we were at sea, before we had reached
    land.
The wind rose, and made an endless howling,
and with it a swell of eight cubits.
Only the mast broke it for me.
Then the boat died.

Those in it – not one of them survived, except me.
And look, I am beside you.

Then I was brought to this island
by a wave of the sea."
And he said to me, "Fear not,
fear not, young man!
Do not be pale, for you have reached me!
Look, God has let you live,
and has brought you to this island of the spirit;
there is nothing which is not within it,
and it is full of every good thing.
Look, you will spend month upon month,
until you have completed four months in the interior of this island.
A ship will come from home,
with sailors in it whom you know,
and you will return home with them,
and die in your city.

How happy is he who can tell of his experience, so that the calamity
    passes!
I shall tell you something similar,
that happened on this island,
where I was with my kinsmen,
and with children amongst them.
With my offspring and my kinsmen, we were 75 serpents in all –
I shall not evoke the little daughter,
whom I had wisely brought away.

Then a star fell,
and because of it they went up in flames.
Now this happened when I wasn't with them;
they were burnt when I wasn't among them.
Then I died for them, when I found them as a single heap of corpses.
If you are brave, master your heart,
and you will fill your embrace with your children,
kiss your wife, and see your house!
This is better than anything.
You will reach home, and remain there,
amongst your kinsmen."

Stretched out prostrate was I,
and I touched the ground in front of him.

I said to him, "I shall tell your power to the sovereign.
I shall cause him to comprehend your greatness.
I shall have them bring you laudanum and malabathrum,
terebinth and balsam,
and the incense of the temple estates with which every God is
    content.
I shall tell what has happened to me, as what I have seen of your
    power.
They will thank God for you in the city
before the council of the entire land.

I shall slaughter bulls for you as a burnt offering.
I shall strangle fowls for you.
I shall have boats brought for you
laden with all the wealth of Egypt,
as is done for a God who loves mankind,
in a far land, unknown to mankind."

Then he laughed at me, at the things I had said,
which were folly to his heart.
He said to me, "Do you have much myrrh,
or all existing types of incense?
For I am the ruler of Punt;
myrrh is mine;
that malabathrum you speak of bringing
is this island's plenty.
And once it happens that you have left this place,
you will never see this island again, which will have become
    water."

Then that boat came,
as he had foretold previously.
Then I went and put myself up a tall tree,
and I recognized those inside it.
Then I went to report this,
and I found that he knew it.
Then he said to me, "Fare well,
fare well, young man,

to your house, and see your children!
Spread my renown in your city! Look, this is my due from you."

Then I prostrated myself,
my arms bent in front of him.
Then he gave me a cargo
of myrrh and malabathrum,
terebinth and balsam,
camphor, *shaasekh*-spice, and eye-paint,
tails of giraffes,
a great mound of incense,
elephant tusks,
hounds and monkeys,
apes and all good riches.

Then I loaded this onto the ship,
and it was then that I prostrated myself to thank God for him.
Then he said to me, "Look, you will arrive
within two months!
You will fill your embrace with your children.
You will grow young again at home, and be buried."
Then I went down to the shore nearby this ship.
Then I called to the expedition which was in this ship,
and I on the shore gave praises
to the lord of this island,
and those who were aboard did the same.

We then sailed northwards,
to the Residence of the sovereign,
and we reached home
in two months, exactly as he had said.
Then I entered before the sovereign,
and I presented him with this tribute
from the interior of this island.
Then he thanked God for me before the council of the entire land.
Then I was appointed as a Follower;
I was endowed with 200 persons.
Look at me, after I have reached land, and have viewed my past
   experience!
Listen to my [speech]!

[7]

Look, it is good to listen to men.'
Then he said to me, 'Don't act clever, my friend!
Who pours water [for] a goose,
when the day dawns for its slaughter on the morrow?'

So it ends, from start to finish,
as found in writing,
[as] a writing of the scribe with clever fingers,
Ameny son of Amenyaa (l.p.h.!).

Source: *The Tale of Sinuhe and Other Ancient Egyptian Poems, 1940–1640 BC,*
translated with an introduction and explanatory notes by R. B. Parkinson, Oxford
University Press, 1997.

Golden Ages and Elysiums

The myth of a long-lost Golden Age goes far back in human culture. A common feature of the myth is that the earth bore fruit without cultivation, so work was unnecessary. This has led some scholars to speculate that the Golden Age may represent a racial memory of the time when man was a hunter-gatherer, before the beginning of agriculture.

The earliest Western account is in the poem *Works and Days* by the Greek poet Hesiod, a farmer's son living on the slopes of Mount Helicon in central Greece, probably in the eighth century BC. He divides history into four ages – golden, silver, bronze and iron – of which his own age of peasant toil, strife and hunger is the last. But long ago things were different.

> In the beginning, the immortals
> 　　who have their homes on Olympos
> created the golden generation of mortal people.
> These lived in Kronos' time, when he
> 　　was king in heaven.
> They lived as if they were gods,
> 　　their hearts free from sorrow,
> by themselves, and without hard work or pain;
> 　　no miserable
> old age came their way; their hands, their feet,
> 　　did not alter.
> They took their pleasure in festivals,
> 　　and lived without troubles.
> When they died, it was as if they fell asleep.
> 　　All goods
> were theirs. The fruitful grainland
> 　　yielded its harvest to them
> of its own accord; this was great and abundant,
> 　　while they at their pleasure

> quietly looked after their works
> in the midst of good things.

Some scholars think the myth of the four ages came to Hesiod from the East – from Indian or Zoroastrian mythology.

The Roman poet Ovid included a more elaborate Golden Age, based partly on Hesiod, in his *Metamorphoses* (finished in AD 7).

The first age was golden. People kept faith and did what was right of their own accord, without compulsion, without law. Punishment and intimidation were unknown. No one read threatening decrees inscribed in brass. No suppliants cowered in fear before their judge. They lived safely, without judges. As yet no pine tree, felled on its native mountain side, had been carried down to the bright waves to visit foreign lands. People knew of no other shores than their own. Cities were not ringed with break-neck moats. There were no trumpets of straight, or horns of curved brass, no swords, no helmets. With no use for armies, nations passed the time carelessly in gentle ease. The earth herself, untouched by hoe, unwounded by ploughshares, gave all things freely; and men, content with food produced with no effort, gathered fruits from the strawberry-tree, wild strawberries from the mountains, wild cherries, blackberries that clustered on prickly brambles, and acorns that fell from Jove's spreading tree. Spring was eternal. Soft zephyrs soothed with warm breaths flowers that bloomed unsown. The untilled earth brought forth early harvests, and the fields, though never left fallow, grew white with heavy ears of wheat. Rivers flowed now with milk, now with nectar, and yellow honey trickled from the green oak.

Perfection, in myth, lies in the future as well as the past. There was a Golden Age, and there will be bliss (for some) in Elysium or Paradise or Fortunate Isles. Hesiod predicts a privileged afterlife for heroes.

> There they have their dwelling place,
>   and hearts free of sorrow
> in the islands of the blessed
>   by the deep-swirling streams of ocean,
> prospering heroes, on whom in every year
>   three times over

the fruitful grainland bestows its sweet yield.
   These live
far from the immortals, and Kronos is
   king among them.

A similar myth is preserved in Homer's *Odyssey* (probably eighth century BC). The favoured dead will be conveyed to the Elysian Fields:

where there is made the easiest life for mortals,
for there is no snow, nor much winter there, nor is there ever
rain, but always the stream of Ocean sends up breezes
of the West Wind blowing briskly for the refreshment of mortals.

Paradises, like utopias, tend to be on islands. This may be because they suggest seclusion and purity. But it has also been pointed out that the human foetus is an island. So the island-paradise may reflect man's longing for the protective fluid that once surrounded him.

Sources: Hesiod, *Works and Days*, translated by Richard Lattimore, University of Michigan Press, 1959; *The Odyssey of Homer*, translated with an introduction by Richard Lattimore, New York: Harper and Row, 1967.

Philosophers Rule

Plato's *Republic*, written about 360 BC, is the earliest surviving European utopia. It does not seem very utopian to modern readers. Plato believed in compulsion and authority. The Peloponnesian war had ended, when he was twenty-three, with the defeat of his homeland, Athens, and the victory of Sparta. The *Republic* shows his admiration for the iron discipline of the victors. Other philosophers of his day were preaching freedom. They dreamed of a past golden age of communal happiness with no government and no inequality. Zeno, founder of the Stoics, wrote a *Republic* (now lost) in which, apparently, temples, law-courts, schools and money were abolished. In place of such benign idealism, Plato proposes rigorous control.

Slaves, who were not citizens and had no civil rights, made up a third of the population of Athens at the time. In Plato's *Republic* slavery will continue, though only foreigners, not Greeks, will be slaves. There will be strict class-distinction, the three classes being Rulers, Auxiliaries (soldiers, police, government officials), and workers (tradesmen, craftsmen, farmers, etc.). The Rulers and Auxiliaries will collectively be called Guardians. To prop up the class system, everyone will be encouraged to believe a 'convenient fiction' or 'noble lie', spread by the Rulers, to the effect that the different classes are physically different. The gods have mixed gold in the composition of Rulers, silver in Auxiliaries, and iron and brass in workers. However (the 'noble lie' continues) the gods decree that if golden parents produce a child with an alloy of iron or brass they must 'without the smallest pity' thrust him out to live with workers, whereas if a working-class couple have a gold or silver child he must become a Guardian. Despite this gesture towards social mobility, Plato makes no provision for lower-class education.

There will be strict censorship, to ensure mental health. The works of Homer, and others who tell ugly, immoral tales about gods and heroes, will be banned. No one will be allowed to teach that Zeus (the top god) is responsible for evil as well as for good. Far from spreading tales of violence, writers and artists must (if possible) instil the belief that no one has ever had a quarrel with a fellow citizen, and that it would be a sin to do so. Playwrights will not be allowed to imitate low and vulgar types, only people of well-regulated character. Craftsmen who produce unseemly or licentious paintings or sculptures will be banished. This will prevent children growing up among representations of moral deformity. Poetry and art in general will be discouraged, since they are remote from reality. 'Art is a form of play, not to be taken seriously.' Poetry encourages emotions we are ashamed to give way to in real life. So poets will be excluded from Plato's well-ordered state.

Bodily health, like mental, will be vigorously encouraged. To need medical aid simply as a result of one's unhealthy life-style is disgraceful, Plato states. Medicine in his utopia will not be used to save sickly intemperate people who are likely to beget unhealthy children. They will be left to die. Doctors will actually put to death those who are incurably corrupt in mind. Medical aid will be available only to those sound in body and soul. A further incentive to keep oneself fit is that it will be considered a man's duty to defend himself against possible assailants. Law-suits for assault will not be allowed.

The life envisaged for the Guardians embodies Plato's most revolutionary social ideas. It will be tough, austere and communist. Private property and families – frequent causes of favouritism and corruption – will be banned. Male and female Guardians will not be allowed to set up house together. 'Wives are to be held in common by all; so, too, are children.' Guardians will be maintained by the state, but they will own no personal possessions. They will scorn luxuries. They will share the same dwellings and eat at common tables. Female Guardians will undergo exactly the same training, physical and mental, as male. They will exercise naked with the men, and fight in war. The finest and most intelligent Guardians will be selected for education as Rulers (a lengthy process, comprising ten years of advanced maths, followed by a five-year philosophy course). Women as well as men will be eligible as Rulers. They will constitute a true aristocracy (rule by the best), as opposed to democracy and tyranny – forms of government Plato detested.

Breeding will be strictly controlled, to produce strong, intelligent children. The Rulers will pair off male and female Guardians on eugenic lines – though, to avoid complaint by disappointed wooers, they will pretend the pairings have resulted from drawing lots. Further, in order to eliminate families, no parent will know his or her child, nor any child his or her parent.

As soon as children are born, they will be taken in charge by officers appointed for the purpose, who may be men or women or both, since offices are to be shared by both sexes. The children of the better parents [i.e. more fit to breed] they will carry to the crèche to be reared in the care of nurses living apart in a certain quarter of the city. Those of inferior parents, and any children of the rest that are born defective, will be hidden away, in some appropriate manner that must be kept secret . . .

These officers will also superintend the nursing of children. They will bring the mothers to the creche when their breasts are full, while taking every precaution that no mother shall know her own child; and if the mothers have not enough milk, they will provide wet-nurses. They will limit the time during which the mothers will suckle their children, and hand over all the hard work and sitting up at night to nurses and attendants . . .

Children should be born from parents in the prime of life . . . A woman should bear children for the commonwealth from her twentieth to her fortieth year; a man should begin to beget them when he has 'passed the racer's prime in swiftness' [a disputable phrase, meaning probably 'in his early thirties'] and continue till he is fifty-five . . .

If a man either above or below this age meddles with the begetting of children for the commonwealth, we shall hold it as an offence against divine and human law. He will be begetting for his country a child conceived in darkness and dire incontinence, whose birth, if it escape detection, will not have been sanctioned by the sacrifices and prayers offered at each marriage festival, when priests and priestesses join with the whole community in praying that the children to be born may be even better and more useful citizens than their parents.

The same law will apply to any man within the prescribed limits who touches a woman also of marriageable age when the Ruler has not paired them. We shall say that he is foisting on the commonwealth a bastard, unsanctioned by law or religion.

As soon, however, as the men and women have passed the age prescribed for producing children, we shall leave them free to form a connection with whom they will . . . after we have exhorted them to see that no child, if any be conceived, shall be brought to light, or if they cannot prevent its birth, to dispose of it on the understanding that no such child can be reared.

In this free-for-all stage of sexual life, it will obviously be tricky to avoid incest given that parents do not know their own children. Plato, however, evolves a scheme for coping with this difficulty. Men and women will regard the whole generation-group of those who are of an age to be their sons and daughters as if they were their sons and daughters, and will refrain from sex with them. Brothers and sisters in the same generation-group will not know they are related, so may commit incest. But Plato does not seem to have thought sibling-sex necessarily wrong.

Source: *The Republic of Plato*, translated with an introduction and notes by Francis MacDonald Cornford, Oxford University Press, 1941, pp. 156–8.

Pure Germans

The Roman historian Cornelius Tacitus wrote the *Germania* in AD 98. At the time Trajan's legions were still locked in battle with the Teutonic tribes. Tacitus concedes that the Romans have, indeed, been trying unsuccessfully to subdue the Germans for 210 years. His tract is more than just an account of the history and character of the German people. He contrasts the sturdy worth of the Germans, their love of freedom, their chaste marriage customs, with the effete luxury of Rome. In that respect the *Germania* is a work of political and moral exhortation.

In modern times it has become a key document of German nationalism, as Simon Schama shows, tracing its ascendancy in *Landscape and Memory* (1995). At the Reformation, German humanists urged Germans to reassume their ancient spirit, as glorified by Tacitus, and cast off Italian sensuality. The defeats of Roman legions by German tribes were celebrated. The forest, dark and perilous, became the authentic German landscape. After the First World War, German philologists, obsessed with the tribal origins of the Reich, scrutinized the *Germania* to demonstrate the historical as well as the biological basis of Aryan superiority. It was required reading in German schools and universities. Himmler and other National Socialist leaders emphasized Tacitus's testimonial to the purity of the German race.

They particularly coveted a fine manuscript of the *Germania*, a fifteenth-century copy of an eighth-century original, known as the Codex Aesinas. Inconveniently, this belonged to an Italian nobleman and was housed in his palazzo near Ancona. In 1936, when Mussolini visited Berlin, Hitler asked that the Codex should be returned to Germany. Mussolini agreed. But a storm of protest at home persuaded him to renege on his offer. In autumn 1943, after the Duce's fall, an SS detachment was despatched to the palazzo to repatriate the Codex. They smashed the house, pulverizing mosaic floors and stripping frescoes from the walls. But the manuscript was hidden in another of the family's houses nearby, and escaped them.

For myself, I accept the view that the peoples of Germany have never contaminated themselves by intermarriage with foreigners but remain

of pure blood, distinct and unlike any other nation. One result of
this is that their physical characteristics, in so far as one can gen-
eralize about such a large population, are always the same: fierce-
looking blue eyes, reddish hair, and big frames – which, however,
can exert their strength only by means of violent effort. They are less
able to endure toil or fatiguing tasks and cannot bear thirst or heat,
though their climate has inured them to cold spells and the poverty
of their soil to hunger.

The appearance of the country differs considerably in different
parts; but in general it is covered either by bristling forests or by foul
swamps. It is wetter on the side that faces Gaul, windier on the side
of Noricum and Pannonia. A good soil for cereal crops, it will not
grow fruit-trees. It is well provided with live-stock; but the animals
are mostly undersized, and even the cattle lack the handsome heads
that are their natural glory. It is the mere number of them that the
Germans take pride in; for these are the only form of wealth they
have, and are much prized. Silver and gold have been denied them –
whether as a sign of divine favour or of divine wrath, I cannot say.
Yet I would not positively assert that there are no deposits of silver
or gold in Germany, since no one has prospected for them. The
natives take less pleasure than most people do in possessing and
handling these metals; indeed, one can see in their houses silver
vessels, which have been presented to chieftains or to ambassadors
travelling abroad, put to the same everyday uses as earthenware ...

Even iron is not plentiful; this has been inferred from the sort of
weapons they have. Only a few of them use swords or large lances:
they carry spears – called *frameae* in their language – with short and
narrow blades, but so sharp and easy to handle that they can be
used, as required, either at close quarters or in long-range fighting.
Their horsemen are content with a shield and a spear; but the foot-
soldiers also rain javelins on their foes: each of them carries several,
and they hurl them to immense distances, being naked or lightly clad
in short cloaks. There is nothing ostentatious about their equipment:
only their shields are picked out in the colours of their choice. Few
have breastplates, and only one here and there a helmet of metal or
hide. Their horses are not remarkable for either beauty or speed, and
are not trained to execute various evolutions as ours are; they ride
them straight ahead, or with just a single wheel to the right, keeping
their line so well that not a man falls behind the rest. Generally

speaking, their strength lies in infantry rather than cavalry. So foot-soldiers accompany the cavalry into action, their speed of foot being such that they can easily keep up with the charging horsemen. The best men are chosen from the whole body of young warriors and placed with the cavalry in front of the main battle-line. The number of these is precisely fixed: a hundred are drawn from each district, and 'The Hundred' is the name they bear among their fellow-countrymen. Thus what was originally a mere number has come to be a title of distinction. The battle-line is made up of wedge-shaped formations. To give ground, provided that you return to the attack, is considered good tactics rather than cowardice. They bring back the bodies of the fallen even when a battle hangs in the balance. To throw away one's shield is the supreme disgrace, and the man who has thus dishonoured himself is debarred from attendance at sacrifice or assembly. Many such survivors from the battlefield have ended their shame by hanging themselves.

They choose their kings for their noble birth, their commanders for their valour. The power even of the kings is not absolute or arbitrary. The commanders rely on example rather than on the authority of their rank – on the admiration they win by showing conspicuous energy and courage and by pressing forward in front of their own troops. Capital punishment, imprisonment, even flogging, are allowed to none but the priests, and are not inflicted merely as punishments or on the commanders' orders, but as it were in obedience to the god whom the Germans believe to be present on the field of battle. They actually carry with them into the fight certain figures and emblems taken from their sacred groves. A specially powerful incitement to valour is that the squadrons and divisions are not made up at random by the mustering of chance-comers, but are each composed of men of one family or clan. Close by them, too, are their nearest and dearest, so that they can hear the shrieks of their womenfolk and the wailing of their children. These are the witnesses whom each man reverences most highly, whose praise he most desires. It is to their mothers and wives that they go to have their wounds treated, and the women are not afraid to count and compare the gashes. They also carry supplies of food to the combatants and encourage them. It stands on record that armies already wavering and on the point of collapse have been rallied by the women, pleading heroically with their men, thrusting forward their bared bosoms, and making them realize the imminent prospect of enslavement – a fate which the Germans fear more desperately for their women than for themselves. Indeed, you can secure a surer hold on these nations if you compel them to include among a consignment of hostages some girls of noble family. More than this, they believe that there resides in women an element of holiness and a gift of prophecy; and so they do not scorn to ask their advice, or lightly disregard their replies. In the reign of the emperor Vespasian we saw Veleda long honoured by many Germans as a divinity; and even earlier they showed a similar reverence for Aurinia and a number of others – a reverence untainted by servile flattery or any pretence of turning women into goddesses . . .

On matters of minor importance only the chiefs debate; on major affairs, the whole community. But even where the commons have the decision, the subject is considered in advance by the chiefs. Except in case of accident or emergency, they assemble on certain particular days, either shortly after the new moon or shortly before the full moon. These, they hold, are the most auspicious times for embarking on any enterprise. They do not reckon time by days, as we do, but by nights. All their engagements and appointments are made on this system. Night is regarded as ushering in the day. It is a drawback of their independent spirit that they do not take a summons as a command: instead of coming to a meeting all together, they waste two or three days by their unpunctuality. When the assembled crowd thinks fit, they take their seats fully armed. Silence is then commanded by the priests, who on such occasions have power to enforce obedience. Then such hearing is given to the king or state-chief as his age, rank, military distinction, or eloquence can secure – more because his advice carries weight than because he has the power to command. If a proposal displeases them, the people shout their dissent; if they approve, they clash their spears. To express approbation with their weapons is their most complimentary way of showing agreement.

The Assembly is competent also to hear criminal charges, especially those involving the risk of capital punishment. The mode of execution varies according to the offence. Traitors and deserters are hanged on trees; cowards, shirkers, and sodomites are pressed down under a wicker hurdle into the slimy mud of a bog. This distinction in the punishments is based on the idea that offenders against the state should be made a public example of, whereas deeds of shame should be buried out of men's sight . . .

On the field of battle it is a disgrace to a chief to be surpassed in courage by his followers, and to the followers not to equal the courage of their chief. And to leave a battle alive after their chief has fallen means lifelong infamy and shame. To defend and protect him, and to let him get the credit for their own acts of heroism, are the most solemn obligations of their allegiance. The chiefs fight for victory, the followers for their chief. Many noble youths, if the land of their birth is stagnating in a long period of peace and inactivity, deliberately seek out other tribes which have some war in hand. For the Germans have no taste for peace; renown is more easily won among perils, and a large body of retainers cannot be kept together except by means of violence and war. They are always making demands on the generosity of their chief, asking for a coveted war-horse or a spear stained with the blood of a defeated enemy. Their meals, for which plentiful if homely fare is provided, count in lieu of pay. The wherewithal for this openhandedness comes from war and plunder. A German is not so easily prevailed upon to plough the land and wait patiently for harvest as to challenge a foe and earn wounds for his reward. He thinks it tame and spiritless to accumulate slowly by the sweat of his brow what can be got quickly by the loss of a little blood.

When not engaged in warfare they spend a certain amount of time in hunting, but much more in idleness, thinking of nothing else but sleeping and eating. For the boldest and most warlike men have no regular employment, the care of house, home, and fields being left to the women, old men, and weaklings of the family. In thus dawdling away their time they show a strange inconsistency – at one and the same time loving indolence and hating peace . . .

The universal dress in Germany is a cloak fastened with a brooch or, failing that, a thorn. They pass whole days by the fireside wearing no garment but this. It is a mark of great wealth to wear under-garments, which are not loose like those of the Sarmatians and Parthians, but fit tightly and follow the contour of every limb. They also wear the skins of wild animals – the tribes near the river frontiers without any regard to appearance, the more distant tribes with some refinement of taste, since in their part of the country there is no finery to be bought. These latter people select animals with care, and after stripping off the hides decorate them with patches of the skin of creatures that live in the unknown seas of the outer ocean. The dress of the women differs from that of the men in two respects only: women often wear outer garments of linen ornamented with a purple pattern; and as the upper part of these is sleeveless, the whole of their arms, and indeed the parts of their breasts nearest the shoulders, are exposed.

Their marriage code, however, is strict, and no feature of their morality deserves higher praise. They are almost unique among barbarians in being content with one wife apiece – all of them, that is, except a very few who take more than one wife not to satisfy their desires but because their exalted rank brings them many pressing offers of matrimonial alliances. The dowry is brought by husband to wife, not by wife to husband. Parents and kinsmen attend and approve the gifts – not gifts chosen to please a woman's fancy or gaily deck a young bride, but oxen, a horse with its bridle, or a shield, spear, and sword. In consideration of such gifts a man gets his wife, and she in her turn brings a present of arms to her husband. This interchange of gifts typifies for them the most sacred bond of union, sanctified by mystic rites under the favour of the presiding deities of wedlock. The woman must not think that she is excluded from aspirations to manly virtues or exempt from the hazards of warfare. That is why she is reminded, in the very ceremonies which bless her marriage at its outset, that she enters her husband's home to be the partner of his toils and perils, that both in peace and in war she is to share his sufferings and adventures. That is the meaning of the team of oxen, the horse ready for its rider, and the gift of arms. On these terms she must live her life and bear her children. She is receiving something that she must hand over intact and undepreciated to her children, something for her sons' wives to receive in their turn and pass on to her grandchildren.

By such means is the virtue of their women protected, and they live uncorrupted by the temptations of public shows or the excitements of banquets. Clandestine love-letters are unknown to men and women alike. Adultery is extremely rare, considering the size of the population. A guilty wife is summarily punished by her husband. He cuts off her hair, strips her naked, and in the presence of kinsmen turns her out of his house and flogs her all through the village. They have in fact no mercy on a wife who prostitutes her chastity. Neither beauty, youth, nor wealth can find her another husband. No one in Germany finds vice amusing, or calls it 'up-to-date' to seduce and be seduced. Even better is the practice of those states in which only virgins may marry, so that a woman who has once been a bride has finished with all such hopes and aspirations. She takes one husband, just as she has one body and one life. Her thoughts must not stray beyond him or her desires survive him. And even that husband she must love not for himself, but as an embodiment of the married state. To restrict the number of children, or to kill any of those born after the heir, is considered wicked. Good morality is more effective in Germany than good laws are elsewhere.

In every home the children go naked and dirty, and develop that strength of limb and tall stature which excite our admiration. Every mother feeds her child at the breast and does not depute the task to maids or nurses. The young master is not distinguished from the slave by any pampering in his upbringing. They live together among the same flocks and on the same earthen floor, until maturity sets apart the free and the spirit of valour claims them as her own. The young men are slow to mate, and thus they reach manhood with vigour unimpaired. The girls, too, are not hurried into marriage. As old and full-grown as the men, they match their mates in age and strength, and the children inherit the robustness of their parents . . .

As soon as they wake, which is often well after sunrise, they wash, generally with warm water – as one might expect in a country where winter lasts so long. After washing they eat a meal, each man having a separate seat and table. Then they go out to attend to any business they have in hand, or, as often as not, to partake in a feast – always with their weapons about them. Drinking-bouts lasting all day and all night are not considered in any way disgraceful. The quarrels that inevitably arise over the cups are seldom settled merely by hard words, but more often by killing and wounding. Nevertheless, they often make a feast an occasion for discussing such affairs as the ending of feuds, the arrangement of marriage alliances, the adoption of chiefs, and even questions of peace or war. At no other time, they think, is the heart so open to sincere feelings or so quick to warm to noble sentiments. The Germans are not cunning or sophisticated enough to refrain from blurting out their inmost thoughts in the freedom of festive surroundings, so that every man's soul is laid completely bare. On the following day the subject is reconsidered, and thus due account is taken of both occasions. They debate when they are incapable of pretence but reserve their decision for a time when they cannot well make a mistake.

Source: Tacitus, *The Agricola and the Germania*, translated with an introduction by H. Mattingly; translation revised by S. A. Handford, Penguin, 1970.

Spartan Conditions

Plutarch's *Life of Lycurgus* has influenced utopian thought almost as much as Plato's *Republic*. But whereas Plato's ideal people are philosopher-kings, Plutarch's are soldiers. *The Life of Lycurgus* is an account of how to make a nation into a war-machine. Plutarch (who died *c.* AD 120) was a historian. However, in describing Lycurgus, the semi-mythical law-giver of ancient Sparta, he probably relied on his own imagination, as well as oral tradition.

His *Life* relates that Lycurgus seized power by a military coup, replacing the existing government with a senate of twenty-eight members. He next turned his attention to the inequality between rich and poor, and the evils of 'insolence, envy, avarice and luxury' this gave rise to. To remedy these he carried out a compulsory redistribution of land. All existing land-boundaries were cancelled, and the territory of Sparta was divided into 9000 equal lots, one for each citizen. Abolishing inequality in money and other possessions proved more difficult. But Lycurgus hit on a cunning ploy.

First he stopped the currency of gold and silver coin, and ordered that the Spartans should make use of iron money only. Then he assigned only a small value to a great quantity and weight of this iron money – so that to store the equivalent of ten silver coins you would need a whole room, and to move it would require a yoke of oxen. When this iron money became current, many kinds of injustice ceased in Sparta. For who would steal or take a bribe, who would defraud or rob, when he could not conceal his booty – when he could not gain any glory from the possession of it, nor even use the iron if he broke it in pieces? For we are told that when the iron being made into currency was hot, they dipped it in vinegar to make it brittle and unmalleable, and so unfit for any other use. In the next place, he took steps to eliminate unprofitable and superfluous arts. Even if he had not done so, they would mostly have died out anyway when the new iron money became current, because luxury goods could no longer find buyers. The iron coins were not accepted in the rest of Greece, but were ridiculed and despised, so that the Spartans had no means of purchasing foreign curiosities, and merchant ships no longer landed cargoes in their harbours. No longer were there to be found in the whole of Sparta con-men, or wandering fortune tellers, or brothel keepers, or dealers in gold and silver trinkets – because there was no money. So luxury, gradually losing the means that had cherished and supported it, died away of itself.

Another of Lycurgus's anti-luxury laws directed that the ceilings of houses should be made with no tool but the axe, and the doors with no tool but the saw. So elegant interiors became in effect illegal, and there was no temptation to put costly furniture into these rough-hewn settings. His final anti-luxury measure obliged all Spartans to eat at common tables, where all would consume the same food, appointed by law. This banished greed, self-indulgence, and *cordon bleu* catering. Fifteen people sat at each common table, and each brought, as a month's supply, a bushel of meal, 8 gallons of wine, 5lb of cheese, 2.5lb of figs, and a little money to buy meat or fish. Lycurgus aimed at tip-top physical fitness for all citizens, and evidently considered this an ideal diet. Steps were taken, too, to improve the health and genetic qualities of the children born, to weed out the deformed and weak, to toughen the young, and to direct and intensify sexual desire.

He ordered the virgins to exercise themselves in running, wrestling, and throwing quoits and darts, so that their bodies being strong and vigorous, the children afterwards produced from them might be the same, and that, fortified by this exercise, they might be able better to support the pangs of childbirth and be delivered with safety. So as to overcome the excessive tenderness and delicacy of the female sex, which are the consequences of a sheltered life, he accustomed the virgins occasionally to be seen naked, as well as the young men, and to dance and sing in their presence on certain festivals. There the girls sometimes indulged in a little raillery, directed against boys who had misbehaved themselves, and sometimes they sung the praises of boys who deserved it, so stirring up in the young men a useful emulation and love of glory. For he who was praised for his bravery and celebrated among the virgins went away perfectly happy, while their satirical glances, thrown out only in sport, were really just as cutting as serious admonitions – especially as the senate went with the other citizens to see all that happened on these occasions. As for the virgins appearing naked, there was nothing disgraceful in it, because everything was conducted with modesty, and without one indecent word or action . . . These public dances and other exercises of young naked maidens, in sight of the young men, were, moreover, incentives to marriage, and – to use Plato's expression – drew them almost as necessarily to the attractions of love as a geometrical conclusion follows from its premises. To encourage them still more, some marks of infamy were set upon those young men who remained unmarried. They were no longer allowed to see the naked virgins exercise, and the magistrates commanded them to march naked themselves round the marketplace in winter, and to sing a song composed against themselves, which expressed how justly they were punished for disobeying the laws . . .

In their marriages, the bridegroom carried off the bride by violence – and brides were never of a tender age, but fully mature. When the time came, the woman who had direction of the wedding cut the bride's hair close to her scalp, dressed her in man's clothes, laid her upon a mattress and left her in the dark. The bridegroom – neither overcome with wine nor softened by luxury, but hardy and sober from always eating at the common table – went in privately, untied her girdle, and carried her to another bed. Having stayed there a short time, he modestly retired to his usual apartment, to sleep with the other young men. That is how the marriage would continue. The husband would spend the day with his men friends, and lie down with them at night, not even visiting his bride except with great caution, and apprehension of being discovered by the rest of her family. The bride, for her part, would exercise all her cunning to contrive convenient opportunities for their private meetings. They carried on in this way not just for a short time but habitually – some of them had children born to them before they so much as saw their wives by daylight. These marriage arrangements not only exercised their temperance and chastity, but also kept their bodies fruitful, and kept the first ardour of love fresh and unabated. For they did not become sated, like husbands who are always with their wives, but were still fired by unextinguished desire.

When Lycurgus had established a proper regard for modesty and decorum in marriage, he was equally concerned to banish from the marital relationship the vain and womanish passion of jealousy. He did this by making it perfectly reputable to share the parentage of one's children with people of merit. He laughed at those who looked upon a married woman's infidelity as an occasion for fighting and bloodshed. On the contrary, he allowed that if an elderly man had a young wife he might introduce her to some handsome and honest young man, whom he approved of, and when she had a child of this promising stock, bring it up as his own. Likewise he allowed that if a man of character should entertain a passion for a married woman on account of her modesty and the beauty of her children, he might treat with her husband for admission to her company, so that by planting his seed in a beauty-bearing soil, he might produce excellent children – the superior offspring of high-grade parents. For, firstly, Lycurgus considered children not so much the property of their parents as of the state, and therefore he would not have them begotten by ordinary people, but by the best men in it. Secondly, he observed the vanity and absurdity of other nations, where people take steps to have their horses or dogs of the finest breed they can procure, by money or personal influence, and yet they keep their wives shut up, so that they may have children by none but themselves, even if they happen to be in their dotage, or decrepit, or infirm. As if children, when sprung from a bad stock, and consequently good for nothing, are no detriment to those whom they belong to, and who have the trouble of bringing them up, or as if they are not, on the other hand, a great boon when well descended and of a generous disposition. These regulations, designed to secure healthy offspring, advantageous to the state, were so far from encouraging licentious-ness that adultery was not known among them . . .

It was not left to the father to rear what children he pleased. He was obliged to carry his newborn child to a place called Lesche, to be examined by the oldest men of the tribe, who assembled there. If it was strong and well-proportioned, they gave orders for its edu-cation, and assigned to it one of the nine thousand shares of land. But if it was weakly and deformed they ordered it to be thrown into the place called Apothetae, which is a deep cavern near mount Taygetus, concluding that its life could be no advantage either to itself or to the public, since nature had not equipped it with strength or constitutional fitness. For the same reason the women did not wash their newborn infants with water, but with wine, to make trial of their bodily fitness, for they imagined that sickly or epileptic children would faint and die under this experiment, while healthy children would become more vigorous and hardy . . .

Nor were the parents at liberty to educate them as they pleased. But as soon as they were seven years old, Lycurgus ordered them to be enrolled in companies, where they were all kept under the same order and discipline, and had their exercises and recreations in common. The boy who showed the most alertness and courage amongst them was made captain of the company. The rest kept their eyes on him, obeyed his orders, and bore with patience the punishments he inflicted, so that their whole education was an exercise of obedience. The old men were present at their diversions, and often suggested some occasion of dispute or quarrel, so that they might observe with exactness the spirit of each boy, and their firmness in battle.

As for learning, they had just what was absolutely necessary. All the rest of their education was calculated to make them subject to command, to endure labour, to fight and to conquer. They made their discipline more rigorous as they grew up, cutting their hair very close, obliging them to go barefoot, and play, for the most part, quite naked. At twelve years of age their undergarment was taken away, and only one upper garment a year was allowed them. As a result they were necessarily dirty in their persons, and were not indulged with baths or body-oils except as a great favour on some particular days of the year. They slept in companies, in beds made of the tops of reeds, which they gathered with their own hands, without knives, and carried from the banks of the river Eurotas. In winter they were permitted to add a little thistledown, as that seemed to have some warmth in it . . .

After the age of twelve, the boys are transferred to companies, each under the command of a twenty-year-old, who trains them to be tough, cunning marauders – as they will need to be in warfare.

He gives orders to those under his command in their little battles, and has them to serve him at his house. He sends the oldest of them to fetch wood, and the younger to gather pot-herbs. These they steal where they can find them, either slyly getting into gardens, or else craftily and warily creeping to the common tables. But if any one is caught he is severely flogged for his negligence and want of dexterity. They steal, too, whatever food they can, ingeniously contriving to do it when the owners are asleep, or not on the watch. If they are caught, they are punished not only with whipping but with hunger. Their rations are meagre at the best of times, so that, to keep famine at bay, they are forced to exercise their courage and quickness ... The boys steal with such resolute secrecy that one of them, having hidden a young fox under his tunic, allowed the creature to tear out his bowels with its teeth and claws, choosing rather to die than to be detected ...

Lycurgus's Spartans were, in effect a leisured military caste. When they were not actually fighting, they spent their time dancing, hunting, training the young, or meeting to exercise or converse. Work of any productive kind was forbidden to them. That was left to the underclass of slaves ('helots') who grew their food and performed all manual labour. Young Spartans would carry out mass murders of helots either as sport or as part of their military training. Plutarch, though generally admiring, does not approve of this.

The governors of the youth ordered the shrewdest of them from time to time to disperse themselves in the countryside, equipped only with daggers and some basic provisions. In the daytime they hid, lying in wait in the most secret places. But at night they sallied forth onto the roads, and killed all the helots they could find. Sometimes they even fell upon them in the open fields in broad daylight, and murdered the ablest and strongest ... In other respects they treated them with great inhumanity. Sometimes they made them drink till they were incapable, and in that condition led them into the public halls, to show the young men what drunkenness was. They ordered them, too, to sing mean songs and dance ridiculous dances, not allowing them to meddle with any that were serious or graceful.

Source: Plutarch, *Life of Lycurgus*, in *Ideal Commonwealths*, edited by Henry Morley, Routledge, 1885 (modified).

Arrangements in the Beyond

In the last book of the Bible, the *Revelation of St John the Divine*, Chapter 20, it is foretold that at Christ's second coming the devil will be cast into a bottomless pit, and then the righteous will reign with Christ for a thousand years. Imagining this joyful 'millennium' became a rich source of Christian utopian fantasy. An agricultural approach was favoured by St Irenaeus (*c.* AD 140–*c.*202), whose vision suggests that concern about the food and drink supply was common in second-century Gaul. Irenaeus became Bishop of Lyons, and was of crucial importance in the development of Christian theology. He attributes his account of the millennium to Jesus Christ himself.

The elders who saw John, the disciple of the Lord, related that they had heard from him how the Lord used to teach in regard to these times, and say: 'The days will come in which vines shall grow, each having ten thousand branches, and in each branch ten thousand twigs, and in each twig ten thousand shoots, and in each one of the shoots ten thousand clusters, and on every one of the clusters ten thousand grapes, and every grape when pressed will give five and twenty metretes [about 225 gallons] of wine. And when any one of the saints shall lay hold of a cluster, another shall cry out, "I am a better cluster, take me; bless the Lord through me." ' In like manner the Lord declared that a grain of wheat would produce ten thousand ears, and that every ear should have ten thousand grains, and every grain would yield ten pounds of clear, pure, fine flour: and that all other fruit-bearing trees and seeds and grass would produce in similar proportions.

The unknown authors of the *Revelation* (written *c.* AD 75–100) describe the heavenly city, New Jerusalem. Built out of gold, and walled with jasper, it has twelve gates.

And the foundations of the walls of the city were garnished with all manner of precious stones. The first foundation was jasper; the second, sapphire; the third, a chalcedony; the fourth, an emerald; the fifth, sardonyx; the sixth, sardius; the seventh, chrysolite; the eighth, beryl; the ninth, a topaz; the tenth, a chrysoprasus; the eleventh, a jacinth; the twelfth, an amethyst. And the twelve gates were twelve pearls; every several gate was of one pearl; and the street of the city was pure gold, as it were transparent glass . . . And he showed me a pure river of water of life, clear as crystal, proceeding out of the throne of God and of the Lamb. In the midst of the street of it, and on either side of the river, was there the tree of life, which bare twelve manner of fruits, and yielded her fruit every month . . . And there shall be no night there; and they need no candle, neither light of the sun; for the Lord giveth them light: and they shall reign for ever and ever.

The Greek satirist Lucian (born in Syria *c.* AD 17) clearly intended the Isles of the Blessed in his spoof travelogue *The True History* to be a caricature of the New Jerusalem, as well as of other paradises. Indignant Christian readers denounced him as a blasphemer and gave it out that he was torn to pieces by mad dogs for being so rabid against the truth. *The True History*'s narrator is swallowed by a whale (like Jonah). But he and his shipmates escape and land, quite by mistake, on islands normally reserved for the souls of the blessed, where they proceed to the main town.

The town in question is built entirely of gold, except for the outer wall, which is of emerald and contains seven gates, each composed of a solid chunk of cinnamon. The whole area inside the wall is paved with ivory, all the temples are constructed of beryl, and the altars, on which they usually sacrifice a hundred oxen at a time, consist of single slabs of amethyst. The town is encircled by a river of best-quality perfume, nearly two hundred feet across and approximately ninety feet deep, so that you can swim about in it without any risk of stubbing your toe on the bottom. By way of Turkish baths, they have large glass houses heated by burning cinnamon, with hot and cold dew laid on.

Their clothes are made of very fine cobwebs, dyed crimson, but they have not any bodies to put them on, for the town is exclusively inhabited by disembodied spirits. However, insubstantial as they are, they give an impression of complete solidity, and move and think and speak like ordinary human beings. Altogether, it is as if their naked souls were walking about clothed in the outward semblance of their bodies, for until you try touching them, it is quite impossible to detect their incorporeal nature. I suppose the best way of putting it would be to say that they are like walking shadows – except, of course, that they are not black.

Nobody grows old there, for they all stay the age they were when they first arrived, and it never gets dark. On the other hand, it never gets really light either, and they live in a sort of perpetual twilight, such as we have just before sunrise. Instead of four seasons they have only one, for with them it is always spring, and the only wind that blows comes from the west. All kinds of flowers grow there, and all kinds of garden-trees, especially shady ones. The vines bear fruit twelve times a year – in other words, once a month – and we were given to understand that the pomegranate-trees, the apple-trees, and all the other fruit-trees bore fruit no fewer than thirteen times a year, for two separate crops were normally produced in the month of Minober [called after Minos, judge of the dead]. As for the corn, instead of ordinary ears it sprouts mushroom-shaped loaves of bread, all ready to eat.

Scattered about the town are three hundred and sixty-five water-springs, an equal number of honey-springs, five hundred scent-springs (but these, I admit, are rather smaller than the others), seven rivers of milk, and eight rivers of wine. In spite of these urban amenities, however, most of the social life goes on outside the town, in a place called the Elysian Fields, which is a meadow beautifully situated in the middle of a wood. Under the shade of this wood, which is full of all sorts of different trees, a delightful party is permanently in progress.

The guests recline at their ease on beds of flowers, and are waited on by the winds, which do everything but serve the wine. However, there is no difficulty about that, for there are plenty of big glass-trees all round. In case you do not know what glass-trees are, they are trees made of very clear glass, which bear fruit in the form of wine-glasses of every conceivable shape and size. So every guest picks one or two of these glasses the moment he arrives, and puts them down beside him, whereupon they immediately become full of wine. That takes care of the drink problem, and the floral decorations are arranged by the nightingales and other song-birds from the neighbouring meadows, which pick up flowers in their beaks and rain them down over the guests, singing sweetly all the while.

Finally the heroes are even saved the trouble of putting on their own scent by the following ingenious system: specially absorbent clouds suck up perfume from the five hundred springs and from the river, after which they go and hover over the party; then the winds give them a gentle squeeze, and down comes the scent in a fine spray like dew.

Sources: *The Ante-Nicene Fathers. Translations of the Writings of the Fathers down to AD 325*, edited by the Revd Alexander Roberts DD and James Donaldson LL D, T. T. Clark, Edinburgh, and Wm B. Eerdmans, Grand Rapids, Michigan, 1989 (for Irenaeus); Lucian, *Satirical Sketches*, translated by Paul Turner, Penguin, 1961.

Watching the Damned Fry

Tertullian (*c.* AD 160–*c.*220) was one of the founders of Western Christianity. He was a Roman citizen, but born in Africa, in the city of Carthage. His father was possibly a Roman army officer, and the boy was brought up as a pagan. Highly educated, he went to Rome in his twenties, perhaps to pursue a legal career. The courage and determination of Christian martyrs in the Roman amphitheatre may have been a factor in his conversion to Christianity. His theological and controversial writings are marked by passion, wit and sarcasm. In the *De Spectaculis* (*Concerning Spectacles*) he warns Christians against attending theatres, gymnastic displays and other shows. Instead, he urges them to look forward to the Day of Judgment when he and they will be able to enjoy watching the torments of the damned, and taunting them for their hostility to Christian truths. This will be far better than any earthly spectacle – and will last for ever.

What exultation there will be among the angels, what glory among the souls of the blessed as they rise again! What a reign of the righteous will follow! What a city, the New Jerusalem! Yes, and there will be other spectacles too – that last and eternal Day of Judgment, which the pagans believed would never happen, which they scoffed at and ridiculed, when all the ages of the world and all its generations will be consumed in one fire. What a panorama it will be! And, watching it, what will strike me with wonder? What will make me laugh? I shall rejoice, I shall exult, to see so many kings and emperors – who, we were told, would be taken up into heaven with Jove when they died – groaning in the deepest darkness along with those who foretold their heavenly glory. And the magistrates who persecuted the name of Our Lord – to see them melting in flames fiercer than their own fierceness when they raged against Christians. What else? Those pillars of wisdom, the philosophers, blushing bright red in the presence of their pupils (whom they persuaded that God was nothing, that the soul didn't exist, that it would never be reunited with the body) as they all blaze together in one single conflagration. Then there will be the poets, trembling not before the imaginary judges of their pagan underworld, but before – surprise! – the judgment seat of Jesus Christ. And there will be the tragic actors to listen to, bellowing more loudly in their personal calamity than they ever did on the stage. There will be acrobats to watch, jumping about much more nimbly on account of the fire. There will be charioteers to gaze at, red all over in wheels of flame, and gymnasts to enjoy, flying through the air not in a fairground but in an inferno – though perhaps I shall choose not to watch their antics even then, because I shall prefer to turn my relentless gaze on those who spewed out their wild slanders against our Lord. 'This is he,' I shall say, 'that son of a carpenter and a whore, that Sabbath-breaker, that Samaritan possessed by devils; this is the man you bought from Judas, who was struck with a reed and pummelled, who was defiled with spittle, who was made to drink gall and vinegar. This is he whose body the disciples secretly stole away, so that they could pretend he had risen from the dead – or maybe it was the gardener who smuggled his corpse away, in case his lettuces should be trampled by crowds of sightseers.'

These are the sights and joys that await you. What earthly impresario, however lavish, can offer you anything to rival them?

Source: Tertullian, *De Spectaculis* (editor's translation of the Latin text).

In a Chinese Mountain

Tao Qian (AD 365–427) is the most famous early Chinese poet. He was born into the minor gentry, and held some public offices, but decided to resign and return to 'his garden and his fields'. This renunciation inspired much of his poetry. Preference for the personal life, untouched by statecraft or politics, is the subject, too, of his 'Account of Peach Blossom Spring'. One of the best loved stories in the Chinese tradition, it contrasts with Western utopias in that the happiness it describes consists in *not* being reorganized or reformed, but simply living as you always have.

The 'upheavals during the Qin', mentioned in the story, refer to the unification of China under the Qin Dynasty in 221 BC, when the Qin emperor instigated draconian measures to eliminate cultural and regional diversity. The other dynasties mentioned are the Han (206 BC–AD 220), the Wei (AD 220–65) and the Jin, responsible for reunifying China in AD 280. So the villagers have been in their hideout for six centuries.

During the Tai-yuan Reign of the Jin (376–396), there was a native of Wu-ling who made his living catching fish. Following a creek, he lost track of the distance he had traveled when all of a sudden he came upon forests of blossoming peach trees on both shores. For several hundred paces there were no other trees mixed in. The flowers were fresh and lovely, and the falling petals drifted everywhere in profusion. The fisherman found this quite remarkable and proceeded on ahead to find the end of this forest. The forest ended at a spring, and here he found a mountain. There was a small opening in the mountain, and it vaguely seemed as if there were light in it. He then left his boat and went in through the opening. At first it was very narrow, just wide enough for a person to get through. Going on further a few dozen paces, it spread out into a clear, open space.

The land was broad and level, and there were cottages neatly arranged. There were good fields and lovely pools, with mulberry, bamboo, and other such things. Field paths crisscrossed, and dogs and chickens could be heard. There, going back and forth to their work planting, were men and women whose clothes were in every way just like people elsewhere. Graybeards and children with their hair hanging free all looked contented and perfectly happy.

When they saw the fisherman, they were shocked. They asked where he had come from, and he answered all their questions. Then they invited him to return with them to their homes, where they served him beer and killed chickens for a meal. When it was known in the village that such a person was there, everyone came to ask him questions.

Of themselves they said that their ancestors had fled the upheavals during the Qin and had come to this region bringing their wives, children, and fellow townsmen. They had never left it since that time and thus had been cut off from people outside. When asked what age it was, they didn't know of even the existence of the Han, much less the Wei or Jin. The fisherman told them what he had learned item by item, and they all sighed, shaking their heads in dismay. Each person invited him to their homes, and they all offered beer and food.

After staying there several days, he took his leave. At this people said to him, 'There's no point in telling people outside about us.'

Once he left, he found his boat; and then as he retraced the route by which he had come, he took note of each spot. On reaching the regional capital, he went to the governor and told him the story as I have reported. The governor immediately sent people to follow the way he had gone and to look for the spots he had noticed. But they lost their way and could no longer find the route.

Liu Zi-ji of Nan-yang was a gentleman of high ideals. When he heard of this, he was delighted and planned to go there. Before he could realize it, he grew sick and passed away. After that no one tried to find the way there.

Source: *An Anthology of Chinese Literature: Beginnings to 1911*, edited and translated by Stephen Owen, W. W. Norton, 1996.

More's Conundrum

Thomas More (1478–1535) published *Utopia* in 1516. There have been endless debates about how seriously he meant it. Maybe this uncertainty was what he aimed to provoke. Deadpan humour was always his speciality. The book is presented as a travel-account by a voyager called Raphael Hythloday, whom More says he met in Antwerp, and the first part takes the form of a conversation between Hythloday, More and a real-life Antwerp civil servant, Peter Gilles.

Readers in favour of taking *Utopia* as a serious proposal for an ideal society point out that in this first part Hythloday attacks the injustices of European society, without any trace of humour. He describes a system in which greedy landlords, intent on lucrative sheep-farming, evict peasants, who must then starve – or steal, and be hanged. The social arrangements on the island of Utopia, where Hythloday says he lived for five years, can be read as a blueprint for righting these very real wrongs. In Utopia there is no poverty, no exploitation, no luxury, no idle rich.

It is a land of happy, healthy, public-spirited communists. Money and private property are extinct. Anyone can enter any house at any time: doors are never locked. Everyone works at a trade (clothwork, masonry or carpentry) and takes a turn at agricultural labour in the countryside. Idleness is forbidden. A six-hour working day is the rule, and provides amply for everyone. Leisure is spent sensibly – attending lectures, gardening, or playing brain-stretching board games, resembling chess. There are no taverns or ale-houses. Everyone goes to bed at eight o'clock.

All produce is collected into common storehouses, from which the officials of each district freely draw supplies. Families can eat at home if they like, but everyone usually eats in the communal halls where the food is excellent (cooked by the women on a rota system) and accompanied by music and educational reading. To the starving European peasants Hythloday pities, Utopia would seem like heaven.

Readers opposed to taking Utopia as a serious ideal, however, argue that, as a devout Catholic and future persecutor of heretics, More would have found many Utopian practices unacceptable. The Utopians are not Christians

– though they believe in a Supreme Being and in rewards and punishments after death. They practise complete religious toleration. Their priests can marry, and may be either men or women. Divorce is allowed, in cases of adultery, or by mutual consent where partners find each other incompatible. All of this would shock a sixteenth-century Catholic. So would the Utopian practice of euthanasia, as Raphael describes it.

As I told you, when people are ill, they're looked after most sympathetically, and given everything in the way of medicine or special food that could possibly assist their recovery. In the case of permanent invalids, the nurses try to make them feel better by sitting and talking to them, and do all they can to relieve their symptoms. But if, besides being incurable, the disease also causes constant excruciating pain, some priests and government officials visit the person concerned, and say something like this:

'Let's face it, you'll never be able to live a normal life. You're just a nuisance to other people and a burden to yourself – in fact you're really leading a sort of posthumous existence. So why go on feeding germs? Since your life's a misery to you, why hesitate to die? You're imprisoned in a torture-chamber – why don't you break out and escape to a better world? Or say the word, and we'll arrange for your release. It's only common sense to cut your losses. It's also an act of piety to take the advice of a priest, because he speaks for God.'

If the patient finds these arguments convincing, he either starves himself to death, or is given a soporific and put painlessly out of his misery. But this is strictly voluntary, and, if he prefers to stay alive, everyone will go on treating him as kindly as ever.

Another argument against *Utopia*'s seriousness is that the proper names in it are jokes. Utopia means 'no place'; Hythloday, 'dispenser of nonsense', and so on. However, this could be More's double bluff, simulating jocularity as self-defence, in a society where spreading new ideas could be dangerous.

Aspects of Utopia that irk modern readers might well have seemed desirable to More, who had monastic leanings as a young man, and wore a hair shirt under his Lord Chancellor's robes. In Utopia there is no frivolity and little freedom. Clothing is uniform, and made of undyed homespun wool. You need a permit to travel, and must go in a group. If you travel without a permit, you are arrested as a runaway and severely punished. Marital arrangements are strict and unsentimental.

Girls aren't allowed to marry until they're eighteen – boys have to wait four years longer. Any boy or girl convicted of pre-marital intercourse is severely punished, and permanently disqualified from marrying, unless this sentence is remitted by the Mayor. The man and woman in charge of the household in which it happens are also publicly disgraced, for not doing their jobs properly. The Utopians are particularly strict about that kind of thing, because they think very few people would want to get married – which means spending one's whole life with the same person, and putting up with all the inconveniences that this involves – if they weren't carefully prevented from having any sexual intercourse otherwise.

When they're thinking of getting married, they do something that seemed to us quite absurd, though they take it very seriously. The prospective bride, no matter whether she's a spinster or a widow, is exhibited stark naked to the prospective bridegroom by a respectable married woman, and a suitable male chaperon shows the bridegroom naked to the bride. When we implied by our laughter that we thought it a silly system, they promptly turned the joke against *us*.

'What we find so odd,' they said, 'is the silly way these things are arranged in other parts of the world. When you're buying a horse, and there's nothing at stake but a small sum of money, you take every possible precaution. The animal's practically naked already, but you firmly refuse to buy until you've whipped off the saddle and all the rest of the harness, to make sure there aren't any sores underneath. But when you're choosing a wife, an article that for better or worse has got to last you a lifetime, you're unbelievably careless. You don't even bother to take it out of its wrappings.

Adultery is punished with penal servitude. For a second offence, the penalty is death. Once a month, wives have to kneel and confess their faults to their husbands. Children, too, are treated harshly by modern standards. Though all Utopian mothers breast-feed their babies, close parental bonding seems to be discouraged. Each extended family, living together in a single house, is meant to have between ten and sixteen children. Any surplus children are sent to make up the tally of less prolific families. In the dining halls children wait at table or stand in respectful silence, eating only what is given them by the adult diners.

Two classes are exempt from the normal egalitarian regime – slaves and intellectuals. Slavery is the punishment for most major offences. Slaves work in chain gangs, and are slaughtered like wild beasts if they prove recalcitrant. Intellectuals, selected for their aptitude in book-learning, are excused from normal work-regulations so as to devote their lives to study – though if they slack they return to being artisans like everyone else. All higher officials and priests are chosen from among the intellectuals. So is the prince of each Utopian city.

Whether More meant his Utopia seriously is unanswerable – and perhaps too simple a question. Human complexity is bred out of the oppositions we harbour within ourselves. We know from More's book some of those that harboured within him. Whether he approved of them or not is, by comparison, of little importance.

The brilliance and novelty of his thinking are nowhere more apparent than in Raphael's account of Utopian attitudes to wealth and warfare.

Silver and gold, the raw materials of money, get no more respect from anyone than their intrinsic value deserves – which is obviously far less than that of iron. Without iron human life is simply impossible, just as it is without fire or water – but we could easily do without silver and gold, if it weren't for the idiotic concept of scarcity-value. And yet kind Mother Nature has deliberately placed all her greatest blessings, like earth, air, and water, right under our noses, and tucked away out of sight the things that are no use to us.

Now if they locked these metals up in a strong-room, the man in the street might get some silly idea into his head – you know what a talent he has for that kind of thing – that the Mayor and the Bencheaters [elected officials] were cheating him, and somehow making a profit out of the stuff. It could, of course, be converted into ornamental bowls or other *objets d'art*. But then people would grow so fond of them that, if they ever had to melt them down and pay soldiers with them, it would be a terrible wrench.

To get around these difficulties, they've devised a system, which, while perfectly consistent with their other conventions, is diametrically opposed to ours – especially to the way we treasure up gold. So you'll probably think it incredible, until you've actually seen it for yourself. According to this system, plates and drinking-vessels, though beautifully designed, are made of quite cheap stuff like glass or earthenware. But silver and gold are the normal materials, in private houses as well as communal dining-halls, for the humblest items of domestic equipment, such as chamber-pots. They also use chains and fetters of solid gold to immobilize slaves, and anyone who commits a really shameful crime is forced to go about with gold rings on his ears and fingers, a gold necklace round his neck, and a crown of gold on his head. In fact they do everything they can to bring these metals into contempt. This means that if they suddenly had to part with all the gold and silver they possess – a fate which in any other country would be thought equivalent to having one's guts torn out – nobody in Utopia would care two hoots.

It's much the same with jewels. There are pearls to be found on the beaches, diamonds and garnets on certain types of rock – but they never bother to look for them. However, if they happen to come across one, they pick it up and polish it for some toddler to wear. At first, children are terribly proud of such jewellery – until they're old enough to register that it's only worn in the nursery. Then, without any prompting from their parents, but purely as a matter of self-respect, they give it up – just as our children grow out of things like dolls, and conkers, and lucky charms. This curious convention is liable to cause some equally curious reactions, as I realized most vividly in the case of the Flatulentine diplomats.

These diplomats visited Aircastle while I was there, and, as they were coming to discuss a matter of great importance, each town had sent its three members of parliament to meet them. Now all foreign diplomats who'd been there before had come from places just across the channel, and were therefore quite familiar with Utopian ideas. They knew it was a country where expensive clothes were not admired, silk was despised, and gold was a dirty word, so they'd dressed as simply as they could for the occasion. But these Flatulentines lived too far away to have had much contact with the Utopians. All they knew was that everyone in Utopia wore the same sort of clothes, and pretty crude ones at that – presumably because they'd nothing better to wear. So they adopted a policy more arrogant than diplomatic, which was to array themselves in positively godlike splendour, and dazzle the wretched Utopians with their magnificence.

When the legation arrived, it consisted of only three men, but these were escorted by a hundred retainers, all wearing multi-coloured clothes, mostly made of silk. As for the great men themselves – for they *were* great men in their own country – they wore cloth of gold, with great gold chains round their necks, gold ear-rings dangling from their ears, and gold rings on their fingers. Their very hats were festooned with glittering ropes of pearls and other jewels. In fact they were fully equipped with all the things used in Utopia for punishing slaves, humiliating criminals, or amusing small children.

Well, I wouldn't have missed it for anything. There were these three gentlemen, looking terribly pleased with themselves, as they compared their own appearance with that of the local inhabitants – for of course the streets were packed with people. And there was the actual effect that they were producing – so very unexpected and disappointing. You see, from the Utopians' point of view – apart from a few who'd had occasion to go abroad – all that splendour was merely degrading. So they reserved their most respectful greeting for the least distinguished members of the party, and completely ignored the diplomats themselves, assuming from their gold chains that they must be slaves.

Oh, but you should have seen the faces of the older children, who'd grown out of things like pearls and jewels, when they saw the ones on the envoys' hats. They kept nudging their mothers and whispering:

'I say, Mother, just look at that great baby! Fancy wearing jewellery at his age!'

To which the mother would reply, very seriously:

'Sh, dear! I imagine he must be a clown attached to the embassy.' . . .

And that brings us to the subject of war. Well, fighting is a thing they absolutely loathe. They say it's a quite subhuman form of activity, although human beings are more addicted to it than any of the lower animals. In fact, the Utopians are practically the only people on earth who fail to see anything glorious in war. Of course, both sexes are given military training at regular intervals, so that they won't be incapable of fighting if they ever have to do it. But they hardly ever go to war, except in self-defence, to repel invaders from friendly territory, or to liberate the victims of dictatorship – which they do in a spirit of humanity, just because they feel sorry for them . . .

They don't like bloody victories – in fact they feel ashamed of them, for they consider it stupid to pay too high a price for anything, however valuable it is. What they're really proud of is outwitting the enemy. They celebrate any success of this kind by a triumphal procession, and by putting up a trophy, as for some feat of heroism. You see, their idea of quitting themselves like men is to achieve victory by means of something which only man possesses, that is, by the power of the intellect. They say any animal can fight with its body – bears, lions, boars, wolves, dogs can all do it, and most of them are stronger and fiercer than we are – but what raises us above them is our reason and intelligence.

Their one aim in wartime is to get what they've previously failed to get by peaceful means – or, if that's out of the question, to punish the offenders so severely that nobody will ever dare to do such a thing again. They make for these objectives by the shortest possible route – but always on the principle of safety first, and national prestige second. So the moment war's declared they arrange through secret agents for lots of posters to go up simultaneously at all points on enemy territory where they're most likely to be seen. These posters carry the official seal of the Utopian government, and offer a huge reward for killing the enemy king. They also offer smaller, but still very considerable sums for killing certain individuals, whose names appear on a list, and who are presumed to be the chief supporters, after the king, of anti-Utopian policies. The reward for bringing such people in alive is twice as much as for killing them – and they themselves are offered the same amount of money, plus a free pardon, for turning against their own associates.

The immediate result is that everyone mentioned on the list becomes suspicious of everything in human shape. They all stop trusting one another, and stop being trustworthy. They live in a constant state of terror, which is perfectly justified – for it's often been known to happen that all of them, including the king himself, are betrayed by the very person that they pinned most faith on. The fact is, people will do anything for money, and there's no limit to the amount of money that the Utopians are prepared to give. Bearing in mind the risks that they're inviting each traitor to run, they're very careful to offer him compensating advantages. So, in addition to vast quantities of gold, they also promise him the freehold of a valuable estate in safe and friendly territory – and such promises they invariably keep.

This system of making take-over bids for the enemy is generally considered mean and cruel, but the Utopians are very proud of it. They say it's extremely sensible to dispose of major wars like this without fighting a single battle, and also most humane to save thousands of innocent lives at the cost of a few guilty ones. They're thinking of all the soldiers who would have been killed in action, on one side or the other – for they feel almost as much sympathy for the mass of the enemy population as they do for their own. They realize that these people would never have started a war if they hadn't been forced into it by the insanity of their rulers.

If this method fails, they sow and foster the seeds of discord among their enemies, by encouraging the king's brother or some other member of the aristocracy to aspire to the throne. If internal dissension shows signs of flagging, they inflame hostility in some adjacent country by digging up one of those ancient claims that kings are always so well provided with. They promise to support the claimant's war effort, and do it by supplying plenty of money and very little manpower – for they're much too fond of one another to be willing to sacrifice a single Utopian citizen, even in exchange for the enemy king himself. But they're perfectly happy to hand out silver and gold, because that's all they keep it for, and they know it won't make any difference to their standard of living if they spend the whole lot . . .

So most of their fighting is done by mercenaries. They recruit them from all over the world, but especially from a place called Venalia [probably Switzerland: the chief source of mercenaries in More's Europe], which is about five hundred miles to the east of Utopia. The Venalians are extremely primitive and savage – like the wild forests and rugged mountains among which they grow up. They're very tough, and can stand any amount of heat, cold, and physical hardship. They've no idea of enjoying themselves, never do any farming, and are equally careless about their clothes and their houses. Apart from looking after cattle, they live mostly by hunting and stealing. In fact, they seem naturally designed for nothing but war. They're always looking for a war to fight in, and when they succeed in finding one they go rushing off in their thousands to offer their services cheap to anyone who needs soldiers. For taking lives is the only method they know of earning a living . . .

These people will fight for the Utopians against any nation in the world, because no one else is prepared to pay them so much. You see, the Utopians are just as anxious to find wicked men to exploit as good men to employ. So when necessary they tempt Venalians with lavish promises to engage in desperate enterprises, from which most of them never come back to claim their earnings. But those who do are always paid in full, so that they'll think it worth while to take similar risks in future. For the Utopians don't care how many Venalians they send to their deaths. They say, if only they could wipe the filthy scum off the face of the earth completely, they'd be doing the human race a very good turn.

Source: Thomas More, *Utopia*, translated by Paul Turner, Penguin, 1965.

Moon Landing

Accounts of moon landings became popular in the 1630s, following Galileo's announcement (1610) that the moon, seen through his telescope, was not a smooth ball, as had been thought, but had mountains and valleys quite like the earth. Francis Godwin (1562–1633) seems, however, to have been ahead of the field, since he wrote his moontrip while a student at Oxford in the late 1570s. He later became Bishop of Hereford. His *The Man in the Moon, or A Discourse of a Voyage Thither* was published posthumously in 1638.

The astronaut in Godwin's narrative is a Spaniard called Gonzales, who discovers that he can leave the ground by tying twenty-five large swans to a light framework, on which he sits. The book's frontispiece shows him perched on a cross-bar, dressed in ruff and cloak, while the swans bear him up into the stratosphere. Once clear of the earth's gravitational field, he and his swans experience weightlessness, suspended in space 'as easily and quietly as a fish in the middle of water'. Unimpeded by gravity, a very small effort on the part of the swans carries him with unimaginable 'swiftness and celerity'. He reaches the moon (despite having to pass through a region of devils and wicked spirits) in eleven days.

His account of the lunar inhabitants is rather muddled, perhaps because of space-shock. He reports that they come in different sizes, some giants, some dwarfs. The dwarfs are used as labourers and, being less light-tolerant than the giants, have to sleep during the lunar day (equivalent to fourteen earth days). All lunars are Christians.

Lunar language consists not of words but of tunes. Gonzales prints some samples, using musical notation. Lunar clothes are of an indescribable colour, unlike any in our earthly spectrum. This anticipates Hugh Lofting's Doctor Dolittle, who also finds a dazzling range of new colours on the moon. In fact, however, a traveller to another world would take his eyes and brain with him and so could see only that part of the spectrum that had been accessible to him back on earth. Godwin's science is more dependable on the question of weight loss. Weak lunar gravity allows lunars to fly, as Gonzales explains.

Unto every one of us there was delivered at our first setting forth two fans of feathers, not much unlike unto those that our ladies do carry in Spain, to make a cool air unto themselves in the heat of summer. The use of which fans before I declare unto you, I must let you understand that the globe of the moon is not altogether destitute of an attractive power, but it is so far weaker than that of the earth as if a man do but spring upward with all his force (as dancers do when they show their activity by capering) he shall be able to mount 50 or 60 foot high, and then he is quite beyond all attraction of the moon's earth, falling down no more, so as by the help of these fans, as with wings, they convey themselves in the air in a short space (although not with that swiftness that birds do) even whither they list.

How the lunars return to the moon's surface again, Gonzales does not divulge. He later reveals, though, that they have a magic stone that can make them heavier or lighter at will, so perhaps they use this.

Climate, medical resourcefulness and unusual sexual restraint on the part of lunar males combine to make the moon an ideal habitat, Gonzales reports. Any lunars who happen to be born with an evil disposition are sent to a place where it will not be noticed.

Food groweth everywhere without labour, and that of all sorts to be desired. For raiment, housing, or anything else that you may imagine possible for a man to want or desire, it is provided by the command of superiors, though not without labour, yet so little that they do nothing but as it were playing, and with pleasure.

Again, their females are all of an absolute beauty: and I know not how it cometh to pass by a secret disposition of nature there that a man having once known a woman never desireth any other. As for murder, it was never heard of amongst them, neither is it a thing almost possible to be committed. For there is no wound to be given that may not be cured, they assured me (and I for my part did believe it), that although a man's head be cut off, yet if any time within the space of three moons it be put together and joined to the carcass again, with the appointment of the juice of a certain herb there growing, it will be joined together again, so as the party wounded shall become perfectly whole in a few hours.

But the chief cause is that through an excellent disposition of that nature of people there, all, young and old, do hate all manner of vice, and do live in such love, peace and amity as it seemeth to be another paradise. True it is that some are better disposed than others – but that they discern immediately at the time of their birth. And because it is an inviolable decree amongst them never to put anyone to death, perceiving by the stature and some other notes they have who are likely to be of a wicked or imperfect disposition, they send them away (I know not by what means) into the Earth, and change them for other children, before they shall have either ability or opportunity to do amiss amongst them.

Source: Domingo Gonzales, *The Man in the Moon, or A Discourse of a Voyage Thither,* 1638.

Utopian Cannibals

The voyages of discovery of the late fifteenth and early sixteenth centuries revolutionized utopia. Alternative cultures came to light which, to open-minded Europeans, raised challenging questions about the good life and their own civilization. No European was more open-minded than Michel de Montaigne (1533–92). His *Essays*, written in the 1570s and 80s, are a unique blend of scepticism and self-knowledge, at once learned and distrustful of learning. Nothing so intellectually adventurous had been written before; little has since.

Montaigne knew about the New World partly from reading, partly from travellers' accounts, and partly from a meeting in 1562 with three Brazilian Indians whom the explorer Nicolas Durand de Villegagnon had brought back to France. His essay *On Cannibals* argues that the Brazilian Indians are 'wild' only in the sense that wild flowers are – that is, the most useful and natural virtues and properties are alive and vigorous in them. By contrast, the products of European culture are unnatural and inferior. 'With all our efforts we cannot imitate the nest of the very smallest bird, its structure, its beauty, or the suitability of its form, nor even the web of the lowly spider.' The Indians are still governed by natural laws.

They are in such a state of purity that it sometimes saddens me to think we did not learn of them earlier, at a time when there were men who were better able to appreciate them than we. I am sorry that Lycurgus and Plato [see pp. 12 and 24] did not know them, for I think that what we have seen of these people with our own eyes surpasses not only the pictures with which poets have illustrated the golden age, and all their attempts to draw mankind in the state of happiness, but the ideas and the very aspirations of philosophers as well. They could not imagine an innocence as pure and simple as we have actually seen; nor could they believe that our society might be maintained with so little artificiality and human organization.

This is a nation, I should say to Plato, in which there is no kind of commerce, no knowledge of letters, no science of numbers, no title of magistrate or of political superior, no habit of service, riches or poverty, no contracts, no inheritance, no division of property, only leisurely occupations, no respect for any kinship but the common ties, no clothes, no agriculture, no metals, no use of corn or wine. The very words denoting lying, treason, deceit, greed, envy, slander, and forgiveness have never been heard. How far from such perfection would he find the republic that he imagined: 'men fresh from the hands of the gods' [Seneca, *Letters* xc] . . .

For the rest, they live in a land with a very pleasant and temperate climate, and consequently, as my witnesses inform me, a sick person is a rare sight; and they assure me that they never saw anyone palsied or blear-eyed, toothless or bent with age. These people inhabit the seashore, and are shut in on the landward side by a range of high mountains, which leave a strip about a hundred leagues in depth between them and the sea. They have a great abundance of fish and meat which bear no resemblance to ours, and they eat them plainly cooked, without any other preparation. The first man who brought a horse there, although he had made friends with them on some earlier voyages, so terrified them when in the saddle that they shot him to death with arrows before recognizing him.

Their buildings are very long and capable of holding two or three hundred people. They are covered with strips of bark from tall trees, tethered at one end to the ground and attached at the other for mutual support to the roof beam, after the manner of some of our barns whose roofing comes down to the ground and serves for side walls. They have a wood so hard that they can cut with it, and make it into swords and grills to roast their meat. Their beds are of woven cotton, hung from the roof like those on our ships; and each has his own, for the women sleep apart from their husbands. They get up with the sun, and immediately after rising they eat for the whole day, for they have no other meal. They do not drink at the same time, but like some Eastern peoples described by Suidas, always apart from their meals. They drink several times a day, and a great deal. Their beverage is made of some root, and is of the colour of our red wine. They drink it only warm, and it will not keep for more than two or three days. It is rather sharp in taste, not at all heady, good for the stomach, and laxative to those who are not used to it; it is a very pleasant drink to those who are. Instead of bread they use a white stuff like preserved coriander, which I have tasted; the flavour is sweetish and rather insipid.

They spend the whole day dancing. Their young men go hunting after wild beasts with bows and arrows. Some of their women employ themselves in the meantime with the warming of their drink, which is their principal duty. In the morning, before they begin to eat, one of their old men preaches to the whole barnful, walking from one end to the other, and repeating the same phrase many times, until he has completed the round – for the buildings are quite a hundred yards long. He enjoins only two things upon them: valour against the enemy and love for their wives. And he never fails to stress this obligation with the refrain that it is they who keep their drink warm and well-seasoned for them.

There may be seen in a number of places, including my own house, examples of their beds, of their ropes, of their wooden swords, of the wooden bracelets with which they protect their wrists in battle, and of the great canes, open at one end, which they sound to beat time for their dancing. They are close-shaven all over, and perform the operation much more cleanly than we, with only a razor of wood or stone. They believe in the immortality of the soul, and that those who have deserved well of the gods have their abode in that part of the sky where the sun rises; and those who are damned in the West.

They have some sort of priests and prophets, who very seldom appear among the people, but have their dwelling in the mountains. When they come, a great festival and solemn assembly of several villages is held. Each of these barns which I have described forms a village, and they are about one French league apart. The prophet speaks to them in public, exhorting them to virtue and to do their duty. But their whole ethical teaching contains only two articles; resolution in battle and affection for their wives.

Montaigne particularly commends their valour in battle.

As for flight and terror, they do not know what they are. Every man brings home for a trophy the head of an enemy he has killed, and hangs it over the entrance of his dwelling. After treating a prisoner well for a long time, and giving him every attention he can think of, his captor assembles a great company of his acquaintances. He then ties a rope to one of the prisoner's arms, holding him by the other end, at some yards' distance for fear of being hit, and gives his best friend the man's other arm, to be held in the same way; and these two, in front of the whole assembly, despatch him with their swords. This done, they roast him, eat him all together, and send portions to their absent friends. They do not do this, as might be supposed, for nourishment as the ancient Scythians did, but as a measure of extreme vengeance.

Montaigne concedes that cannibalism is barbarous. But, he argues, it is less savage than many European tortures and punishments. He finds the Indians' fighting 'beautiful' because it is entirely noble and disinterested. Their only motive for war is to display their valour. They do not need, or seek, new territories, and as they hold all their goods in common the soldiers have no use for the spoils of conquest. Courage is their one ideal.

They ask no ransom of their prisoners but only the confession and acknowledgement that they have been beaten: but there has never been one, in a whole century, who has not chosen death rather than yield, either by word or behaviour, one single jot of their magnificent and invincible courage; not one of them has ever been known who has not preferred to be killed and eaten rather than beg to be spared. Prisoners are treated with all liberality so that their lives may be the more dear to them, and are usually plied with threats of their imminent death. They are reminded of the tortures that they are to suffer, of the preparations then being made to that end, of the lopping off of their limbs, and of the feast that will be held at their expense. All this is done solely in order to extort from their lips some weak or despondent word, or to rouse in them a desire to escape; its only purpose is to gain the advantage of having frightened them and shaken their constancy . . .

These prisoners are so far from giving in, whatever their treatment, that all through these two or three months of their captivity they show a cheerful face, and urge their masters to be quick in putting them to the test. They defy them, insult them, and reproach them with cowardice, counting over the number of battles in which their own people have defeated them. I have a ballad made by one prisoner in which he tauntingly invites his captors to come boldly forward, every one of them, and dine off him, for they will then be eating their own fathers and grandfathers, who have served as food and nourishment to his body. 'These muscles,' he says, 'this flesh, and these veins are yours, poor fools that you are! Can you not see that the substance of your ancestors' limbs is still in them? Taste them carefully, and you will find the flavour is that of your own flesh.' A shaft of wit that by no means savours of barbarism. Those who tell us how they die, and describe their executions, depict the prisoner spitting in the faces of his killers and grimacing defiantly. In fact, up to their last gasp they never cease to brave and defy them with word and gesture. Here are men who compared with us are savages indeed. They must be so, indubitably, if we are not, for there is an amazing difference between their characters and ours.

Their men have many wives; the higher their reputation for valour the larger the number; and one very beautiful thing about their marriages is that whereas our wives anxiously keep us from enjoying the friendship and kindliness of other women, their wives are equally anxious to procure just those favours for their husbands. Being more concerned for the honour of their men than for anything else, they take pains to find and keep as many companions as they can, in as much as this is a testimony to their husband's worth.

Our wives will exclaim that this is a miracle. It is not. It is a proper marital virtue, but of the highest order ...

Not knowing how costly a knowledge of this country's corruptions will one day be to their happiness and repose, and that from inter-course with us will come their ruin – which, I suppose, is far advanced already – three men of their nation – poor fellows to allow themselves to be deluded by the desire for things unknown, and to leave the softness of their own skies to come and gaze at ours – were at Rouen at the time when the late King Charles the Ninth visited the place. The King talked with them for some time; they were shown our way of living, our magnificence, and the sights of a fine city. Then someone asked them what they thought about all this, and what they had found most remarkable. They mentioned three things, of which I am sorry to say I have forgotten the third. But I still remember the other two. They said that in the first place they found it very strange that so many tall, bearded men, all strong and well armed, who were around the King – they probably meant the Swiss of his guard – should be willing to obey a child [Charles IX was twelve years old], rather than choose one of their own number to command them. Secondly – they have a way in their language of speaking of men as halves of one another – that they had noticed among us some men gorged to the full with things of every sort while their other halves were beggars at their doors, emaciated with hunger and poverty. They found it strange that these poverty-stricken halves should suffer such injustice, and that they did not take the others by the throat or set fire to their houses.

Shakespeare read Montaigne's essay *On Cannibals* in John Florio's translation, published in 1603. In *The Tempest*, act II, scene i, when a party of modern Italians are shipwrecked on a desert island, one of their number, 'honest old' Gonzalo, tries to cheer up his master, King Alonso, with a little utopian fantasizing, borrowed from Montaigne. The treacherous and corrupt Sebastian and Antonio mock and interrupt him.

GONZALO (*to Alonso*): Had I plantation of this isle, my lord –
ANTONIO (*to Sebastian*): He'd sow't with nettle-seed.
SEBASTIAN: Or docks, or mallows.
GONZALO: And were the king on't, what would I do?
SEBASTIAN (*to Antonio*): Scape being drunk, for want of wine.
GONZALO: I'th' commonwealth I would by contraries
            Execute all things. For no kind of traffic
            Would I admit, no name of magistrate;
            Letters should not be known; riches, poverty,
            And use of service, none; contract, succession,
            Bourn, bound of land, tilth, vineyard, none;
            No use of metal, corn, or wine, or oil;
            No occupation, all men idle, all;
            And women too – but innocent and pure;
            No sovereignty –
SEBASTIAN (*to Antonio*): Yet he would be king on't.
ANTONIO: The latter end of his commonwealth forgets the
            beginning.
GONZALO: All things in common nature should produce
            Without sweat or endeavour. Treason, felony,
            Sword, pike, knife, gun, or need of any engine,
            Would I not have; but nature should bring forth
            Of it own kind all foison, all abundance,
            To feed my innocent people.
SEBASTIAN (*to Antonio*): No marrying 'mong his subjects?

[55]

ANTONIO: None, man, all idle: whores and knaves.
GONZALO: I would with such perfection govern, sir,
            T'excel the Golden Age.

Critics disagree as to whether anything can be deduced from this, or from *The Tempest* as a whole, about Shakespeare's attitude to Montaigne's essay. Needless to say, nothing can. Gonzalo's account sounds like a send-up, but it may be Gonzalo's send-up not Shakespeare's, and the fact that the slimy pair Sebastian and Antonio deride it counts in its favour. Caliban, the native inhabitant of the island, is an anagram of (seventeenth-century spelling) 'canibal'. But whether he is to be seen as an uncivilized brute, or as a hapless victim of colonialism living in exemplary accord with nature, is a matter of endless dispute among Shakespeareans. As usual with Shakespeare, we are left to decide for ourselves. What we decide will reveal something about our own utopian assumptions.

Source: Michel de Montaigne, *Essays*, translated with an introduction by J. M. Cohen, Penguin, 1958.

My America

Love poems are not usually utopias. But John Donne (1572–1631) was singular in imagining the woman he loved as a land to be discovered, explored and exploited. No ordinary land could compare with her; no ordinary prince with him.

> She is all states, and all princes, I,
> Nothing else is.
> Princes do but play us.

This valiant boast comes in Donne's poem 'The Sun Rising'. Some have conjectured that it was the crushing of his worldly hopes that made him turn women into sites of success, wealth and conquest. In 1601 he contracted a secret marriage with an heiress, and when it was discovered he was imprisoned (briefly), thrown out of his job, and forced to live on her relatives' charity. But he almost certainly wrote 'To His Mistress Going to Bed' before this disaster occurred, and it is his most exuberant celebration of woman as utopia.

One or two phrases may need explanation for a modern reader. The 'harmonious chime' is from a chiming watch – a very expensive bauble indeed in the 1590s, which marks out the woman as upper-class. The references to being 'tired with standing', to the 'busk' (corset) that can 'stand' so stiffly and so long, and to the angels that set 'flesh upright', all allude to the male erection. The mention of 'penance' and 'white linen', towards the end, alludes to the practice of making sinners stand in a white sheet in church. The last line is ambiguous: she needs no more covering than a man has (he is naked already); or, she needs no more covering than a man lying on top of her.

> Come, Madam, come, all rest my powers defy,
> Until I labour, I in labour lie.
> The foe oft-times, having the foe in sight,

Is tired with standing though they never fight.
Off with that girdle, like heaven's zone glistering,
But a far fairer world encompassing.
Unpin that spangled breastplate, which you wear
That th' eyes of busy fools may be stopped there:
Unlace yourself, for that harmonious chime
Tells me from you that now 'tis your bed-time.
Off with that happy busk, which I envy,
That still can be, and still can stand so nigh.
Your gown going off, such beauteous state reveals,
As when from flowery meads th' hill's shadow steals.
Off with your wiry coronet and show
The hairy diadem which on you doth grow.
Off with those shoes: and then safely tread
In this love's hallowed temple, this soft bed.
In such white robes heaven's angels used to be
Received by men; thou angel bring'st with thee
A heaven like Mahomet's paradise; and though
Ill spirits walk in white, we easily know
By this these angels from an evil sprite,
They set our hairs, but these our flesh upright.
   Licence my roving hands, and let them go
Behind, before, above, between, below.
O my America, my new found land,
My kingdom, safeliest when with one man manned,
My mine of precious stones, my empery,
How blessed am I in this discovering thee.
To enter in these bonds is to be free,
Then where my hand is set my seal shall be.
   Full nakedness, all joys are due to thee.
As souls unbodied, bodies unclothed must be,
To taste whole joys. Gems which you women use
Are like Atlanta's balls, cast in men's views,
That when a fool's eye lighteth on a gem
His earthly soul may covet theirs, not them.
Like pictures, or like books' gay coverings made
For laymen, are all women thus arrayed;
Themselves are mystic books, which only we
Whom their imputed grace will dignify

Must see revealed. Then since I may know,
As liberally as to a midwife show
Thyself; cast all, yea this white linen hence,
Here is no penance, much less innocence.
　　To teach thee, I am naked first: why then
What needst thou have more covering than a man?

Source: *John Donne*, edited by John Carey, Oxford University Press, 1990.

Sun City

Tommaso Campanella (1568–1639) was the son of an illiterate cobbler of Stilo, Calabria. He joined the Dominican order at fourteen, and became known for his prodigious learning. He was drawn to the physical sciences, but also to astrology and magic. Resenting the Spanish government of southern Italy, and prophesying that the year 1600 would herald apocalyptic wonders, he put himself at the head of a popular uprising. It proved abortive, and he was arrested, interrogated by the Inquisition, tortured, and sentenced to life imprisonment. Though for much of his incarceration he was chained hand and foot in the damp underground dungeon of Castel S. Elmo, he managed a voluminous literary output. His most famous book, *The City of the Sun*, was finished in 1602, the first year of his imprisonment, though not published till 1623. He clearly believed this hopelessly utopian utopia could become reality – indeed, had his uprising succeeded, it seems probable that the Calabrian peasants would have found themselves organized in theocratic communes, along the lines described in his book. He repeatedly urged the Catholic authorities to start building a City of the Sun. Released from prison after twenty-seven years, he went to Paris where he made the same proposal to Richelieu, with similar lack of success.

Indebted for many of its ideas to Plato and More, Campanella's City has a unique architectural design. Its walls, named after the seven planets, form seven concentric circles around a central temple. The inhabitants, called Solarians, are virtuous, obedient, and devoted to the common good. They have no private property, private houses or family life, work a four-hour day (all that is needed to support their frugal life-style), and wear unisex military uniforms which they wash once a month. Women have equal status with men, receive the same education, and are similarly subject to compulsory military service. Campanella's is the first utopia to abolish slave labour. All Solarians help in tilling the fields and growing crops. They use 'wagons fitted with sails which are borne along by the wind, even when it is contrary, by the marvellous contrivance of wheels within wheels'.

Solarians worship the sun as the image of God. Their prince is a priest, as are all the subordinate governors. This is convenient because, as priests, they hear confession, so have a close knowledge of the city's moral health. The prince's official title is Sun. He must be over thirty-five, and is elected because he is the person most proficient at learning all the arts and sciences. His tenure lasts till someone with greater knowledge and ability comes along.

Solarians are so purged of self-love that there is virtually no crime. If they show ingratitude or malice they are temporarily banished from the common table or from conversation with the opposite sex. Murder carries the death penalty, so does cowardice in battle. Anyone who disobeys a military order is given a club and put in an enclosure with lions and bears. If he survives he is pardoned. It is a capital offence for a woman to wear cosmetics, high-heeled shoes, or a particular kind of gown with a train which Campanella seems to have considered immodest. Fortunately these accessories are not easily procurable. There is no executioner. Execution is by stoning or burning and all the people take part.

Solarians lead an active life. Children wrestle. Adults play football and field sports. Games played sitting down (cards, dice, chess) are forbidden. Consequently there is no disease and the average life-span is 170 years.

Great importance is attached to education, of which a revolutionary feature (which influenced educational thinkers later in the seventeenth century) is the use of visual aids. All seven walls of the city are painted with pictures and diagrams illustrating astronomy, geology, anthropology, zoology, botany, and the other sciences, with show-cases containing specimens where appropriate. The mechanical arts (metalwork, building, painting) are also illustrated. This means that the streets are classrooms and museums. Children learn, without realizing it, while they play. They know all the sciences before they are ten years old, and can pick up any mechanical art in two days.

The basis of Campanella's whole enterprise is a birth-control programme that ensures healthy, intelligent, astrologically favoured offspring.

No female ever submits to a male until she is nineteen years of age, nor does any male seek to have children until he is twenty-one or, if he is pale and delicate, even older. Before that age some of them are permitted to have intercourse with barren or pregnant women so as to avoid illicit usages. The matrons and seniors in charge of pro-creation are responsible for providing in accordance with what those who are most troubled by Venus reveal to them in secret. Those who commit sodomy are disgraced and are made to walk about for two days with a shoe tied to their necks as a sign that they perverted natural order, putting their feet where the head belongs. With each repetition of the offence the sentence is increased until finally the punishment is death. On the other hand, those who abstain from every form of sexual intercourse until they reach twenty-one are honoured, and odes are written in their praise.

Since both males and females, in the manner of the ancient Greeks, are completely naked when they engage in wrestling exercises, their teachers may readily distinguish those who are able to have intercourse from those who are not and can determine whose sexual organs may best be matched with whose. Consequently, every third night, after they have all bathed, the young people are paired off for intercourse. Tall handsome girls are not matched with any but tall brave men, while fat girls are matched with thin men and thin girls with fat ones, so as to avoid extremes in their offspring. On the appointed evening, the boys and girls prepare their beds and go to bed where the matron and senior direct them. Nor may they have intercourse until they have completely digested their food and have said their prayers. There are fine statues of illustrious men that the women gaze upon. Then both male and female go to a window to pray to the God of Heaven for good issue. They sleep in separate neighbouring cells until they are to have intercourse. At the proper time, the matron goes around and opens the cell doors. The exact hour when this must be done is determined by the Astrologer and the Physician, who always endeavour to choose a time when Mercury and Venus are oriental to the Sun in a benefic house and are seen by Jupiter, Saturn, and Mars with benefic aspect.

The officials, all of whom are priests, and the learned do not try to procreate without first submitting to numerous conditions and restrictions stretching over many days. The reason for this is that those who are much given to speculation tend to be deficient in animal spirits and fail to bestow their intellectual powers upon their progeny because they are always thinking of other matters. Thus they produce offspring of poor quality. As a consequence, they take care to mate with energetic, spirited, handsome women.

Source: Tommaso Campanella, *La Citta del Sole: Dialogo Poetico. The City of the Sun: A Poetic Dialogue*, translated with an introduction and notes by Daniel J. Donno, University of California Press, 1981.

The Island of Scientists

Though not strictly a scientist, Francis Bacon (1561–1626) was the first man to see that science would transform life on earth, and the first to envisage it as the centre of a nation's cultural effort. The European scientific movement of the seventeenth and eighteenth centuries looked back to him as its founder. His *New Atlantis* (1627), the first science-fiction novel, is set on a Pacific island, Bensalem, where scientific research is, as in our modern world, the major intellectual enterprise. To allay fears, already current in the seventeenth century, that science would make people godless and ungovernable, Bacon presents his Bensalemites as exemplary citizens. They are devoutly Christian, and much given to ritual and ceremony. They are also remarkably chaste ('no stews, no dissolute houses, no courtesans, nor anything of that kind') and heterosexual ('As for masculine love, they have no touch of it').

Their 'science' contains a good deal of semi-magical belief, still popular in Bacon's day. But it also anticipates modern scientific advances. They have developed synthetic perfumes and flavours, robots which imitate men, animals and fish, sound-synthesizers, submarines, engines that travel faster than a bullet, flying machines, telephones, explosives more destructive than any available in the seventeenth century, and something that sounds remarkably like napalm.

Four centuries before the DNA revolution, Bacon also anticipates the results (though not the means) of genetic engineering. His scientists can modify plants and animals, as modern gene-splicing can. They can also design new life forms, in line with the ambitions of present-day biogeneticists, who hope to create entirely new species of 'transgenic' animals. Already a race of 'supermice' and (in 1995) fruit flies with eyes on their wings, legs and antennae have been developed. The Bensalemite experimenters are almost as adventurous.

We make, by art, in . . . orchards and gardens, trees and flowers to come earlier or later than their seasons; and to come up and bear more speedily than by their natural course they do. We make them

[63]

also by art greater much than their nature; and their fruit greater and sweeter and of differing taste, smell, colour and figure, from their nature ... We have also parks and enclosures of all sorts of beasts and birds, which we use not only for view or rareness, but likewise for dissections and trials, that thereby we may take light what may be wrought upon the body of man. Wherein we find many strange effects, as, continuing life in them, though divers parts which you account vital be perished and taken forth; resuscitating of some that seem dead in appearance, and the like. We also try all poisons and other medicines upon them ... By art likewise we make them greater or taller than their kind is, and contrariwise dwarf them and stay their growth. We make them more fruitful and bearing than their kind is, and contrariwise barren and not generative. And we also make them differ in colour, shape, activity, many ways. We find means to make commixtures and copulations of different kinds, which have produced many new kinds, and them not barren, as the general opinion is. We make a number of kinds of serpents, worms, flies, fishes, of putrefaction, whereof some are advanced (in effect) to be perfect creatures, like beasts or birds, and have sexes, and do propagate. Neither do we this by chance, but we know beforehand of what matter and commixture what kind of those creatures will arise.

Bacon also foresees the dilemma of the modern scientist whose knowledge, if it gets into the hands of politicians, may wreak havoc. The Bensalemite scientist explains:

We have consultations, which of the inventions and experiences which we have discovered shall be published, and which not; and take an oath of secrecy for the concealing of those which we think fit to keep secret, though some of those we do reveal sometimes to the state, and some not.

Source: Francis Bacon, *New Atlantis*, 1627.

Honours for Schoolteachers

In 1648 Samuel Gott (1614–71), a London ironmonger's son, published a huge Latin romance-cum-utopia called *New Jerusalem*. It is set at some indefinite time in the future when the Jews have been converted to Christianity. They now enjoy 'wonderful prosperity'. The capital of their Hebrew-speaking Jewish state is New Jerusalem, a walled city with twelve gates all of solid brass, built on the ruins of Old Jerusalem. Gott's book is full of admiration for the Jewish people. They live austere, efficient lives. They value hard work and commercial success. Beggars are despised. Education is accorded great importance.

The Jews of New Jerusalem do not hold schoolmasters in contempt, as so many other nations do, nor do they class them simply as superior servants to see chiefly that the children are kept safe, and do not get into mischief. On the contrary they are classed with the chief magistrates of the nation, and especially are those schoolmasters held in honour who have the charge of the very young and untrained, for they are invested with the Order of the Sun, appropriately enough too, for the sun is the dispeller of all darkness . . .

The earliest faults that show themselves in children are passion and an over-readiness to cry and yell, and afterwards obstinacy, pride and envy. These are the vices we first of all try to master. We foster a voluntary habit of endurance and good temper, more by contrivance and the giving of prizes than by moral precepts. We do not allow anything to be wrung from us by tears – nothing is less likely to affect us. Obstinacy is made to yield to fear and reverence. We take great care not to encourage a too haughty temper by empty flattery. Kindness and liberality are commended. None are allowed to take pleasure in others' misfortunes or to mock at them, whether they be in real life or only, maybe, on the stage. Especially do we try to restrain the violent desires of the child's nature within the bonds

[65]

of temperance and chastity. We put special restrictions on eating and sleeping too much. All must rise early and eat whatever happens to be set before them. Hardly ever do they get the chance of delicacies. But sometimes to create disgust we allow them to gorge to repletion. By such training good manners can be best formed.

Source: Samuel Gott, *Nova Solyma. The Ideal City; or Jerusalem Regained*, translated by Walter Begley, John Murray, 1902.

The Earth Shall Be Made a Common Treasury

The Diggers, who also called themselves the 'True Levellers', were one of the radical political splinter-groups to emerge from the turmoil of the English Civil War. They were egalitarian communists and pacifists. Their leader, Gerrard Winstanley (1609–76), was a cloth merchant, born in Wigan, whose business had been ruined by the war. His political programme came as a mystical revelation. He wrote in 1649:

Not a full year since, being quiet at my work, my heart was filled with sweet thoughts, and many things were revealed to me which I never read in books, nor heard from the mouth of any flesh. And when I began to speak of them, some people could not bear my words; and amongst those revelations this was one, that the earth shall be made a common treasury of livelihood to whole mankind, without respect of persons. And I had a voice within me bade me declare it all abroad . . . There shall be no buying nor selling, no fairs or markets . . . There shall be none lords over others, but everyone shall be a lord of himself.

Winstanley obeyed his voice. In April 1649 he and twenty or thirty other poor men began to cultivate the waste ground at St George's Hill near Cobham, Surrey, sowing corn, parsnips, carrots and beans. 'They invite all to come in and help them,' an observer noted, 'and promise them meat, drink and clothes.' At the time between one-third and two-thirds of England was waste land. The Digger answer to poverty was the communal cultivation of this. The conditions they faced were severe. The rural poor suffered acutely in the period 1620–50. Wages were officially fixed below the cost of subsistence. The average agricultural wage was sixpence a day, which was the cost of a single loaf. 'Divers of us having 5, 6, 7, 8, 9 in family,' a Digger pamphlet reads, 'we cannot get bread for one of them by our labour.' By cultivating the waste land, Winstanley and his Diggers were seen to be infringing the property rights of local landlords, and swift reprisals followed.

The landlords applied successfully to the Council of State for military assistance, though some soldiers of Cromwell's New Model Army seem, when they arrived, to have been sympathetic to the commune. A mob of rich landowners, including the local parson, organized attacks on the colony, raking up their seeds, driving off their cows, pulling down and burning the cottages they had built – 'not pitying', Winstanley records, 'the cries of many little children and their frighted mothers'. When the unresisting Diggers asked why they were being persecuted, the landowners replied, 'Because you do not know God, nor will not come to church.' Even after these depredations the Diggers remained patient and cheerful. 'They have,' Winstanley reported early in 1650, 'built them some few little hutches, like calf-cribs, and there they lie anights.' But the persecutors were too powerful and persistent to be resisted. By Easter 1650 the Digger colony had ceased to exist. We do not even know where or when Winstanley died. His pamphlets, however, remain, and contain some of the most forceful prose of the seventeenth century. He is a devout communist. The two greatest sins, he says, are private property and the defending of private property by law.

These curses are not found in man's infancy:

Look upon a child that is new born, or till he grows up to some few years. He is innocent, harmless, humble, patient, gentle, easy to be entreated, not envious. And this is Adam or mankind in his innocency. And this continues till outward objects entice him to pleasure or seek content without him. And when he consents or suffers the imaginary covetousness within to close with the objects, then he falls and is taken captive.

Winstanley hates cruelty, and in his early pamphlets he takes the advanced position of complete opposition to capital punishment:

If a man can say he can give life, then he hath power to take away life. But if the power of life and death be only in the hand of the Lord, then surely he is a murderer of the Creation that takes away the life of his fellow creature man, by any law whatsoever.

Experience of bitter persecution made Winstanley less tolerant. His last work, *The Law of Freedom* (1651), addressed to Cromwell, takes the form of a blueprint for an ideal commonwealth. In Winstanley's utopia anyone who administers the law for money or reward, and anyone who buys or sells anything, will be executed. Money is abolished. All produce and manufactures are taken to common state storehouses, from which all families will freely draw their supplies. Doctors, too, will serve everyone freely: there will be, in effect, a National Health Service. To prevent the system being unfairly exploited by the lazy, everyone will be forced to learn a practical trade, and pursue it – till age forty, which will be the universal retirement age. Any slackness will be punished by slavery. There will be no leisured class. No one will be allowed to devote himself merely to book learning, which, besides being equivalent, in Winstanley's view, to idleness, produces clergy and lawyers who 'advance themselves to be lords and masters above their labouring brethren'. Wealth in Winstanley's eyes is theft. So is ownership of land.

No man can be rich but he must be rich either by his own labours or by the labours of other men, helping him. If a man have no help from his neighbour he shall never gather an estate of hundreds and thousands a year. If other men help him to work, then are those riches his neighbour's as well as his; for they be the fruit of other men's labours as well as his own . . . Rich men receive all they have from the labourer's hand, and what they give, they give away other men's labours, not their own; therefore they are not righteous actors in the earth . . .

True freedom lies where a man receives his nourishment and pres- ervation, and that is in the use of the earth. For as man is compounded of the four materials of the creation, fire, water, earth, and air, so is he preserved by the compounded bodies of these four . . . Surely then, oppressing lords of manors, exacting landlords, and tithe-takers, may as well say their brethren shall not breathe in the air nor enjoy warmth in their bodies, nor have the moist waters to fall upon them in showers, unless they will pay them rent for it; as to say, their brethren shall not work upon earth, nor eat the fruits thereof, unless they will hire that liberty of them. For he that takes upon him to restrain his brother from the liberty of the one, may upon the same ground restrain him from the liberty of all four, viz., fire, water, earth and air.

A man had better have no body, than to have no food for it. Therefore this restraining of the earth from brethren by brethren is oppression and bondage; but the free enjoyment thereof is true freedom.

Source: *Gerrard Winstanley. Selections from his Works*, edited by Leonard Hamilton, with an introduction by Christopher Hill, The Cresset Press, 1949.

On Not Being a Round Quadrangle

Thomas Hobbes (1588–1679) lived through the English Civil War. This made him value peace and stability, and the effect on his political thinking is evident. He had acted as unofficial secretary to Sir Francis Bacon (see p. 63), and like Bacon he aimed at scientific knowledge. But it was the science of government he studied. If properly worked out, he believed, politics could be just as scientific as mathematics: 'The skill of making and maintaining commonwealths consisteth in certain rules, as doth arithmetic and geometry.' In *Leviathan* (1651) he starts from first principles. All men are selfish. If a man seems to act unselfishly, his motives are nevertheless selfish, namely 'to gain the reputation of charity or magnanimity, or to deliver his mind from the pain of compassion'. Even seemingly attractive aspects of human conduct, like humour, are completely selfish.

Joy, arising from imagination of a man's own power and ability, is that exultation of the mind which is called glorying . . . Sudden glory is the passion which maketh those grimaces called laughter, and is caused either by some sudden act of their own that pleaseth them, or by the apprehension of some deformed thing in another, by comparison whereof they suddenly applaud themselves.

A consequence of man's selfishness, Hobbes argues, is that if there were no law and no government, men would be perpetually at one another's throats.

It is manifest that during the time men live without a common power to keep them all in awe, they are in that condition which is called war; and such a war as is of every man against every man . . . In such condition, there is no place for industry, because the fruit thereof is uncertain; and consequently no culture of the earth, no navigation, no use of the commodities that may be imported by sea, no commodious building, no instruments of moving and removing such things as require much force, no knowledge of the face of the earth, no account of time, no arts, no letters, no society, and that which is worst of all, continual fear and danger of violent death, and the life of man solitary, poor, nasty, brutish and short.

Hobbes calls this primitive state the state of nature. Rather confusingly, however, he proceeds to argue that it is actually incompatible with man's nature to live in such a state. For man's nature drives him to find a way of living that can provide security and contentment – namely, a governed state, with laws. It looks as if Hobbes is saying that it is natural for man to live in a primitive, lawless state *and* natural for him not to. The confusion is (just about) soluble, if we assume Hobbes to be saying that it *used to be* natural for man to live in a primitive lawless state, but that with the growth of reason it became clear that such a state was against man's nature. However, deep down the confusion remains. Hobbes has to concede that laws and government are not natural to man, because primitive man in his state of perpetual war did not have them. But he wants to argue that they are so necessary to peace and security that they must count as natural. The peace and security that laws and government give are obtainable, he argues, only if men agree to found a commonwealth.

The only way to erect such a common power as may be able to defend them from the invasions of foreigners, and the injuries of one another, and thereby to secure them in such sort as that by their own industry and by the fruits of the earth they may nourish themselves and live contentedly, is to confer all their power and strength upon one man, or upon one assembly of men, that may reduce all their wills, by plurality of voices, unto one will. Which is as much as to say, to appoint one man, or assembly of men, to bear their person [i.e., to represent them], and every one to own and acknowledge himself to be author of whatsoever he that so beareth their person shall act, or cause to be acted, in those things that concern the common peace and safety; and therein to submit their wills, every one to his will, and their judgements to his judgement. This is more than consent or concord. It is a real unity of them all in one and the same person, made by covenant of every man with every man, in such a manner as if every man should say to every man, *I authorise and give up my right of governing myself to this man, or to this assembly of men, on this condition, that thou give up thy right to him, and authorise all his actions in like manner.* This done, the multitude so united in one person is called a Commonwealth, in

Latin, *civitas*. This is the generation of that great Leviathan, or rather (to speak more reverently) of that mortal God, to which we owe, under the immortal God, our peace and defence.

Since, for Hobbes, the formation of men into commonwealths is a scientific consequence of human nature, it can be expressed as a law of nature. Similarly, the conventions that allow men to live peaceably in commonwealths are not just (he argues) desirable habits, but laws of nature, as inevitable as the laws of physics. Hobbes spells out these laws.

A Law of Nature (*Lex Naturalis*) is a precept or general rule, found out by reason, by which a man is forbidden to do that which is destructive of his life, or taketh away the means of preserving the same, and to omit that by which he thinketh it may be best preserved . . . The first branch of which rule containeth the first and fundamental Law of Nature, which is *to seek peace and follow it.* The second, the sum of the right of nature, which is *by all means we can to defend ourselves.*

If men try to defend themselves without a central government, the result (see above) is perpetual war, and a life 'nasty, brutish and short'. It follows that to give up one's individual right of self-defence to the government is to obey natural law – that 'Law of Nature', as Hobbes puts it, 'by which we are obliged to transfer to another, such rights as, being retained, hinder the peace of mankind'. Similarly, to behave in ways that destroy the peace of the commonwealth, by arrogantly claiming privileges, or refusing justice to others, is unscientific, as well as immoral. It abrogates natural law just as much, say, as trying to walk on the ceiling.

The Laws of Nature are immutable and eternal. For injustice, ingratitude, arrogance, pride, iniquity, acception of persons [i.e., not distributing to each man what reasonably belongs to him] and the rest can never be made lawful. For it can never be that war shall preserve life and peace destroy it.

So far Hobbes's reasoning seems entirely benign – even if it seems strange to us to talk about 'laws of nature' that can be disobeyed. However, his scientific theory starts to show its teeth when the question of dissent, or opposition to the government, arises. The idea that people can live under government and be free is, he points out, ridiculous. To talk of a 'free subject' is just as illogical 'as if a man should talk to me of a round quadrangle . . . I should not say he were in error, but that his words were without meaning, that is to say, absurd'. Similarly, the notion that we are capable of freely deciding what is right or wrong, or that we have a duty to obey our consciences, is pernicious.

The diseases of a commonwealth proceed from the poison of seditious doctrines, whereof one is *That every private man is judge of good and evil actions* . . . It is manifest that the measure of good and evil actions is the civil law, and the judge, the legislator, who is always representative of the commonwealth. From this false doctrine men are disposed to debate with themselves and dispute the commands of the commonwealth, and afterwards to obey or disobey them, as in their private judgements they shall think fit. Whereby the commonwealth is distracted and weakened. Another doctrine repugnant to civil society is that *whatsoever a man does against his conscience is sin.*

It will be seen that in effect Hobbes advocates totalitarianism. One authority alone is allowable within the Hobbesian state.

In particular, a second, 'spiritual' authority (e.g. the Christian church) cannot be permitted. Whether or not Hobbes was an atheist is debatable. Some contemporaries suspected he was, though he is careful to include respectful references to God in his published writing. But he mocks the idea of a spiritual realm, beyond the reach of the state and the law. To believe in this, he insists, is like believing in 'a Kingdom of Fairies, in the dark'. For the church to pretend it has access to such a 'higher' realm, and can therefore justifiably oppose the dictates of the state, is to 'set up a supremacy against the sovereignty'. For Hobbes, the state alone has the right to declare what is right and wrong. 'Sin is nothing but the transgression of the law.' Private morality is an illusion. Any dictator would happily agree.

Source: Thomas Hobbes, *The Leviathan, or The Matter, Form, and Power of a Commonwealth, Ecclesiastical and Civil,* 1651 (modernized).

Holy and Cheerful

Andrew Marvell (1621–78) must have known that the facts were less idyllic than he makes out in his poem 'Bermudas'. The islands were originally discovered by the Spaniards in the early sixteenth century. But they remained uninhabited until 1609 when the English admiral Sir George Somers beached his flagship *Sea Venture* after hitting one of the reefs. When he died in Bermuda the following year, his body was taken back to Devon, and three men and a dog were left in possession. According to a contemporary report, they ruled their 'little commonwealth for a while with brotherly regency', planting corn and other crops. But they fell out when they found, on the beach, a valuable lump of ambergris (a secretion of the sperm whale, used in perfume manufacture). They fought, and one of them was bitten by the dog. Their desperate plan to build a boat and sail to Virginia, so that they could cash in on their find, was thwarted by the arrival of sixty English settlers. Bitter religious disputes soon broke out among the new arrivals. Drunkenness and debauchery were problems, and the poor were dispossessed by greedy profiteers. In 1616 a black and an Indian were brought to the island as slaves, and the slave population rapidly increased. A mid-century report narrates 'the unhappy divisions' that have fallen out among the islanders.

In 1653 Marvell stayed with the Puritan divine John Oxenbridge, who had gone to the Bermudas twenty years earlier to escape the persecution of nonconformists by Charles I's Archbishop Laud (the 'prelate's rage' referred to in the poem). No doubt Oxenbridge told him the unhappy truth. Despite this, his poem celebrates a utopia of plenty and divine blessedness, in the spirit of his contemporary, Lewis Hughes, who reflected that 'The islands have been kept from the beginning of the world for the English nation and no other'. The 'apples' the poem refers to are pineapples.

> Where the remote Bermudas ride
> In the ocean's bosom unespied,
> From a small boat, that rowed along,
> The listening winds received this song.

'What should we do but sing his praise
That led us through the watery maze,
Unto an isle so long unknown,
And yet far kinder than our own?
Where he the huge sea-monsters wracks,
That lift the deep upon their backs,
He lands us on a grassy stage,
Safe from the storms, and prelate's rage.
He gave us this eternal spring,
Which here enamels everything,
And sends the fowl to us in care,
On daily visits through the air.
He hangs in shades the orange bright,
Like golden lamps in a green night,
And does in the pom'granates close
Jewels more rich than Ormus shows.
He makes the figs our mouths to meet,
And throws the melons at our feet,
But apples plants of such a price,
No tree could ever bear them twice.
With cedars, chosen by his hand,
From Lebanon, he stores the land,
And makes the hollow seas, that roar,
Proclaim the ambergris on shore.
He cast (of which we rather boast)
The gospel's pearl upon our coast,
And in these rocks for us did frame
A temple, where to sound his name.
Oh let our voice his praise exalt,
Till it arrive at heaven's vault:
Which thence (perhaps) rebounding, may
Echo beyond the Mexique Bay.'
    Thus sung they, in the English boat,
An holy and a cheerful note,
And all the way, to guide their chime,
With falling oars they kept the time.

Source: Andrew Marvell, *Miscellaneous Poems*, 1681 (spelling modernized).

Paradise Regained

Thomas Traherne (1637–74), poet and mystic, was the first English writer to try to describe how children see the world. Further, he maintained that we can all regain the child's luminous vision, and re-enter paradise, if only we learn to value the 'great, common and simple' things – the sun, the sky, the air – instead of hankering after honours and riches. So for Traherne utopia is here and now, but before it reveals itself as utopia it has to be seen with a child's love and wonder. He was the son of a shoemaker in Hereford, and it is probably Hereford and its surroundings that he recalls in this famous passage from his *Centuries of Meditation*.

Certainly Adam in paradise had not more sweet and curious apprehensions of the world than I when I was a child . . . The corn was orient and immortal wheat, which never should be reaped, nor was ever sown. I thought it had stood from everlasting to everlasting. The dust and stones of the street were as precious as gold. The gates were at first the end of the world. The green trees, when I saw them first through one of the gates, transported and ravished me; their sweetness and unusual beauty made my heart to leap, and almost mad with ecstasy, they were such strange and wonderful things. The men! O what venerable and reverend creatures did the aged seem! Immortal cherubims! And the young men glittering and sparkling angels; and maids strange and seraphic pieces of life and beauty! Boys and girls tumbling in the street and playing were moving jewels. I knew not that they were born or should die. But all things abided eternally, as they were in their proper places. Eternity was manifest in the light of the day, and something infinite behind everything appeared, which talked with my expectation and moved my desire. The city seemed to stand in Eden, or to be built in heaven. The streets were mine, the temple was mine, the people were mine, their clothes and gold and silver was mine, as much as their sparkling eyes, fair skins and ruddy faces. The skies were mine, and so were the sun and moon and stars, and all the world was mine, and I the only spectator and enjoyer of it. I knew no churlish proprieties, nor bounds nor divisions. But all proprieties and divisions were mine, all treasures and the possessors of them. So that with much ado I was corrupted, and made to learn the dirty devices of this world. Which now I unlearn, and become as it were a little child again, that I may enter into the Kingdom of Heaven.

Source: Thomas Traherne, *Centuries of Meditation*, edited by Bertram Dobell, 1908 (modernized)

The Empress's New Clothes

The Blazing World (1666) by Margaret Cavendish (1623–76) is the first known English utopia written by a woman. It would be encouraging to be able to report that it takes new strides towards humanity and social justice. Alas, the contrary is true. Not only is it tedious and rambling. It also strongly endorses tyranny, aristocratic privilege, opulence, and self-aggrandizement. Cavendish was a noted and flamboyant eccentric. One woman contemporary remarked that there were 'many soberer people in Bedlam'. Though almost wholly uneducated, she was a prolific author, her works encompassing a bizarre medley of philosophy, scientific speculation, oratory, poetry and unactable plays. During the English Civil War she was maid-of-honour to Charles I's queen, Henrietta Maria, and went into exile with her to Paris when the cavaliers were defeated. There she married the Marquis of Newcastle, who had been one of Charles I's army commanders. After the war the childless couple returned and lived on his estate in Nottinghamshire.

The heroine of *The Blazing World* is a young lady, abducted by a merchant, who sails with her to the North Pole. There the merchant and all the crew die from the cold. The ship, however, enters another world (the 'Blazing World') which is joined to our own at the pole. This new world is inhabited by men in the shapes of bears, foxes, geese, worms, fish, flies, magpies, ants and (writes Cavendish) 'many more, which I cannot all remember'. The emperor is absolute monarch. All his government officials are castrated, because they cause less trouble if they do not have wives and families. As soon as the emperor sets eyes on the young lady he marries her and makes her his empress. Most of the book is taken up with a series of debates in which the new empress questions and harangues representatives of the bearmen, fox-men etc. on subjects ranging from whether insects have blood to the nature of the soul. On all these topics both she and they are loquaciously unenlightening. She also questions a number of immortal spirits whom she summons to converse with her. Among these is the spirit of Margaret Cavendish, Duchess of Newcastle, who thus becomes a character in her own fiction. The empress and the duchess feel strong mutual attraction and (we are told) 'became platonic lovers, although they were both female'. Towards the end of the book the empress hears that in the world she left behind (i.e., our real world) the king of her country is under attack by foreign fleets. Accordingly she returns to the real world, taking with her a Blazing-World army and supplies of a Blazing-World chemical that ignites on contact with water. With this she systematically and ruthlessly burns the fleets and cities of every nation that will not pay tribute to her king, and so makes him absolute monarch of the whole world.

The account of the empress's first meeting with her future husband illustrates Cavendish's obsession with power, wealth, privilege and display.

The first part of the palace was, as the imperial city, all of gold, and when it came to the Emperor's apartment, it was so rich with diamonds, pearls, rubies, and the like precious stones, that it surpasses my skill to enumerate them all. Amongst the rest, the imperial room of state appeared most magnificent; it was paved with green diamonds (for in that world are diamonds of all colours) so artificially as it seemed but of one piece. The pillars were set with diamonds so close, and in such a manner, that they appeared most glorious to the sight. Between every pillar was a bow or arch of a certain sort of diamonds, the like whereof our world does not afford; which being placed in every one of the arches in several rows, seemed just like so many rainbows of several different colours. The roof of the arches was of blue diamonds, and in the midst thereof was a carbuncle, which represented the sun. The rising and setting sun at the east and west side of the room were made of rubies. Out of this room there was a passage into the Emperor's bed-chamber, the walls whereof were of jet, and the floor of black marble; the roof was of mother of pearl, where the moon and blazing stars were represented by white diamonds, and his bed was made of diamonds and carbuncles.

No sooner was the Lady brought before the Emperor, but he conceived her to be some goddess, and offered to worship her; which she refused, telling him (for by that time she had pretty well learned their language) that although she came out of another world, yet was she but a mortal. At which the Emperor rejoicing, made her his wife, and gave her an absolute power to rule and govern all that world as she pleased. But her subjects, who could hardly be persuaded to believe her mortal, tendered her all the veneration and worship due to a deity.

Her accoutrement after she was made Empress was as followeth:

on her head she wore a cap of pearl, and a half-moon of diamonds just before it; on the top of her crown came spreading over a broad carbuncle, cut in the form of the sun; her coat was of pearl, mixed with blue diamonds, and fringed with red ones; her buskins and sandals were of green diamonds. In her left hand she held a buckler, to signify the defence of her dominions, which buckler was made of that sort of diamond as has several different colours, and being cut and made in the form of an arch, showed like a rainbow. In her right hand she carried a spear made of a white diamond, cut like the tail of a blazing star, which signified that she was ready to assault those that proved her enemies.

None was allowed to use or wear gold but those of the imperial race, which were the only nobles of the state; nor durst anyone wear jewels but the Emperor, the Empress, and their eldest son.

Source: Margaret Cavendish, Duchess of Newcastle, *The Description of a New World Called the Blazing World*, 1666.

Perfect Humans?

The depiction of Adam and Eve's life in Eden by John Milton (1608–74) in his epic poem *Paradise Lost* (1667) represents the primal utopia. But Milton's account was in several respects unusual. His Adam and Eve are obliged to work, because their garden is so rampant that it needs constant pruning, whereas in the Genesis account work is part of God's curse on mankind following the Fall. Further, Milton's Adam and Eve enjoy sexual intercourse in Eden, another departure from Genesis and from the Christian tradition which tended to depict them as pure, pre-sexual or childlike. Milton's unfallen Adam even admits that he feels sexual passion, which Christian commentators had always condemned as an unmistakable mark of fallen man. These changes make Milton's Eden more like our world than his readers would have expected. In other respects, though, his Adam and Eve conform to established Garden-of-Eden conventions. They are naked, unashamed vegetarians, surrounded by tame animals. Adam, as male, has God-given authority over the female, a right signified by his hairstyle, among other features. Modern feminist critics have severely censured this aspect of Milton's imaginings.

We first see the human pair through the eyes of Satan, who has flown up from Hell to the newly created earth, and finds it full of living creatures, such as he has never encountered before.

> Two of far nobler shape erect and tall,
> Godlike erect, with native honour clad
> In naked majesty seemed lords of all,
> And worthy seemed, for in their looks divine
> The image of their glorious maker shone,
> Truth, wisdom, sanctitude severe and pure,
> Severe but in true filial freedom placed;
> Whence true authority in men; though both
> Not equal, as their sex not equal seemed;
> For contemplation he and valour formed,

For softness she and sweet attractive grace,
He for God only, she for God in him:
His fair large front [forehead] and eye sublime declared
Absolute rule; and hyacinthine locks
Round from his parted forelock manly hung
Clustering, but not beneath his shoulders broad:
She as a veil down to the slender waist
Her unadorned golden tresses wore
Dishevelled, but in wanton ringlets waved
As the vine curls her tendrils, which implied
Subjection, but required with gentle sway,
And by her yielded, by him best received,
Yielded with coy submission, modest pride,
And sweet reluctant amorous delay.
Nor those mysterious parts were then concealed,
Then was not guilty shame, dishonest shame
Of nature's works, honour dishonourable,
Sin-bred, how have ye troubled all mankind
With shows instead, mere shows of seeming pure,
And banished from man's life his happiest life,
Simplicity and spotless innocence.
So passed they naked on, nor shunned the sight
Of God or angel, for they thought no ill:
So hand in hand they passed, the loveliest pair
That ever since in love's embraces met,
Adam the goodliest man of men since born
His sons, the fairest of her daughters Eve.
Under a tuft of shade that on a green
Stood whispering soft, by a fresh fountain side
They sat them down, and after no more toil
Of their sweet gardening labour than sufficed
To recommend cool zephyr, and made ease
More easy, wholesome thirst and appetite
More grateful, to their supper fruits they fell,
Nectarine fruits which the compliant boughs
Yielded them, sidelong as they sat recline
On the soft downy bank damasked with flowers:
The savoury pulp they chew, and in the rind
Still as they thirsted scoop the brimming stream;

Nor gentle purpose, nor endearing smiles
Wanted, nor youthful dalliance as beseems
Fair couple, linked in happy nuptial league,
Alone as they. About them frisking played
All beasts of the earth, since wild, and of all chase
In wood or wilderness, forest or den;
Sporting the lion ramped, and in his paw
Dandled the kid; bears, tigers, ounces, pards,
Gambolled before them, the unwieldly elephant
To make them mirth used all his might, and wreathed
His lithe proboscis.

Though Milton's Eden is blissful, it is – unlike many utopias – not static. His Adam and Eve were capable of improvement and, if they had not fallen, would have improved. This is explained to them by Raphael, a visiting angel. He accepts Adam's offer of refreshment, and tells him that:

... from these corporal nutriments perhaps
Your bodies may at last turn all to spirit,
Improved by tract of time, and winged ascend
Ethereal, as we ...

It seems then that Milton's Adam and Eve, although they could and should have resisted Satan's temptation, were not created perfect. They could have been created better, and being better would entail being able to fly like an angel. Raphael's prediction brings into Milton's epic the common utopian desire for air-travel.

Source: John Milton, *Paradise Lost*, 1667 (modernized).

Increase and Multiply

Henry Neville (1620–94), the Oxford-educated son of a diplomat, was a doctrinaire republican and became a member of Cromwell's Council of State. In 1658 he was charged with atheism and blasphemy, but the charges were dropped. His *The Isle of Pines* (1668) was extremely popular, and translated into French, German, Dutch and Italian. It purports to be a 'true relation' by a Dutch seaman, Henry Cornelius Van Sloetten, whose ship is driven off course by a storm. It anchors off a southern island which, Van Sloetten finds, has a population of some 12,000 people, all descended from an Englishman, George Pine, who was shipwrecked there with four women in 1569. Many of the book's original readers seem to have taken it to be a factual account. Van Sloetten relates that the islanders all speak English and walk around naked, except that the women weave scanty coverings out of grass and flowers. The king, William Pine, George Pine's grandson, gives Van Sloetten a copy of his grandfather's personal narrative. This records that he was a book-keeper, in the service of a wealthy English merchant, sailing out to set up a trading post in the East Indies. When they were shipwrecked, all the crew and passengers drowned, except for Pine, his master's fifteen-year-old daughter, two maidservants and a Negro female slave.

The place, as we after found, being a large island, and disjoined, and out of sight of any other land, was wholly uninhabited by any people, neither was there any hurtful beast to annoy us. But on the contrary, the country was so very pleasant, being always clothed with green, and full of pleasant fruits, and variety of birds, ever warm and never colder than in England in September, so that this place (had it the culture that skillful people might bestow on it) would prove a paradise.

The woods afforded us a sort of nuts, as big as a large apple, whose kernel being pleasant and dry, we made use of instead of bread, and a sort of water-fowl like ducks, and their eggs, and a beast about the size of a goat, and almost such a like creature, which brought [gave birth to] two young ones at a time, and that twice a year, of which the lowlands and woods were very full, being a very harmless creature and tame, so that we could easily take and kill them. Fish also, especially shellfish, which we could best come by, we had great store of, so that in effect as to food we wanted nothing. And thus, and by suchlike helps, we continued six months, without any disturbance or want.

Idleness and fullness of everything begot in me a desire of enjoying the women. Beginning now to grow more familiar, I had persuaded the two maids to let me lie with them, which I did at first in private, but after, custom taking away shame (there being none but us) we did it more openly, as our lusts gave us liberty. For we wanted no food, and living idly, and seeing us at liberty to do our wills, without hope of ever returning home, made us bold. One of the first of my consorts, with whom I first accompanied (the tallest and handsomest) proved presently with child. The second was my master's daughter, and the other also not long after fell into the same condition, none now remaining but my Negro who, seeing what we did, longed also for her share. One night, I being asleep, my Negro, with the consent of the others, got close to me, thinking, it being dark, to beguile me. But I awaking, and feeling her, and perceiving who it was, yet willing to try the difference, satisfied myself with her as well as with one of the rest. That night, although the first time, she proved also with child. So that in the year of our being here all my women were with child by me, and they all coming at different seasons were a great help to one another. The first brought me a brave boy. My master's daughter was the youngest: she brought me a girl. So did the other maid, who being something fat sped worse at her labour. The Negro had no pain at all and brought me a fine white girl. So I had one boy and three girls. The women were soon well again, and the two first with child again before the two last were brought to bed – my custom being not to lie with any of them after they were with child, till others were so likewise, and not with the black at all after she was with child, which commonly was at the first time I lay with her – which was in the night and not else, my stomach would not serve me, although she was one of the handsomest blacks I had seen, and her children as comely as any of the rest. We had no clothes for them, and therefore, when they had sucked, we laid them in moss to sleep, and took no further care of them, for we knew when they were gone more would come, the women never failing once a year at least, and none of the children (for all the hardship we put them to) were ever sick. So that wanting now nothing but clothes, nor them much neither, other than for decency, the warmth of the country and custom supplying that defect, we were now well satisfied with our condition. Our family beginning to grow large, there being nothing to hurt us, we many times lay abroad on mossy banks, under the shelter of some trees, or suchlike – for having nothing else to do I had made me several arbours to sleep in with my women in the heat of the day. In these I and my women passed the time away, they being never willing to be out of my company.

And having now no thought of ever returning home, as having resolved and sworn to each other never to part or leave one another, or the place; having by my several wives forty-seven children, boys and girls, but mostly girls, and growing up apace, we were all of us very fleshly, the country so well agreeing with us that we never ailed anything. My Negro having had twelve was the first that left bearing, so I never meddled with her more. My master's daughter, by whom I had most children, being the youngest and handsomest, was most fond of me, and I of her. Thus we lived for sixteen years, till, perceiving my eldest boy to mind the ordinary work of nature, by seeing what we did, I gave him a mate, and so I did to all the rest, as fast as they grew up and were capable. My wives having left bearing, my children began to breed apace, so we were like to be a multitude. My first wife brought me thirteen children, my second seven, my master's daughter fifteen, and the Negro twelve, in all forty-seven.

After we had lived there 22 years, my Negro died suddenly, but I could not perceive anything that ailed her. Most of my children being grown, as fast as we married them I sent them and placed them over the river by themselves severally, because we would not pester one another, and now, they being all grown up and gone and married (after our manner), except some two or three of the youngest, for, growing myself into years, I liked not the wanton annoyance of young company. Thus having lived to the sixtieth year of my age, and the fortieth of my coming thither, at which time I sent for all of them to bring their children, and there were in number descended from me by these four women, of my children, grandchildren, and great-grandchildren, five hundred and sixty-five of both sorts. I took off the males of one family, and married them to the females of another, not letting any to marry their sisters, as we did formerly out of necessity. So blessing God for his providence and goodness I dismissed them. I having taught some of my children to read formerly, for I had left still the Bible, I charged it should be read once a month at a general meeting. At last one of my wives died, being sixty-eight years of age, which I buried in a place set out on purpose – and within a year after, another. So I had none left now but my master's daughter, and we lived together twelve years longer. At length she died also, so I buried her also next the place where I purposed to be buried myself, and the tall maid, my first wife, next me on the other side, the Negro next without her, and the other maid next my master's daughter. I had now nothing to mind but the place whither I was to go, being very old, almost eighty years. I gave my cabin and furniture that was left to my eldest son after my decease, who had married my eldest daughter by my beloved wife, whom I made king and governor of all the rest. I informed them of the manners of Europe, and charged them to remember the Christian religion, after the manner of them that spake the same language [i.e., the Church of England], and to admit no other, if hereafter any should come to find them out.

And now, once for all, I summoned them to come to me, that I might number them, which I did, and found the estimate to contain, in or about the eightieth year of my age, and the fifty-ninth of my coming there, in all, of all sorts, one thousand five hundred and eighty nine. Thus, praying God to multiply them and send them the true light of the gospel, I last of all dismissed them. For, being now very old, and my sight decayed, I could not expect to live long. I gave this narration (written with my own hand) to my eldest son, who now liveth with me, commanding him to keep it, and if any strangers should come hither by chance, to let them see it and take a copy of it, if they would, that our name be not lost from the earth. I gave these people, descended from me, the name of the *ENGLISH PINES*, *George Pine* being my name, and my master's daughter's name *Sarah English*, my two other wives were *Mary Sparkes* and *Elizabeth Trevor*, so their several descendants are called the *ENGLISH*, the *SPARKES*, and the *TREVORS*, and the *PHILLS*, from the Christian name of the Negro, which was *Philippa*, she having no surname. And the general name of the whole the *ENGLISH PINES*, whom God bless with the dew of heaven, and the fat of the earth, AMEN.

William Pine, George's grandson, tells Van Sloetten about the events that followed the death of George, during the reign of George's eldest son, Henry.

But as it is impossible but that in multitudes disorders will grow, the stronger seeking to oppress the weaker, no tie of religion being strong enough to chain up the depraved nature of mankind, even so amongst them mischiefs began to rise, and they soon fell from those good orders prescribed them by my grandfather. The source from whence those mischiefs sprang was at first, I conceive, the neglect of hearing the Bible read which, according to my grandfather's prescription, was once a month at a general meeting. But now, many of them wandering far up into the country, they quite neglected the coming to it, with all other means of Christian instruction, whereby, the sense of sin being quite lost in them, they fell to whoredoms, incests and adulteries – for that what my grandfather was forced to do for necessity, they did for wantonness, nay, not confining themselves within the bound of any modesty, but brother and sister lay openly together. Those who would not yield to their lewd embraces were by force ravished, yea, many times endangered of their lives. To redress those enormities my father assembled all the company near unto him, to whom he declared the wickedness of those their brethren – who all with one consent agreed that they should be severely punished. And so arming themselves with boughs, stones, and suchlike weapons, they marched against them, who, having notice of their coming, and fearing their deserved punishment, some of them fled into woods, others passed over a great river, which runneth through the heart of our country, hazarding drowning to escape punishment. But the grandest offender of them all was taken, whose name was *John Phill*, the second son of the *Negro-woman* that came with my grandfather into this island. He being proved guilty of divers ravishings and tyrannies committed by him, was adjudged guilty of death, and accordingly was thrown down from a high rock into the sea, where he perished in the waters. Execution being done upon him, the rest were pardoned for what was past, which being notified abroad they returned from those deserts and obscure places wherein they were hidden.

Now as seed being cast into stinking dung produceth good and wholesome corn for the sustentation of man's life, so bad manners produceth good and wholesome laws for the preservation of human society. Soon after my father, with the advice of some few others of his counsel, ordained and set forth these laws to be observed by them.

1. That whosoever should blaspheme or talk irreverently of the name of God should be put to death.
2. That who should be absent from the monthly assembly to hear the Bible read, without sufficient cause shown to the contrary, should for the first default be kept without any victuals or drink for the space of four days, and if he offend therein again, then to suffer death.
3. That who should force or ravish any maid or woman should be burnt to death, the party so ravished putting fire to the wood that should burn him.
4. Whosoever should commit adultery, for the first crime the male shall lose his privities, and the woman have her right eye bored out. If after that she was again taken in the act, she should die without mercy.
5. That whoso injured his neighbour, by laming of his limbs, or taking anything away which he possesseth, shall suffer in the same kind himself by loss of limb, and for defrauding his neighbour, to become servant to him, whilst [until] he had made him double satisfaction.
6. That who should defame or speak evil of the Governor, or refuse to come before him upon summons, should receive a punishment by whipping with rods, and afterwards be exploded from [hissed out of] the city of [by] all the rest of the inhabitants.

Van Sloetten relates that, before leaving the island and sailing home, he and his men intervened, at the request of the Governor, in a civil war between the Phills and the Trevors. Their firearms, which filled the islanders with terror, made it easy for them to restore order. The war had begun when Henry Phill, head of the Phill family, raped a Trevor wife. He was captured and executed.

Like many utopias, Neville's seems to be ambivalent. The first part, recounting George's early days on the island, resonates with sexual liberation and sensual fruition. The old repressions are overthrown. The boundaries of class and race are triumphantly transgressed, as George beds his master's daughter, and responds to black Philippa's advances. Though Philippa was a slave back in England, there is no slavery on the island. Yet in the second part the grim prohibitions of law, religion and racism reassert themselves. That it is the Phills, descendants of the Negro Philippa, who commit sexual outrage, and have to be subdued by European weaponry, reflects the inbuilt neuroses of seventeenth-century white supremacy. That the black woman's sexual appetite drove her into George's arms, whereas with the white women he had to take the initiative, accords with white mythology about the sexual voracity of blacks.

Henry Neville, from whose imagination the prolific Pines sprang, married, but had no children.

Source: Henry Cornelius Van Sloetten [Henry Neville], *The Isle of Pines, or, A Late Discovery of a Fourth Island near Terra Australis Incognita*, 1668.

Reasonable Behaviour

Denis Vairasse (*c*.1630–*c*.1700) was a Huguenot, exiled from France because of his religion. In England he scraped a living by teaching languages, history and geography, and by practising a little espionage. He also wrote an innovative five-book utopia, spiced with romance and mild pornography, called *The History of the Sevarambians* (1677–9). This tells how a Captain Siden (anagram of Denis) and his shipwrecked shipmates get ashore in Australia and discover an advanced civilization, founded, some centuries before, by a great lawgiver Sevarias (anagram of Vairasse). Like the Incas in pre-Conquest Peru, the Sevarambians are communist sun-worshippers. They have a rich language with ten vowels and thirty consonants, but can also speak European languages and Latin. Their observers, disguised as Persians, are stationed all over Europe and send back news of the latest developments.

Two strikingly modern principles dictate social arrangements in Sevarambia. The first is that it is bad for you, especially when young, not to have frequent and regular sex. The second is that religion (insofar as it means belief in the supernatural, contrary to the dictates of reason) breeds ignorance, cruelty, perversion, warfare and tyranny, and should be rooted out of all civil societies.

Contact is first made with the Sevarambians when the search party that Siden sends into the interior, led by a lieutenant called Maurice, is picked up by some Sevarambian border guards and conducted to the city of Sporunde. They are courteously received, and an official called Sermodas explains to them the superiority of Sevarambian civilization.

At night we had a good supper, and two hours after we were all carried to a great hall, where we found fifteen young women who waited there for us. They were most of them very tall and proper women, in painted calico gowns, wearing their black hair in long and thick braids hanging down upon their breasts and shoulders. We were a little surprised to find so many of them in a row, and did much admire at them, not knowing what they stood there for, when Sermodas spoke to us in this manner.

'You wonder, Maurice, to see here so many proper women together, and little understand the reason why you find them in this posture and habit, somewhat different from other women's dress. Know you therefore that these are our slaves, and that they are here to wait upon you and your comrades. You have your several customs in Europe, and so have other countries their own. Some are bad and vicious in nature, and others only seem to be good or bad according to men's prejudices and apprehensions. But there are some that are grounded upon reason, and are truly good in themselves if we rightly consider them. Ours are for the most part, if not all, of this kind, and we hardly have any one which is not established upon Reason. You know, I suppose, that the moderate use of those good things nature hath appointed for all living creatures is good, and that there is nothing but the abuse of them, either in the excess or in the defect, that may be termed bad . . . Among those good things we conceive there are two of the greatest importance viz. the preservation and happy being of every living creature, and the propagation of its species. The means to attain to the first are all those natural actions without which no creature can subsist, and such are eating, drinking, sleeping etc. . . . . For the preservation of every species, Nature hath likewise appointed that every male should be united to a female, that by their union their kind should be preserved, which is her chiefest end. And that they may be the more inclined to accomplish her noble design she hath given them a mutual love and desire of conjunction, and annexed a pleasure to the actual union of the two sexes for the preservation of the species, as a pleasure also in eating and drinking in every animal. These are the eternal laws of God in Nature, and these two ends, together with the pleasure we take in the means through which we may attain them, are not only lawful and necessary but also laudable and commanded . . . Those considerations induced our great lawgiver Sevarias (whose glorious name and love of his incomparable virtues shall ever be sweet and precious to us) to fit his government as near as he could to the laws of nature established upon reason, carefully avoiding to forbid anything that is naturally good in itself, and allowing the moderate use of them to all his subjects. Among the rest of his laws there is one that commands marriage to all men and women as soon as they are come to an age fit for generation, which law and custom we inviolably observe in all our dominions. But because many among us are sometimes obliged to travel and leave their wives at home, we keep in all cities a number of women slaves appointed for their use, so that we do not only give every traveller meat, drink and lodging, but also a woman to lie with him as openly and lawfully as if she were his wife. According to this laudable custom, and being willing to use you as well as any of our own nation, we have appointed so many women as you are men to come and lie with you every other night so long as you remain here with us, if you can find in your hearts to use this privilege.'

You may easily imagine that these reasons quickly prevailed, and that he needed not use any further arguments to persuade us to accept of the proffer. We gave him most humble thanks, told him his reasons were very powerful, and the custom of this country much better than that of Europe in our judgment.

'Well,' saith he, 'use the privilege if you please, find out a method to agree among yourselves, and so I wish you good night.'

As soon as he was gone there came in two men who spake to us in French, and bid us welcome to Sporunde. One of them told us that he was a physician, and his companion a surgeon. He desired us very earnestly to be sincere with him, and to tell him whether any of us had any venereal distemper upon him.

'Gentlemen, I am appointed to examine every one of you upon that score, and if any deny the truth it will turn to his damage and shame; but if he confess it ingeniously he will get love, esteem and a speedy cure.'

Every one of the company said he was free from any such thing. But notwithstanding our saying so, the man would not be satisfied till he had seen and carefully examined every one of us apart in a room next to the hall we stood in.

During the night the travellers are locked in their bedrooms with their chosen bedfellows to prevent 'permutation' (promiscuity), which Sevarambians disapprove of because it causes problems in establishing the paternity of children.

Sevarambian sex laws combine liberty with compulsion. Women must offer themselves for marriage at eighteen, men at twenty-one. There are regular communal marriage ceremonies where young men and women are lined up, and a priest asks each woman to choose a man. She walks down the row of men and takes her pick. If he accepts her, they make till-death-us-do-part promises, and pair off. Any women left over at the end comes back and tries again at the next ceremony. Should she still not have found a husband after three ceremonies, she is accepted among the wives of one of the senators or officials (who, as a perk of office, are allowed several wives). What happens to young men who are unable to find a partner is not revealed. Possibly they are given a female slave.

For the first three years of marriage couples can sleep together only one night in three; then two nights in three till they are twenty-eight, after which it is open season. This reflects the common seventeenth-century belief that too-frequent sexual intercourse produces feeble children. Adultery carries a penalty of seven to ten years in prison, and premarital sex, three years. During imprisonment all prisoners are periodically paraded in public, stripped to the waist, and whipped. Maurice describes one of these punishment sessions, in a style clearly designed to recapture the reader's wandering attention ('I remember that one of the women, who had committed adultery, was a very proper and lusty woman, not above one or two and twenty years of age. She had a very beautiful face, black eyes, brown hair, and a delicate clear skin. But her breasts, which we saw quite naked, were the loveliest I ever beheld . . .').

Mothers are honoured and allowed to wear a purple sash for each child who survives to the age of seven. Barren women are despised: after five years of marriage their husbands are permitted to choose another wife. Wife-swapping is sanctioned by the state, provided that both the husbands and both the wives concerned agree. It often proves an effective way of solving marital discord.

The utopian fixation with sameness and regimentation appears in the laws governing education and dress. At the age of seven, all children are adopted by the state. The parents sign away their rights at a special ceremony. Then both boys and girls attend state schools for four years, learning to read and write, and do military training. At eleven they spend three years farming (and going to school four hours a day). At fourteen they choose a trade. Only the gifted (it is a strictly meritocratic society) go on to higher education.

Everyone (except state officials, who are rather grandly dressed) wears similar clothes, and the colour changes every seven years, working through a spectrum of white, yellow, green, blue, red and black (for the elderly). All citizens have two new suits of clothes every year, and a warm bath once every ten days.

Lying is severely punished. If vicious types do not improve after punishment, they are sent to work in the mines and shut away from the company of honest folk. Deformed or maimed people live in separate cities. Drunkenness is rare, because there are no inns or taverns and the unmarried are forbidden to touch alcohol.

Females as well as men do military service, and Vairasse supplies elaborate descriptions of women's regiments and their uniforms. For some unexplained reason the golden Sevarambian rule of sex-every-night does not apply to soldiers. As might be expected, this leads to infringements of military discipline. The travellers become aware of this while touring an army camp.

As soon as the exercise was over, three young men were brought up under guard, who had been surprised at the maids' camp in the night, on a visit to their mistresses, but had made a shift to get out of the bounds before they were taken. They could not by any means whatever be prevailed on to name the girls they had been to see, choosing rather to suffer alone the punishment which their discipline prescribed for offences of this nature than, by accusing their mistresses, to expose them to the same, which they must have undergone if they could have been discovered. They were all three disarmed and stripped naked to the waist, in which condition they were to run the gauntlet through a lane of all the young women in the army, who had been drawn up, both horse and foot, in two lines for that purpose. Each of the women had a long switch in her hand, which she gave every criminal a stroke with as he passed by her – but they were not allowed to give more than one, and that was enough to have flayed the poor lovers sufficiently, if they had all laid it home. But the greatest part of them tapped so gently that it was plain enough to be perceived they were not so angry as at the beginning they appeared.

The second grand principle of Sevarambian society is contempt for superstition. In this respect Sevarias, the people's first lawgiver, was also their saviour. For before he arrived and conquered them they had been in the grip of a religious tyranny. This is the most daring part of Vairasse's narrative, since the false religion Sevarias roots out has distinct affinities with Catholic Christianity. It was founded by a fraud called Stroukaras, who taught that there was a world of invisible spirits, with whom he was in touch; that he was the son of the Sun; and that he communed with his divine father by means of eagles which he had trained to carry messages. Doubters who questioned his sacred authority were denounced by his priests and massacred. When he died, it was given out that he had ascended to heaven, and was there with his father. Under cover of a show of sanctity, his priests became ruthless exploiters. One of their favourite tricks was to seduce beautiful young women, promising them that the divine Stroukaras would return from heaven and make them his brides. Vairasse's account of what really happened on these occasions illustrates the overheated imaginings about the depravity of the Catholic clergy that persecuted Protestants were prey to.

These ceremonies being performed, the girl was left alone with an old priest, who made her strip herself naked, and taught her to throw herself into a hundred lascivious postures, to solicit Stroukaras to come, see and take possession of her. While she was going through this course of impure ceremonies, the rest of the priests who had retired and left her with the old director for this very purpose, being hid behind a lattice, from whence they could see the whole temple without being themselves seen, indulged their wanton eyes with a view of her person in every attitude. After they had sufficiently satisfied themselves this way, they cast lots who should first enjoy her; and when night was come the girl was conducted into a dark place, set apart for this use, where she was commanded to lie on a bed, and expect, with great devotion, the descent of her celestial love. In a little time, after she was thus posted, artificial lightnings began to flash in her eyes, which inspired her with respect and astonishment. These lightnings were followed with thunder, every clap of which filled her with fear and admiration, for she had been taught to look on all these tricks as the forerunners of the arrival of her glorious lover. However, notwithstanding this apparatus, he always came in obscurity, after having well perfumed himself, and so united his false divinity with the real humanity of this credulous and devoted virgin. After this they kept her on in the same manner till she proved with child, when they restored her to her parents, who received her with great humility and gratitude.

The great king and lawgiver Sevarias put a stop to these corrupt goings-on, banished superstition, and introduced Reason. His religion assumes that there is a God who created the universe (evidently Vairasse felt no reasonable person could doubt that) but everything else is considered uncertain, and all other supernatural beliefs are dismissed. A black veil hangs behind the altar in Sevarambian temples to represent the invisible and eternal God whom humans cannot know. They worship the Sun as a living god, believing him to be God's viceroy in their part of the universe, and the giver of all life on earth. Accordingly a replica of the sun takes its place beside the black veil in their temples. An image of a mother nursing many children is also displayed there. These three symbols, representing the unknown God, the sun, and motherhood, are Vairasse's challenging alternative to the Christian Trinity. As king, Sevarias called himself viceroy of the sun, and his successors do the same.

Though sun-worship is the state religion, many other creeds are tolerated, and opinions vary on such questions as the immortality of the soul. There is even a small sect of Christians, though they are generally laughed at for their absurd beliefs in miracles and mysteries. Sevarambians respect the memory of Jesus Christ, but hold that he was merely a good man with valuable ethical ideas. They believe the universe is infinite and everlasting, but that the various worlds it contains are all temporary, including our own, and that from the destruction of existing stars and heavenly bodies others will be born. Modern astrophysics tells us the same, so here, too, the Sevarambians were surprisingly up to date.

Source: Denis Vairasse, *The History of the Sevarites or Sevarambi*, 1675, and *The History of the Sevarambians*, 1738.

Unisex Australians

Gabriel de Foigny (?1640–?92) was a renegade monk who became a Protestant and settled in Geneva. In constructing his utopia, he seems to have asked himself: 'How could men live in brotherly concord?' His answer was that it would be necessary to eliminate the things men quarrel over – money, possessions, women. Moreover, it would be necessary to remove not just those things, but the need for them. De Foigny shows how this can be done in *A New Discovery of Terra Incognita Australis*; which recounts the adventures of a shipwrecked French mariner, James Sadeur, in Australia – a land then unknown to Europeans.

The Australians, Sadeur finds, live in conditions of such idyllic plenty that they have never developed the idea of money or possessions. The climate is perfect – all-year-round sunshine, no rain – so they are confirmed nudists: 'They are so accustomed to go naked, that they think they cannot speak of covering themselves without being declared enemies to nature, and deprived of reason.' Their trees bear many varieties of nutritious and medicinal fruits, unknown in Europe, so food is no problem. You just reach out your hand and take a meal from the nearest branch. Australians never cook, and the notion of eating meat disgusts them. Their ability to do without women results from a more unusual characteristic.

All the Australians are of both sexes, or hermaphrodites, and if it happen that a child is born but of one, they strangle him as a monster. They are nimble, very active, their flesh is more upon the red than vermilion. They are commonly eight foot high . . . Beard and hair always black, which they never cut because they grow but little . . . They have very little breasts, placed very low, a little redder than vermilion . . . Everyone is obliged to present at least one child to the Heb [the House of Education]. But they bring them forth in so private a manner that it is accounted a crime amongst them to speak of the necessary conjunction in the propagation of mankind. In all the time that I was there I could never discover how generation work was performed amongst them. I have only observed that they all loved one another with a cordial love, and that they never loved any one more than another. I can affirm that in 30 years that I have been with them I neither saw quarrel or animosity amongst them. They know not how to distinguish between mine and thine; they have all things in common amongst them.

Despite the ignorance about Australian parturition that Sadeur expresses here, he later learns from an old Australian that 'children grow within them like fruits upon a tree'. He also discovers, somehow, the rituals that surround childbirth.

As soon as an Australian has conceived, he quits his apartment, and is carried to the Hab [Town Hall], where he is received with testimonies of extraordinary bounty ... They have a certain high place upon which they go to bring forth their child, which is received upon certain balsamic leaves; after which the mother (or person that bore it) takes it and rubs it with those leaves, and gives it suck, without any appearance of having suffered any pain.

The Australians explain to Sadeur that they take pride in their lack of passion. They consider Europeans like him, who have only one gender, to be mere 'half-men'. For it is the nature of man to be reasonable, without passion. Whereas half-men, and the lower animals, are prey to gluttony, lust and other vices, as a consequence of their defective sexual nature.

We live without being sensible of any of these animal ardours one for another, and we cannot bear them spoke of without horror. Our love has nothing carnal nor brutal in it. We are sufficiently satisfied in ourselves; we have no need to seek any happiness from without, and live contented, as you see we do.

The Australians disdain bodily functions. They eat only in secret, and sleep very little, regarding sleep as an animal action from which men should if possible wholly abstain.

As de Foigny's book proceeds, the debit side of their lack of passion begins to appear. Because they despise their bodies, and realize, rationally, that death is inevitable in the long run, they all yearn to get out of life as quickly as possible. This is easy, because among the native fruits is one, in appearance like an olive, which gives happy death. Those who eat it expire

[99]

'with all the signs of the greatest joy and pleasure in the world'. In the past, suicide became so common that there was a serious risk the race would die out. It is still popular, but now no Australian can get permission to go to his 'long rest' unless he has produced at least one child to replace him.

Lack of passion also debars pity, or compassion. The Australians' conduct of warfare appears to Sadeur appallingly cruel. When a neighbouring people, the Fondins, attack them, the Australians exterminate them. Fondin women and children have their throats cut by the thousand, and are left in huge rotting heaps for the birds and beasts to devour. The Fondin island is annihilated – the earth that formed it is carried away, so that the sea flows over the site. Sadeur tries to save some captured Fondin women, but their throats are cut, and he is condemned to death for having pity on them. He manages to escape by taming a gigantic bird, of a sort common in Australia, that carries him to safety in its talons.

Though he does not spell it out, de Foigny's moral seems to be that mercy and joy in life are rooted in human passion, as are vice and lust. Pure reason is incompatible with happiness and love, just as it is with those animal appetites the Australians condemn.

Source: James Sadeur [Gabriel de Foigny], *A New Discovery of Terra Incognita Australis*, 1693.

Alchemists Rule

The Sophick Constitution, an anonymous English utopia published in 1700, is singular in that it envisages a state ruled by alchemists, who can turn base metal into gold. This will solve all revenue problems. The alchemists will, however, keep their useful skill secret, and encourage their subjects to be industrious, frugal and clean. Hygienic town-planning will be introduced. Factories and burial grounds will be prohibited in urban areas. Every house will have a garden, 'that the air of towns and cities should not be choked, as it is ordinarily'. Waste disposal will be efficiently organized. Most streets will have public lavatories, guarded by 'sentinels' to keep them neat. As the book proceeds, precautions against unseemliness and excess become more severe.

No persons extraordinarily frightful and deformed should be suffered to go in the streets, such objects striking with horror the beholders, and being dangerous to women big with child. If those miserable persons were not able to maintain themselves, by reason of their confinement, they should be taken into some hospital, built for that purpose ... All unnecessary trades should be abolished, and unnecessary expenses spared, to be applied to better purposes. All house furniture should be plain. There should be no such thing as fringe, lace, embroidery, nor the like; or else, those that would have them should be fined the fourth part of their revenues ... If there were no more horses and dogs kept than were absolutely necessary; if it was not only permitted but enjoined to everyone to destroy all wild fowls and wild beasts, as much as possible, there would be more corn, more fruit, more sheep and cows, and consequently a better provision for the generality of men ... All those things which are superfluous and cause unnecessary expenses should be forbidden by express laws. Even excess in clothes and apparel should be punishable, and those that should bring up their children in any pride or vanity should be fined. Those that would wear rings or jewels, long wigs, and longer garments than is necessary, and women that would have ribbons, high dress, long trains, and the like, should be taxed a considerable part of their revenues for it.

Source: Anon., *Annus Sophiae Jubilaeus or The Sophick Constitution*, 1700.

Paradise Found

Milton's description of Adam and Eve in *Paradise Lost* (see p. 81) hovers behind the noble savages who populate many eighteenth-century utopias. In Ambrose Evans's *The Adventures and Surprising Deliverances of James Dubourdieu* (1719), the narrator and a priest are shipwrecked on an island, which they proceed to explore.

We advanced to the brow of a hill, whence we had a full survey or prospect of the most beautiful and charming country that our eyes ever beheld. Hence we began our progress down through pleasant groves, or frequent groups of trees, for above a mile together. Proceeding on still, near the end of another mile, we were surprised, and frightened too, to see at our backs three huge animals, that at first appeared to us to be lions. But coming up with us, they did no more than take hold of the lappet of our coats, or linen garments we had on, and thus led us down to the foot of the hill, above half a mile farther. They at last brought us into a plain, where there were thousands of people, some in an adjacent pool or pond, and others on its banks, men, women, and children, and all stark naked. The men were all tall, and seemed to us of a larger size than generally our Europeans are, but of a perfect symmetry, and their eyes seemed to carry a perfect awe and majesty in them. Their hair was generally of a light brown, curling in ringlets a little below their shoulders; that of the women, something more yellow, and falling down even to their waists, not without frequent curls, which made it the more graceful. The women were all crowned with chaplets of beautiful flowers, and the men had no weapon in their hands but a sort of white staff, about seven foot in length, at the end of which was fixed a sort of cutting hook, with which I found afterwards they sheared and trimmed the trees.

The travellers discover that these people have no knowledge of money, private property, ships or clothes. They sing beautifully, and live in perfect love without formal goverment. They are monogamous, and adultery is unknown. Their 'lions' are more like huge dogs, and vegetarian. They believe in a benign all-powerful Creator. The priest's account of Christianity, with its God divided into three parts, and one of the three parts dying on a cross, shocks them so much that they expel the travellers as 'Children of Wrath'.

Source: Ambrose Evans, *The Adventures and Surprising Deliverances of James Dubourdieu, and His Wife,* 1719.

Desert Island Discontent

Daniel Defoe (1660–1731) was sixty when he wrote *Robinson Crusoe* (1719). In many respects he was an unlikely author of fiction, and particularly of fiction that pretends to be fact, as *Crusoe* does. A devout Puritan, he had suffered several spells of imprisonment, and been locked for three days in the pillory, for his courageous defence of freedom of worship. He did not care much for art and literature, quite the contrary. Like many Puritans he considered theatre and opera devilish, and believed bubonic plague was invented by God expressly to punish playgoers. He was a keen, though persistently unsuccessful, businessman, and his views epitomize commercialism at its ugliest. Five-year-old children labouring in textile mills struck him as a wholesome and heartening sight. He eagerly predicted the spread of industrial cities, and urged ever more vigorous English participation in the African slave trade.

Along with this rapacity went blood-curdling bigotry on questions of sexual conduct. He admired the Scots because they still hanged adulterers – a 'necessary severity' – and he recommended that homosexuals should be secretly exterminated, lest news of their 'hellish' behaviour should leak out and corrupt others. For married couples to seek pleasure in sex, instead of being intent on procreation, was mere 'lewdness', and the contraceptive devices married women resorted to to escape the hazards of annual childbirth smacked of 'witchcraft and the Devil'.

Despite this bigotry, he was an imaginative genius and a prodigiously fluent writer. In 1704 he founded a newspaper, *The Review*, writing it single-handed three times a week until 1713. He is credited with the invention of several features of modern tabloid journalism, including the agony aunt, the gossip column, and the spoof reader's letter. *Robinson Crusoe* was his first attempt at fiction, and was a phenomenal success. It has been translated into almost every language, and has never gone out of print. It spawned innumerable imitations, adaptations and sequels, creating a new literary genre known to contemporaries as the *robinsonade*. There were German, French, Italian, female and Jesuit Robinsons.

The gulf between stern Puritanism and imaginative artistry suggests some deep division in Defoe himself, and is reflected in *Robinson Crusoe*. The novel continually see-saws between the material and the spiritual. Modern adaptations tend to leave the spiritual out, concentrating on the desert-island adventure, with Robinson building his own little kingdom out of native wit and salvaged wreckage. It is this that attracts children to the story, appealing to the same instinct that makes them improvise dens and tree-houses – juvenile utopias, beyond parental control.

Robinson himself is a disobedient child. His parents forbid him to go to sea, but he does. After a few preliminary adventures (capture by pirates, a spell of slavery in Morocco) he sets up as a sugar-planter in Brazil and fits out a ship to fetch Negro slaves from the Guinea coast. It goes aground in a dreadful storm off an uncharted Caribbean island. They take to the boats, but only Robinson gets ashore alive. The realism of the next section, describing his settling-in on the island, was an entirely new thing in the English novel, and hoodwinked many readers – though some noted suspiciously that after pulling off all his clothes to swim to the ship Crusoe is able to fill his pockets with biscuit a few lines later.

Crusoe spends his first night in a tree, for safety. In the morning he discovers that the ship has run aground not far from the shore, and, constructing a raft, he proceeds to empty it of its most useful stores and provisions, including firearms and gunpowder.

My next work was to view the country, and seek a proper place for my habitation, and where to stow my goods to secure them from whatever might happen; where I was, I yet knew not, whether on the continent or on an island, whether inhabited or not inhabited, whether in danger of wild beasts or not. There was a hill not above a mile from me, which rose up very steep and high, and which seemed to overtop some other hills, which lay as in a ridge from it northward; I took out one of the fowling pieces, and one of the pistols, and an horn of powder, and thus armed I travelled for discovery up to the top of that hill, where after I had with great labour and difficulty got to the top, I saw my fate to my great affliction, viz. that I was in an island environed every way with the sea, no land to be seen, except some rocks which lay a great way off, and two small islands less than this, which lay about three leagues to the west.

I found also that the island I was in was barren, and, as I saw good reason to believe, uninhabited, except by wild beasts, of whom however I saw none, yet I saw abundance of fowls, but knew not their kinds, neither when I killed them could I tell what was fit for food, and what not; at my coming back, I shot at a great bird which I saw sitting upon a tree on the side of a great wood. I believe it was the first gun that had been fired there since the creation of the world; I had no sooner fired, but from all the parts of the wood there arose an innumerable number of fowls of many sorts, making a confused screaming, and crying every one according to his usual note; but not one of them of any kind that I knew. As for the creature I killed, I took it to be a kind of a hawk, its colour and beak resembling it, but had no talons or claws more than common; its flesh was carrion, and fit for nothing.

Contented with this discovery, I came back to my raft, and fell to work to bring my cargo on shore, which took me up the rest of that day, and what to do with myself at night I knew not, nor indeed where to rest; for I was afraid to lie down on the ground, not knowing but some wild beast might devour me, though, as I afterwards found, there was really no need for those fears.

However, as well as I could, I barricadoed myself round with the chests and boards that I had brought on shore, and made a kind of a hut for that night's lodging; as for food, I yet saw not which way to supply myself, except that I had seen two or three creatures like hares run out of the wood where I shot the fowl.

I now began to consider that I might yet get a great many things out of the ship, which would be useful to me, and particularly some of the rigging, and sails, and such other things as might come to land, and I resolved to make another voyage on board the vessel, if possible; and as I knew that the first storm that blew must necessarily break her all in pieces, I resolved to set all other things apart, till I got everything out of the ship that I could get; then I called a council, that is to say, in my thoughts, whether I should take back the raft, but this appeared impracticable; so I resolved to go as before, when the tide was down, and I did so, only that I stripped before I went from my hut, having nothing on but a chequered shirt, and a pair of linen drawers, and a pair of pumps on my feet.

I got on board the ship, as before, and prepared a second raft, and having had experience of the first, I neither made this so unwieldy, nor loaded it so hard, but yet I brought away several things very useful to me; as first, in the carpenter's stores I found two or three bags full of nails and spikes, a great screw-jack, a dozen or two of hatchets, and above all, that most useful thing called a grindstone; all these I secured together, with several things belonging to the gunner, particularly two or three iron crows, and two barrels of musket bullets, seven muskets, and another fowling piece, with some small quantity of powder more; a large bag full of small shot, and a great roll of sheet lead. But this last was so heavy I could not hoist it up to get it over the ship's side.

Besides these things, I took all the men's clothes that I could find, and a spare fore-top-sail, a hammock, and some bedding; and with this I loaded my second raft, and brought them all safe on shore to my very great comfort.

I was under some apprehensions during my absence from the land, that at least my provisions might be devoured on shore; but when I came back, I found no sign of any visitor, only there sat a creature like a wild cat upon one of the chests, which when I came towards it, ran away a little distance, and then stood still; she sat very composed and unconcerned, and looked full in my face, as if she had a mind to be acquainted with me. I presented my gun at her, but as she did not understand it, she was perfectly unconcerned at it, nor did she offer to stir away; upon which I tossed her a bit of biscuit, though by the way I was not very free of it, for my store was not great. However, I spared her a bit, I say, and she went to it, smelled of it, and ate it, and looked (as pleased) for more, but I thanked her, and could spare no more, so she marched off.

Having got my second cargo on shore, though I was fain to open the barrels of powder and bring them by parcels, for they were too heavy, being large casks, I went to work to make me a little tent with the sail and some poles which I cut for that purpose, and into this tent I brought everything that I knew would spoil, either with rain or sun, and I piled all the empty chests and casks up in a circle round the tent, to fortify it from any sudden attempt, either from man or beast.

When I had done this I blocked up the door of the tent with some boards within, and an empty chest set up on end without, and spreading one of the beds upon the ground, laying my two pistols just at my head, and my gun at length by me, I went to bed for the first time, and slept very quietly all night, for I was very weary and heavy, for the night before I had slept little, and had laboured very hard all day, as well to fetch all those things from the ship, as to get them on shore . . .

I had been now thirteen days on shore, and had been eleven times on board the ship; in which time I had brought away all that one pair of hands could well be supposed capable to bring, though I believe verily, had the calm weather held, I should have brought away the whole ship piece by piece. But preparing the 12th time to go on board, I found the wind begin to rise; however, at low water I went on board, and though I thought I had rummaged the cabin so effectually, as that nothing more could be found, yet I discovered a locker with drawers in it, in one of which I found two or three razors, and one pair of large scissors with some ten or a dozen of good knives and forks; in another I found about thirty-six pounds value in money, some European coin, some Brazil, some pieces of eight, some gold, some silver.

I smiled to myself at the sight of this money. 'O drug!' said I aloud, 'what art thou good for? Thou art not worth to me, no, not the taking off of the ground; one of those knives is worth all this heap; I have no manner of use for thee, e'en remain where thou art, and go to the bottom as a creature whose life is not worth saving.' However, upon second thoughts, I took it away, and wrapping all this in a piece of canvas, I began to think of making another raft, but while I was preparing this, I found the sky overcast, and the wind began to rise, and in a quarter of an hour it blew a fresh gale from the shore; it presently occurred to me that it was in vain to pretend to make a raft with the wind off shore, and that it was my business to be gone before the tide of flood began, otherwise I might not be able to reach the shore at all. Accordingly I let myself down into the water, and swam across the channel which lay between the ship and the sands, and even that with difficulty enough, partly with the weight of the things I had about me, and partly the roughness of the water, for the wind rose very hastily, and before it was quite high water it blew a storm.

But I was gotten home to my little tent, where I lay with all my wealth about me very secure. It blew very hard all that night, and in the morning when I looked out, behold, no more ship was to be seen; I was a little surprised, but recovered myself with this satisfactory reflection, viz. that I had lost no time, nor abated no diligence to get everything out of her that could be useful to me, and that indeed there was little left in her that I was able to bring away if I had had more time.

I now gave over any more thoughts of the ship, or of anything out of her, except what might drive on shore from her wreck, as indeed divers pieces of her afterwards did; but those things were of small use to me.

My thoughts were now wholly employed about securing myself against either savages, if any should appear, or wild beasts, if any were in the island; and I had many thoughts of the method how to do this, and what kind of dwelling to make, whether I should make me a cave in the earth, or a tent upon the earth: and, in short, I resolved upon both, the manner and description of which it may not be improper to give an account of. I soon found the place I was in was not for my settlement, particularly because it was upon a low moorish ground near the sea, and I believed would not be wholesome, and more particularly because there was no fresh water near it, so I resolved to find a more healthy and more convenient spot of ground.

I consulted several things in my situation which I found would be proper for me: 1st health and fresh water I just now mentioned; 2dly shelter from the heat of the sun; 3dly security from ravenous creatures, whether men or beasts; 4thly a view to the sea, that if God sent any ship in sight, I might not lose any advantage for my deliverance, of which I was not willing to banish all my expectation yet.

In search of a place proper for this, I found a little plain on the side of a rising hill, whose front towards this little plain was steep as a house-side, so that nothing could come down upon me from the top; on the side of this rock there was a hollow place worn a little way in like the entrance or door of a cave, but there was not really any cave or way into the rock at all.

On the flat of the green, just before this hollow place, I resolved to pitch my tent. This plain was not above an hundred yards broad, and about twice as long, and lay like a green before my door, and at the end of it descended irregularly every way down into the low-grounds by the sea side. It was on the NNW side of the hill, so that I was sheltered from the heat every day, till it came to a W and by S sun, or thereabouts, which in those countries is near the setting.

Before I set up my tent, I drew a half circle before the hollow place which took in about ten yards in its semi-diameter from the rock, and twenty yards in its diameter, from its beginning and ending.

In this half circle I pitched two rows of strong stakes, driving them into the ground till they stood very firm like piles, the biggest end being out of the ground about five foot and a half, and sharpened on the top. The two rows did not stand above six inches from one another.

Then I took the pieces of cable which I had cut in the ship, and I laid them in rows one upon another, within the circle, between these two rows of stakes, up to the top, placing other stakes in the inside, leaning against them, about two foot and a half high, like a spur to a post, and this fence was so strong that neither man or beast could get into it or over it. This cost me a great deal of time and labour, especially to cut the piles in the woods, bring them to the place, and drive them into the earth.

The entrance into this place I made to be not by a door, but by a short ladder to go over the top, which ladder, when I was in, I lifted over after me, and so I was completely fenced in, and fortified, as I thought, from all the world and consequently slept secure in the night, which otherwise I could not have done, though, as it appeared afterward, there was no need of all this caution from the enemies that I apprehended danger from.

Into this fence or fortress, with infinite labour, I carried all my riches, all my provisions, ammunition, and stores, of which you have the account above; and I made me a large tent, which, to preserve me from the rains that in one part of the year are very violent there, I made double, viz. one smaller tent within, and one larger tent above it, and covered the uppermost with a large tarpaulin which I had saved among the sails.

And now I lay no more for a while in the bed which I had brought on shore, but in a hammock, which was indeed a very good one, and belonged to the mate of the ship.

Into this tent I brought all my provisions, and everything that would spoil by the wet, and having thus enclosed all my goods, I made up the entrance, which till now I had left open, and so passed and re-passed, as I said, by a short ladder.

When I had done this, I began to work my way into the rock, and bringing all the earth and stones that I dug down out through my tent, I laid them up within my fence in the nature of a terrace, that so it raised the ground within about a foot and a half; and thus I made me a cave just behind my tent, which served me like a cellar to my house.

Although the island puts Crusoe back in touch with nature, *Robinson Crusoe* is not a back-to-nature utopia. Quite the reverse. During his twenty-eight years on the island Crusoe never ceases wanting to get off it, and he spends his time reinventing Western agriculture and technology from the bottom up. He tames and breeds goats, using tallow from their meat to make candles, and manufacturing his own butter and cheese from their milk. He grows corn – by mistake at first. Some old bird-seed he throws away sprouts green shoots, and within a few years he has mastered cereal-production. Then, after an interval constructing his own pestle and mortar, and sieves for separating the chaff, he is able to embark on flour-milling and bread-baking. Finding clay, he builds a kiln, learns to make glaze from sand, and soon has fireproof ovenware. He finds grapes growing wild, cultivates them, and learns to make wine and raisins. His most ingenious achievement is a retractable umbrella, made of goat-skin. There are turtles on the island, which he catches for flesh and eggs, but as his own industries prosper he relies less and less on mere hunter-gatherer techniques.

However, his resourceful pursuit of material improvement is counter-pointed by a spiritual development, which encourages him to contemn the merely material. His vacillation between the two sets of values shows up comically in the above excerpt, when he first scorns the money he finds, then decides to take it after all. Spirituality gains strength as time goes on. After an attack of ague, which almost kills him, he undergoes a full-scale religious conversion. He realizes that God is punishing him for his 'dreadful mis-spent life'. Penitence and gratitude for his salvation overwhelm him. He discovers what genuine prayer is, and proceeds to structure his life around a framework of religious observation. He says grace before meals, sets aside time for reading the Bible three times each day, and keeps the anniversary of his landing on the island (30 September) as a day of solemn prayer and thanksgiving.

It is this spiritual growth that makes the island a utopia rather than a dystopia – as Crusoe himself explains.

In the middle of this work, I finished my fourth year in this place, and kept my anniversary with the same devotion, and with as much comfort as ever before; for by a constant study and serious application of the word of God, and by the assistance of His grace, I gained a different knowledge from what I had before. I entertained different notions of things. I looked now upon the world as a thing remote, which I had nothing to do with, no expectation from, and indeed no desires about: in a word, I had nothing indeed to do with it, nor was ever like to have; so I thought it looked as we may perhaps look upon it hereafter, viz. as a place I had lived in, but was come out of it; and well might I say, as Father Abraham to Dives, *Between me and thee is a great gulf fixed* [Luke 16: 26].

In the first place, I was removed from all the wickedness of the world here. I had neither *the lust of the flesh, the lust of the eye, or the pride of life* [1 John 2: 16]. I had nothing to covet; for I had all that I was now capable of enjoying; I was lord of the whole manor; or if I pleased, I might call myself king or emperor over the whole country which I had possession of. There were no rivals; I had no competitor, none to dispute sovereignty or command with me. I might have raised ship-loadings of corn; but I had no use for it; so I let as little grow as I thought enough for my occasion. I had tortoise or turtles enough; but now and then one was as much as I could put to any use. I had timber enough to have built a fleet of ships. I had grapes enough to have made wine, or to have cured into raisins, to have loaded that fleet when they had been built.

But all I could make use of was all that was valuable. I had enough to eat and to supply my wants, and what was all the rest to me? If I killed more flesh than I could eat, the dog must eat it, or the vermin. If I sowed more corn than I could eat, it must be spoiled. The trees that I cut down were lying to rot on the ground. I could make no more use of them than for fuel; and that I had no occasion for, but to dress my food.

In a word, the nature and experience of things dictated to me, upon just reflection, that all the good things of this world are no farther good to us than they are for our use; and that whatever we may heap up indeed to give others, we enjoy just as much as we can use and no more. The most covetous griping miser in the world would have been cured of the vice of covetousness, if he had been in my case; for I possessed infinitely more than I knew what to do with. I had no room for desire, except it was of things which I had not, and they were but trifles, though indeed of great use to me. I had, as I hinted before, a parcel of money, as well gold as silver, about thirty-six pounds sterling. Alas! there the nasty sorry useless stuff lay; I had no manner of business for it; and I often thought with myself that I would have given a handful of it for a gross of tobacco-pipes, or for a hand-mill to grind my corn; nay, I would have given it all for sixpennyworth of turnip and carrot seed out of England, or for a handful of peas and beans, and a bottle of ink. As it was, I had not the least advantage by it, or benefit from it; but there it lay in a drawer, and grew mouldy with the damp of the cave in the wet season; and if I had had the drawer full of diamonds, it had been the same case; and they had been of no manner of value to me, because of no use.

I had now brought my state of life to be much easier in itself than it was at first, and much easier to my mind, as well as to my body. I frequently sat down to my meat with thankfulness, and admired the hand of God's providence, which had thus spread my table in the wilderness. I learned to look more upon the bright side of my condition, and less upon the dark side, and to consider what I enjoyed, rather than what I wanted; and this gave me sometimes such secret comforts, that I cannot express them; and which I take notice of here, to put those discontented people in mind of it, who cannot enjoy comfortably what God has given them; because they see and covet something that He has not given them. All our discontents about what we want appeared to me to spring from the want of thankfulness for what we have.

The struggle between spiritual and material continues to be evident here, of course. Crusoe's yearning for material comfort (tobacco pipes etc.) is acknowledged even when he is expressly rejecting the material. Defoe makes us aware how fragile even genuine repentance and conversion are. This is the point of the famous footprint episode. As soon as Crusoe sees the footprint in the sand, he loses both his sense of security and his trust in God.

You are to understand that now I had, as I may call it, two plantations in the island; one my little fortification or tent, with the wall about it under the rock, with the cave behind me, which by this time I had enlarged into several apartments or caves, one within another. One of these, which was the driest and largest, and had a door out beyond my wall or fortification, that is to say, beyond where my wall joined to the rock, was all filled up with the large earthen pots, of which I have given an account, and with fourteen or fifteen great baskets, which would hold five or six bushels each, where I laid up my stores of provision, especially my corn, some in the ear cut off short from the straw, and the other rubbed out with my hand.

As for my wall, made, as before, with long stakes or piles, those piles grew all like trees, and were by this time grown so big, and spread so very much, that there was not the least appearance to anyone's view of any habitation behind them.

Near this dwelling of mine, but a little farther within the land, and upon lower ground, lay my two pieces of corn-ground, which I kept duly cultivated and sowed, and which duly yielded me their harvest in its season; and whenever I had occasion for more corn, I had more land adjoining as fit as that.

Besides this, I had my country seat, and I had now a tolerable plantation there also; for first, I had my little bower, as I called it, which I kept in repair; that is to say, I kept the hedge which circled it in constantly fitted up to its usual height, the ladder standing always in the inside; I kept the trees, which at first were no more than my stakes, but were now grown very firm and tall; I kept them always so cut, that they might spread and grow thick and wild, and make the more agreeable shade, which they did effectually to my mind. In the middle of this I had my tent always standing, being a piece of a sail spread over poles set up for that purpose, and which never wanted any repair or renewing; and under this I had made me a squab or couch, with the skins of the creatures I had killed, and with other soft things, and a blanket laid on them, such as belonged to our sea-bedding, which I had saved, and a great watch-coat to cover me; and here, whenever I had occasion to be absent from my chief seat, I took up my country habitation.

Adjoining to this I had my enclosures for my cattle, that is to say, my goats. And as I had taken an inconceivable deal of pains to fence and enclose this ground, so I was so uneasy to see it kept entire, lest the goats should break through, that I never left off till with infinite labour I had stuck the outside of the hedge so full of small stakes, and so near to one another, that it was rather a pale than a hedge, and there was scarce room to put a hand through between them, which afterwards when those stakes grew, as they all did in the next rainy season, made the enclosure strong like a wall, indeed stronger than any wall.

This will testify for me that I was not idle, and that I spared no pains to bring to pass whatever appeared necessary for my comfortable support; for I considered the keeping up a breed of tame creatures thus at my hand would be a living magazine of flesh, milk, butter, and cheese for me as long as I lived in the place, if it were to be forty years; and that keeping them in my reach depended entirely upon my perfecting my enclosures to such a degree that I might be sure of keeping them together; which by this method indeed I so effectually secured that, when these little stakes began to grow, I had planted them so very thick, I was forced to pull some of them up again.

In this place also I had my grapes growing, which I principally depended on for my winter store of raisins, and which I never failed to preserve very carefully, as the best and most agreeable dainty of my whole diet; and indeed they were not agreeable only, but physical [medicinal], wholesome, nourishing, and refreshing to the last degree.

As this was also about half-way between my other habitation and the place where I had laid up my boat, I generally stayed and lay here in my way thither; for I used frequently to visit my boat, and I kept all things about or belonging to her in very good order; sometimes I went out in her to divert myself, but no more hazardous voyages would I go, nor scarce ever above a stone's cast or two from the shore, I was so apprehensive of being hurried out of my knowledge again by the currents, or winds, or any other accident. But now I come to a new scene of my life.

It happened one day about noon going towards my boat, I was exceedingly surprised with the print of a man's naked foot on the shore, which was very plain to be seen in the sand. I stood like one thunder-struck, or as if I had seen an apparition; I listened, I looked round me, I could hear nothing, nor see anything; I went up to a rising ground to look farther; I went up the shore and down the shore, but it was all one, I could see no other impression but that one. I went to it again to see if there were any more, and to observe if it might not be my fancy; but there was no room for that, for there was exactly the very print of a foot, toes, heel, and every part of a foot; how it came thither I knew not, nor could in the least imagine. But after innumerable fluttering thoughts, like a man perfectly confused and out of myself, I came home to my fortification, not feeling, as we say, the ground I went on, but terrified to the last degree, looking behind me at every two or three steps, mistaking every bush and tree, and fancying every stump at a distance to be a man; nor is it possible to describe how many various shapes affrighted imagination represented things to me in, how many wild ideas were found every moment in my fancy, and what strange unaccountable whimsies came into my thoughts by the way.

When I came to my castle, for so I think I called it ever after this, I fled into it like one pursued; whether I went over by the ladder as first contrived, or went in at the hole in the rock which I called a door, I cannot remember; no, nor could I remember the next morning, for never frighted hare fled to cover, or fox to earth, with more terror of mind than I to this retreat.

I slept none that night; the farther I was from the occasion of my fright, the greater my apprehensions were, which is something contrary to the nature of such things, and especially to the usual practice of all creatures in fear: but I was so embarrassed with my own frightful ideas of the thing, that I formed nothing but dismal imaginations to myself, even though I was now a great way off of it. Sometimes I fancied it must be the devil; and reason joined in with me upon this supposition; for how should any other thing in human shape come into the place? Where was the vessel that brought them? What marks was there of any other footsteps? And how was it possible a man should come there? But then to think that Satan should take human shape upon him in such a place where there could be no manner of occasion for it, but to leave the print of his foot behind him, and that even for no purpose too, for he could not be sure I should see it; this was an amusement the other way; I considered that the devil might have found out abundance of other ways to have terrified me than this of the single print of a foot; that as I lived quite on the other side of the island, he would never have been so simple to leave a mark in a place where 'twas ten thousand to one whether I should ever see it or not, and in the sand too, which the first surge of the sea upon a high wind would have defaced entirely. All this seemed inconsistent with the thing itself, and with all the notions we usually entertain of the subtlety of the devil.

Abundance of such things as these assisted to argue me out of all apprehensions of its being the devil; and I presently concluded then, that it must be some more dangerous creature, viz. that it must be some of the savages of the mainland over-against me, who had wandered out to sea in their canoes, and, either driven by the currents or by contrary winds, had made the island; and had been on shore, but were gone away again to sea, being as loth, perhaps, to have stayed in this desolate island as I would have been to have had them.

While these reflections were rolling upon my mind, I was very thankful in my thoughts that I was so happy as not to be thereabouts at that time, or that they did not see my boat, by which they would have concluded that some inhabitants had been in the place, and perhaps have searched farther for me. Then terrible thoughts racked my imagination about their having found my boat, and that there were people here; and that if so, I should certainly have them come again in greater numbers, and devour me; that if it should happen so that they should not find me, yet they would find my enclosure, destroy all my corn, carry away all my flock of tame goats, and I should perish at last for mere want.

Thus my fear banished all my religious hope; all that former confidence in God, which was founded upon such wonderful experience as I had had of His goodness, now vanished, as if He that had fed me by miracle hitherto, could not preserve by His power the provision which He had made for me by His goodness. I reproached myself with my easiness, that would not sow any more corn one year than would just serve me till the next season, as if no accident could intervene to prevent my enjoying the crop that was upon the ground; and this I thought so just a reproof, that I resolved for the future to have two or three years' corn beforehand, so that whatever might come, I might not perish for want of bread. . . .

After his adventures with the cannibals and Man Friday, and his escape from the island, Crusoe returns to England to find himself a rich man. His Brazilian sugar plantation has prospered. Enormous profits have accrued in his absence. To some readers it may seem that the truly utopian thing about Crusoe is his ability to reconcile his possession of a large fortune with his Christian piety. Just as he seems to have thought there was nothing un-Christian about running a sugar plantation with slave labour, so his high-minded rejection of gold and silver on the island does not prevent him from slipping into the role of a nabob on his return. The assumption that you can have treasure on earth as well as treasure in heaven was, of course, shared by many respectable Christians in his day and since. But it has encouraged his more austere modern critics to denounce him as the epitome of exploitative and hypocritical colonialism.

Source: Daniel Defoe, *The Life and Strange Surprising Adventures of Robinson Crusoe, of York, Mariner, Written by Himself,* 1719 (spelling modernized).

How to Discourage Adultery

The poet Ambrose Philips (1674–1749), mocked by Alexander Pope for his foppery and red stockings, was a friend of Addison and Swift and eventually became a judge in Ireland. He is the probable author of *The Fortunate Shipwreck* (1720), describing a utopia in Australia. The Australians live according to virtuous and rational precepts. All books, for example, are published anonymously, to ensure that they are prized for their own merit and not for the author's name. Criminals are banished to the far side of a lofty range of mountains. Philips's utopians are devout Christians: 'the precepts of the Gospel are the laws of the land, and a breach of them is punished by the civil magistrate'. The treatment of adulterers is not, however, gospel-based.

Adultery . . . is a vice not so common there as in most other parts of the world, and perhaps the punishment very much lessens the number of offenders. For when it is discovered, the man is banished beyond the mountains, and the woman has a sort of composition rubbed over her face, which immediately infects it with tumours and swellings, to that degree that the most beautiful face is made the most ugly and forbidding; and she herself degraded from her quality, though never so high, and sent into that quarter of the town where the washer-women are, and under them kept a slave to hard work as long as she lives.

Source: Maurice Williams [Ambrose Philips], *The Fortunate Shipwreck, or a Description of New Athens*, in *Miscellanea Aurea; or The Golden Medley*, 1720.

Horse Sense

Jonathan Swift's *Gulliver's Travels* (1726) is the most famous imaginary voyage ever written. It has bred innumerable imitations and endless debate about what Swift (1667–1745) really believed. Gulliver's last voyage is to the land of the Houyhnhnms. These are rational horses (their name is a transliteration of a horse's whinny), and they live in friendship, decency and civility. The evils of human life – including money, alcohol, luxury, disease, warfare and lawyers – are unknown to them. Their language has no word for a lie: the nearest they can get is 'the thing that is not'. They converse in neighs, and are marvellously adept at using the hollow between the pastern and the hoof as a hand. With this they can make flint tools and earthenware vessels, and even thread a needle. The other inhabitants of their country are a race of disgusting beasts called Yahoos – obscene, vicious, greedy and quarrelsome – who closely resemble human beings. The Houyhnhnms use them as draught animals, and seriously debate whether to exterminate them – though they eventually decide it would be better simply to castrate all the young males, so that the race will die out naturally. Gulliver feels deep reverence for the Houyhnhnms, and affection for his 'master', a grey horse, who receives him into his house. When he returns to England, he cannot bear the sight or smell of his wife and family, and retires to the stable to live with his horses.

The Houyhnhnms' rationality is most evident in areas where, with humans, emotion is paramount – family love, sex and death.

They have no fondness for their colts or foals; but the care they take in educating them proceedeth entirely from the dictates of reason. And I observed my master to show the same affection to his neighbour's issue that he had for his own. They will have it that nature teacheth them to love the whole species, and it is reason only that maketh a distinction of persons where there is a superior degree of virtue.

When the matron Houyhnhnms have produced one of each sex,

they no longer accompany with their consorts, except they lose one of their issue by some casualty, which very seldom happens. But in such case they meet again. Or when the like accident befalls a person whose wife is past bearing, some other couple bestows on him one of their own colts, and then go together a second time, until the mother be pregnant. This caution is necessary to prevent the country from being overburdened with numbers. But the race of inferior Houyhnhnms bred up to be servants is not so strictly limited upon this article. These are allowed to produce three of each sex, to be domestics in the noble families.

In their marriages, they are exactly careful to choose such colours as will not make any disagreeable mixture in the breed. Strength is chiefly valued in the male, and comeliness in the female – not upon the account of love, but to preserve the race from degenerating. For when a female happens to excel in strength, a consort is chosen with regard to comeliness. Courtship, love, presents, jointures, settlements, have no place in their thoughts, or terms whereby to express them in their language. The young couple meet and are joined merely because it is the determination of their parents and friends. It is what they see done every day, and they look upon it as one of the necessary actions of a reasonable being . . .

If they can avoid casualties, they die only of old age, and are buried in the obscurest places that can be found, their friends and relations expressing neither joy nor grief at their departure. Nor does the dying person discover the least regret that he is leaving the world, any more than if he were upon returning home from a visit to one of his neighbours. I remember my master having once made an appointment with a friend and his family to come to his house upon some affair of importance. On the day fixed, the mistress and her two children came very late. She made two excuses, first for her husband, who, as she said, happened that very morning to *Ihduwhn*. The word is strongly expressed in their language, but not easily rendered into English. It signifies *to retire to his first mother*. Her excuse for not coming sooner was that, her husband dying late in the morning, she was a good while consulting her servants about a convenient place where his body should be laid. And I observed she behaved herself at our house as cheerfully as the rest. She died about three months after.

Gulliver's description of his first encounter with Yahoos exposes the disgust Swift felt, or professed to feel, for the human body.

At last, I beheld several animals in a field, and one or two of the same kind sitting in trees. Their shape was very singular, and deformed, which a little discomposed me, so that I lay down behind a thicket to observe them better. Some of them coming forward near the place where I lay, gave me an opportunity of distinctly marking their form. Their heads and breasts were covered with a thick hair, some frizzled and others lank; they had beards like goats, and a long ridge of hair down their backs, and the fore parts of their legs and feet; but the rest of their bodies were bare, so that I might see their skins, which were of a brown buff colour. They had no tails, nor any hair at all on their buttocks, except about the *anus*; which, I presume, nature had placed there to defend them as they sat on the ground, for this posture they used, as well as lying down, and often stood on their hind feet. They climbed high trees as nimbly as a squirrel, for they had strong extended claws before and behind, terminating on sharp points, hooked. They would often spring, and bound, and leap with prodigious agility. The females were not so large as the males; they had long lank hair on their heads, and only a sort of down on the rest of their bodies, except about the *anus*, and *pudenda*. Their dugs hung between their fore feet, and often reached almost to the ground as they walked. The hair of both sexes was of several colours, brown, red, black and yellow. Upon the whole, I never beheld in all my travels so disagreeable an animal, or one against which I naturally conceived so strong an antipathy. So, that thinking I had seen enough, full of contempt and aversion, I got up and pursued the beaten road . . . I had not gone far, when I met one of these creatures full in my way, and coming up directly to me. The ugly monster, when he saw me, distorted several ways every feature of his visage, and stared, as at an object he had never seen before; then, approaching nearer, lifted up his fore paw, whether out of curiosity or mischief, I could not tell: but I drew my hanger, and gave him a good blow with the flat side of it; for I durst not strike him with the edge, fearing the inhabitants might be provoked against me, if they should come to know, that I had killed or maimed any of their cattle. When the beast felt the smart, he drew back, and roared so loud, that a herd, of at least forty, came flocking about me from the next field, howling and making odious faces; but I ran to the body of a tree, and leaning my back against it, kept them off, by waving my hanger. Several of this cursed brood getting hold of the branches behind, leaped up into the tree; from whence they began to discharge their excrements on my head: however, I escaped pretty well, by sticking close to the stem of the tree, but was almost stifled with the filth; which fell about me on every side.

Gulliver's admiration for the Houyhnhnms naturally leads him to behave as much like a horse as possible. However, a shameful incident betrays his true kinship with the Yahoos.

Being one day abroad with my protector the sorrel nag, and the weather exceeding hot, I entreated him to let me bathe in a river that was near. He consented, and I immediately stripped myself stark naked, and went down softly into the stream. It happened that a young female Yahoo standing behind a bank, saw the whole proceeding; and inflamed by desire, as the nag and I conjectured, came running with all speed, and leaped into the water within five yards of the place where I bathed. I was never in my life so terribly frighted; the nag was grazing at some distance, not suspecting any harm; she embraced me after a most fulsome manner; I roared as loud as I could, and the nag came galloping towards me, whereupon she quitted her grasp, with the utmost reluctancy, and leaped upon the opposite bank, where she stood gazing and howling all the time I was putting on my clothes.

This was matter of diversion to my master and his family, as well as of mortification to myself. For now I could no longer deny, that I was a real Yahoo, in every limb and feature, since the females had a natural propensity to me as one of their own species: neither was the hair of this brute of a red colour (which might have been some excuse for an appetite a little irregular) but black as sloe, and her countenance did not make an appearance altogether so hideous as the rest of the kind; for, I think, she could not be above eleven years old.

Source: Jonathan Swift, *Gulliver's Travels*, 1735.

Wise Trees

Ludwig Holberg (1684–1754), 'the Molière of the North', was a leading figure in the European Enlightenment, a prolific comic playwright, and the founder of Danish literature. Published in Latin in 1741, his utopia *Niels Klim's Journey to the World Under Ground* was inspired by Swift's *Gulliver's Travels*, and may have influenced *Alice in Wonderland*. Klim, the narrator, is a penniless graduate of Copenhagen University. He drops through a hole in the ground, and after falling a considerable distance, finds himself in a subterranean universe, with its own sun and stars, where he goes into orbit around a large planet. A biscuit, which he pulls from his pocket, goes into orbit round him, making him, he proudly tells himself, into a heavenly body with its own moon. Landing eventually on the surface of the new planet he is chased by a bull, and tries to climb a tree to escape. But the tree shrieks in a female voice and boxes him on the ear. He finds that the planet's inhabitants are walking, talking trees, and that he is under arrest for assaulting the sheriff's wife. After this matter has been cleared up, he stays with the trees, observing and admiring their slow but rational procedures. They regard his human quick-wittedness as a sign of great folly. But as his legs are longer than is normal with trees, he is given the rather lowly job of royal messenger. Among the trees' many wise ordinances is one that makes metaphysics and theology punishable offences.

It is forbidden, under pain of being banished, to expound the sacred writings, and if any person ventures to dispute concerning the essence and attributes of the Divinity, and about the nature of ghosts, the soul, and such spiritual matters, he is sentenced to be immediately phlebotomized [surgically bled], and put into the public hospital or madhouse of the town. 'For it is perfectly absurd and preposterous,' say they, 'for us to attempt to describe and define that wherein our understandings are as blind as an owlet in the sunshine.' They are all united and agree in the adoration and worship of one supreme Being, whose omnipotence has created, and whose providence keeps and preserves, all things. Respecting the form of worshipping this Being, everyone is allowed to think and act as he will; but those who openly attack the established religion of the State are punished as public disturbers of the peace.

Source: Lewis Holberg, *Journey to the World Under Ground; Being the Subterraneous Travels of Niels Klim*, Thomas North, 1828 (from the Latin).

Difficulties with a Flying Suit

The Life and Adventures of Peter Wilkins, A Cornish Man (1751) by Robert Paltock (1697–1767) was admired by Coleridge and Southey, and tells of a Robinson Crusoe style castaway (Wilkins) who creates his private 'kingdom' on a desert island. One day a beautiful woman lands on his roof. She has wings, and appears to be clad in tight silk clothing. Later Wilkins finds that this is actually her skin, and that her people, whom he meets, all have a similar outer membrane, with large, curved wings attached, which double as boats when they lie on their backs in the water. Wilkins and his airborne visitor undergo a form of marriage, but, not yet understanding her physique, he finds his wedding night perplexing at first.

After supper, in order to give my bride the opportunity of undressing alone, which I thought might be most agreeable the first night, I withdrew into the antechamber, till I thought she was laid; and then, having first disposed of my lamp, I moved softly towards her, and stepped into bed too – when, on my nearer approach to her, I imagined she had her clothes on. This struck me a thorough damp all over, and asking her the reason of it, not being able to touch the least bit of her flesh but her face and hands, she burst out laughing, and running her hand along my naked side, soon perceived the difference she before had made such doubt of, between herself and me. Upon which she fairly told me that neither she or any person she had ever seen before had any other covering than what they were born with, and which they would not willingly part with but with their lives. This shocked me terribly, not from the horror of the thing itself, or any distaste I had to this covering, for it was quite smooth, warm, and softer than velvet or the finest skin imaginable, but from an apprehension of her being so wholly encased in it that though I had so fine a companion, and now a wife, yet I should have no conjugal benefit from it, either to my own gratification or the increase of our species.

In the height of my impatience I made divers essays for unfolding this covering, but unsuccessfully. Surely, says I, there must be some way of coming at my wishes, or why should she seem so shy of me at first, and now we are under engagements to each other, meet me half way with such a yielding compliance. I could, if I had had time to spare, have gone on, starting objections and answering them in my own breast a great while longer (for I knew not what to make of it), but being prompted to act as well as think, and feeling as tenderly as possible upon her bosom for the folds or plaits of her garment – she lying perfectly still – and perceiving divers fat, broad ledges, like whalebone, seemingly under her covering, which closely enfolded her body, I thought it might be all laced together, somewhat like stays, and felt behind for the lacing. At length, perceiving me so puzzled and beyond conception vexed at my disappointment, of a sudden, lest I should grow outrageous, which I was almost come to, she threw down all those seeming ribs flat to her side, so imperceptibly to me that I knew nothing of the matter, though I lay close to her, till putting forth my hand again to her bosom, the softest skin and most delightful body, free from all impediment, presented itself to my wishes and gave up itself to my embraces.

Source: Robert Paltock, *The Life and Adventures of Peter Wilkins, A Cornish Man*, 1751.

The Happy Savage

Jean-Jacques Rousseau (1712–78), one of the dominant thinkers of modern times, and a major influence behind the French Revolution and the Romantic movement, was the son of a watchmaker, and grew up in a Protestant artisan family in Geneva. He moved to Paris in 1742 where he became known to Diderot and other leading French intellectuals. Largely self-taught, he maintained himself as a young man by various secretarial and tutorial posts. He also wrote comedies, a ballet and an opera. In 1745 he began a relationship with Thérèse le Vasseur, a servant at his hotel. She bore him five children, all of whom he sent to a foundling hospital. Later, when he became a famous moralist, and a proponent of liberal educational ideas (in *Emile*, 1762), his abandonment of his children caused him acute guilt and remorse.

In his writings he persistently prefers man's 'natural' state to the civilized condition, which, as he sees it, has bred corruption, inequality, luxury, idleness and vice – in short, mid-eighteenth-century France. In 1750 his *Discourse on the Sciences and the Arts* argued that art and science merely served the interests of the rich. It raised a storm of controversy.

Though Rousseau conceded that return to primitive innocence was impossible, he urged that some improvement could be effected by introducing equality before the law, and distributing wealth more equitably. In *The Social Contract* (1762) he argued that government should reflect 'the general will', and be exercised for the common good. These opinions outraged the French authorities, and he was forced to flee to England.

He never wrote a formal utopia, but he came close to writing one in his *Discourse on the Origin of Inequality* (1754) – or, rather, he came close to writing two. For as the following extracts show, Rousseau in the *Discourse* was attracted to two alternative ideas of primitive man. The second of these was based on the reports of savages brought back by explorers from America, the Caribbean and elsewhere. But the first was (as he admits) Rousseau's own invention, or rather his imaginative reconstruction of life as it was lived by primitive human beings in the trackless wastes of prehistory, before men began to gather together into communities. These true, original savage men, Rousseau imagines, lived alone, roaming the forests like animals, and coupling with any females they came across. They were enormously superior to civilized man in strength and agility, and in the keenness of their sight, smell and hearing. They were also far happier.

Being a solitary, Rousseau's savage man did not need to communicate, so he had not developed language. Consequently he was incapable of what civilized man calls thought. But this was one reason for his greater happiness, for it freed him from the anxieties with which civilized man torments himself. ('I venture to declare that a state of reflection is a state contrary to nature, and that a thinking man is a depraved animal'). The only goods savage man recognized in the universe were food (mainly acorns), a female and sleep. He was wholly absorbed in the feeling of his present existence, without any idea of the future. He was independent, needing neither clothes nor dwelling. Having no possessions, he had no idea of justice or crime. If a stronger man or animal took his food or a woman from him, he regarded it as a natural mishap. Instead of seeking revenge, he simply found other food and another woman. Attachment to one particular female, and the notion of staying with her after copulation, were still unknown.

Since savage man was completely independent, and unable to communicate with others, he was also free, and freely satisfied all his needs. In such a state, social inequality could not develop.

Despite his solitary life, savage man was (Rousseau liked to think) capable of feeling compassion: 'an innate repugnance at seeing a fellow-creature suffer'. Rousseau believed wild animals feel this too. Further, compassion was stronger in savage man than it is in civilized man. For savage man did not have reason, and it is reason that tells civilized man not to worry about the sufferings of others, so long as they do not threaten him ('The human race would long since have ceased to be, had its preservation depended only on the reasonings of the individuals composing it').

Unlike other animals, savage man had free will. In some respects this was an advantage. He could choose, for example, to eat food he was not accustomed to. Other animals could not ('A pigeon would starve to death beside a dish of choice meat, and a cat on a heap of fruit or grain'). But allied to free will was savage man's capacity for self-improvement, another characteristic denied to animals. This was to become the source of all human misfortune. For it drew mankind out of his original savage state, in which he spent his days in peace, innocence and happiness.

In the second part of his *Discourse*, Rousseau undertakes to trace how happy savage man became unhappy civilized man. He starts with a challenging scenario.

The first man who, having enclosed a piece of ground, bethought himself of saying 'This is mine,' and found people simple enough to believe him, was the real founder of civil society. From how many crimes, wars, and murders, from how many horrors and misfortunes might not any one have saved mankind, by pulling up the stakes, or filling up the ditch, and crying to his fellows: 'Beware of listening to this impostor; you are undone if you once forget that the fruits of the earth belong to us all, and the earth itself to nobody.' But there is great probability that things had then already come to such a pitch, that they could no longer continue as they were; for the idea of property depends on many prior ideas, which could only be acquired successively, and cannot have been formed all at once in the human mind. Mankind must have made very considerable progress, and acquired considerable knowledge and industry which they must also have transmitted and increased from age to age, before they arrived at this last point of the state of nature.

Rousseau proceeds to trace mankind's gradual progress from savagery to civilization. Increase in population led to a degree of competition between men, and to the development of primitive tools and weapons. It also led man to compare himself with other men and animals. He learnt to outwit animals by snares and other stratagems, and so he first felt the emotion of pride. He began to combine with other men for hunting, and this required a language (though 'not much more refined than that of rooks or monkeys'). Tools allowed men to build huts, and they began to live in families with parents and children under one roof. This gave rise to feelings of love and affection. But it also enervated both body and mind, for man began to surround himself with comforts his predecessors had not needed.

Everything now begins to change its aspect. Men, who have up to now been roving in the woods, by taking to a more settled manner of life, come gradually together, form separate bodies, and at length in every country arises a distinct nation, united in character and manners, not by regulations or laws, but by uniformity of life and food, and the common influence of climate. Permanent neighbourhood could not fail to produce, in time, some connection between different families. Among young people of opposite sexes, living in neighbouring huts, the transient commerce required by nature soon led, through mutual intercourse, to another kind not less agreeable, and more permanent. Men began now to take the difference between objects into account, and to make comparisons; they acquired imperceptibly the ideas of beauty and merit, which soon gave rise to feelings of preference. In consequence of seeing each other often, they could not do without seeing each other constantly. A tender and pleasant feeling insinuated itself into their souls, and the least opposition turned it into an impetuous fury: with love arose jealousy; discord triumphed, and human blood was sacrificed to the gentlest of all passions.

As ideas and feelings succeeded one another, and heart and head were brought into play, men continued to lay aside their original wildness; their private connections became every day more intimate as their limits extended. They accustomed themselves to assemble before their huts round a large tree; singing and dancing, the true offspring of love and leisure, became the amusement, or rather the occupation, of men and women thus assembled together with nothing else to do. Each one began to consider the rest, and to wish to be considered in turn; and thus a value came to be attached to public esteem. Whoever sang or danced best, whoever was the handsomest, the strongest, the most dextrous, or the most eloquent, came to be of most consideration; and this was the first step towards inequality, and at the same time towards vice. From these first distinctions arose on the one side vanity and contempt and on the other shame and envy: and the fermentation caused by these new leavens ended by producing combinations fatal to innocence and happiness.

As soon as men began to value one another, and the idea of consideration had got a footing in the mind, everyone put in his claim to it, and it became impossible to refuse it to any with impunity. Hence arose the first obligations of civility even among savages; and every intended injury became an affront; because, besides the hurt which might result from it, the party injured was certain to find in it a contempt for his person, which was often more insupportable than the hurt itself.

Thus, as every man punished the contempt shown him by others, in proportion to his opinion of himself, revenge became terrible and men bloody and cruel. This is precisely the state reached by most of the savage nations known to us: and it is for want of having made a proper distinction in our ideas, and seen how very far they already are from the state of nature, that so many writers have hastily concluded that man is naturally cruel, and requires civil institutions to make him more mild; whereas nothing is more gentle than man in his primitive state, as he is placed by nature at an equal distance from the stupidity of brutes, and the fatal ingenuity of civilized man. Equally confined by instinct and reason to the sole care of guarding himself against the mischiefs which threaten him, he is restrained by natural compassion from doing any injury to others, and is not led to do such a thing even in return for injuries received. For, according to the axiom of the wise Locke, 'There can be no injury, where there is no property.'

But it must be remarked that the society thus formed, and the relations thus established among men, required of them qualities different from those which they possessed from their primitive constitution. Morality began to appear in human actions, and every one, before the institution of law, was the only judge and avenger of the injuries done him, so that the goodness which was suitable in the pure state of nature was no longer proper in the new-born state of society. Punishments had to be made more severe, as opportunities of offending became more frequent, and the dread of vengeance had to take the place of the rigour of the law. Thus, though men had become less patient, and their natural compassion had already suffered some diminution, this period of expansion of the human faculties, keeping a just mean between the indolence of the primitive state and the petulant activity of our egoism, must have been the happiest and most stable of epochs. The more we reflect on it, the more we shall find that this state was the least subject to revolutions, and altogether the very best man could experience; so that he can have departed from it only through some fatal accident, which, for the public good, should never have happened. The example of savages, most of whom have been found in this state, seems to prove that men were meant to remain in it, that it is the real youth of the world, and that all subsequent advances have been apparently so many steps towards the perfection of the individual, but in reality towards the decrepitude of the species.

So long as men remained content with their rustic huts, so long as they were satisfied with clothes made of the skins of animals and sewn together with thorns and fish-bones, adorned themselves only with feathers and shells, and continued to paint their bodies different colours, to improve and beautify their bows and arrows, and to make with sharp-edged stones fishing boats or clumsy musical instruments; in a word, so long as they undertook only what a single person could accomplish, and confined themselves to such arts as did not require the joint labour of several hands, they lived free, healthy, honest, and happy lives, so long as their nature allowed, and as they continued to enjoy the pleasures of mutual and independent intercourse. But from the moment one man began to stand in need of the help of another; from the moment it appeared advantageous to any one man to have enough provisions for two, equality disappeared, property was introduced, work became indispensable, and vast forests became smiling fields, which man had to water with the sweat of his brow, and where slavery and misery were soon seen to germinate and grow up with the crops.

Metallurgy and agriculture were the two arts which produced this great revolution. The poets tell us it was gold and silver, but, for the philosophers, it was iron and corn, which first civilized men, and ruined humanity.

Cultivation of the ground led to its being divided up, Rousseau explains. This introduced the idea of property. Further, both metalwork and agriculture made inequalities in skill apparent, as they had not been when savage man hunted by himself. Some could gain a great deal by their work, others could barely support themselves. So poverty and wealth developed, and with them constant antagonism between the poor and the rich.

It is impossible that men should not at length have reflected on so wretched a situation, and on the calamities that overwhelmed them. The rich, in particular, must have felt how much they suffered by a constant state of war, of which they bore all the expense; and in which, though all risked their lives, they alone risked their property. Besides, however speciously they might disguise their usurpations, they knew that they were founded on precarious and false titles; so that, if others took from them by force what they themselves had gained by force, they would have no reason to complain. Even those who had been enriched by their own industry, could hardly base their proprietorship on better claims. It was in vain to repeat: 'I built this well; I gained this spot by my industry.' Who gave you your standing, it might be answered, and what right have you to demand payment of us for doing what we never asked you to do? Do you not know that numbers of your fellow-creatures are starving, for want of what you have too much of? You ought to have had the express and universal consent of mankind, before appropriating more of the common subsistence than you needed for your own maintenance. Destitute of valid reasons to justify and sufficient strength to defend himself, able to crush individuals with ease, but easily crushed himself by a troop of bandits, one against all, and incapable, on account of mutual jealousy, of joining with his equals against numerous enemies united by the common hope of plunder, the rich man, thus urged by necessity, conceived at length the profoundest plan that ever entered the mind of man: this was to employ in his favour the forces of those who attacked him, to make allies of his adversaries, to inspire them with different maxims, and to give them other institutions as favourable to himself as the law of nature was unfavourable.

With this view, after having represented to his neighbours the horror of a situation which armed every man against the rest, and made their possessions as burdensome to them as their wants, and in which no safety could be expected either in riches or in poverty, he readily devised plausible arguments to make them close with his design. 'Let us join,' said he, 'to guard the weak from oppression, to restrain the ambitious, and secure to every man the possession of what belongs to him: let us institute rules of justice and peace, to which all without exception may be obliged to conform; rules that may in some measure make amends for the caprices of fortune, by subjecting equally the powerful and the weak to the observance of reciprocal obligations. Let us, in a word, instead of turning our forces against ourselves, collect them in a supreme power which may govern us by wise laws, protect and defend all the members of the association, repulse their common enemies, and maintain eternal harmony among us.'

Far fewer words to this purpose would have been enough to impose on men so barbarous and easily seduced; especially as they had too many disputes among themselves to do without arbitrators, and too much ambition and avarice to go long without masters. All ran headlong to their chains, in hopes of securing their liberty; for they had just wit enough to perceive the advantages of political institutions, without experience enough to enable them to foresee the dangers. The most capable of foreseeing the dangers were the very persons who expected to benefit by them; and even the most prudent judged it not inexpedient to sacrifice one part of their freedom to ensure the rest; as a wounded man has his arm cut off to save the rest of his body.

Such was, or may well have been, the origin of society and law, which bound new fetters on the poor, and gave new powers to the rich; which irretrievably destroyed natural liberty, eternally fixed the law of property and inequality, converted clever usurpation into unalterable right, and, for the advantage of a few ambitious individuals, subjected all mankind to perpetual labour, slavery, and wretchedness. It is easy to see how the establishment of one community made that of all the rest necessary, and how, in order to make head against united forces, the rest of mankind had to unite in turn. Societies soon multiplied and spread over the face of the earth, till hardly a corner of the world was left in which a man could escape the yoke, and withdraw his head from beneath the sword which he saw perpetually hanging over him by a thread. Civil right having thus become the common rule among the members of each community, the law of nature maintained its place only between different communities, where, under the name of the right of nations, it was qualified by certain tacit conventions, in order to make commerce practicable, and serve as a substitute for natural compassion, which lost, when applied to societies, almost all the influence it had over individuals. . . .

But bodies politic, remaining thus in a state of nature among themselves, presently experienced the inconveniences which had obliged individuals to forsake it; for this state became still more fatal to these great bodies than it had been to the individuals of whom they were composed. Hence arose national wars, battles, murders, and reprisals, which shock nature and outrage reason; together with all those horrible prejudices which class among the virtues the honour of shedding human blood. The most distinguished men hence learned to consider cutting each other's throats a duty; at length men massacred their fellow-creatures by thousands without so much as knowing why, and committed more murders in a single day's fighting, and more violent outrages in the sack of a single town, than were committed in the state of nature during whole ages over the whole earth. Such were the first effects which we can see to have followed the division of mankind into different communities . . .

The savage and the civilized man differ so much in the bottom of their hearts and in their inclinations, that what constitutes the supreme happiness of one would reduce the other to despair. The former breathes only peace and liberty; he desires only to live and be free from labour; even the *ataraxia* [freedom from passion] of the Stoic falls far short of his profound indifference to every other object. Civilized man, on the other hand, is always moving, sweating, toiling, and racking his brains to find still more laborious occupations: he goes on in drudgery to his last moment, and even seeks death to put himself in a position to live, or renounces life to acquire immortality. He pays his court to men in power, whom he hates, and to the wealthy, whom he despises; he stops at nothing to have the honour of serving them; he is not ashamed to value himself on his own meanness and their protection; and, proud of his slavery, he speaks with disdain of those, who have not the honour of sharing it. What a sight would the perplexing and envied labours of a European minister of State present to the eyes of a Caribbean! How many cruel deaths would not this indolent savage prefer to the horrors of such a life, which is seldom even sweetened by the pleasure of doing good! But for him to see into the motives of all this solicitude, the words 'power' and 'reputation' would have to bear some meaning in his mind; he would have to know that there are men who set a value on the opinion of the rest of the world who can be made happy and satisfied with themselves rather on the testimony of other people than on their own. In reality, the source of all these differences is, that the savage lives within himself, while social man lives constantly outside himself, and only knows how to live in the opinion of others, so that he seems to receive the consciousness of his own existence merely from the judgment of others concerning him . . .

It has indeed cost us not a little trouble to make ourselves as wretched as we are. When we consider, on the one hand, the immense labours of mankind, the many sciences brought to perfection, the arts invented, the powers employed, the deeps filled up, the mountains levelled, the rocks shattered, the rivers made navigable, the tracts of land cleared, the lakes emptied, the marshes drained, the enormous structures erected on land, and the teeming vessels that cover the sea; and, on the other hand, estimate with ever so little thought, the real advantages that have accrued from all these works to mankind, we cannot help being amazed at the vast disproportion there is between these things, and deploring the infatuation of man, which, to gratify his silly pride and vain self-admiration, induces him eagerly to pursue all the miseries he is capable of feeling, though beneficent nature had kindly placed them out of his way.

That men are actually wicked, a sad and continual experience of them proves beyond doubt: but, all the same, I think I have shown that man is naturally good. What then can have depraved him to such an extent, except the changes that have happened in his constitution, the advances he has made, and the knowledge he has acquired? We may admire human society as much as we please; it will be none the less true that it necessarily leads men to hate each other in proportion as their interests clash, and to do one another apparent services, while they are really doing every imaginable mischief . . .

Savage man, when he has dined, is at peace with all nature, and the friend of all his fellow-creatures. If a dispute arises about a meal, he rarely comes to blows, without having first compared the difficulty of conquering his antagonist with the trouble of finding subsistence elsewhere: and, as pride does not come in, it all ends in a few blows; the victor eats, and the vanquished seeks provision somewhere else, and all is at peace. The case is quite different with man in the state of society, for whom first necessaries have to be provided, and then superfluities; delicacies follow next, then immense wealth, then subjects, and then slaves. He enjoys not a moment's relaxation; and what is yet stranger, the less natural and pressing his wants, the more headstrong are his passions, and, still worse, the more he has it in his power to gratify them; so that after a long course of prosperity, after having swallowed up treasures and ruined multitudes, the hero ends up by cutting every throat till he finds himself, at last, sole master of the world. Such is in miniature the moral picture, if not of human life, at least of the secret pretensions of the heart of civilized man.

Source: Jean-Jacques Rousseau, *The Social Contract: Discourses*, with an introduction by G. D. H. Cole, J. M. Dent & Sons, 1913.

Utopian Fishing

In the anonymous utopia *A Voyage to the World in the Centre of the Earth* (1755), the narrator falls into the crater of Mount Vesuvius and arrives in an idyllic region, light and airy, where the inhabitants are strict observers of animal rights. As an elder explains: 'Next after the worshipping and adoring our creator, it is the principal part of our religion to protect what he has been pleased to give life to.' Consequently wildlife has no fear of man. When the narrator walks through the countryside, birds perch all over him and put their beaks to his lips. When he meets a lion, it drops a stone at his feet and looks up appealingly for him to throw it, like a dog. He is taken to visit a lady, and learns that her husband is in the garden fishing.

After we had entered the garden, and passed through the most delightful walks and groves I ever beheld, we discovered her husband at a small distance, sitting by the side of a large pond. As soon as he saw us, he rose to meet us; and . . . was, by his wife, introduced to me. Having heard my story before, he received me with the utmost complaisance. Then addressing himself to his wife, 'My dear,' says he, 'I have had good sport since I saw you; and if you please to bring our visitors along with you, I will show them the success I have met with; for I verily believe, I have made a thousand fish happy, by filling their bellies.' We followed him to the pond, and found a cistern near it full of clear water, with several fish in it of different sorts, flouncing and playing about; at the side of it was a vessel full of a sort of grain, of which he every now and then threw a handful or two in, to feed the fish he had caught. He then went to the pond-side, and said he would show us what diversion he had. Upon his approach, he stirred the water with a stick, and hundreds of fish, of different sorts, appeared on the surface, and came so near him, that he might take them out with his hand; which having done, he put them into the cistern, and threw several handfuls of grain in, to feed them. After he had for some time entertained us with his dexterity, in first catching the fish, and then filling their bellies, he took the cistern, and delivered the fish again to the pond . . .

In our passage to the house, I could not help reflecting how much more pleasure it must give one to protect life than to take it away; and how much happier he must be in catching the fish with no other intention than to feed them, than it can be with us, to first torture them with hooks and then throw them on the ground to expire in agonies. Surely, if we were to make it our own case, we should refrain from many barbarities, that we look upon as amusements, and not entertain ourselves by tormenting any thing that has life, when we are sensible how terrible it would be to us to be served in the same manner; for every thing that has life as naturally endeavours to preserve it, and feels pain as severely as we, the great self-conceited lords of the universe.

Source: Anon., *A Voyage to the World in the Centre of the Earth*, 1755.

Eldorado

Voltaire's *Candide* (1758) is a satire on the philosophical doctrine of Optimism. According to this doctrine, since the Creator is benevolent and all-powerful, what appear to be the disasters and catastrophes of human life must all be for the best, and if only we could see them from a divine perspective we should realize this. Traceable in part to the German philosopher Leibniz, Optimism was popularized in England and France by Alexander Pope's poem *An Essay, on Man* (1732–4), of which the first 'Epistle' concludes:

> All Nature is but art, unknown to thee;
> All chance, direction which thou canst not see;
> All discord, harmony not understood;
> All partial evil universal good:
> And spite of pride, in erring reason's spite,
> One truth is clear, Whatever is, is RIGHT.

Dr Johnson famously remarked of Pope's *Essay*, 'Never were penury of knowledge and vulgarity of sentiment so happily disguised.'

In Voltaire's satire a young German, Candide, living at the country house of Baron Thunder-ten-tronckh in Westphalia, is introduced to Optimism by the family tutor, Dr Pangloss, who is philosophically convinced that all is for the best in the best of all possible worlds. Candide is cast penniless upon the world when he is caught kissing the daughter of the family, the beauteous Cunégonde. Pangloss soon joins him in his wanderings. So, later, does Cunégonde. They experience a succession of betrayals, persecutions and calamities – including the Lisbon earthquake of 1755, which killed fifty thousand people. Through it all Pangloss persists in his Optimism, until he is hanged by the Inquisition. In fact he survives. But while he is absent from the narrative Candide, his servant Cacambo, and Cunégonde visit the New World. There Cunégonde is abducted by the governor of Buenos Aires, and Candide and Cacambo have a utopian adventure while sailing down a river.

The stream took them several miles between banks which at one point were smooth and covered with flowers, and at another were rocky and sterile. The river grew wider and wider, and at last disappeared into a cave under some cliffs of terrifying height, whose summits seemed to touch the sky. The two travellers were courageous enough to trust themselves to the stream as it rushed under the cliffs, while the river, narrowing once more, carried them on with frightening speed and noise. At the end of twenty-four hours they emerged into the light of day; but their boat was dashed to pieces against some boulders and they had to creep from rock to rock for three whole miles, until at length they reached a vast open plain, surrounded by inaccessible mountains. The farmer and the landscape gardener had been equally busy in this countryside, and everything which served the needs of man was pleasing to the sight. The roads were crowded, or rather adorned, with carriages, magnificent in appearance and material, drawn by huge red sheep faster than the finest horses of Andalusia, Tetuan, or Mequinez, and in them sat men and women of matchless beauty.

'This is a better sort of country than Westphalia,' said Candide, while he and Cacambo were making for the nearest village.

As they approached they noticed some children, covered with tattered gold brocade, playing at ninepins; and our two visitors from the other world stopped to watch them. Their skittles were large round objects of striking brilliance, some of them yellow, some red, and some green. The travellers had the curiosity to pick some up, and found that they were gold nuggets, emeralds, and rubies, the least of which would have been the grandest ornament in the Mogul throne.

'These children playing at ninepins,' said Cacambo, 'are no doubt the sons of the King of this country.'

At that moment the village schoolmaster appeared to send the children back to school.

'That must be the tutor to the Royal Family,' said Candide.

The little urchins stopped playing, and left their skittles and other toys in the road. Candide picked them up and, running after the tutor, handed them to him with a deep bow and made signs to show that Their Royal Highnesses had forgotten their gold nuggets and precious stones. The village schoolmaster smiled and threw them away, surveying Candide for a moment with great surprise before continuing his walk.

The travellers did not fail to pick up the gold, emeralds, and rubies.

'Where can we have got to?' cried Candide. 'The children of the Kings of this country must be well brought up, if they are taught to despise gold and precious stones.' And Cacambo was as surprised as Candide.

In due course they approached the largest house in the village, which looked like a European palace. A crowd of people was standing round the door, and there were more inside. Strains of delightful music could be heard, and a delicious smell of cooking reached them. Cacambo went up to the door, and heard Peruvian spoken. It was his mother tongue, for you will remember that Cacambo was born in an Argentine village where that was the only language they knew.

'I will be your interpreter,' said he to Candide. 'Let's go inside. This is an inn.'

Two waiters and two waitresses, dressed in cloth of gold with their hair tied in ribbons, invited them to sit down to table and put before them four tureens of soup, each garnished with two parakeets, a boiled vulture weighing about two hundred pounds, two delicious roast monkeys, three hundred doves on one plate, and six hundred humming-birds on another, as well as exquisite stews and luscious pastries, all served on plates of a sort of rock crystal. And the waiters and waitresses offered them several kinds of liqueurs to drink made from sugar cane.

The guests were tradesmen and waggoners for the most part and were all extremely polite. They put several questions to Cacambo with delicate tact, and answered the enquiries he made to his complete satisfaction.

When the meal was over, Cacambo thought – as indeed did Candide – that two of the large gold nuggets they had picked up would amply pay their bill, but when they placed them on the table the landlord and his wife laughed so long and so loud that they had to hold their sides. They recovered their composure at last, and the landlord said:

'Gentlemen, it is obvious that you are strangers here, and we are not used to foreigners. So please excuse our laughter at your offering to pay us with stones off the road. I dare say you haven't any of our money, but you don't need any to dine here. All inns run for the convenience of tradespeople are paid for by the Government. You have fared badly here because this is a poor village, but everywhere else you will be received as you deserve to be.'

Cacambo interpreted the landlord's remarks to Candide, and Candide heard them with the same wonder and bewilderment that his friend Cacambo showed in translating them.

'What country can this be?' said one to the other. 'It must be unknown to the rest of the world, because everything is so different from what we are used to. It is probably the country where all goes well; for there must obviously be some such place. And whatever Professor Pangloss might say, I often noticed that all went badly in Westphalia.'

Cacambo tried to satisfy his curiosity by questioning the landlord, but all the landlord would say was: 'I am an ignorant fellow and quite content to be so. But we have an old man in the neighbourhood who has retired from Court; he is the most learned person in the kingdom, and he will certainly be able to satisfy you.' So he took Cacambo to call on the old man, while Candide played a minor part and accompanied his valet. They walked over to a modest little house, and went in. The door was mere silver, and the rooms were panelled with nothing better than gold; but the workmanship was in such good taste as to vie with the richest panelling. It is true that the hall was incrusted only with rubies and emeralds, but everything was so well designed as to compensate for this extreme simplicity.

The old man was seated on a couch stuffed with humming-bird feathers when the two strangers were shown in. He begged them to sit down, and offered them liqueurs in diamond glasses. After this refreshment he began to satisfy their curiosity as follows:

'I am one hundred and seventy-two years old,' he said. 'It was from my late father, who was equerry to the King, that I learned about the astonishing Peruvian revolution of which he was an eye-witness. The kingdom where we live used to be inhabited by the Incas, who imprudently left it to subdue another part of the world, and were finally exterminated by the Spaniards.

'A few noblemen had been wise enough to stay behind in their native country. With the agreement of the whole nation, they made a law that no inhabitant should ever leave our little kingdom; and that is how our innocence and happiness have been preserved. The Spaniards had a confused knowledge of the existence of this country, which they named Eldorado, and an English nobleman called Ralegh nearly reached it about a hundred years ago; but as we are surrounded by unscalable rocks and precipices, we have so far been sheltered from the greed of European nations, who have a quite irrational lust for the pebbles and dirt found in our soil, and would kill every man of us to get hold of them.'

Their conversation was a long one and covered the form of government in Eldorado, local customs, behaviour towards women, public ceremonies, and the arts. At last Candide, whose taste for metaphysics was insatiable, told Cacambo to ask whether any religion was practised in the country.

The old man blushed slightly. 'Religion!' he exclaimed. 'Why, of course there's a religion. Do you suppose we are lost to all sense of gratitude?'

Cacambo humbly asked him what the religion of Eldorado was. The old man blushed once more.

'Can there be two religions, then?' said he. 'I have always believed that we hold the religion of all mankind. We worship God from morning till night.'

'Do you worship only one God?' asked Cacambo, interpreting Candide's doubts.

'Of course we do,' said the old man. 'There is only one God, not two, three, or four. What odd questions you foreigners ask!'

Candide was indefatigable in plying the good old man with questions. He wanted to know how prayers were offered to God in Eldorado.

'We never pray,' said this good and venerable man; 'we have nothing to ask of God, since He has given us everything we need. But we thank Him unceasingly.'

Candide was curious to see some of their priests, and told Cacambo to ask where they could be found.

The old man smiled. 'My friends,' said he, 'we are all priests; the King and the heads of each family perform solemn hymns of thanksgiving every morning, with an orchestra of five or six thousand musicians to accompany them.'

'Do you mean to say you have no monks teaching and disputing, governing and intriguing, and having people burned if they don't subscribe to their opinions?'

'We should be stupid if we had,' said the old man; 'we are all of the same opinion here, and we don't know what you mean by monks.'

Candide was delighted with all he heard, and said to himself: 'This is quite different from Westphalia and the Baron's mansion: if our friend Pangloss had seen Eldorado, he would not have kept on saying that Castle Thunder-ten-tronckh was the loveliest house on earth; it shows that people ought to travel.'

When this long conversation was over, the good old man had a carriage and six sheep made ready, and commissioned twelve of his servants to take the two travellers to Court.

'I must beg you,' said he, 'to excuse me from accompanying you; my great age deprives me of that honour. You will have no reason, I am sure, to be discontented with your reception from the King; but if any of the customs of this country should happen to displease, no doubt you will make allowances.'

Candide and Cacambo took their seats in the carriage, and the six sheep made such speed that in less than four hours they reached the King's palace, which stood at one end of the capital. The portico was two hundred feet high and one hundred broad, but it is impossible to describe what it was made of. Nevertheless, the prodigious superiority of its materials over the sand and pebbles which we call gold and precious stones was clearly manifest.

Twenty maidservants of surpassing beauty welcomed Candide and Cacambo as they alighted from their carriage, and led them to a dressing-room, where they fitted them out with garments of humming-bird down. Dressed in these robes of State, they were conducted by lords and ladies of the Court to wait upon His Majesty, and passed through an antechamber, on each side of which two ranks of a thousand musicians had been placed, in accordance with the normal custom. As they approached the throne room, Cacambo asked one of the lords-in-waiting how he should behave in saluting His Majesty; should he fall on his knees or should he grovel, should he put his hands on his head or his behind, or should he lick the dust off the floor; in short, what was the procedure?

'The custom is,' said the lord-in-waiting, 'to embrace the King and kiss him on both cheeks.'

Accordingly, Candide and Cacambo fell on His Majesty's neck, and were most graciously received by him and invited to supper that evening.

To pass away the time before supper they were shown the sights of the city. The public buildings were so lofty that their roofs seemed to touch the sky, and the marketplaces were adorned with endless colonnades. Fountains of pure water, rose-water, and sugar-cane liqueur played unceasingly in the public squares, which were paved with a kind of precious stone smelling of cloves and cinnamon. Candide asked to see the Law Courts and the Court of Appeal, but was told that there were none; court cases, in fact, were unknown. He enquired whether there were any prisons, and his guide answered no. What surprised and delighted him most of all was the Palace of Science, where he saw a gallery two thousand feet long filled with mathematical and scientific instruments.

The afternoon had passed, and they had seen little more than a thousandth part of the city, but it was time to go back to the royal palace for supper. Candide sat down to table with His Majesty, and Cacambo and several Court ladies were of the company. Never was entertainment so lavish as that supper party, and never was anyone so witty as His Majesty. Cacambo interpreted the King's witticisms to Candide, who found them still witty in translation, a point which surprised him as much as anything he heard or saw.

They spent a month at the palace, but not a day passed without Candide saying to Cacambo: 'It is quite true, my good fellow, that the house where I was born won't bear comparison with the mansions of this country; but still, I shall never be happy without Lady Cunégonde, and I dare say you have some mistress or other in Europe. If we stay here, we shall be no different from anybody else; but if we go back to the old world with a mere twelve sheep laden with Eldorado stones, we shall be richer than all the kings of Europe put together. We shall have nothing to fear from Inquisitors, and we shall easily rescue Lady Cunégonde.'

Cacambo was pleased at this, for, like Candide, he had a restless spirit. They were both anxious, also, to show their friends how rich they had grown and to boast about what they had seen in their travels. So these happy men decided to be happy no longer and to take leave of His Majesty.

'This is a foolish scheme of yours,' said the King; 'I realize that my country is not much to boast of, but a man should be satisfied with what works moderately well. I have no right to detain strangers against their will; that would be a tyranny which neither our customs nor our laws could justify. All men are free. Go when you wish, but you will find it difficult to get out. It is impossible to make your way against that torrent which so miraculously brought you here through subterranean caves. The mountains which surround my entire kingdom are ten thousand feet high, and as sheer as a wall. Each of them covers an area of more than thirty square miles, and when you reach the top, you can only clamber down precipices. However, since you are absolutely determined to leave, I will give orders to my engineers to make a machine to transport you in comfort. When you have been carried over the mountains, no one can accompany you any further; for my subjects have sworn never to cross the border, and they are too wise to break their oath. But apart from providing you with guides, you may ask me for anything you wish.'

'All we ask of Your Majesty,' said Cacambo, 'is a few sheep saddled with food and with the stones and mud of your country.'

The King laughed. 'I don't understand your European taste for our yellow mud,' he said; 'but take all you want, and much good may it do you.'

He immediately gave orders to his engineers to make a machine for hoisting these two extraordinary men out of his kingdom. Three thousand celebrated scientists set to work, and it was finished in fifteen days at a cost of not more than twenty thousand pounds sterling in the money of that country. Candide and Cacambo were placed on the machine with two large red sheep, saddled and bridled for riding after they had crossed the mountains, and in addition twenty sheep with pack-saddles full of food, thirty to carry exquisitely chosen presents, and fifty laden with gold, diamonds, and precious stones. Before they left, the King tenderly embraced the two wanderers.

Their departure was a beautiful sight, and the ingenious way in which they and their sheep were lifted over the tops of the mountains was worth watching. The scientists took leave of them after placing them in safety, and Candide had no other wish or object in view than to go and present his sheep to Lady Cunégonde.

'We can now pay off the Governor of Buenos Ayres,' he remarked, 'if Lady Cunégonde should be held to ransom. Let's go to Cayenne and set sail, and we will then see what kingdom we can buy.'

Needless to say, they soon meet fresh disasters and lose all their money. Voltaire's allusions to More's *Utopia* (see p. 38) are obvious. But his satire embraces standbys of the utopian genre – universal politeness, luxuries on tap, friendly rulers – that extend far beyond More. Voltaire's own opinions of such hopes may be gathered from an exchange, a little later in the narrative, between Candide and an old scholar called Martin.

'Do you think,' said Candide, 'that men have always massacred each other, as they do today, that they have always been false, cozening, faithless, ungrateful, thieving, weak, inconstant, mean-spirited, envious, greedy, drunken, miserly, ambitious, bloody, slanderous, debauched, fanatic, hypocritical, and stupid?'

'Do you think,' said Martin, 'that hawks have always eaten pigeons when they could find them?'

'Of course I do,' said Candide.

'Well,' said Martin, 'if hawks have always had the same character, why should you suppose that men have changed theirs?'

Source: Voltaire, *Candide, or Optimism*, translated by John Butt, Penguin, 1947.

A Pastoral Idyll

Samuel Johnson's *Rasselas* (1759), written in a week to pay the expenses of his mother's funeral, is perhaps the wisest book ever written. It is a satire against hope. Rasselas, Prince of Abyssinia, grows up, like all Abyssinian royals, in the Happy Valley. There, all his wants are supplied. But he feels constricted, and escapes, with his sister Princess Pekuah and his tutor, the poet Imlac, to find happiness in the world outside. He mixes with all sorts and conditions of men, but finds none of them happy. An early encounter is with some shepherds, whom he expects to find enjoying pastoral contentment.

Their way lay through fields, where shepherds tended their flocks, and the lambs were playing upon the pasture. 'This,' said the poet, 'is the life which has been often celebrated for its innocence and quiet: let us pass the heat of the day among the shepherds' tents, and know whether all our searches are not to terminate in pastoral simplicity.'

The proposal pleased them, and they induced the shepherds, by small presents and familiar questions, to tell their opinion of their own state. They were so rude and ignorant, so little able to compare the good with the evil of the occupation, and so indistinct in their narratives and descriptions, that very little could be learned from them. But it was evident that their hearts were cankered with discontent; that they considered themselves as condemned to labour for the luxury of the rich, and looked up with stupid malevolence towards those that were placed above them.

The princess pronounced with vehemence that she would never suffer these envious savages to be her companions, and that she should not soon be desirous of seeing any more specimens of rustic happiness.

After many adventures among the unhappy inhabitants of the world, the travellers return, disillusioned, to the Happy Valley. 'We are long,' Johnson concludes, 'before we are convinced that happiness is never to be found, and each believes it possessed by others, to keep alive the hope of obtaining it for himself.'

Source: Samuel Johnson, *The History of Rasselas Prince of Abyssinia*, 1759.

An American in London

In the anonymous *Private Letters from an American in England to his Friends in America* (1769), set towards the end of the eighteenth century, the seat of government has been transferred to America, England is largely depopulated, and the contents of the British Museum have been sold to buy food. Though some of its predictions are still to be fulfilled, it was well ahead of its time in anticipating the replacement of Britain by America as the dominant world power.

After passing a place called Leicester Square, where the pedestal only of an equestrian statue still remained, I found nothing but unroofed buildings, common sewers open to the air – and, of course, very offensive, grass growing between the interstices of the stones on the footway, and, in short, everything symptomatic of desolation . . .

I naturally made my first pilgrimage to St Paul's. I was determined to walk, as the rubbish of old uninhabited houses made it difficult for a carriage to pass . . . On approaching the west door – for I most exactly followed the plan in my hand – I saw a kind of harlequin walking to and fro, and a sort of Italian playing on a guitar. I asked them if I could be admitted to see the church. My answer was – If you mean to see the pantomime, the other door leads you to it, but if you intend being at the concert, with the latest favourite burletta, this is the entrance.

Source: Anon., *Private Letters from an American in England to his Friends in America*, 1769.

In the South Seas

Louis Antoine, Comte de Bougainville (1729–1811), who gave his name to the exotic climber Bougainvillaea which he brought back to Europe, commanded the two ships *La Boudeuse* and *L'Etoile* that made the first French circumnavigation of the world. His narrative of this voyage, published in French in 1771, introduced European readers to a new version of paradise-on-earth, the island of Tahiti.

As we came nearer the shore, the number of islanders surrounding our ships increased. The periaguas [canoes] were so numerous all about the ships that we had much ado to warp in amidst all the crowd of boats and the noise. All these people came crying out *tayo*, which means friend, and gave a thousand signs of friendship. They all asked nails and ear-rings of us. The periaguas were full of females who, for agreeable feature, are not inferior to most European women, and who in point of beauty of the body might, with much reason, vie with them. Most of these fair females were naked, for the men and the old women that accompanied them had stripped them of the garments which they generally dress themselves in. The glances which they gave us from their periaguas seemed to discover some degree of uneasiness, notwithstanding the innocent manner in which they were given, perhaps because nature has everywhere embellished their sex with a natural timidity, or because even in those countries where the ease of the golden age is still in use, women seem least to desire what they most wish for. The men, who were more plain, or rather more free, soon explained their meaning very clearly. They pressed us to choose a woman and to come on shore with her, and their gestures, which were nothing less than equivocal, denoted in what manner we should form an acquaintance with her. It was very difficult, amidst such a sight, to keep at their work four hundred young French sailors, who had seen no women for six months. In spite of all our precautions, a young girl came on board and placed herself upon the quarter-deck near one of the hatchways which was open, in order to give air to those who were heaving at the capstan below it. The girl carelessly dropped a cloth which covered her, and appeared to the eyes of all beholders such as Venus showed herself to the Phrygian shepherd [Paris], having, indeed, the celestial form of that goddess. Both sailors and soldiers endeavoured to come to the hatchway, and the capstan was never hove with more alacrity than on this occasion . . .

Bougainville and his party go ashore, and are welcomed by a native chief, Ereti.

The chief then proposed that we should sit down upon the grass before his house, where he ordered some fruit, broiled fish, and water to be set before us. During the meal he sent for some pieces of cloth, and for two great collars or gorgets of osiers, covered with black feathers and shark's teeth. They are pretty like in form to the immense ruffs worn in the time of Francis I. One of these he put upon the neck of the Chevalier d'Oraison, another upon mine, and distributed the cloths. We were just going to return on board when the Chevalier de Suzannet missed a pistol, which had been very dextrously stolen out of his pocket. We informed the chief of it, who immediately was for searching all the people who surrounded us, and even treated some of them very harshly. We stopped his researches, endeavouring only to make him understand that the thief would fall a victim to his own crime, and that what he had stolen could kill him.

The chief and all his people accompanied us to our boats. We were almost come to them when we were stopped by an islander, of a fine figure, who, lying under a tree, invited us to sit down by him on the grass. We accepted his offer. He then leaned towards us, and with a tender air he slowly sung a song, without doubt of the Anacreontic kind [in the style of the Greek lyric poet Anacreon], to the tune of a flute which another Indian blew with his nose. This was a charming scene and worthy the pencil of a Boucher [François Boucher, French rococo artist]. Four islanders came with great confidence to sup and lie on board. We let them hear the music of our flutes, bass-viols and violins, and we entertained them with a firework of skyrockets and fire-snakes. This sight caused a mixture of surprise and horror in them . . .

The French set up a camp on shore, which the islanders freely visit.

The only constraint which their presence put upon us was that they obliged us to have our eyes upon everything that was brought on shore, and even to look to our pockets. For even in Europe itself one cannot see more expert filchers than the people of this country. However, it does not appear that stealing is usual among themselves. Nothing is shut up in their houses. Every piece of furniture lies on the ground or is hung up without being under any person's care. Doubtless their curiosity for new objects excited violent desires in them . . .

All our transactions were carried on in as friendly a manner as possible, if we except thieving. Our people were daily walking in the isle without arms, either quite alone or in little companies. They were invited to enter the houses, where the people gave them to eat. Nor did the civility of their landlords stop at a slight collation. They offered them young girls. The hut was immediately filled with a curious crowd of men and women who made a circle round the guest and the young victim of hospitality. The ground was spread with leaves and flowers, and their musicians sung an hymeneal song to the tune of their flutes. Here Venus is the goddess of hospitality, her worship does not admit of any mysteries, and every tribute paid to her is a feast for the whole nation. They were surprised at the confusion which our people appeared to be in, as our customs do not admit of these public proceedings. However, I would not answer for it that every one of our men found it impossible to conquer his repugnance and conform to the customs of the country.

I have often, in company with only one or two of our people, been out walking in the interior parts of the isle. I thought I was trans- ported into the Garden of Eden. We crossed a turf, covered with fine fruit trees, and intersected by little rivulets, which keep up a pleasant coolness in the air, without any of those inconveniences which humidity occasions. A numerous people there enjoy the blessings which nature showers liberally down upon them. We found com- panies of men and women sitting under the shade of their fruit-trees. They all greeted us with signs of friendship. Those who met us upon the road stood aside to let us pass by. Everywhere we found hospitality, ease, innocent joy, and every appearance of happiness amongst them . . .

On the 10th [of April] an islander was killed, and the natives came to complain of this murder. I sent some people to the house, whither they had brought the dead body. It appeared very plain that the man had been killed by a firearm. However, none of our people had been suffered to go out of the camp or to come from the ships with firearms. The most exact inquiries which I made to find out the author of this villainous action proved unsuccessful. The natives doubtless believed that their countryman had been in the wrong, for they continued to come to our quarters with their usual confidence. However, I received intelligence that many of the people had been seen carrying off their effects to the mountains, and that even Ereti's house was quite unfurnished. I made him some presents, and this good chief continued to testify the sincerest friendship for us . . .

One misfortune never comes alone. As we were occupied with a piece of work upon which our safety depended, I was informed that three of the natives had been killed or wounded with bayonets in their huts, that the alarm was spread in the country, that the old men, the women and the children fled towards the mountains with their goods, and even the bodies of the dead, and that we should perhaps be attacked by an army of these enraged men . . .

Bougainville sends a lieutenant to reassure the natives. He is met by a party of women.

The women, who were all in tears, fell at his feet, kissed his hands, weeping and repeating several times, *Tayo, mate*, You are our friends, and you kill us. By his caresses and demonstrations of friendship he at last succeeded in regaining their confidence. I saw from on board a crowd of people running to our quarters: fowls, coconuts, and branches of bananas embellished this procession and promised a peace. I immediately went ashore with an assortment of silk stuffs and tools of all sorts. I distributed them among the chiefs, expressing my concern to them on account of the disaster which had happened the day before, and assuring them I would punish the perpetrators. The good islanders loaded me with caresses. The people applauded the reunion, and in a short time the usual crowd and the thieves returned to our quarters, which looked like a fair . . .

Some weeks after leaving Tahiti Bougainville was disconcerted to find that a number of his crew-members had contracted venereal disease on the paradise isle. He laid the blame for this on the sailors from an English ship, the *Dolphin*, which had visited Tahiti in 1767.

The French philosopher Denis Diderot (1713–84) put these facts together, and added reinforcement from his own imagination, to produce his *Supplement to Bougainville's Voyage* (published posthumously in 1796). This is a passionate denunciation of 'civilized' values. It presents Tahiti as a haven of innocence, despoiled by European lust, disease and murder. According to Diderot, the islanders follow the pure instincts of nature. That is why they see nothing vicious or shameful in sex – including promiscuity, adultery and incest. Every act of love is for them a joyful communal celebration of fertility. Further, crime is unknown, and they hold all property in common.

The truth was less idyllic, as Diderot knew. For Bougainville goes on to recount, in his *Voyage*, that a Tahitian named Aotourou (who, at his own request, returned to France with the travellers) gave them a first-hand account of the island's laws and customs.

I have mentioned above that the inhabitants of Tahiti seemed to live in an enviable happiness. To be almost equal in rank amongst themselves, or at least enjoying a liberty which was only subject to the laws established for their common happiness. I was mistaken. The distinction of ranks is very great at Tahiti, and the disproportion very tyrannical. The kings and grandees have power of life and death over their servants and slaves, and I am inclined to believe they have the same barbarous prerogative with regard to the common people, whom they call *Tat-einou*, vile men. So much is certain, that the victims for human sacrifices are taken from this class of people. Flesh and fish are reserved for the tables of the great; the commonalty live upon mere fruits and pulse. Even the very manner of being lighted at night shows the difference in the ranks. For the kind of wood which is burnt for people of distinction is not the same with that which the common people are allowed to make use of.

Source: Lewis [Louis] de Bougainville, *A Voyage Round the World. Performed by Order of His Most Christian Majesty, in the Years 1766, 1767, 1768 and 1769*, translated by John Reinhold Forster, 1772.

Happy Taxpayers

The French dramatist and social critic Louis-Sébastien Mercier (1740–1814) attacked the licentious manners of the nobility in his *Tableau de Paris* (1781) and was forced to flee to Switzerland. He saw himself as 'the true prophet of the French Revolution', and on return from exile became a member of the Convention. His utopia, *The Year 2440* (1771), was one of the great clandestine best-sellers of pre-Revolutionary France, going through twenty-five editions. Mercier did not dare acknowledge his authorship till 1791. It relates how a contemporary of Mercier awakes 700 years in the future, and finds Paris – and the human race – transformed. Avarice, vanity and ostentation are no more. People have become reasonable and public-spirited. A Temple of Clemency stands on the site of the Bastille. Paris has beautiful straight streets. Parisians wear loose simple clothes – no swords, powdered wigs or gold lace. Traffic keeps to the right of the road and obeys a strict speed limit. The city is largely pedestrianized. Even the king and nobles walk rather than use carriages. The only honour, replacing all orders and decorations, is an embroidered hat, awarded for outstanding public services (e.g. saving the life of a fellow citizen). Unless they have earned the right to wear it, even princes and dukes are not honoured.

There are no slums or air pollution. Fountains flow with pure drinking water. Twenty new, clean, hygienic hospitals provide free medication even for the poorest patients. Fragrant roof gardens have replaced the old pitched roofs. The evil institutions that have become obsolete include colonialism, the Catholic church and Negro slavery. We learn that a heroic black freedom fighter, now accorded almost divine honours, organized simultaneous uprisings in which all slave-owners, French, Spanish, English, Dutch and Portuguese, were slaughtered.

Censorship has ceased. There is a free press. But the state expects men of letters to improve the virtues and develop the sensibilities of mankind. The theatre is a 'school of morality'. An author who is judged by the public to have written an immoral book wears a mask, to signify his shame, till he has atoned by writing something more rational. He is daily visited by two worthy citizens who dispute with him and help him to amend. Everyone is an author, in that everyone publishes a book of his best thoughts towards the end of his life. This is regarded as his 'soul', and read at his funeral, replacing pompous mausoleums and memorials. Libraries are contemned as places of idleness and extravagance, and most books from previous centuries have been burned. A few abridgements of their contents are alone preserved. Volumes of theology and jurisprudence are kept behind bars in library basements. Their only use is as weapons: sent among enemy nations, they undermine their good sense.

Schoolchildren are not taught Greek, Latin or history ('the disgrace of humanity, being crowded with crimes and follies'), but they all learn algebra, to encourage rigorous thought, and physics ('the key to nature'). Science and religion are closely linked. When a young man comes of age, he is taken to an observatory and shown the stars through a telescope. Then a microscope is brought and he is shown the 'new universe' it reveals. Meanwhile a pastor enjoins him to reverence the Supreme Being who created the wonders he sees. Apparently the young initiates never ask what evidence there is for a Supreme Being. The narrator is informed that there is probably not a single atheist in the whole kingdom. If one were found, he would be despised as a 'stupid wretch', and banished if he persevered, 'but first we should enjoin him to go through an assiduous course of experimental physics'. Seemingly the rites-of-passage Mercier describes apply only to males. Women in the new Paris are expected to be subservient, seeking no distinction except what is reflected on them from their husbands. They should take particular care to avoid being witty, since it annoys men.

Capital punishment is rare and humane, and requires unusually co-operative offenders. The narrator witnesses an execution – the first for thirty years. The criminal, a young man who has killed his rival in love, is paraded in a bloody shirt amid weeping citizens. He is not fettered, tortured or kept long in prison. Nor, apparently, is he given a trial. After confessing his crime, he is addressed by the magistrate: 'It is still in your power to choose. If you will to live, you may. But it must be in disgrace, and loaded with our indignation.' The man bows his head, signifying he prefers death, whereupon his friends and relatives gather round congratulating him. His bloody shirt is replaced by a white robe, to show he dies pardoned, and six fusiliers shoot him.

The taxation system is not the least of the wonders the narrator encounters:

'Tell me, I beseech you, how are your public taxes levied? For let the legislature be as perfect as it may, taxes, I think, must always be paid.' As a full answer, the worthy man, my conductor, took me by the hand, and led me to a spacious place, formed by the termination of four streets. I observed a strong chest that was twelve feet high. It was supported on four wheels. There was a small opening at the top, which was screened from the rain by a kind of awning. On this chest was written: *Tribute due to the king representing the state.* Hard by was another chest, of smaller size, with these words: *Free gifts.* I saw several people, with easy, cheerful, contented looks, throw sealed packets into the chest, as in our day they threw letters into the post office . . . 'That large coffer you see,' they said, 'is our receiver general of the finances. It is there that every citizen deposits his contribution for the support of the state. We are obliged to deposit the fiftieth part of our annual income. He that has no property, or what is only just sufficient for his maintenance, is exempt . . . In the other coffer are voluntary offerings, intended for useful designs, for the execution of such projects as have been approved by the public. This sometimes is richer than the other, for we love liberality in our gifts, and no other motive is necessary to excite it than equity and a love for the state.' . . . 'How,' said I, 'do you leave it to the good will of the people to pay their taxes? There must be a great number who pay nothing, without your knowing it.' 'Not at all; your fears are vain. In the first place we give with a free will. Our tribute is not by compulsion, but founded on reason and equity. There is scarce a man amongst us who does not esteem it a point of honour to discharge the most sacred and most legitimate of all debts. Besides, if a man in condition to pay should dare to neglect it, you there see the table on which the name of the head of every family is engraved, by which we should soon see who had not thrown in his packet, on which should be his seal. In that case he covers himself with an eternal infamy, and we regard him as you regarded a thief. The appellation of a bad citizen follows him to the grave. Examples of this sort are very rare.'

Source: Louis-Sebastien Mercier, *Memoirs of the Year Two Thousand Five Hundred,* translated by W. Hooper, W. Jones, 1802.

Mathematical Perfectibility

The Marquis Jean-Antoine-Nicolas Caritat de Condorcet (1743–94) was a mathematical genius. A member of the famous society of *philosophes* grouped around Voltaire and the Encyclopaedia project, he was known to his friends as a 'snow-capped volcano' because of the passions lurking beneath his rational exterior. Encouraged by his young wife Sophie de Grouchy he took up the republican cause, and at the Revolution he presided over the Legislative Assembly. But he opposed the execution of Louis XVI, and was hunted down by Robespierre's police. While in hiding he wrote his *Sketch for a Historical Picture of the Progress of the Human Mind* (published posthumously in 1795).

Composed in the shadow of the guillotine, this has been called 'one of the few really great monuments of liberal thought', and it is filled with an ardent belief in human perfectibility. It charts the progress of mankind from hunter-gatherer to civilized modern. The driving force behind this progress, Condorcet argues, has always been reason, which naturally pursues what is useful and pleasurable. Its obstacles have been tyranny and religion (though Condorcet concedes that Islam has shown itself less absurd and more tolerant than other religions). He portrays humanity as benefiting from the occasional brainwaves of geniuses (such as the unknown inventors of the bow and arrow and the alphabet). But the innate reasonableness of people, when freed from the grip of priests and despots, has been just as important in ensuring advance. It is this that will inevitably spread the principles of the French Revolution – liberty, equality, fraternity – worldwide. 'The time will come when the sun will shine only on free men, who know no other master but their reason.' So, too, our perspective on mankind will be transformed. 'Up till now the history of politics, like that of philosophy or science, has been the history only of a few individuals: that which really constitutes the human race has been forgotten.'

Science, he predicts, will alter this. Science, not metaphysics, is the only true knowledge, and Condorcet explains that it is just as applicable to human affairs as it is to the natural world. 'All that is necessary to reduce the whole of nature to laws similar to those which Newton discovered with the aid of calculus, is to have a sufficient number of observations and a mathematics that is complex enough.' Systematic observation of the mass of mankind, backed up by scientific knowledge, will solve all medical and moral and social problems. It will also allow the establishment of old-age pensions and national insurance schemes on sound actuarial principles. Virtually all aspects of human behaviour will become mathematically computable. The calculus of probability will develop techniques for forecasting public opinion and majority decisions. (For example, anticipating that science would make it possible to predetermine the sex of children, Condorcet worked it out mathematically that the numbers of the two sexes would nevertheless remain about the same.) History, too, will become a precise science, allowing accurate prediction. It will be possible to 'tame the future'. Mass education will reduce the inequality between people to negligible proportions, and will greatly increase the supply of scientific geniuses. Indeed, the production of science and scientists will become the organizing principle behind society. Altruistic white Europeans will bear scientific knowledge to the backward nations of Africa and Asia, uprooting their barbaric traditions. 'I have proved the possibility,' Condorcet claimed, 'and indicated the means of resolving what is perhaps the most important problem for the human species: perfectibility of the broad masses, that is to say, the problem of rendering right judgement, an independent sound reason, an enlightened conscience, a habitual submission to the rules of humanity and justice, almost universal qualities.'

Condorcet's *Sketch* became a blueprint for nineteenth-century belief in human progress. It also spurred Thomas Malthus to write his *Essay on Population* (1798) warning utopians that unless they could check population growth their utopias would end in starvation. Condorcet had, in fact, already thought of this, and (with characteristic optimism) put his faith in common sense and contraception.

We can assume that men will know that, if they have a duty towards those who are not yet born, that duty is not to give them existence but to give them happiness. Their aim should be to promote the general welfare of the human race ... rather than foolishly to encumber the world with useless and wretched beings.

Sexual equality and universal peace will also characterize the new, rational era.

Among the causes of the progress of the human mind that are of the utmost importance to the general happiness, we must number

[162]

the complete annihilation of the prejudices that have brought about an inequality of rights between the sexes, an inequality fatal even to the party in whose favour it works. It is vain for us to look for a justification of this principle in any differences of physical organization, intellect or moral sensibility between men and women. This inequality has its origin solely in an abuse of strength, and all the later sophistical attempts that have been made to excuse it are vain . . .

Once people are enlightened they will know that they have the right to dispose of their own life and wealth as they choose; they will gradually learn to regard war as the most dreadful of scourges, the most terrible of crimes . . .

Nations will learn that they cannot conquer other nations without losing their own liberty; that permanent confederations are their only means of preserving their independence; and that they should seek not power but security.

There will, too, be a universal language, or rather many universal languages, each one devoted to the development and discussion of a particular art or science.

We shall show that the formation of such a language, if confined to the expression of those simple, precise propositions which form the system of a science or the practice of an art, is no chimerical scheme; that even at the present time it could be readily introduced to deal with a large number of objects; and that, indeed, the chief obstacle that would prevent its extension to others would be the humiliation of having to admit how very few precise ideas and accurate, unambiguous notions we actually possess.

We shall show that this language, ever improving and broadening its scope all the while, would be the means of giving to every subject embraced by the human intelligence, a precision and a rigour that would make knowledge of the truth easy and error almost impossible. Then the progress of every science would be as sure as that of mathematics, and the propositions that compose it would acquire a geometrical certainty, as far, that is, as is possible granted the nature of its aim and method.

In conclusion Condorcet observes that so far he has been considering the human species only as it exists at present, with its limited natural faculties and imperfect physical organization.

How much greater would be the certainty, how much vaster the scheme of our hopes if we could believe that these natural faculties themselves and this organization could also be improved? This is the last question that remains for us to ask ourselves.

Organic perfectibility or deterioration amongst the various strains in the vegetable and animal kingdom can be regarded as one of the general laws of nature. This law also applies to the human race. No one can doubt that, as preventative medicine improves and food and housing become healthier, as a way of life is established that develops our physical powers by exercise without ruining them by excess, as the two most virulent causes of deterioration, misery and excessive wealth, are eliminated, the average length of human life will be increased and a better health and a stronger physical constitution will be ensured. The improvement of medical practice, which will become more efficacious with the progress of reason and of the social order, will mean the end of infectious and hereditary diseases and illnesses brought on by climate, food, or working conditions. It is reasonable to hope that all other diseases may likewise disappear as their distant causes are discovered. Would it be absurd then to suppose that this perfection of the human species might be capable of indefinite progress; that the day will come when death will be due only to extraordinary accidents or to the decay of the vital forces, and that ultimately the average span between birth and decay will have no assignable value? Certainly man will not become immortal, but will not the interval between the first breath that he draws and the time when in the natural course of events, without disease or accident, he expires, increase indefinitely? Since we are now speaking of a progress that can be represented with some accuracy in figures or on a graph, we shall take this opportunity of explaining the two meanings that can be attached to the word *indefinite*.

In truth, this average span of life which we suppose will increase indefinitely as time passes, may grow in conformity either with a law such that it continually approaches a limitless length but without ever reaching it, or with a law such that through the centuries it reaches a length greater than any determinate quantity that we may assign to it as its limit. In the latter case such an increase is truly indefinite in the strictest sense of the word, since there is no term on this side of which it must of necessity stop. In the former case it is equally indefinite in relation to us, if we cannot fix the limit it always approaches without ever reaching, and particularly if, knowing only that it will never stop, we are ignorant in which of the two senses the term 'indefinite' can be applied to it. Such is the present condition of our knowledge as far as the perfectibility of the human race is concerned; such is the sense in which we may call it indefinite.

So, in the example under consideration, we are bound to believe that the average length of human life will for ever increase unless this is prevented by physical revolutions; we do not know what the limit is which it can never exceed. We cannot tell even whether the general laws of nature have determined such a limit or not.

But are not our physical faculties and the strength, dexterity and acuteness of our senses, to be numbered among the qualities whose perfection in the individual may be transmitted? Observation of the various breeds of domestic animals inclines us to believe that they are, and we can confirm this by direct observation of the human race.

Finally may we not extend such hopes to the intellectual and moral faculties? May not our parents, who transmit to us the benefits or disadvantages of their constitution, and from whom we receive our shape and features, as well as our tendencies to certain physical affections, hand on to us also that part of the physical organization which determines the intellect, the power of the brain, the ardour of the soul or the moral sensibility? Is it not probable that education, in perfecting these qualities, will at the same time influence, modify and perfect the organization itself? Analogy, investigation of the human faculties and the study of certain facts, all seem to give substance to such conjectures which would further push back the boundaries of our hopes.

These are the questions with which we shall conclude this final stage. How consoling for the philosopher who laments the errors, the crimes, the injustices which still pollute the earth and of which he is often the victim is this view of the human race, emancipated from its shackles, released from the empire of fate and from that of the enemies of its progress, advancing with a firm and sure step along the path of truth, virtue and happiness! It is the contemplation of this prospect that rewards him for all his efforts to assist the progress of reason and the defence of liberty. He dares to regard these strivings as part of the eternal chain of human destiny; and in this persuasion he is filled with the true delight of virtue and the pleasure of having done some lasting good which fate can never destroy by a sinister stroke of revenge, by calling back the reign of slavery and prejudice. Such contemplation is for him an asylum, in which the memory of his persecutors cannot pursue him; there he lives in thought with man restored to his natural rights and dignity, forgets man tormented and corrupted by greed, fear or envy; there he lives with his peers in an Elysium created by reason and graced by the purest pleasures known to the love of mankind.

In March 1794, having completed his *Sketch*, Condorcet tried to leave Paris, was identified as an aristocrat, arrested and imprisoned. He was found dead in his cell the following day, possibly having taken poison.

Source: Antoine Nicolas de Condorcet, *Sketch for a Historical Picture of the Progress of the Human Mind*, translated by June Barraclough, with an introduction by Stuart Hampshire, Weidenfeld and Nicolson, 1955.

Sanctuaries for Sadists

The Marquis de Sade (1740–1814) was born into a noble family, became an army officer at fifteen, serving in the war against Prussia, and married the wealthy Mlle de Montreuil in 1763. In 1768 he was arrested for assaulting Rose Keller, an out-of-work cotton spinner, whom he had stripped and flogged. In 1772, after an escapade involving four young women, he was condemned to death for sodomy. He escaped, but there were further incidents involving prostitutes and hired women. Incarcerated for the first time in 1777, he spent thirty-four years in various prisons and lunatic asylums. Much of his enormous literary output (only about a quarter of which has survived) was written in these institutions. At the Revolution he was one of the prisoners liberated from the Bastille.

De Sade was obsessed with the idea of flagellating, torturing and sodomizing women. His letters to his wife from prison make no secret of his abnormalities. Rather than renounce his 'principles and tastes', he declares, he would 'sacrifice a thousand lives and a thousand liberties'. However, these letters also stress his good works. He is, he protests, neither a criminal nor a murderer. Several families on his estates live off his charity, and he once saved a child from being crushed by a runaway horse.

These gestures towards conventional morality are wildly out of key with the doctrine put across by de Sade in his novels and philosophical writings. These (though sometimes under a thin veneer of piety) recommend absolute egotism. The only rule of conduct is to gratify one's own desires, however cruel or perverse they might appear. Compared to this self-gratification, the greatest atrocities inflicted on other people are utterly negligible. Christianity, with its ideals of mercy and charity, is an absurdity, concocted by that 'grubby Nazarene fraud', Jesus, with the purpose of allowing the weak to subdue the strong. God is an illusion, and all religious constraints on conduct are baseless. Murder, rape, theft, arson, infanticide and all other so-called crimes, are perfectly justifiable, because they satisfy natural impulses. 'Were Nature offended by these proclivities she would not have inspired them in us.' To illustrate what he means by 'Nature' de Sade frequently cites the behaviour of savages or wild animals. Just as the wolf obeys nature when it devours the lamb, so the strong obey nature by pleasuring themselves at the expense of the weak. The heroic lechers in de Sade's fiction persistently explain that they are behaving entirely naturally when they torture women in their gloomy châteaux and monasteries. They often lecture their victims, between bouts of flagellation and gang-rape, on the philosophical correctness of their actions. In *Justine* (1791) the monk Clément, having thrashed the heroine on every conceivable part of her body, explains that he is merely obeying his nature and cannot be blamed.

If in this world there exist persons whose tastes conflict with accepted prejudices, not only must one not be surprised by the fact, not only must one not scold these dissenters or punish them, but one must aid them, procure them contentment, remove obstacles which impede them, and afford them, if you wish to be just, all the means to satisfy themselves without risk; because they are no more responsible for having this curious taste than you are responsible for being live-spirited or dull-witted, prettily made or knock-kneed.

A weakness of de Sade's philosophy is that, since any action we feel impelled to do can be ascribed to 'nature', it has no special force as a justification. The authorities responsible for imprisoning him and destroying his books, for example, could plead that they, like him, were merely obeying the dictates of their natures. His basic principle can, in other words, be invoked by both sides, and is consequently of no use in defending particular actions.

The Surrealist poet Guillaume Apollinaire, who revived interest in de Sade at the start of the twentieth century, applauded him as 'the freest spirit who ever lived'. The impression given by his prolix and repetitive pornographic works, however, is just the contrary – of a man stuck in the groove of a ludicrous and humiliating sexual perversion. His heroes, though nominally all-powerful in their subjugation of naked, quivering womanhood, also come across as helplessly programmed to pursue a goal that always eludes them. Whatever atrocities they invent (one character gets pleasure only from decap-itating women; another takes two bowlfuls of blood from his wife every three days, and can get satisfaction no other way; another needs two fresh children each day to glut his appetites on), the limited number of surfaces and orifices that the human body offers, and the limited sufferings that can be inflicted on them, create an air of frenzied constriction. This finds a reflection in the vaults and fortresses where the orgies take place, and also in the strict rules and timetables imposed on both the libertines and their victims in de Sade's huge programmatic pornotopia, *The 120 Days of Sodom*.

De Sade's world is, of course, quite as unreal and artificial as Disneyland. It obeys its own narrow conventions, and could exist nowhere but in a book. However, his *Philosophy in the Bedroom* (1795) contains a pamphlet entitled 'Yet Another Effort, Frenchmen, If You Would Become Republicans', which is addressed to the beneficiaries of the French Revolution, and which proposes various utopian schemes, including specialist state-run brothels. This proposal is unusual in its consideration for women as well as men. Generally de Sade takes the view that men, being stronger, have a natural right to subjugate women.

Now that we have got back upon our feet and broken with the host of prejudices that held us captive; now that, brought closer to Nature by the quantity of prejudices we have recently obliterated, we listen only to Nature's voice, we are fully convinced that if anything were criminal, it would be to resist the penchants she inspires in us, rather than to come to grips with them. We are persuaded that lust, being a product of those penchants, is not to be stifled or legislated against, but that it is, rather, a matter of arranging for the means whereby passion may be satisfied in peace. We must hence undertake to introduce order into this sphere of affairs, and to establish all the security necessary so that, when need sends the citizen near the objects of lust, he can give himself over to doing with them all that his passions demand, without ever being hampered by anything, for there is no moment in the life of man when liberty in its whole amplitude is so important to him. Various stations, cheerful, sanitary, spacious, properly furnished and in every respect safe, will be erected in divers points in each city; in them, all sexes, all ages, all creatures possible will be offered to the caprices of the libertines who shall come to divert themselves, and the most absolute subordination will be the rule of the individuals participating; the slightest refusal or recalcitrance will be instantly and arbitrarily punished by the injured party. I must explain this last more fully, and weigh it against republican manners; I promised I would employ the same logic from beginning to end, and I shall keep my word . . .

First of all, what right have you to assert that women ought to be exempted from the blind submission to men's caprices Nature dictates? and, secondly, by what other right do you defend their subjugation to a continence impossible to their physical structure and of perfect uselessness to their honor?

[169]

I will treat each of these questions separately.

It is certain, in a state of Nature, that women are born *vulguivaguous*, that is to say, are born enjoying the advantages of other female animals and belonging, like them and without exception, to all males; such were, without any doubt, both the primary laws of Nature and the only institutions of those earliest societies into which men gathered. *Self-interest, egoism,* and *love* degraded these primitive attitudes, at once so simple and so natural; one thought oneself enriched by taking a woman to wife, and with her the goods of her family: there we find satisfied the first two feelings I have just indicated; still more often, this woman was taken by force, and thereby one became attached to her – there we find the other of the motives in action, and in every case, injustice.

Never may an act of possession be exercised upon a free being; the exclusive possession of a woman is no less unjust than the possession of slaves; all men are born free, all have equal rights: never should we lose sight of those principles; according to which never may there be granted to one sex the legitimate right to lay monopolizing hands upon the other, and never may one of these sexes, or classes, arbitrarily possess the other. Similarly, a woman existing in the purity of Nature's laws cannot allege, as justification for refusing herself to someone who desires her, the love she bears another, because such a response is based upon exclusion, and no man may be excluded from the having of a woman as of the moment it is clear she definitely belongs to all men. The act of possession can only be exercised upon a chattel or an animal, never upon an individual who resembles us, and all the ties which can bind a woman to a man are quite as unjust as illusory.

If then it becomes incontestable that we have received from Nature the right indiscriminately to express our wishes to all women, it likewise becomes incontestable that we have the right to compel their submission, not exclusively, for I should then be contradicting myself, but temporarily.* It cannot be denied that we have the right to decree

* Let it not be said that I contradict myself here, and that after having established, at some point further above, that we have no right to bind a woman to ourselves, I destroy those principles when I declare now we have the right to constrain her; I repeat, it is a question of enjoyment only, not of property: I have no right of possession upon that fountain I find by the road, but I have certain rights to its use; I have the right to avail myself of the limpid water it offers my thirst; similarly, I have no real right of possession

laws that compel woman to yield to the flames of him who would have her; violence itself being one of that right's effects, we can employ it lawfully. Indeed! has Nature not proven that we have that right, by bestowing upon us the strength needed to bend women to our will?

It is in vain women seek to bring to their defense either modesty or their attachment to other men; these illusory grounds are worthless; earlier, we saw how contemptible and factitious is the sentiment of modesty. Love, which may be termed the *soul's madness*, is no more a title by which their constancy may be justified: love, satisfying two persons only, the beloved and the loving, cannot serve the happiness of others, and it is for the sake of the happiness of everyone, and not for an egotistical and privileged happiness, that women have been given to us. All men therefore have an equal right of enjoyment of all women; therefore, there is no man who, in keeping with natural law, may lay claim to a unique and personal right over a woman. The law which will oblige them to prostitute themselves, as often and in any manner we wish, in the houses of debauchery we referred to a moment ago, and which will coerce them if they balk, punish them if they shirk or dawdle, is thus one of the most equitable of laws, against which there can be no sane or rightful complaint.

A man who would like to enjoy whatever woman or girl will henceforth be able, if the laws you promulgate are just, to have her summoned at once to duty at one of the houses; and there, under the supervision of the matrons of that temple of Venus, she will be surrendered to him, to satisfy, humbly and with submission, all the fancies in which he will be pleased to indulge with her, however strange or irregular they may be, since there is no extravagance which is not in Nature, none which she does not acknowledge as her own. There remains but to fix the woman's age; now, I maintain it cannot be fixed without restricting the freedom of a man who desires a girl of any given age.

He who has the right to eat the fruit of a tree may assuredly pluck it ripe or green, according to the inspiration of his taste. But, it will be objected, there is an age when the man's proceedings would be

over such-and-such a woman, but I have incontestable rights to the enjoyment of her; I have the right to force from her this enjoyment, if she refuses me it for whatever the cause may be.

decidedly harmful to the girl's well-being. This consideration is utterly without value; once you concede me the proprietary right of enjoyment, that right is independent of the effects enjoyment produces; from this moment on, it becomes one, whether this enjoyment be beneficial or damaging to the object which must submit itself to me. Have I not already proven that it is legitimate to force the woman's will in this connection? and that immediately she excites the desire to enjoy she has got to expose herself to this enjoyment, putting all egotistical sentiments quite aside? The issue of her well-being, I repeat, is irrelevant. As soon as concern for this consideration threatens to detract from or enfeeble the enjoyment of him who desires her, and who has the right to appropriate her, this consideration for age ceases to exist; for what the object may experience, condemned by Nature and by the law to slake momentarily the other's thirst, is nothing to the point; in this study, we are only interested in what agrees with him who desires. But we will redress the balance.

Yes, we will redress it; doubtless we ought to. These women we have just so cruelly enslaved – there is no denying we must recompense them, and I come now to the second question I proposed to answer.

If we admit, as we have just done, that all women ought to be subjugated to our desires, we may certainly allow them ample satisfaction of theirs. Our laws must be favorable to their fiery temperament. It is absurd to locate both their honor and their virtue in the antinatural strength they employ to resist the penchants with which they have been far more profusely endowed than we; this injustice of manners is rendered more flagrant still since we contrive at once to weaken them by seduction, and then to punish them for yielding to all the efforts we have made to provoke their fall. All the absurdity of our manners, it seems to me, is graven in this shocking paradox, and this brief outline alone ought to awaken us to the urgency of exchanging them for manners more pure.

I say then that women, having been endowed with considerably more violent penchants for carnal pleasure than we, will be able to give themselves over to it wholeheartedly, absolutely free of all encumbering hymeneal ties, of all false notions of modesty, absolutely restored to a state of Nature; I want laws permitting them to give themselves to as many men as they see fit; I would have them accorded the enjoyment of all sexes and, as in the case of men, the enjoyment of all parts of the body; and under the special clause prescribing their surrender to all who desire them, there must be subjoined another guaranteeing them a similar freedom to enjoy all they deem worthy to satisfy them . . .

There will then be houses intended for women's libertinage and, like the men's, under the government's protection; in these establishments there will be furnished all the individuals of either sex women could desire, and the more constantly they frequent these places the higher they will be esteemed.

Source: The Marquis de Sade, *Justine, Philosophy in the Bedroom, Eugénie de Franval and Other Writings*, Arrow Books, 1991.

Equality

Francois-Noel Babeuf (1760–97) was the first revolutionary communist of modern times. In the *Communist Manifesto* he is recognized as the spokesman for the proletariat in the French Revolution. The son of a tax-official in St Quentin, Picardy, he started work as an agent of the feudal system. But the 1789 Revolution put an end to this employment and he devoted himself to the political struggle. He published a newspaper criticizing the conservative members of the Convention who seized power after the death of Robespierre. With other opposition leaders he planned an armed rising, aiming to restore the democratic Constitution of 1793, and so secure the elementary democratic rights to meet, debate and organize. This was scarcely a 'utopian' project, though, as Babeuf's modern translator points out, in the USA workers did not win legal recognition of these rights until 1938, after a struggle lasting nearly three-quarters of a century that cost hundreds of lives. The so-called Conspiracy of the Equals was betrayed, and Babeuf and his confederates were taken in iron cages to trial in Vendome. His speech in his own defence – a classic of egalitarian rhetoric – quotes from an article he had written in his newspaper, which he refers to as 'the frank confession of my political faith'. The following extract is from this.

Man's condition ought not to have deteriorated in passing from a state of nature to a state of social organization. In the beginning the soil belonged to none, its fruits to all. The introduction of private property was a piece of trickery put over on the simple and unsuspecting masses. The laws that buttressed property operated inevitably to create social classes – privileged and oppressed, masters and slaves.

The law of inheritance is a sovereign wrong. It breeds misery even from the second generation. Two sons of a rich man receive equal shares of their father's fortune. One son has but one child, the other, twelve. Of these twelve each receives only a twelfth part of the fortune of his uncle and the twenty-fourth part of the fortune of his grandfather. This portion is not enough to live on; and so twelve poor men must work for one rich one. Hence we find masters and servants among the grandchildren of a single man.

The law of alienability is no less unjust. This one man, already master over all the other grandchildren in the same line, pays what he will for the work that they must do for him. Their wages are insufficient to maintain life and they are obliged to sell their meager inheritance to their master. They become landless men; and if they have children of their own, these inherit nothing.

The gulf between rich and poor, rulers and ruled, proceeds from yet another cause, the difference in value and in price that arbitrary opinion attaches to the diverse products of toil and manufacture. Thus a watchmaker's working day has been valued twenty times higher than a ploughman's or laborer's. The wages of the watchmaker enable him to get possession of the inheritance of twenty ploughmen whom he is thus in a position to expropriate, and enhance his own condition.

These three roots of our public woes – heredity, alienability, and the differing values which arbitrary opinion assigns to different types of social product – proceed from the institution of private property. All the evils of society flow from them. They isolate the people from each other; they convert every family into a private commonwealth, pit it against society at large, and dedicate it with an ever growing emphasis to inequality in all its vicious, suicidal forms . . .

If the earth belongs to none and its fruits to all; if private ownership of public wealth is only the result of certain institutions that violate fundamental human rights; then it follows that this private ownership is a usurpation; and it further follows that all that a man takes of the land and its fruits beyond what is necessary for sustenance is theft from society . . .

All that a citizen lacks for the satisfaction of his various daily needs, he lacks because he has been deprived of a natural property right by the engrossers of the public domain. All that a citizen enjoys beyond what is necessary for the satisfaction of his daily needs he enjoys as a result of a theft from the other members of society. In this way a more or less numerous group of people is deprived of its rightful share in the public domain.

Inheritance and alienability are institutions destructive of basic human rights.

The plea of superior ability and industry is an empty rationaliz-ation to mask the machinations of those who conspire against human equality and happiness. It is ridiculous and unfair to lay claim to a higher wage for the man whose work requires more concentrated thought and more mental effort. Such effort in no way expands the capacity of the stomach. No wage can be defended over and above what is necessary for the satisfaction of a person's needs.

The worth of intelligence is only a matter of opinion, and it still remains to be determined if natural, physical strength is not of equal worth. Clever people have set a high value upon the creations of their minds; if the toilers had also had a hand in the ordering of things, they would doubtless have insisted that brawn is entitled to equal consideration with brain and that physical fatigue is no less real than mental fatigue.

If wages are not equalized, the clever and persevering are given a licence to rob and despoil with impunity those less fortunately endowed with natural gifts. In this way the economic equilibrium of society is upset, for nothing has been more conclusively proven than the maxim: *a man only succeeds in becoming rich through the spoli-ation of others.*

All our civic institutions, our social relationships, are nothing else but the expression of legalized barbarism and piracy, in which every man cheats and robs his neighbor. In its festering swamp our swind-ling society generates vice, crime, and misery of every kind. A handful of well-intentioned people band together and wage war on these evils, but their efforts are futile. They can make no headway because they do not tackle the problem at its roots, but apply palliatives based upon the distorted thinking of a sick society.

It is clear from the foregoing that whatever a man possesses over and above his rightful share of the social product has been stolen. It is therefore right and proper to take this wealth back again from those who have wrongfully appropriated it. Even a man who shows that he can do the work of four, and who consequently demands the wages of four, will still be an enemy of society; he is using criminal means to shake the social order and to obliterate its sacred equality. Common sense tells us, with no small emphasis, that we should curb a man of this type and drive him out as if he had the plague. At the very least he should be allowed to perform no more than one man's work and to lay claim to no more than one man's pay. The human species alone has made insane value distinctions between one of its members and another. As a result, the human species alone has been obliged to experience misery and want. There is no need for men to lack those things which nature has provided for all, though, of course, if want should arise as a result of the unavoidable calamities of wind, storm, flood, or famine, such privation must be borne and shared equally by all.

The creations of the human hand and mind become the property of society, part of the nation's capital, from the very moment that thinkers and workers bring these creations into being. Invention is the fruit of prior investigation and effort. The most recent workers in the field reap their reward as a result of the social labors of their predecessors in a society that nurtures invention and that aids the scientific worker in his task. It is clear that if knowledge is a social product it must be shared by all alike.

It is a truth, which only ignorant or prejudiced people are likely to contest, that if knowledge were made available to all alike, it would serve to make men roughly equal in ability and even in talent. Education is a monstrosity when it is unequally shared, since then it becomes the exclusive patrimony of a section of society; it becomes, in the hands of this section, a set of tools, an ideological armory, with the help of which the privileged make war upon the defenseless masses. In this way the rich succeed, with little difficulty, in stifling and deceiving and robbing the people, thus subjecting them to a shameful servitude.

One thinker [Abbé Morelly, reputed author of a utopian tract, the *Code de la Nature*, 1773] expressed a profound truth when he wrote: 'Talk as long as you will of the forms of government; it will all be idle speculation until you destroy the seeds of human greed and acquisitiveness.' Society must be made to operate in such a way that it eradicates once and for all the desire of a man to become richer, or wiser, or more powerful than others.

Putting this more exactly, we must try to *bring our fate under control*, try to make the lot of every member of society independent of accidental circumstances, happy or unhappy. We must try to guarantee to each man and his posterity, however numerous, a sufficiency of the means of existence, and nothing more. We must try and close all possible avenues by which a man may acquire more than his fair share of the fruits of toil and the gifts of nature.

The only way to do this is to organize a communal regime which will suppress private property, set each to work at the skill or job he understands, require each to deposit the fruits of his labor in kind at the common store, and establish an agency for the distribution of basic necessities. This agency will maintain a complete list of people and of supplies, will distribute the latter with scrupulous fairness, and will deliver them to the home of each worker.

A system such as this has been proven practicable by actual experience, for it is used by our twelve armies with their 1,200,000 men. And what is possible on a small scale can also be done on a large one. A regime of this type alone can ensure the general welfare, or, in other words, the permanent happiness of the people – the true and proper object of organized society.

Such a regime will sweep away iron bars, dungeon walls, and bolted doors, trials and disputations, murders, thefts and crimes of every kind; it will sweep away the judges and the judged, the jails and the gibbets – all the torments of body and agony of soul that the injustice of life engenders; it will sweep away enviousness and gnawing greed, pride and deceit, the very catalogue of sins that Man is heir to; it will remove – and how important is this! – the brooding, omnipresent fear that gnaws always and in each of us concerning our fate tomorrow, next month, next year, and in our old age; concerning the fate of our children and of our children's children.

Of the defendants who were found guilty, only Babeuf and Augustin Darthé were condemned to death. On the announcement of the sentence, they stabbed themselves with daggers they had earlier improvised from brass candle-holders and concealed in their clothing. Though the wounds were serious, they did not prove mortal. There was a delay of twenty-four hours while the guillotine was fetched from Blois, and Babeuf spent the last day of his life in agony. He was executed in the early morning of 27 May 1797.

Source: *The Defense of Gracchus Babeuf before the High Court of Vendome*, edited and translated by John Anthony Scott, with an Essay by Herbert Marcuse and Illustrations by Thomas Cornell, University of Massachusetts Press, 1967. Originally published by Leonard Baskin's Gehenna Press, Northampton, Massachusetts, 1964, this volume was designed as a contribution to pedagogy, illustrating 'how graphic and literary art may be used to illuminate and humanize the teaching of history'.

The Punishment Fits the Crime

In *Libellus: or A Brief Sketch of the Kingdom of Gotham* (1798), the anonymous author presents a mirror-image view of England, in which wrongs are righted. The penal system is conducted on rational, eye-for-eye lines. To add solemnity, he breaks into verse to deliver the penalty for rape.

The police of this happy race of people is worthy of imitation by every nation on earth. Their penal laws are as little Draconic [i.e. resembling those of the severe Athenian law-giver Draco] as possible, there being only two cases where the culprit is to be deprived of life, and those are for murder – or the attempt to perpetrate that horrid crime – and for arson, or setting fire to tenements which are either inhabited, or contiguous to houses which are so. Indeed, the burning of a solitary uninhabited edifice (not belonging to the incendiary) is not punished with certain death, but by the *lex talionis* [law of revenge], requiring the offender's left hand to be burnt off (unless he happen to be left-handed, and then the punishment is inflicted on the right hand): when he is immediately put under the care of a skilful surgeon. If he recovers he is at liberty to get a livelihood where he can, with honesty and one hand. If he dies, nobody will lament his loss, except the surgeon, who is always well paid for successful management of his patient, but has very little if he fails to recover. If however any person's life should be lost in the fire that is wilfully occasioned, the incendiary is himself to be burnt alive. Setting fire to any house in a town where no life is lost thereby, the punishment is death by hanging.

In the case of murder, the *lex talionis* is resorted to as nearly as possible. He who destroys his fellow-creature by firearms or a bludgeon, is destroyed by the same means. The assassin who stabs and cuts is obliged to be stabbed and wounded in like manner, enduring, as nearly as possible, a similar kind of torture in degree, and also in duration, as far as a public execution will admit. And that most diabolical wretch who takes away life by the infusing of poison is obliged to drink poison himself on a public stage, and there remain tortured with all the agonies of the most dreadful bodily sufferings, and his misery rendered still more acute with the idea of being thus exposed a public spectacle, and yet deprived of the assistance of any fellow creature with a view to alleviate his torments . . .

As the strength of women is commonly insufficient to defend them against personal assault, therefore (that they may be protected as far as law can protect them, so as not to have their chastity reluctantly violated):

> Those rampant males, those savage human brutes,
> Who will not put a curb upon their lust,
> But *force* enjoyment from the unwilling fair,
> Are here deprived (deservedly deprived!)
> Of pow'r to perpetrate such carnal deeds.
> Thus wisely making their offence the cause
> Of infamy, and bitter self-reproach
> So long as life and memory endure!
> A punishment far more severely felt,
> More dreaded, than the common hangman's hand!

Source: Anon., *Libellus: or, A Brief Sketch of the Kingdom of Gotham*, 1798.

The Paradise of Single Mothers

The utopia described in James Lawrence's *The Empire of the Nairs* (published in Britain in 1811) was based (loosely) on reality. The Nairs (or Nayars), were a Hindu caste, inhabiting the Indian state of Kerala, and they had highly unusual marriage customs, which attracted the attention of European free-thinkers. Nair women could receive as many visiting lovers as they chose. The men had no rights over either the women or the children born from these unions. Mothers were the heads of families. They and their children were maintained by their matrilineal groups.

An Etonian, and the son of a Jamaican landowner, Lawrence (1773–1840) led a wandering (and single) life. In the preface to *The Empire of the Nairs* he opposes marriage on the grounds that it is unnatural, and known to no animals except humans. The promises it entails are unrealistic, for no man can guarantee lasting fidelity – 'the voice of an opera girl may disturb the peace of a family'. Its abolition will, Lawrence predicts, increase the liberty and happiness of both sexes. His novel was first published in Germany in 1801, and enthusiastically received by the modern-minded. Schiller and Shelley both admired it.

It is set in the Nair kingdom of Calicut, where women rule. All property (houses, estates etc.) belongs to them and passes to their daughters at death. They enjoy absolute freedom in love. A man may propose sex to any woman and be sure of 'a gracious compliance or a polite refusal'. Social gatherings usually end in love-making, partners in the last waltz generally spending the night together. All mothers are single mothers, and the care and management of children is their concern. They receive money from the public treasury, corresponding to the number of their children. Motherhood is publicly honoured – soldiers, for example, salute pregnant women. The name of father is, however, unknown. Children may speak of their mothers' lovers, but they have no notion of a father. Nair women have emancipated themselves from the false modesty that (as Lawrence saw it) helped to keep women subjugated in Europe and Islam (both vigorously criticized in the novel). They appear naked before men without a second thought, and at one of their great annual ceremonies their queen strips and bathes in public

– commemorating an occasion when Samora, the founder of their empire, went straight from her bath to quell an insurrection, without bothering to dress. The Englishman De Grey, the novel's hero, attends this ceremony with his hostess, the Countess of Raldabar.

The crowd was so great that the Countess's carriage could advance but slowly. The whole nation seemed animated with one enthusiasm of glory; every individual appeared conscious of the advantages that he enjoyed; all the streets, through which the procession was to pass, had been richly decorated; the sportive fancy of a lively people had produced a variety of matriotic devices, and the magnificence that reigned on every side was worthy of a city that fame had proclaimed the capital of the East. After having passed the Samorina's palace, a pile of building spacious and magnificent as Versailles, they arrived at the Temple of Samora, an edifice not inferior to St Peter's. The Countess conducted De Grey to a gallery, destined for strangers, and left him to join the suite of her august mistress. De Grey's eyes wandered from object to object; he could not sufficiently admire the stupendous monument of Syrian architecture.

A hundred instruments and a thousand voices announce the appearance of the Samorina. She comes! sovereign princes in her suite, surrounded by the ministers of state, attended by the first officers of her household. Among the ladies of the court the Countess of Raldabar shines unrivalled for her elegance and beauty.

The high priest flings the censer on high, the air is filled with frankincense, an awful silence reigns. The Samorina approaches the bath, below the high altar. The chamberlains assist her to lay aside her purple robe, the muslin falls; she stands in her nakedness, majestic, under the statue of her divine ancestress. She descends the marble steps, and, triumphing over age, disdains to touch the golden balustrade.

Meanwhile a flute in Lydian measure accompanies the sweetest voice that ever sung the praise of love: the Princess reaches the middle of the bath; the voice stops – the soft notes of the flute are drowned in the loud clangours of the martial trumpet – the fife plays an air of defiance and the drum beats to arms. The whole concert imitates the commotion which threatened Samora's throne.

The Princess passes with a tranquil mien, and ascends the opposite steps. The music ceases as if awe-struck at her presence – a perfect

[182]

silence – the Persian and Chinese ambassadors, according to immemorial custom, fall prostrate at her feet. This is the great annual triumph of Calicut. At length she beckons them to rise; and they, however indignant, must each produce a silken towel (the Persian's towel must be green, the colour of Mahomet), they must wipe her before the eyes of the Nairs. A knight of the phoenix, deputed by the grand master, receives these towels; they will be converted into flags for the order, and, preceding them in their excursions against the Polygamists [i.e. Islam, against whom the Nairs wage constant war], will raise their enthusiasm for their own glory, and augment their contempt of the enemy.

But now, while the solemn organ is celebrating the re-established tranquillity of the empire, the Samorina re-assumes her habits.

Perhaps a man of pleasure, who might have expected to have seen the figure of Venus rising from the water, would have been disappointed. The respectable Samorina, though of a dignified deportment, was old enough to be a great grandmother, and consequently was no object of desire; yet De Grey, as an observer of mankind, was happy in seeing this ceremony, which at Calicut was not considered an object of curiosity, but an act of devotion, to which the bigoted part of the nation flocked from every part.

Source: James Lawrence, *The Empire of the Nairs; or, The Rights of Women. An Utopian Romance, in Twelve Books*, printed for T. Hookham, Jr and E. T. Hookham, 1811.

The Gospel of Industrialism

In his own day Claude-Henri de Saint-Simon (1760–1825) was ignored or mocked. He is now seen as a prophet of scientific-industrial society and the welfare state, and one of the founders of social science and Socialism.

Born into an aristocratic family, he converted to the Enlightenment as a student. When he refused to take his first communion, his father had him imprisoned. But he escaped, joined the army, and fought against the British in the American War of Independence. In America he was impressed by the religious toleration and absence of social privilege, which influenced his future thinking. At the outbreak of the French Revolution he renounced his title, and underwent a 'republican baptism' ceremony. The future of mankind, he decided, lay with science. He took courses in physics, maths and physiology, and started to formulate a science of man and society which would be as precise and objective as the physical sciences. In his *Letters from an Inhabitant of Geneva* (1802–3), he proposed a plan for human society in which 'All men will work; they will regard themselves as workers attached to a workshop.'

A major factor in his programme was the transfer of power from the idle rich, the titled, the clergy, and other drones, to the 'industrials' (*industriels*). This latter class comprised everyone who worked in useful employment. It included directors of industry just as much as artisans. Saint-Simon's belief that workers and bosses could unite for the common good led Marx and Engels to label him utopian (i.e. hopelessly idealistic), since he denied the inevitability of the class-war. They were, nevertheless, indebted to his thinking. The distinction between the idle and the useful in society was made sharply in his *Extracts from L'Organisateur* (1819).

Let us suppose that all of a sudden France loses fifty each of its best physicists, chemists, physiologists, mathematicians, poets, painters, sculptors, musicians, authors, mechanics, civil and military engineers, artillerymen, architects, doctors, surgeons, pharmicists, sailors, clock-makers, bankers; its two hundred best merchants and six hundred best farmers; fifty each of its best iron-masters, arms manufacturers, tanners, dyers, miners, manufacturers of cloth, cotton, silk, linen, ironmongery, earthenware and porcelain, crystal- and glass-ware; shipowners, carriers, printers, engravers, goldsmiths, and other met-alworkers; masons, carpenters, joiners, blacksmiths, locksmiths, cutlers, foundrymen, and one hundred other persons in various unspecified posts, eminent in the sciences, fine arts, and arts and crafts, making in all the three thousand best scientists, artists, and artisans in France.*

As these Frenchmen are the most essential producers, those who provide the most important products, who direct the work which is most useful to the nation, and who are responsible for its productivity in the sciences, fine arts, and arts and crafts, they are really the flower of French society. Of all Frenchmen they are the most useful to their country, bringing it the most glory and doing most to promote civilization and its prosperity. The nation would become a lifeless corpse as soon as it lost them. It would immediately fall into a state of inferiority *vis-à-vis* its present rivals, and it would remain their subordinate as long as this loss was left unretrieved, as long as it was waiting for a new head to emerge. It would take France at least one whole generation to make up for this disaster, as the men who distinguish themselves in work of positive utility are really the exception, and nature is not prodigious in producing the exceptional, especially in this species.

Let us proceed to another supposition. Let us say that France retains all its men of genius in the sciences, fine arts, and arts and crafts, but has the misfortune to lose on the same day Monsieur the King's brother, Monseigneur the duc d'Angoulême, Monseigneur the duc de Berry, Monseigneur the duc d'Orléans, Monseigneur the duc de Bourbon, Madame the duchesse d'Angoulême, Madame the duchesse de Berry, Madame the duchesse d'Orléans, Madame the duchesse de Bourbon, and Mademoiselle de Condé.

Let us suppose that at the same time it loses all the great officers of the Crown, all Ministers of State (with or without portfolio), all

---

* Usually the term 'artisan' is only used to refer to ordinary workmen. In order to avoid circumlocution, we shall take this expression to mean everyone involved in material production, i.e. farmers, manufacturers, merchants, bankers, and all the clerks or workmen employed by them.

Councillors of State, all chief magistrates, all its marshals, all its cardinals, archbishops, bishops, vicars-general, and canons, all prefects and sub-prefects, all ministerial employees, all judges, and, on top of all that, the ten thousand richest property owners who live in the style of nobles.

This accident would certainly distress the French, because they are good, and could not regard with indifference the sudden disappearance of such a large number of their fellow countrymen. But this loss of the thirty thousand individuals who are deemed the most important in the State would grieve them only from a purely sentimental point of view, for it would not result in any political harm to the State.

This is because, first of all, it would be very easy to fill the vacancies. There are many Frenchmen who could perform the functions of the King's brother as well as Monsieur can. There are many who could fill the princely positions just as well as Monseigneur the duc d'Angoulême, Monseigneur the duc de Berry, Monseigneur the duc d'Orléans, Monseigneur the duc de Bourbon. Many Frenchwomen would make just as good princesses as Madame the duchesse d'Angoulême, Madame the duchesse de Berry, Mesdames d'Orléans, de Bourbon, and de Condé.

The antechambers of the palace are full of courtiers ready to replace the great officers of the Crown. The army has many soldiers who would make just as good captains as our present marshals. How many clerks there are who are just as good as our Ministers of State; how many administrators who could manage departmental affairs better than the prefects and sub-prefects; how many advocates who would make just as good lawyers as our judges; how many clergymen who are just as capable as our cardinals, archbishops, bishops, vicars-general, and canons. As for the ten thousand property owners living like nobles, their heirs will need no apprenticeship to do the honours of their drawing-rooms as well as they.

The prosperity of France can only be achieved through the progress of the sciences, fine arts, and arts and crafts. Now, the princes, the great officers of the Crown, the bishops, the marshals of France, the prefects, and the idle property owners do not work directly for the progress of the sciences, fine arts, and arts and crafts. Far from contributing to this progress, they can only hinder it, since they endeavour to prolong the supremacy hitherto exercised by conjectural theories over positive knowledge. They inevitably hinder the nation's prosperity by depriving, as they do, the scientists, artists, and artisans of the highest degree of respect to which they are legitimately entitled; by employing their financial resources in a way which is not directly useful to the sciences, fine arts, and arts and crafts; and by costing the nation's taxpayers an annual sum of three to four hundred millions under the headings of appointments, pensions, gratuities, indemnities, etc. as payment for their work which is of no use to the nation.

For naming members of the royal family among the drones, Saint-Simon was arrested and found guilty of subversion, but acquitted on appeal.

The realization that science and industry were the true agents of progress led Saint-Simon to the conviction that religion must be remodelled. It could no longer be based on outworn superstitions and supernatural beliefs. He proposed a 'Religion of Newton', recognizing Isaac Newton's role as founder of modern science. The world's most eminent scientists and artists would head this new church, dispensing a 'cult of Reason', which would put an end to metaphysics and theology. A new 'terrestrial morality', in line with modern science and conducive to industrialism, would replace Catholicism. These plans offended conservatives, as did Saint-Simon's far-sighted scheme of European unification. His proposal of a preliminary unification of England and France seemed, in the aftermath of Waterloo, tactlessly unpatriotic to the French.

In his later work, plans for a new morality are combined with a new Christianity. Saint-Simon stresses that the aim of 'industrialism' is to eradicate the poverty, both spiritual and material, of the working class, ensuring that all men are properly educated and gainfully employed. This, he contests, precisely concurs with the original teaching of Christ.

Moreover, since a positive science of man and society could reveal the scientific laws of social organization, the realization of utopia became not a dream but a perfectly rational possibility.

In utopia, the new priesthood of scientists and artists (*savants*) will cater for mankind's spiritual needs, while the industrials and captains of industry will take over the organization of production. Politics will become essentially the 'science of production', replacing old notions of government.

It is evident that the most certain way to promote the prosperity of agriculture, commerce, and manufacturing is to give the farmers, merchants, and manufacturers the task of directing the administration of public affairs, that is, of framing the budget.

[187]

Public revenue, instead of being squandered on the army, the aristocracy, the police and the courts, will be invested in science and industry, and consequently promote social welfare. A non-militaristic, peace-loving social system will evolve, within which industrialism can flourish. Saint-Simon's plan was that it should spread not just throughout Europe but to all corners of the civilized world.

He worked out the distribution of power between the *savants* (the new secular priesthood) and the captains of industry in great detail, as can be seen from the proposed reorganization of the French parliament in his *Sketch of a New Political System* (1819).

A first Chamber will be formed and called the Chamber of *Invention*.

This Chamber will consist of three hundred members, and will be divided into three sections which may meet separately but whose work will only be official when they deliberate together.

Each section will be able to call a joint meeting of the three sections.

The first section will consist of two hundred civil engineers; the second of fifty poets and other literary inventors; and the third of twenty-five painters, fifteen sculptors and architects, and ten musicians.

This Chamber will apply itself to the following tasks:

At the end of the first year of its formation it will present a project for public works to be undertaken in order to increase France's wealth and improve the condition of its inhabitants in every useful and pleasing respect. Then, each year it will give its advice on additions to be made to its original project and on ways in which it thinks it might be improved.

Drainage, land clearance, road building, the opening up of canals will be considered the most important part of this project. The roads and canals to be built should not be conceived only as a means of facilitating transport; their construction should be planned so as to make them as pleasant as possible for travellers.*

---

* Fifty thousand acres of land (more, if it is thought right) will be chosen from the most picturesque sites crossed by roads or canals. This ground will be authorized for use as resting-places for travellers and holiday resorts for the inhabitants of the neighbourhood.

Each of these gardens will contain a museum of both natural and industrial products of the surrounding districts. They will also include dwellings for artists who want to stop there, and a certain number of musicians will always be maintained there to inspire the

This Chamber will present another report providing a project for public festivals.

These festivals will be of two kinds: festivals of *hope* and festivals of *remembrance*.

These festivals will be celebrated successively in the capital and chief towns of the departments and cantons, so that capable orators (who will never be very numerous) may spread the benefits of their eloquence.

In the festivals of *hope* the orators will explain to the people the plans for public works approved by Parliament, and they will encourage the citizens to work with energy, by showing them how their condition will improve once the plans are executed.

In the festivals dedicated to *remembrance* it will be the task of the orators to show the people how their present position is better than that of their ancestors.

The nucleus of the Chamber of Invention will consist of:

The eighty-six chief engineers for bridges and roads in the departments;

The forty members of the French Academy;

The painters, sculptors, and musicians in the Institute.

Each member of this Chamber will enjoy an annual salary of 10,000 francs.

Every year a sum of twelve millions will be placed at the disposal of this Chamber to be employed to promote the inventions it considers useful. The first section will dispose of eight millions, and the other two sections will have two millions each.

---

inhabitants of the canton with that passion whose development is necessary for the greatest good of the nation.

The whole of French soil should be turned into a superb English park, adorned with all that the fine arts can add to the beauties of nature. For a long time luxury has been concentrated in the palaces of kings, the residences of princes, the mansions and châteaux of a few powerful men. This concentration is most detrimental to the general interests of society, because it tends to establish two different grades of civilization, one for persons whose intelligence is developed through habitual viewing of productions of the fine arts, and one for men whose imaginative faculties undergo no development, since the material work in which they are exclusively engaged does not stimulate their intelligence.

Present circumstances favour making luxury national. Luxury will become useful and moral when it is enjoyed by the whole nation. The honour and advantage of employing directly, in political arrangements, the progress of the exact sciences and of the fine arts since the brilliant age of their regeneration, have been reserved for our century.

The nucleus will itself arrange for the rest of the seats in the Chamber to be filled.

The Chamber will constitute itself, that is, it will determine who may vote and who may stand for election. Its members may not be elected for more than five years, but they will be eligible for re-election indefinitely, and the Chamber may adopt whatever method of substitution it chooses.

This Chamber may have one hundred national and fifty foreign associate members. The associates will have the right to sit in the Chamber, and will have a consultative vote.

A second chamber will be formed with the name Chamber of *Examination*.

This Chamber will consist of three hundred members: one hundred physicists working on the physics of organic bodies, one hundred working on the physics of inorganic bodies, and one hundred mathematicians.

This Chamber will be given three tasks:

It will examine all the projects presented by the first Chamber, and will give its detailed and reasoned opinion on each of them.

It will draw up a project for general public education, which will be divided into three grades of teaching, for citizens of three different levels of wealth. Its aim will be to ensure that young people are as capable as possible of conceiving, directing, and carrying out useful work.

As every citizen is at perfect liberty to practise whatever religion he chooses, and may consequently bring up his children in the one he prefers, on no account should there be any question of religion in the Chamber's education project. When the project has been approved by the other two Chambers, the Chamber of Examination will be responsible for its execution and will continue to supervise public education.

The third task involving this Chamber should be a project for public festivals of the following kind: men's festivals, women's festivals, boys' festivals, girls' festivals, fathers' and mothers' festivals, children's festivals, managers' festivals, workers' festivals. In each of these festivals orators nominated by the Chamber of Examination will make speeches on the social duties of those in whose honour the festival is being celebrated.

THE GOSPEL OF INDUSTRIALISM

Each member of this Chamber will enjoy an annual salary of 10,000 francs.

Every year a sum of twenty-five millions will be placed at the disposal of this Chamber, to be employed on the expenditure required by public schools and on ways of hastening the progress of the physical and mathematical sciences.

The Chamber of *Examination* will be constituted according to the same conditions as the Chamber of *Invention*.

The Class of Physical and Mathematical Sciences at the Institute will provide the nucleus of this Chamber.

The Chamber of Examination may have one hundred national and fifty foreign associate members, who will have consultative votes.

The House of Commons will be reconstituted once the first two Chambers have been formed. It will then assume the name Chamber of *Execution*.

This Chamber will take care that in its new composition every branch of industry is represented, and that each branch has a number of deputies proportionate to its importance.

The members of the Chamber of Execution will not have any salary, since they should all be rich, being chosen from the most important heads of industrial houses.

The Chamber of Execution will supervise the execution of all approved projects. It alone will be responsible for the imposition and collection of taxes.

The three Chambers will together form the new Parliament, which will be invested with sovereign power, constitutional as well as legislative.

Each of the three Chambers will have the right to summon Parliament.

The Chamber of Execution will be able to direct the attention of the other two Chambers to those subjects it considers suitable.

Thus, every project will be presented by the first Chamber, examined by the second, and will only be definitely adopted by the third.

If a project presented by the first Chamber is ever rejected by the second, in order to save time it will be sent back to the first without being considered by the third.

The failure of his ideas to gain wide acceptance depressed Saint-Simon. In 1823 he attempted suicide, firing seven bullets at his head in quick succession. Though he lost his right eye, he survived, recovered quickly, and soon launched a new periodical, *The Catechism of Industrials*. He died suddenly of gastro-enteritis in 1825.

The Saint-Simonian movement flourished and diversified after the Master's death. Disciples took different paths. A new sexual order based on free love and an androgynous God, the search for a Female Messiah, the Romantic idealization of brotherly feeling, public works at Ménilmontant where young Saint-Simonians, dressed in symbolic red, white and blue, did manual labour and organized parades celebrating the virtues of work, the spread of Saint-Simonian ideas to radical circles in Russia where they influenced, among others, Dostoevsky – these were aspects of Saint-Simon's legacy. So too was a new age of French industrial expansion and investment, the foundation of the Crédit Mobilier bank and the building of the Suez Canal.

Source: Henri Saint-Simon, *Selected Writings on Science, Industry and Social Organisation*, translated with an introduction and notes by Keith Taylor, Croom Helm, 1975.

How to Run a Cotton-Mill

Unlike most utopians, Robert Owen (1771–1858) put his utopian ideas into practice. The son of a saddler and ironmonger in Newtown, Wales, he was an unusually precocious child. At the age of seven he was already assistant to the local schoolmaster. His parents apprenticed him to a draper. But his acute business sense and dynamic personality brought him early and phenomenal success in the cotton industry. In 1799 he acquired cotton-mills at New Lanark, Scotland, from the wealthy Glasgow merchant David Dale, marrying Dale's daughter.

Owen was a pioneer of humane factory management and working-class education, and within a decade he had made New Lanark famous throughout Europe for its advanced social policy as well as for the quality of its cotton thread. His ideas of Socialism and profit-sharing had not developed at this stage. Though he was a benevolent employer by the standards of his day, New Lanark had high profit-margins and used child labour.

Two ideas permanently dominated Owen's thought. The first was that human nature is infinitely malleable, so that, given efficient education, children may be trained to acquire any character. As he put it:

The infants of any one class in the world may be readily formed into men of any other class, even to believe and declare that conduct to be right and virtuous, and to die in its defence, which their parents had been taught to believe and say was wrong and vicious, and to oppose which those parents would also have willingly sacrificed their lives.

Owen's second idea arose directly from this first one. It was that a person's character is always formed *for* that person, by education and upbringing, and never by that person. Our will has no power over our opinions: we must believe what has been impressed on us by our educators. Consequently it is 'the essence of irrationality to suppose that any human being, from the creation to this day, could deserve praise or blame, reward or punishment'.

In *A New View of Society, or, Essays on the Principle of the Formation of the Human Character, and the Application of the Principle to Practice* (1813–16), Owen tells the story of the New Lanark mills. He is himself, of course, the unnamed reformer in this account.

In the year 1784 the late Mr Dale, of Glasgow, founded a manufactory for spinning of cotton, near the falls of the Clyde, in the county of Lanark, in Scotland; and about that period cotton mills were first introduced into the northern part of the kingdom.

It was the power which could be obtained from the falls of water that induced Mr Dale to erect his mills in this situation; for in other respects it was not well chosen. The country around was uncultivated; the inhabitants were poor and few in number; and the roads in the neighhourhood were so bad, that the Falls, now so celebrated, were then unknown to strangers.

It was therefore necessary to collect a new population to supply the infant establishment with labourers. This, however, was no light task; for all the regularly trained Scotch peasantry disdained the idea of working early and late, day after day, within cotton mills. Two modes then only remained of obtaining these labourers; the one, to procure children from the various public charities of the country; and the other, to induce families to settle around the works.

To accommodate the first, a large house was erected, which ultimately contained about 500 children, who were procured chiefly from workhouses and charities in Edinburgh. These children were to be fed, clothed, and educated; and these duties Mr Dale performed with the unwearied benevolence which it is well known he possessed.

To obtain the second, a village was built; and the houses were let at a low rent to such families as could be induced to accept employment in the mills; but such was the general dislike to that occupation at the time, that, with a few exceptions, only persons destitute of friends, employment, and character, were found willing to try the experiment; and of these a sufficient number to supply a constant increase of the manufactory could not be obtained. It was therefore deemed a favour on the part even of such individuals to reside at the village, and, when taught the business, they grew so valuable to the establishment, that they became agents not to be governed contrary to their own inclinations.

Mr Dale's principal avocations were at a distance from the works, which he seldom visited more than once for a few hours in three or four months; he was therefore under the necessity of committing the management of the establishment to various servants with more or less power.

Those who have a practical knowledge of mankind will readily anticipate the character which a population so collected and constituted would acquire. It is therefore scarcely necessary to state, that the community by degrees was formed under these circumstances into a very wretched society: every man did that which was right in his own eyes, and vice and immorality prevailed to a monstrous extent. The population lived in idleness, in poverty, in almost every kind of crime; consequently, in debt, out of health, and in misery. Yet to make matters still worse – although the cause proceeded from the best possible motive, a conscientious adherence to principle – the whole was under a strong sectarian influence, which gave a marked and decided preference to one set of religious opinions over all others, and the professors of the favoured opinions were the privileged of the community.

The boarding-house containing the children presented a very different scene. The benevolent proprietor spared no expense to give comfort to the poor children. The rooms provided for them were spacious, always clean, and well ventilated; the food was abundant, and of the best quality; the clothes were neat and useful; a surgeon was kept in constant pay, to direct how to prevent or cure disease; and the best instructors which the country afforded were appointed to teach such branches of education as were deemed likely to be useful to children in their situation. Kind and well-disposed persons were appointed to superintend all their proceedings. Nothing, in short, at first sight seemed wanting to render it a most complete charity.

But to defray the expense of these well-devised arrangements, and to support the establishment generally, it was absolutely necessary that the children should be employed within the mills from six o'clock in the morning till seven in the evening, summer and winter; and after these hours their education commenced. The directors of the public charities, from mistaken economy, would not consent to send the children under their care to cotton mills, unless the children were received by the proprietors at the ages of six, seven and eight. And Mr Dale was under the necessity of accepting them at those ages, or of stopping the manufactory which he had commenced.

It is not to be supposed that children so young could remain, with the intervals of meals only, from six in the morning until seven in the evening, in constant employment, on their feet, within cotton mills, and afterwards acquire much proficiency in education. And so it proved; for many of them became dwarfs in body and mind, and some of them were deformed. Their labour through the day and their education at night became so irksome, that numbers of them continually ran away, and almost all looked forward with impatience and anxiety to the expiration of their apprenticeship of seven, eight, and nine years, which generally expired when they were from thirteen to fifteen years old. At this period of life, unaccustomed to provide for themselves, and unacquainted with the world, they usually went to Edinburgh or Glasgow, where boys and girls were soon assailed by the innumerable temptations which all large towns present, and to which many of them fell sacrifices.

Thus Mr Dale's arrangements, and his kind solicitude for the comfort and happiness of these children, were rendered in their ultimate effect almost nugatory. They were hired by him and sent to be employed, and without their labour he could not support them; but, while under his care, he did all that any individual, circumstanced as he was, could do for his fellow creatures. The error proceeded from the children being sent from the workhouses at an age much too young for employment. They ought to have been detained four years longer, and educated; and then some of the evils which followed would have been prevented.

If such be a true picture, not overcharged, of parish apprentices to our manufacturing system, under the best and most humane regulations, in what colours must it be exhibited under the worst?

Mr Dale was advancing in years: he had no son to succeed him; and, finding the consequences just described to be the result of all his strenuous exertions for the improvement and happiness of his fellow creatures, it is not surprising that he became disposed to retire from the cares of the establishment. He accordingly sold it to some English merchants and manufacturers; one of whom, under the circumstances just narrated, undertook the management of the concern, and fixed his residence in the midst of the population. This individual had been previously in the management of large establishments, employing a number of workpeople, in the neighbourhood of Manchester, and, in every case, by the steady application of certain general principles, he succeeded in reforming the habits of those under his care, and who always, among their associates in similar employment, appeared conspicuous for their good conduct. With this previous success in remodelling English character, but ignorant of the local ideas, manners, and customs, of those now committed to his management, the stranger commenced his task.

At that time the lower classes of Scotland, like those of other countries, had strong prejudices against strangers having any authority over them, and particularly against the English, few of whom had then settled in Scotland, and not one in the neighbourhood of the scenes under description. It is also well known that even the Scotch peasantry and working classes possess the habit of making observations and reasoning thereon with great acuteness; and in the present case those employed naturally concluded that the new purchasers intended merely to make the utmost profit by the establishment, from the abuses of which many of themselves were then deriving support. The persons employed at these works were therefore strongly prejudiced against the new director of the establishment – prejudiced, because he was a stranger, and from England – because he succeeded Mr Dale, under whose proprietorship they acted almost as they liked – because his religious creed was not theirs – and because they concluded that the works would be governed by new laws and regulations, calculated to squeeze, as they often termed it, the greatest sum of gain out of their labour.

In consequence, from the day he arrived amongst them every means which ingenuity could devise was set to work to counteract the plan which he attempted to introduce; and for two years it was a regular attack and defence of prejudices and malpractices between the manager and the population of the place, without the former being able to make much progress, or to convince the latter of the sincerity of his good intentions for their welfare. He, however, did not lose his patience, his temper, or his confidence in the certain success of the principles on which he founded his conduct.

These principles ultimately prevailed: the population could not continue to resist a firm well-directed kindness, administering justice to all. They therefore slowly and cautiously began to give him some portion of their confidence; and as this increased, he was enabled more and more to develop his plans for their amelioration. It may with truth be said, that at this period they possessed almost all the vices and very few of the virtues of a social community. Theft and the receipt of stolen goods was their trade, idleness and drunkenness their habit, falsehood and deception their garb, dissensions, civil and religious, their daily practice; they united only in a zealous systematic opposition to their employers.

Here then was a fair field on which to try the efficacy in practice of principles supposed capable of altering any characters. The manager formed his plans accordingly. He spent some time in finding out the full extent of the evil against which he had to contend, and in tracing the true causes which had produced and were continuing those effects. He found that all was distrust, disorder, and disunion; and he wished to introduce confidence, regularity, and harmony. He therefore began to bring forward his various expedients to withdraw the unfavourable circumstances by which they had hitherto been surrounded, and to replace them by others calculated to produce a more happy result. He soon discovered that theft was extended through almost all the ramifications of the community, and the receipt of stolen goods through all the country around. To remedy this evil, not one legal punishment was inflicted, not one individual imprisoned, even for an hour; but checks and other regulations of prevention were introduced; a short plain explanation of the immediate benefits they would derive from a different conduct was inculcated by those instructed for the purpose, who had the best powers of reasoning among themselves. They were at the same time instructed how to direct their industry in legal and useful occupations, by which, without danger or disgrace, they could really earn more than they had previously obtained by dishonest practices. Thus the difficulty of committing the crime was increased, the detection afterwards rendered more easy, the habit of honest industry formed, and the pleasure of good conduct experienced.

Drunkenness was attacked in the same manner; it was discountenanced on every occasion by those who had charge of any department: its destructive and pernicious effects were frequently stated by his own more prudent comrades, at the proper moment when the individual was soberly suffering from the effects of his previous excess;

pot- and public-houses were gradually removed from the immediate vicinity of their dwellings; the health and comfort of temperance were made familiar to them; by degrees drunkenness disappeared, and many who were habitual bacchanalians are now conspicuous for undeviating sobriety.

Falsehood and deception met with a similar fate: they were held in disgrace; their practical evils were shortly explained; and every countenance was given to truth and open conduct. The pleasure and substantial advantages derived from the latter soon overcame the impolicy, error, and consequent misery, which the former mode of acting had created.

Dissensions and quarrels were undermined by analagous expedients. When they could not be readily adjusted between the parties themselves, they were stated to the manager; and as in such cases both disputants were usually more or less in the wrong, that wrong was in as few words as possible explained, forgiveness and friendship recommended, and one simple and easily remembered precept inculcated, as the most valuable rule for their whole conduct, and the advantages of which they would experience every moment of their lives; viz. – 'That in future they should endeavour to use the same active exertions to make each other happy and comfortable, as they had hitherto done to make each other miserable; and by carrying this short memorandum in their mind, and applying it on all occasions, they would soon render that place a paradise, which, from the most mistaken principle of action, they now made the abode of misery.' The experiment was tried: the parties enjoyed the gratification of this new mode of conduct; references rapidly subsided; and now serious differences are scarcely known.

Considerable jealousies also existed on account of one religious sect possessing a decided preference over the others. This was corrected by discontinuing that preference, and by giving a uniform encouragement to those who conducted themselves well among all the various religious persuasions; by recommending the same consideration to be shown to the conscientious opinions of each sect, on the ground that all must believe the particular doctrines which they had been taught, and consequently that all were in that respect upon an equal footing, nor was it possible yet to say which was right or wrong. It was likewise inculcated that all should attend to the essence of religion, and not act as the world was now taught and trained to do; that is, to overlook the substance and essence of religion, and devote their talents, time, and money, to that which is far worse than its shadow sectarianism; another term for something very injurious to society, and very absurd, which one or other well-meaning enthusiast has added to *true religion*, which, without these defects, would soon form those characters which every wise and good man is anxious to see.

Such statements and conduct arrested sectarian animosity and ignorant intolerance; each retains full liberty of conscience, and in consequence each partakes of the sincere friendship of many sects instead of one. They act with cordiality together in the same departments and pursuits, and associate as though the whole community were not of different sectarian persuasions; and not one evil ensues.

The same principles were applied to correct the irregular intercourse of the sexes: such conduct was discountenanced and held in disgrace; fines were levied upon both parties for the use of the support fund of the community. (This fund arose from each individual contributing one sixtieth part of their wages, which, under their management, was applied to support the sick, and injured by accident, and the aged.) But because they had once unfortunately offended against the established laws and customs of society, they were not forced to become vicious, abandoned, and miserable; the door was left open for them to return to the comforts of kind friends and respected acquaintances; and, beyond any previous expectation, the evil became greatly diminished.

The system of receiving apprentices from public charities was abolished; permanent settlers with large families were encouraged, and comfortable houses were built for their accommodation.

The practice of employing children in the mills, of six, seven and eight years of age, was discontinued, and their parents advised to allow them to acquire health and education until they were ten years old. (It may be remarked, that even this age is too early to keep them at constant employment in manufactories, from six in the morning to seven in the evening. Far better would it be for the children, their parents, and for society, that the first should not commence employment until they attain the age of twelve, when their education might be finished, and their bodies would be more competent to undergo the fatigue and exertions required of them. When parents can be trained to afford this additional time to their children without inconvenience, they will, of course, adopt the practice now recommended.)

The children were taught reading, writing, and arithmetic, during five years, that is, from five to ten, in the village school, without expense to their parents. All the modern improvements in education have been adopted, or are in process of adoption. (To avoid the inconveniences which must ever arise from the introduction of a particular creed into a school, the children are taught to read in such books as inculcate those precepts of the Christian religion, which are common to all denominations.) They may therefore be taught and well-trained before they engage in any regular employment. Another important consideration is, that all their instruction is rendered a pleasure and delight to them; they are much more anxious for the hour of school-time to arrive than to end; they therefore make a rapid progress; and it may be safely asserted, that if they shall not be trained to form such characters as may be most desired, the fault will not proceed from the children; the cause will be in the want of a true knowledge of human nature in those who have the management of them and their parents.

During the period that these changes were going forward, attention was given to the domestic arrangements of the community.

Their houses were rendered more comfortable, their streets were improved, the best provisions were purchased, and sold to them at low rates, yet covering the original expense, and under such regulations as taught them how to proportion their expenditure to their income. Fuel and clothes were obtained for them in the same manner; and no advantage was attempted to be taken of them, or means used to deceive them.

In consequence, their animosity and opposition to the stranger subsided, their full confidence was obtained, and they became satisfied that no evil was intended them; they were convinced that a real desire existed to increase their happiness upon those grounds alone on which it could be permanently increased. All difficulties in the way of future improvement vanished. They were taught to be rational, and they acted rationally. Thus both parties experienced the incalculable advantages of the system which had been adopted. Those employed became industrious, temperate, healthy, faithful to their employers, and kind to each other; while the proprietors were deriving services from their attachment, almost without inspection, far beyond those which could be obtained by any other means than those of mutual confidence and kindness. Such was the effect of these principles on the adults; on those whose previous habits had been as ill-formed as habits could be; and certainly the application of the principles to practice was made under the most unfavourable circumstances. (It may be supposed that this community was separated from other society; but the supposition would be erroneous, for it had daily and hourly communication with a population exceeding its own number. The royal borough of Lanark is only one mile distant from the works; many individuals came daily from the former to be employed at the latter; and a general intercourse is constantly maintained between the old and new towns.)

I have thus given a detailed account of this experiment, although a partial application of the principles is of far less importance than a clear and accurate account of the principles themselves, in order that they may be so well understood as to be easily rendered applicable to practice in any community and under any circumstances. Without this, particular facts may indeed amuse or astonish, but they would not contain that substantial value which the principles will be found to possess. But if the relation of the narrative shall forward this object, the experiment cannot fail to prove the certain means of renovating the moral and religious principles of the world, by showing whence arise the various opinions, manners, vices, and virtues of mankind, and how the best or the worst of them may, with mathematical precision, be taught to the rising generation.

Let it not, therefore, be longer said that evil or injurious actions cannot be prevented, or that the most rational habits in the rising generation cannot be universally formed. In those characters which now exhibit crime, the fault is obviously not in the individual, but the defects proceed from the system in which the individual was trained. Withdraw those circumstances which tend to create crime in the human character, and crime will not be created. Replace them with such as are calculated to form habits of order, regularity, temperance, industry; and these qualities will be formed. Adopt measures of fair equity and justice, and you will readily acquire the full and complete confidence of the lower orders. Proceed systematically on principles of undeviating persevering kindness, yet retaining and using, with the least possible severity, the means of restraining crime from immediately injuring society; and by degrees even the crimes now existing in the adults will also gradually disappear: for the worst formed disposition, short of incurable insanity, will not long resist a firm, determined, well-directed, persevering kindness. Such a proceeding, whenever practised, will be found the most powerful and effective corrector of crime, and of all injurious and improper habits.

The experiment narrated shows that this is not hypothesis and theory. The principles may be with confidence stated to be universal, and applicable to all times, persons, and circumstances. And the most obvious application of them would be to adopt rational means to remove the temptation to commit crimes, and increase the difficulties of committing them; while, at the same time, a proper direction should be given to the active powers of the individual; and a due share provided of uninjurious amusements and recreation. Care must also be taken to remove the causes of jealousy, dissensions, and irritation; to introduce sentiments calculated to create union and confidence among all the members of the community; and the whole should be directed by a persevering kindness, sufficiently evident to prove that a sincere desire exists to increase, and not to diminish, happiness.

These principles, applied to the community at New Lanark, at first under many of the most discouraging circumstances, but persevered in for sixteen years, effected a complete change in the general character of the village, containing upwards of 2,000 inhabitants, and into which, also, there was a constant influx of newcomers. But as the promulgation of new miracles is not for present times, it is not pretended that under such circumstances one and all are become wise and good; or, that they are free from error. But it may be truly stated, that they now constitute a very improved society; that their worst habits are gone, and that their minor ones will soon disappear under a continuance of the application of the same principles; that during the period mentioned, scarcely a legal punishment has been inflicted, or an application been made for parish funds by any individual among them. Drunkenness is not seen in their streets; and the children are taught and trained in the institution for forming their character without any punishment. The community exhibits the general appearance of industry, temperance, comfort, health, and happiness. These are and ever will be the sure and certain effects of the adoption of the principles explained; and these principles, applied with judgement, will effectually reform the most vicious community existing, and train the younger part of it to any character which may be desired; and that, too, much more easily on an extended than on a limited scale. To apply these principles, however, successfully to practice, both a comprehensive and a minute view must be taken of the existing state of the society on which they are intended to operate. The causes of the most prevalent evils must be accurately traced, and those means which appear the most easy and simple should be immediately applied to remove them.

In this progress the smallest alteration, adequate to produce any good effect, should be made at one time; indeed, if possible, the change should be so gradual as to be almost imperceptible, yet always making a permanent advance in the desired improvements. By this procedure the most rapid practical progress will be obtained, because the inclination to resistance will be removed, and time will be given for reason to weaken the force of long-established injurious prejudices. The removal of the first evil will prepare the way for the removal of the second; and this facility will increase, not in an arithmetical, but in a geometrical proportion; until the directors of the system will themselves be gratified beyond expression with the beneficial magnitude of their own proceedings.

Nor while these principles shall be acted upon can there be any retrogression in this good work; for the permanence of the amelioration will be equal to its extent.

What then remains to prevent such a system from being immediately adopted into national practice? Nothing, surely, but a general destitution of the knowledge of the practice. For with the certain means of preventing crimes, can it be supposed that British legislators, as soon as these means shall be made evident, will longer withhold them from their fellow subjects? No: I am persuaded that neither prince, ministers, parliament, nor any party in church or state, will avow inclination to act on principles of such flagrant injustice. Have they not on many occasions evinced a sincere and ardent desire to ameliorate the condition of the subjects of the empire, when practicable means of amelioration were explained to them, which could be adopted without risking the safety of the state?

For some time to come there can be but one practicable, and therefore one rational reform, which without danger can be attempted in these realms; a reform in which all men and all parties may join – that is, a reform in the training and in the management of the poor, the ignorant, the untaught and untrained, or ill-taught and ill-trained, among the whole mass of British population; and a plain, simple, practicable plan which would not contain the least danger to any individual, or to any part of society, may be devised for that purpose.

That plan is a national, well-digested, unexclusive system for the formation of character and general amelioration of the lower orders. On the experience of a life devoted to the subject, I hesitate not to say, that the members of any community may by degrees be trained to live *without idleness, without poverty, without crime, and without punishment*; for each of these is the effect of error in the various systems prevalent throughout the world. *They are all necessary consequences of ignorance.*

Train any population rationally, and they will be rational. Furnish honest and useful employments to those so trained, and such employments they will greatly prefer to dishonest or injurious occupations. It is beyond all calculation the interest of every government to provide that training and that employment; and to provide both is easily practicable.

An innovation at New Lanark, introduced in 1816, was an Institute for the Formation of Character, in which Owen's theory of psychological determinism was put to practical use.

They had not been taught the most valuable domestic and social habits: such as the most economical method of preparing food; how to arrange their dwellings with neatness, and to keep them always clean and in order; but, what was of infinitely more importance, they had not been instructed how to train their children to form them into valuable members of the community, or to know that principles existed, which, when properly applied to practice from infancy, would ensure from man to man, without chance of failure, a just, open, sincere, and benevolent conduct.

It was in this stage of the progress of improvement, that it became necessary to form arrangements for surrounding them with circumstances which should gradually prepare the individuals to receive and firmly retain those domestic and social acquirements and habits. For this purpose a building, which may be termed the 'new institution', was erected in the centre of the establishment, with an enclosed area before it. The area is intended for a playground for the children of the villagers, from the time they can walk alone until they enter the school.

It must be evident to those who have been in the practice of observing children with attention, that much of good or evil is taught to or acquired by a child at a very early period of its life; that much of temper or disposition is correctly or incorrectly formed before he attains his second year; and that many durable impressions are made at the termination of the first twelve or even six months of his existence. The children, therefore, of the uninstructed and ill-instructed, suffer material injury in the formation of their characters during these and the subsequent years of childhood and of youth.

It was to prevent, or as much as possible to counteract, these primary evils, to which the poor and working classes are exposed when infants, that the area became part of the New Institution.

Into this playground the children are to be received as soon as they can freely walk alone; to be superintended by persons instructed to take charge of them.

As the happiness of man chiefly, if not altogether, depends on his own sentiments and habits, as well as those of the individuals around him; and as any sentiments and habits may be given to all infants, it becomes of primary importance that those alone should be given to them which can contribute to their happiness. Each child, therefore, on his entrance into the playground, is to be told in language which he can understand, that 'he is never to injure his playfellows; but that, on the contrary, he is to contribute all in his power to make them happy'. This simple precept, when comprehended in all its bearings, and the habits which will arise from its early adoption into practice, *if no counteracting principle be forced upon the young mind*, will effectually supersede all the errors which have hitherto kept the world in ignorance and misery. So simple a precept, too, will be easily taught, and as easily acquired; for the chief employment of the superintendents will be to prevent any deviation from it in practice. The older children, when they shall have experienced the endless advantages from acting on this principle, will, by their example, soon enforce the practice of it on the young strangers: and the happiness, which the little groups will enjoy from this rational conduct, will ensure its speedy and general and willing adoption. The habit also which they will acquire at this early period of life by continually acting on the principle, will fix it firmly; it will become easy and familiar to them, or, as it is often termed, natural.

Thus, by merely attending to the evidence of our senses respecting human nature, and disregarding the wild, inconsistent, and absurd theories in which man has been hitherto trained in all parts of the earth, we shall accomplish with ease and certainty the supposed Herculean labour of forming a rational character in man, and that, too, chiefly before the child commences the ordinary course of education.

Owen was virulently attacked, both by fellow mill-owners, who envied his success, and by the clergy, who resented his dismissal of sectarian differences, and saw his theory of human perfectibility as undermining the doctrine of original sin. In the face of this opposition Owen's ideas grew more progressive and unorthodox. He developed a new political principle, which came to be called Socialism, and attacked the concept of private property and the profit-motive. In place of the old society based on individualism and competition, he insisted that a 'new moral world' would have to be constructed. In this new world everyone would live in co-operative villages, or 'villages of union', containing from five hundred to fifteen hundred people, and combining agricultural life with small-scale manufacture. Big cities, which Owen hated, would cease to exist. Money would also become obsolete. The unit of currency would be 'labour-notes', acquired for time spent at work, and exchangeable for goods.

Owen advertised his campaign for world reform on a continental tour in 1818. To found a pilot economy on his principles, he acquired a site at New Harmony, Indiana, in 1825. But the experiment survived for only a few years, and other Owenite communities in America were also short-lived. Meanwhile, Owen was spurred to ever greater efforts. In the 1820s the London Co-Operative Society was set up to propagate his ideas, and the first co-op store opened in Brighton. There were three hundred, all over the country, by 1830. 'Exchanges', where artisans could barter the products of their labour without using money, also came into being, but did not thrive, because they could not offer a sufficiently wide range of commodities. In 1835 Owen founded the Rational Society, to spread Socialist ideas, and it attracted an enormous following. Tens of thousands attended Sunday lectures at Owenite district branches. In Manchester an interested auditor was Friedrich Engels, who co-authored the *Communist Manifesto* with Karl Marx in 1848.

Source: Robert Owen, *A New View of Society and Other Writings*, edited by Gregory Claeys, Penguin, 1991.

Passions Set Free

Charles Fourier (1772–1837) was one of the most devoted and prolific utopians of all time, and has been seen as a precursor of Marx and Freud. He dreamed of a new world of erotic freedom and joyful, non-compulsory work. By contrast, his own life seems to have been drab and lonely. A Besançon cloth-merchant's son, he was forced to earn his keep in 'the jailhouse of commerce', describing himself as 'an almost illiterate shop-clerk'. He rented rooms in boarding houses, kept cats, and never married or, apparently, had a sexual relationship. But each day after work he spent hours devising his utopian realm, which he called Harmony, and which was based on an astonishingly intricate system of psychological classification. His knowledge of personality-types seems to have been derived largely from newspapers, of which he was an avid reader.

The basic idea of Harmony was that the passions are good and God-given and must be set free. Having lived through (and almost perished in) the French Revolution, Fourier hated the 'rationalist' enlightenment that had inspired it. Civilization, he believed, was a nightmare precisely because it strove to repress the passions – a futile endeavour, which promoted mental disease and criminal outrage. He compared himself favourably to Newton. For whereas Newton's theory of gravitation revealed that every particle of matter in the universe attracted every other particle, he, Charles Fourier, had made the 'great discovery' that every person is passionately attracted to certain activities and certain types of people. The investigation of this 'passionate attraction' could be made into an 'exact science', and could provide the key to the human universe – because passions were ultimately more powerful than reason, duty or prejudice. If an expert psychologist (such as Fourier) could so arrange matters that people lived in a community with people to whom they were passionately attracted, and did jobs which passionately attracted them, mankind would live in 'opulence, sensual pleasures, and global unity'.

He calculated that there were 810 common personality types (leaving aside a further 410 mixed or ambiguous ones), each representing a different combination of the twelve basic passions. So, doubling the figure to include women as well as men, he arrived at 1,620 as the optimal number each Phalanx (commune) should contain if it was to represent the normal gamut of human psychology.

The buildings and grounds occupied by the Phalanx (collectively called the Phalanstery) would be palatial, incorporating meeting halls, dining rooms, libraries, studies, parade grounds, gardens, ballrooms, a temple, an observatory, and commodious coops for carrier pigeons. Prefiguring a modern shopping mall, it would provide all-weather access to its various delights. This would be achieved by means of a special feature, the 'street gallery', heated, glassed-in, and taller than the Louvre ('Once a man has seen the street gallery of a Phalanx he will look upon the most elegant civilized palace as a place of exile, a residence worthy of fools').

In the Phalanx, everyone will be assured of a 'social minimum' (i.e. five meals a day – the normal number in Harmony, clothing, including work and dress uniforms, lodging in a private room with toilet, and access to third-class seats at theatres and concerts) without having to work for it. Work will consequently become a game or erotic activity, not a necessity. People will work at as many tasks as they choose (up to eight a day, in brief periods, never longer than two hours), along with a varied group of friends and lovers (called a 'passionate series') who are spontaneously drawn together by their fondness for the task or its products or one another.

All tasks, however much despised in the old civilized world, will attract eager recruits in Harmony. For example, those born with bloodthirsty inclinations, like the Emperor Nero, will join a butchers' group at the age of three, working in the slaughterhouses, and will become happy, skilful butchers. Thus Harmony will usefully employ the very passions that civilization makes vicious. Even the so-called seven deadly sins are natural, God-given passions, Fourier insisted, and in Harmony they will not be repressed but channelled into salutary directions. Filthy jobs, such as cleaning out latrines, will be performed by children, organized in groups called Little Hordes, 'a kind of half-savage legion', with its own slang, grandiose rituals and uniforms, and dwarf horses to ride on. Two-thirds of male children, and a smaller proportion of female, actually enjoy filth, Fourier observes, and are 'unruly, peevish, scurrilous and overbearing' as well. So the Little Hordes will not lack volunteers.

For large-scale tasks such as cultivating the Sahara desert, digging the Suez and Panama canals (both of which Fourier predicted), or the reforestation and reclamation of regions that civilization has devastated, there will be 'industrial armies' to which millions of 'industrial athletes' will flock. One-third of each army will be young women, belonging to the order of Vestals, who normally remain chaste till they are nineteen, but are quite free to become unchaste when they choose, whereupon they join the order of

Damsels. They will work alongside the men, inspire them, and choose lovers from among them. Other young women known as Bacchantes ('sexual athletes') will solace the men who are not chosen. This combination of work with love-making will be the common pattern in Harmony. Love will no longer be 'a recreation that detracts from work', as it is in civilization. Rather it will be 'the soul and vehicle, the mainspring of all works'.

With everyone in Harmony free to choose what he or she will work at each day, organizational problems abound. Each evening there is a libertarian labour-exchange session, to arrange the next day's schedules. Describing a typical session, Fourier, as often, gives his Harmonians romantic names (Dorimon, Amarinte).

There is much more animation and intrigue at the Exchange of a Phalanx than there is at the stock exchanges of London or Amsterdam. For every individual must go to the Exchange to arrange his work and pleasure sessions for the following days. It is there that he makes plans concerning his gastronomic and amorous meetings and, especially, for his work sessions in the shops and fields. Everyone has at least twenty sessions to arrange, since he makes definite plans for the following day and tentative ones for the day after.

Assuming that 1,200 individuals are present, and that each one has twenty sessions to arrange, this means that in the meeting as a whole there are 24,000 transactions to be concluded. Each of these transactions can involve 20, 40 or 100 individuals who must be consulted and intrigued with or against. It would be impossible to unravel so many intrigues and conclude so many transactions if one proceeded according to the confused methods employed by our commercial exchanges; operating at their rate it would take at least a whole day to organize half the meetings that the Harmonians must plan in half an hour. I will now describe their expeditious methods.

In the center of the hall there is a raised platform on which the director, the directrice and their secretaries are seated. Scattered around the hall are the desks of 24 negotiators, 12 men and 12 women. Each of them handles the affairs of a given number of series and serves as the representative of several neighboring Phalanxes. Each of the four secretaries corresponds with six of the 24 negotiators by means of iron wires whose movements indicate requests and decisions.

Negotiations are carried on quietly by means of signals. Each negotiator holds up the escutcheons of the groups or Phalanxes which he represents, and by certain prearranged signs he indicates the approximate number of members which he has recruited. Everyone else walks around the hall. In one or two circuits a given individual may take part in 20 transactions, since all he has to do is to accept or refuse. Dorimon suggests that a meeting of the bee-keepers be held the next day at ten o'clock. The leaders of this group have taken the initiative according to the customary procedures. Their job is to find out whether or not a majority of the members of the bee-keeping group wish to hold a session. In this case the decision is affirmative. Each of the members takes his peg from the bee-keepers' board which is placed in front of Dorimon's desk . . .

At the other side of the hall Araminte calls for a meeting of the rose-growers to be held at the same time. Since many of Araminte's rose-growers are also members of the bee-keeping group, they raise an objection and notify Dorimon. He conveys their message to the directorate which tells Araminte to halt his negotiations. The rose-growers are obliged to choose another hour, since bee-keeping is a more necessary form of work than rose-growing.

Negotiations frequently become so complicated that three, four or five groups, and even complete series, find themselves in competition. Everything is settled by the signals of the negotiators. Their acolytes confer with the leaders of the various conspiring groups by calling them over to one of the desks. Every time someone tries to initiate an intrigue, either to organize a session or prevent one from being held, a conference takes place at some point outside the main promenade area so as not to disturb those who are still walking around the hall, watching the progress of negotiations and making up their minds . . .

When a session of the Exchange is over everyone writes down a list of the meetings which he has agreed to attend, and the negotiators and directors draw up a summary of all the transactions. This summary is immediately sent to the press and then it is distributed to neighboring communities by a dog who carries it around his neck.

Love in Harmony will be 'free', but highly organized, the aim being to provide universal sexual gratification. Everyone, including the elderly and the deformed, will be assured of a 'sexual minimum'. To effect this, philanthropic corporations composed of outstandingly beautiful and promiscuous erotic priests and priestesses will joyfully minister to the needs of less attractive Harmonians. The qualification for admission to this 'amorous nobility' will be a generous sexual nature, capable of carrying on several affairs at once (this will be tested under examination conditions). Polygamy and adultery will be praiseworthy in Harmony, and they will be open and unashamed – there will be no secrecy – whereas monogamy will be despised as the narrowest sort of love. Polygamy, Fourier believed, was already almost universal – though covert – in our own civilization. He drew up a list of seventy-two distinct varieties of cuckold.

In Harmony, the notion of sexual 'perversion' will be abandoned. Lesbians, pederasts, flagellants, and others with more recondite tastes such as heel-scratching and eating live spiders, will all have their desires recognized and satisfied, and will meet regularly at international convocations. Fourier himself confessed to a fondness for lesbians, and calculated that there were 26,400 men on earth, beside himself, who shared this abnormality.

The amorous affairs of each Phalanx will be organized by an elaborate hierarchy of officials, titled variously high priests, pontiffs, matrons, confessors, fairies, fakirs and genies. They will hold sessions of the court of love each evening, after the children have gone to bed. In arranging relationships, they will depend on a complete knowledge of everyone's likes and dislikes, obtained through confession, and an intricate card-index system of erotic personality-matching.

In the following sample session, Fourier imagines a band of travelling Harmonians arriving at a Phalanx and being entertained.

The band of adventurers moves forward through a cloud of perfume and a rain of flowers. The choral groups and musicians of the Phalanx welcome them with hymns of joy. As soon as the visitors have reached the colonnades of the Phalanstery, bowls of flaming punch are brought in and a hundred different nectars spurt from the opened fountains. All the knights and ladies are wearing their most seductive clothing. Two hundred priests and priestesses, who are dressed no less elegantly, greet their guests and perform the introductions. After refreshments have been served, the whole group mounts to the throne room where the pontiff Isis is seated. The welcoming ceremonies are concluded there and, after washing, all the visitors proceed to the confessional.

The high priests begin to examine the adventurers and to read their written declarations. A few adventurers, who have been examined at their last stop, give the priests the commentaries written by their previous confessors. Everyone hands over a written summary of his or her most recent confession together with whatever observations may have been added by the consistory of the last Phalanx visited.

While the visitors are eating a light snack, the work of analyzing and classifying their confessions goes on in the consistory. A list of five or six sympathetic relationships is drawn up for each knight and lady on the basis of the examinations conducted by the young priests and priestesses who wish to become sympathetic with the adventurers. Before the snack is over the fairies and genies have completed their task of match-making. Their recommendations are delivered to the office of the High Matron along with a summary of each confession. Sympathetic matching takes everything into account, and the final choices made are those which seem most likely to complement previous encounters either through contrast or identity.

I am only speaking here about young adventurers. The amorous affairs of the older adventurers are handled by the fakirs who use other methods . . .

The first moments of the visit are taken up by ceremonial activities which should always include an informal meal. This meal will give everyone a chance to satisfy his curiosity, to move about from one person to another and to form some general impression of the visitors. Of course they too need to see how the land lies. People should get a brief look at one another before amorous affairs get underway. This interlude also allows time for the theoretical determination of sympathies; it enables everyone to have his own list of partners in time for the opening of the court of love. It should be added that up until the opening of the court of love the Vestals and the children are free to mingle with the visitors and to satisfy their curiosity about them. This is a most important precaution since the children might otherwise wish to enter the court of love, which they are not allowed to do. Thus the session does not begin until they have seen all they want of the visitors and are quite ready for bed. Only then do the adventurers go to the office of the High Matron to get back their papers and to look at the portraits of their designated sympathetic partners.

When the preludes are over the adventurers and their hosts gather in the salon. A salvo is fired to announce the opening of the session. On one side of the salon stands the whole band of adventurers. On the other side the priesthood is gathered along with other people who have been designated as sympathetic partners or who have come to take part in the amorous activities. The priests are placed opposite the adventuresses and the priestesses opposite the adventurers.

When the Head Fairy waves her wand a semi-bacchanalia gets underway. The members of both groups rush into each other's arms, and in the ensuing scramble caresses are liberally given and received. Everyone strokes and investigates whatever comes to hand and surrenders himself or herself to the unfettered impulses of simple nature. Each participant flits from one person to another, bestowing kisses everywhere with as much eagerness as rapidity. Everyone also makes a special point of encountering those individuals who caught his or her eye earlier. This brief bacchanalia allows people to verify the physical attributes of those to whom they are attracted, and it can lay the groundwork for the establishment of sympathetic relationships between people who are more inclined to physical than spiritual pleasure.

It would be wrong, however, to suppose that this first confused skirmish exercises a decisive influence on the match-making that is to follow. Indeed, it would be bad form for anyone to make a binding commitment at the outset before formally encountering his designated sympathetic partners. People who have gotten together in the scramble will be able to renew their acquaintance later, and they will only love each other all the more if it turns out that their calculated sympathies, of which they are as yet unaware, are consistent with the preferences revealed in the bacchanalia.

Some of our civilized materialists might wish to conclude their investigations at this point. They would claim that this opening skirmish is all they need to make their choice. It will, in fact, be enough for monogynes [people ruled by a single passion] dominated by the passion of touch; and they will not be prevented from forming sensual relationships with like-minded partners encountered during the bacchanalia. But such relationships, which are no more than simple amorous ties, deriving from purely physical affinities, will satisfy no more than a twentieth of the lovers in Harmony . . . For the goal of Harmony is to establish compound amorous relationships based on both physical and spiritual affinities. Thus while the opening sensual skirmish is indispensable, it is only a prelude. It is the first phase in a process which moves, according to the law of progression, from the simple to the compound. Since nature's first thrust is always towards the physical, it would be contrary to the natural order of things to begin by occupying lovers with transcendent and spiritual illusions. The natural impulse should first be reinforced by a little opening bacchanalia, and then the sentiments should be brought into play with the help of the fairies. When sentimental inclinations are linked to the physical ties already established, pleasure will be compounded.

Let us return to our narrative. The opening caresses and exploratory activities should last no more than a few minutes, barely a quarter of an hour. To break up the skirmish, use should be made of a divisive agent. Since everything is done by attraction in Harmony, mixed or homosexual attractions should be employed. Groups of Sapphists and Spartites [female and male homosexuals] should therefore be thrown into the fray to attack people of their own kind. Such people are easy to recognize in Harmony since everyone wears plumes or epaulettes designating his passions. These two new groups will create a general distraction and disunite a number of couples. At that point the senior confessors will have no difficulty in calling a halt to the skirmish, and everyone will proceed to the reconnoitering-room.

The reconnoitering-room contains two tiered and elevated stands. These stands face each other in such a way that anyone on one stand can get a good look at everyone on the other. All of the adventurers are placed on one side and all the sympathetic candidates on the other.

The actual matching is done by the matrons each of whom takes charge of five or six lovers . . . The matrons point out the various partners who have been designated for each individual. The individual has been given a list with precise information concerning the spiritual affinities and temporary inclinations of each of his potential partners. He is also able to determine their physical attraction since they are right before his eyes and since he has perhaps already gotten acquainted with them during the introductory bacchanalia . . .

When the inspection is over, everyone proceeds to the festival hall where the encounter takes place. The encounter is supervised by the fairies and genies whose tasks are much more delicate than those of the matrons. First of all there will be certain problems to resolve. A number of people may desire the same lover. A given priest may be desired by ten adventuresses and a given priestess by ten adventurers.

Such conflicting claims would be very troublesome in civilized gatherings . . . But anyone who has been in love several times knows that people often develop passionate spiritual sympathies for individuals who did not seem at all attractive to them at first. The whole point of the operations of the court of love is to determine these spiritual sympathies at the very outset in order to minimize competition for the most physically attractive individuals. Such competition leaves some people with throngs of admirers and leaves a great many other people in a state of abandonment.

In Harmony sheer physical attractiveness will not have the colossal influence that it has in civilization where everyone is transfixed by the sight of a beautiful woman. Of course the Harmonians will not fail to appreciate physical beauty; in fact their judgment will be considerably more discerning than ours. But when it comes to the selection of sympathetic partners their choices will not be determined by physical charm. For their desire for sensual gratification will be satisfied in several different ways.

First of all the adventurers will never fail to ask for an exhibition of simple nature, a session in which the amorous notabilities of the area, and of their own band, show off their most remarkable attributes. A woman who has only a beautiful bosom exhibits only the bosom and leaves the rest of her body, covered. Another who has only an attractive waist bares it and leaves the rest covered. Another who wishes to exhibit everything she has appears completely naked. Men do the same. No one can say after this session that he has been denied a chance to admire all the physical attractions of the region.

In addition to this exhibition of simple nature, the visitors will be able to organize orgies to be held the following day. At these orgies, which will be appropriately harmonized, everyone will have ample opportunity to derive satisfaction from the beauties displayed at the exhibition.

The physical needs of the adventurers are satisfied in this way at every Phalanx they visit. Given the human need for variety and contrast, the most pressing desire of the adventurers when they arrive at a new Phalanx will therefore be for spiritual sympathy rather than for mere physical gratification.

It should also be pointed out that if, at the end of a visit, an adventuress takes a fancy to a handsome priest with whom she has not made love, it will be possible for her to obtain satisfaction during the farewell session. Such gestures of traditional courtesy should not be refused to any member of a departing band.

As a result of these measures, no one will suffer from a lack of physical gratification. Thus the important problems to be dealt with at the court of love will concern the establishment of spiritual sympathies . . . The encounters which take place in the festival hall will be run in an alternating pattern. First of all the adventurers and adventuresses will be taken by their fairies to meet the priests and priestesses whom they have chosen as their most desirable sympathetic partners. Then the priests and priestesses will go to meet the adventurers whom they have selected. No final decisions will be made until everyone has had a chance to converse with all his or her candidates. Everyone must have a chance to present himself to those he desires and to inspect the information recorded on their escutcheons concerning their personalities, their habits, current caprices, most recent passions, and their need of alternating and contrasting pleasures.

Little by little, as alliances are established, the group will grow smaller. The first and most rapid matchings will be dictated by romantic inspiration or by pure sensuality. But these sudden alliances may well be compound sympathies since everyone has already had the opportunity to study his list and to scrutinize his potential partners . . . All those who are definitively matched up withdraw in order to permit the others to proceed with their encounters. Although it may be necessary for repeated enquiries to be made, this should be done without undue haste. Some alliances take a long time to form: preliminary discussions may go awry and a couple may only come to terms in the ballroom or even at supper. Such delays are commonplace among the more refined individuals.

Those who are the last to make up their minds do not run the risk of being left out or badly matched, for the fakirs may always intervene to satisfy them. But in general the tardy couples . . . get along particularly well because they have spent a long time flirting with each other. Moreover, if the sympathies which bind the tardy couples are somewhat lacking in intensity, their pleasures are always compound and never simple.

In all of these encounters great care is taken to avoid wounding anyone's pride. This is the particular responsibility of the fairies. Even when they are serving as protectors to just two individuals, they can make sure that no one's feelings are hurt. For if after a conversation one person wishes to refuse his or her suitor, the reason for the refusal is told only to the fairy who explains things to the rejected suitor with the utmost delicacy. The fairies abandon their protégés only when they are no longer needed, when two potential partners have established a sufficiently intimate relationship to reach an agreement of their own accord.

I have only described a single phase in the workings of the court of love. But it is already clear that in just two or three hours' time it can cement a host of happy alliances or compound sympathetic relationships of a sort that it takes months to establish in civilization. For it takes an extremely long time to understand the character of any civilized individual, and especially of a civilized woman.

The sympathetic intrigues which take place on the morning after the arrival of a group of visitors will be even more lively than those of the night before. For affairs which miscarried or failed to ripen will be renewed, and there will also be cases of infidelity to lend a touch of variety. The sympathetic relationships which endure will be particularly noteworthy in view of the fact that there will be many temptations to overcome. During a visit of three days almost all the adventurers and adventuresses will waver in their sympathies, finally returning to partners whom they barely got to know in the opening session. All this of course is quite independent of their participation in the orgies, the expositions of simple nature, the bacchanalias, etc. These material distractions are interludes in which both partners in a sympathetic relationship generally participate by mutual consent. They are moments of respite which do not destroy a relationship and which are not even considered to be acts of infidelity when they have been mutually agreed upon. Momentary respites of this sort are widely practised in Harmony not only by sympathetic partners but also by the most faithful lovers. For on special occasions such as the visit of a band of adventurers . . . there are so many temptations that even the most faithful are likely to succumb. In order to avoid losing the privileges of fidelity they agree to break off their relationship for a stipulated period in accordance with the provisions of the code of love . . .

It is evident that the task of arranging sympathetic relationships cannot be assumed by young people . . . Decisions must be made which can only be entrusted to elderly and experienced individuals.

Without their cooperation a band of visitors would be reduced to forming brutish relationships like the dirty and dangerous orgies of civilization in which partners are chosen uniquely on the basis of simple love and physical attraction . . .

Let us consider the benefits that the elderly will derive from their services as amorous intermediaries. The task will not be at all wearisome for them. A skilled and knowledgeable pontiff will take pride in his or her abilities as a match-maker . . . It will also be common for a traveler to become passionately attached to his confessoress. For apart from the fact that many individuals have an innate penchant for elderly people when they are agreeable, there will also be times when this penchant will be aroused by the methodical progression of sympathies. A skillful confessoress will manage to discern this need in the soul of her client and she will even try to call it forth. No one will be taken by surprise in such cases since, according to the custom of the court of love, the confessoress herself will be wearing medals or epaulettes indicating her own spiritual situation, her character, and her most recent impressions. Whenever the need for a sympathetic union between persons of divergent ages arises, it will be very much to the advantage of the confessors and confessoresses.

They say that no one does anything for nothing in this world; and if it is right for the elderly to assist the young in amorous affairs, it is just as right for them to be repaid for their services . . . I cannot repeat too often, however, that customs so alien to ours cannot be established during the first years of Harmony. It will first be necessary to purge the globe of syphilis and other skin diseases. Until this is accomplished, Harmony will be more circumspect about love than civilization now is.

Fourier believed that 'passionate attraction' ruled minerals, vegetables and the heavenly bodies, as well as human beings. Stars made love. Moreover, the creation of our world was only one of eighteen (or twenty-six) creations which, thanks to God's providence, would bring new and better animal and plant species. Climatic conditions would improve also. Grapes would grow in St Petersburg, oranges in Warsaw, and the northern seas would turn into 'a sort of lemonade'.

Source: *The Utopian Vision of Charles Fourier, Selected Texts on Work, Love, and Passionate Attraction*, translated, edited and with an introduction by Jonathan Beecher and Richard Bienvenu, Jonathan Cape, 1972.

Head-Bumps and Destiny

If our genes, together with our upbringing, determine our actions, can we be held responsible for anything we do? Should we be punished for our crimes, if they are the inevitable outcome of our nature and nurture? Is not 'crime', indeed, an outworn concept, since it implies responsibility and blame? These questions were being asked long before the era of modern genetics. John Trotter's comic utopia, *Travels in Phrenologasto* (1829), presents a country ruled by phrenologists. By examination of head-bumps they can predict a person's abilities and innate tendencies with scientific accuracy. At age sixteen all citizens have their heads shaved, and their bumps examined. White plaster is then applied, and each individual's phrenological configuration drawn in with black lines. After this, it is illegal to wear a hat, and so everyone's character can be seen at a glance. The system allows people to be allocated to jobs that exactly fit their abilities, with a great gain in efficiency and personal fulfilment.

Although character is regarded as fixed from the age of sixteen, children's characters, the Phrenologastons believe, can to some extent be modified, by education, manipulation of the head-bumps, and, occasionally, remedial brain surgery. This, and the consequences for Phrenologaston ideas of crime and punishment, are explained to the narrator (who has landed in Phrenologasto by air balloon) by one of the country's sages.

I made bold to ask him whether he believed that the evil dispositions of mankind were as much beyond their control as the good ones; and whether persons inclined to murder, cheat, betray, pillage, and oppress the rest of the world, must inevitably yield to these propensities? 'It may be admitted,' said the doctor, 'that the heads of infants and children may, in some degree, be fashioned by judicious applications; besides that, in adult cases, my friend Dr Squilini has lately favoured the public with a certain cephalic mixture, which I am told has great efficacy in that way. But when once the skull has taken a precise form, you may be assured, my good friend, you may as well endeavour to remove a stone fast frozen in the ice, as to alter any iota of its necessary propensities.'

'Then, sir, you must acknowledge that the gods who formed one man's head to robbery, murder, poison, assassination, cursing or blasphemy, are themselves guilty of all the crimes that person may commit.'

'Call them not crimes, signor: such a word, thank heaven, is now nearly unknown in this country, or at least is to be heard only in the mouths of the vulgar. Our philosophers have long ago cast off these servile and narrow-minded notions, which you unfortunately retain.'

The doctor goes on to explain that, though these antisocial activities are not called crimes, they are subject to financial penalties.

'Three hundred dollars is the established sum for high treason, two hundred for a murder, but one hundred and fifty for manslaughter; eighty-five is the sum for robbery on the highway; twenty for a pickpocket, and sixteen for a sheep-stealer. I will tell you in what manner these fines are levied. It is an invariable maxim among us, as you already know, that the skull after a certain age, by the induration of the *pia* and *dura mater* and the conjunction of the *ossa bregmatis et occipitis* with the *os eithmoides* or *cibriforme*, acquires a manageable form, in which the faculties of the mind are for ever afterwards fixed. All actions, therefore, perpetrated after that age, are to be attributed, not so much to ourselves, as to the preceptors of our youth, who having under their care the disposal of our heads before the above ossification takes place, are justly answerable for the result. If any person therefore commits for example a burglary (for which the fine is seventy dollars), the government in their wisdom, extending their views to the primary cause from which the evil has arisen, demand the sum, not from the person by whom the burglary is committed, but from those who had the education of him when a boy.'

Source: John Trotter, *Travels in Phrenologasto*, 1829.

Lotos-Eaters

Tennyson (1809–92) based his poem *The Lotos-Eaters* on a story in Homer's *Odyssey*, where Odysseus relates how, on the way home from the Trojan War, he and his men disembarked in 'the land of the Lotos-eaters, who eat a flowery food'. Those who tasted the 'honey-sweet fruit of the lotos' were overcome with dreamy forgetfulness, lost all desire to return home, and had to be dragged back to the ships weeping. Duty, responsibility and social conscience were the watchwords of Tennyson's readers, the Victorian middle class. His poem offers them an imagined escape, in the culturally acceptable disguise of classical legend.

'Courage!' he said, and pointed toward the land,
'This mounting wave will roll us shoreward soon.'
In the afternoon they came unto a land
In which it seemèd always afternoon.
All round the coast the languid air did swoon,
Breathing like one that hath a weary dream.
Full-faced above the valley stood the moon;
And like a downward smoke, the slender stream
Along the cliff to fall and pause and fall did seem.

A land of streams! some, like a downward smoke,
Slow-dropping veils of thinnest lawn, did go;
And some through wavering lights and shadows broke,
Rolling a slumbrous sheet of foam below.
They saw the gleaming river seaward flow
From the inner land: far off, three mountain-tops,
Three silent pinnacles of agèd snow,
Stood sunset-flushed: and, dewed with showery drops,
Up-clomb the shadowy pine above the woven copse.

The charmèd sunset lingered low adown
In the red West: through mountain clefts the dale
Was seen far inland, and the yellow down
Bordered with palm, and many a winding vale
And meadow, set with slender galingale;
A land where all things always seemed the same!
And round about the keel with faces pale,
Dark faces pale against that rosy flame,
The mild-eyed melancholy Lotos-eaters came.

Branches they bore of that enchanted stem,
Laden with flower and fruit, whereof they gave
To each, but whoso did receive of them,
And taste, to him the gushing of the wave
Far far away did seem to mourn and rave
On alien shores; and if his fellow spake,
His voice was thin, as voices from the grave;
And deep-asleep he seemed, yet all awake,
And music in his ears his beating heart did make.

They sat them down upon the yellow sand,
Between the sun and moon upon the shore;
And sweet it was to dream of Fatherland,
Of child, and wife, and slave; but evermore
Most weary seemed the sea, weary the oar,
Weary the wandering fields of barren foam.
Then someone said, 'We will return no more';
And all at once they sang, 'Our island home
Is far beyond the wave; we will no longer roam.'

CHORIC SONG

I

There is sweet music here that softer falls
Than petals from blown roses on the grass,
Or night-dews on still waters between walls
Of shadowy granite, in a gleaming pass;
Music that gentlier on the spirit lies,
Than tired eyelids upon tired eyes;
Music that brings sweet sleep down from the blissful skies.
Here are cool mosses deep,

[223]

And through the moss the ivies creep,
And in the stream the long-leaved flowers weep,
And from the craggy ledge the poppy hangs in sleep.

II

Why are we weighed upon with heaviness,
And utterly consumed with sharp distress,
While all things else have rest from weariness?
All things have rest: why should we toil alone,
We only toil, who are the first of things,
And make perpetual moan,
Still from one sorrow to another thrown:
Nor ever fold our wings,
And cease from wanderings,
Nor steep our brows in slumber's holy balm;
Nor harken what the inner spirit sings,
'There is no joy but calm!'
Why should we only toil, the roof and crown of things?

III

Lo! in the middle of the wood,
The folded leaf is wooed from out the bud
With winds upon the branch, and there
Grows green and broad, and takes no care,
Sun-steeped at noon, and in the moon
Nightly dew-fed; and turning yellow
Falls, and floats adown the air.
Lo! sweetened with the summer light,
The full-juiced apple, waxing over-mellow,
Drops in a silent autumn night.
All its allotted length of days,
The flower ripens in its place,
Ripens and fades, and falls, and hath no toil,
Fast-rooted in the fruitful soil.

IV

Hateful is the dark-blue sky,
Vaulted o'er the dark-blue sea.
Death is the end of life; ah, why
Should life all labour be?

Let us alone. Time driveth onward fast,
And in a little while our lips are dumb.
Let us alone. What is it that will last?
All things are taken from us, and become
Portions and parcels of the dreadful Past.
Let us alone. What pleasure can we have
To war with evil? Is there any peace
In ever climbing up the climbing wave?
All things have rest, and ripen toward the grave
In silence; ripen, fall and cease:
Give us long rest or death, dark death, or dreamful ease.

V

How sweet it were, hearing the downward stream,
With half-shut eyes ever to seem
Falling asleep in a half-dream!
To dream and dream, like yonder amber light,
Which will not leave the myrrh-bush on the height;
To hear each other's whispered speech;
Eating the Lotos day by day,
To watch the crisping ripples on the beach,
And tender curving lines of creamy spray;
To lend our hearts and spirits wholly
To the influence of mild-minded melancholy;
To muse and brood and live again in memory,
With those old faces of our infancy
Heaped over with a mound of grass,
Two handfuls of white dust, shut in an urn of brass!

VI

Dear is the memory of our wedded lives,
And dear the last embraces of our wives
And their warm tears: but all hath suffered change:
For surely now our household hearths are cold:
Our sons inherit us: our looks are strange:
And we should come like ghosts to trouble joy.
Or else the island princes over-bold
Have eat our substance, and the minstrel sings
Before them of the ten years' war in Troy,
And our great deeds, as half-forgotten things.

Is there confusion in the little isle?
Let what is broken so remain.
The Gods are hard to reconcile:
'Tis hard to settle order once again.
There *is* confusion worse than death,
Trouble on trouble, pain on pain,
Long labour unto agèd breath,
Sore task to hearts worn out by many wars
And eyes grown dim with gazing on the pilot-stars.

VII

But, propt on beds of amaranth and moly,
How sweet (while warm airs lull us, blowing lowly)
With half-dropt eyelid still,
Beneath a heaven dark and holy,
To watch the long bright river drawing slowly
His waters from the purple hill –
To hear the dewy echoes calling
From cave to cave through the thick-twinèd vine –
To watch the emerald-coloured water falling
Through many a woven acanthus-wreath divine!
Only to hear and see the far-off sparkling brine,
Only to hear were sweet, stretched out beneath the pine.

VIII

The Lotos blooms below the barren peak:
The Lotos blows by every winding creek:
All day the wind breathes low with mellower tone:
Through every hollow cave and alley lone
Round and round the spicy downs the yellow Lotos-dust is
blown.
We have had enough of action, and of motion we,
Rolled to starboard, rolled to larboard, when the surge was
seething free,
Where the wallowing monster spouted his foam-fountains in the
sea.
Let us swear an oath, and keep it with an equal mind,
In the hollow Lotos-land to live and lie reclined
On the hills like Gods together, careless of mankind.
For they lie beside their nectar, and the bolts are hurled

Far below them in the valleys, and the clouds are lightly curled
Round their golden houses, girdled with the gleaming world:
Where they smile in secret, looking over wasted lands,
Blight and famine, plague and earthquake, roaring deeps and
    fiery sands,
Clanging fights, and flaming towns, and sinking ships, and
    praying hands.
But they smile, they find a music centred in a doleful song
Steaming up, a lamentation and an ancient tale of wrong,
Like a tale of little meaning though the words are strong;
Chanted from an ill-used race of men that cleave the soil,
Sow the seed, and reap the harvest with enduring toil,
Storing yearly little dues of wheat, and wine and oil;
Till they perish and they suffer – some, 'tis whispered – down in
    hell
Suffer endless anguish, others in Elysian valleys dwell,
Resting weary limbs at last on beds of asphodel.
Surely, surely, slumber is more sweet than toil, the shore
Than labour in the deep mid-ocean, wind and wave and oar;
Oh rest ye, brother mariners, we will not wander more.

Source: Alfred, Lord Tennyson, *Poems*, 1832.

Plastic-Wood Paradise

In 1833 a German living in Pittsburgh, John Adolphus Etzler, published *A Paradise Within the Reach of All Men, Without Labor, By Powers of Nature and Machinery*. Printed in the same volume were letters addressed to Congress and to President Jackson, urging them to adopt his plan which would, he prophesied, transform the then wild and sparsely populated United States into a heaven-on-earth, attract millions of immigrants from Europe, and ensure America's 'unparalleled glory and dominion over the world'.

I promise to show the means for creating a paradise within ten years, where everything desirable for human life may be had for every man in superabundance, without labour, without pay; where the whole face of nature is changed into the most beautiful form of which it is capable; where man may live in the most magnificent palaces, in all imaginable refinements of luxury, in the most delightful gardens; where he may accomplish, without his labour, in one year, more than hitherto could be done in thousands of years; he may level mountains, sink valleys, create lakes, drain lakes and swamps, intersect everywhere the land with beautiful canals, with roads for transporting heavy loads of many thousand tons and for travelling 1,000 miles in 24 hours; he may cover the ocean with floating islands moveable in any desired direction with immense power and celerity, in perfect security and in all comfort and luxury, bearing gardens, palaces, with thousands of families, provided with rivulets of sweet water; he may explore the interior of the globe, travel from pole to pole in a fortnight; he may provide himself with means, unheard of yet, for increasing his knowledge of the world, and so his intelligence; he may lead a life of continual happiness, of enjoyments unknown yet; he may free himself from almost all the evils that afflict mankind, except death, and even put death far beyond the common period of human life, and finally render it less afflicting; mankind may thus live in and enjoy a new world, far superior to our present, and raise themselves to a far higher scale of beings.

What mankind must do, Etzler explained, to bring about this amazing transformation of life on earth was simply to harness the planet's cost-free energy sources – the wind, the waves, the tides and the sun. His pamphlet contains detailed mathematical calculations of the power that would accrue and (rather less detailed) descriptions of the machines needed to access and store it. He estimates, for example, that wind-power is potentially eighty thousand times greater than the combined muscle-power of the whole of mankind. All that is necessary to make it available is that every square mile of the earth's surface must be surrounded by a line of windmills two hundred feet high. Along the coastline an unbroken line of rafts, connected to the shore by beams, will convert the huge power-pulsations of the rising and falling of the tide and the waves for domestic use. The sun's rays, intensified by burning-glasses, will turn water to steam and operate enormous steam-engines.

Unlike modern advocates of natural energy, Etzler was not concerned to preserve the environment. Very much the contrary: he wanted to change it entirely. Mountains will be flattened, rivers will flow in vitrified channels, deserts will flower. Mankind will live in an immense sculpture-park, the greenery tastefully interspersed with porticoes, fountains and statues. America's large and monotonous forests will be 'ground to dust', and then 'cemented by a liquor', to provide a 'universal building material', rather like plastic wood. This may be moulded by machinery to any shape and, if required, vitrified, so that it will be virtually indestructible and will 'radiate with a crystal-like brilliancy'. The buildings, columns and statuary of the new world will all be machine-made from this 'vitrified substance'. They will be dazzling to look at and last for ever.

The greatest monuments and wonders known or left us to admire from our progenitors, which required many millions of hands, and many centuries to be finished, are nothing but childish, insignificant trifles, in comparison to the stupendous works that may be effected by these powers.

People will be housed in automated, centrally heated palaces, holding seven thousand inhabitants. Machines will meet every need. Each palace-dweller will be able to 'procure to himself all common articles of his daily wants by a short turn of some crank'. Even walking will be unnecessary. The palaces will be equipped with 'many thousand commodious and most elegant vehicles, in which persons may move up and down, like birds, in perfect security'. Poverty, and with it crime, will disappear, and there will be no need for taxation. Nor for slavery:

The slaves in your country will cease to be slaves without any effort, without any new law, without any loss to their masters; for the new mechanical means will supersede their employment: there will be no use for slaves any longer to any purpose; they will be of no value whatever to their masters; they will have no occasion for them. You may then easily dispose of this unfortunate race of men in the manner you please, send them to some distant part of the world, if you think proper; colonize them, make them as happy as they can be, and make some amends for the grievous wrongs they have suffered in this country. While you are sending away this race for their own benefit, you may fill your country with the most civilized and most intelligent part of the European population.

Though Etzler's schemes were abortive, his book may have had one unexpected positive outcome. The American author Henry David Thoreau read it (in its second edition) with deep disfavour. His notice of it (in the *Democratic Review*, December 1843) deplored its emphasis on 'gross comfort and pleasure' at the expense of the higher life. It seems to have set Thoreau thinking. Little more than a year later he built his wooden hut on the edge of Walden Pond, near Concord, and began the two-year retreat from materialism and the pressures of civilization described in his classic *Walden, or Life in the Woods* (1854).

Source: J. A. Etzler, *A Paradise Within the Reach of All Men, Without Labor, By Powers of Nature and Machinery. An Address to All Intelligent Men. In Two Parts*, second English edition, J. Cleave, 1842.

The Joys of Sameness

Etienne Cabet (1788–1856) was the son of a wine-barrel maker in Dijon. He became a lawyer, then a journalist and propagandist for workers' rights. He founded a workers' party and edited a republican newspaper, *Le Populaire*. In 1834 he was prosecuted for an anti-monarchist article, and exiled in England for five years. There, in the British Museum Reading Room, he carried out the research for his utopia, the *Voyage to Icaria* (1839). This described an ideal communist society, and was an immediate success. At the time the French working class was suffering extremes of hunger, poverty and unemployment. Cabet's book seemed to promise hope. Workers who could not afford a copy clubbed together to buy one. Societies of Icarian communists sprang up all over France, and particularly around Lyons, Vienne and Reims. Money was collected to establish an Icarian community in America, and on 3 February 1848 sixty-nine Icarians, singing an Icarian song, waved goodbye to their comrades on the quayside, en route for New Orleans. After a false start in Texas they settled at Nauvoo, Illinois, in an ex-Mormon colony. Cabet joined them, after playing an important part in the 1848 revolution in Paris. Inner strife weakened the colony, however, and it disintegrated. But other American Icarian communes replaced it, the last persisting until 1898.

Icaria is a land of symmetry, cleanliness and convenience. Streets are straight and wide, and cross at right angles. There are well-marked pedestrian crossings. Street-cars run every two minutes. Passengers wait at covered stops. Everything is fixed by law, from the plan of cities to the shape of hats. All Icarians must pursue a trade and work the same number of hours. Together they form 'a SOCIETY founded on the basis of the most perfect EQUALITY. All of them are *associates and citizens, having equal rights and duties.*' All land, property, produce of industry and natural resources belong to the People. All Icarians have the right to vote, and elect the two thousand deputies of the Popular Assembly. However, politics are not left to the deputies. Government is open. All citizens are expected to take an intelligent interest. 'Divided into 2000 communal assemblies the People takes part in the discussion of its laws, either after or before the deliberations of its Representatives. To ensure that the People is able to discuss with a perfect knowledge of the question, everything is carried out in the full light of Publicity, all the facts are recorded by a department of *statistics*, and everything is published in the popular *Journal* which is distributed to all citizens.'

In Cabet's novel, Icarian life is described by a young French painter, Eugene, who has left France after the July Revolution.

EUGENE'S LETTER TO HIS BROTHER

O my dear Camille, how broken-hearted I feel when I think of France and see the happiness enjoyed by the people of Icaria! You will be able to judge for yourself in learning of their institutions concerning FOOD and *clothes*.

Food

Concerning this first need of man, like all the others, everything in our unfortunate country is abandoned to chance and to monstrous abuses. Here, on the contrary, everything is regulated according to the most enlightened reason and the most generous care.

Imagine first, my dear brother, that everything concerning food has been regulated by the *law*. It is the law which accepts or rejects any type of nourishment.

A *committee* of scientists, set up by the national representatives, with the aid of all the citizens, has made a *list* of all known foods, indicating which are good and which are bad, and the respective qualities of each of them.

They have done more than that: among the good ones they have indicated which are necessary, useful and agreeable, and they have had this list printed in several volumes and each family possesses a copy.

They have done still more: they have indicated the most suitable ways of preparing each food, and each family has also a *Cookery Guide*.

Once the list of good foods had been agreed upon, the Republic undertook the task to have them produced by its agricultural labourers and workers, and distributed them to the families; and as none is able to get any food other than that which is distributed, you will realize that no one can eat anything which the Republic does not approve.

The Republic sees first that what is necessary is produced, then what is useful, and finally, in as great a measure as possible, what is agreeable.

The Republic gives an equal share to everybody, in such a manner that each citizen will receive the same quantity of certain food if there is enough for everyone, and that everyone will receive it in turn if there is only enough, each year or each day, for a section of the population.

Everyone has therefore an equal share of all foods without distinction, from those which we consider most plain to the most delicate: and the whole population of Icaria is nourished not only as well, but even better, than the richest people in other countries . . .

The Committee which I have mentioned before has also discussed and indicated the number of *meals*, the time at which they should be eaten, how long they should last, the number of courses, their nature and the order in which they should be served, varying them continuously, not only according to the seasons and the months but also according to the days, with the result that every meal of the week is different from the other.

At six o'clock in the morning, before they begin work, all the workers, that is to say all the citizens, eat a very simple breakfast in common at their workshops, prepared and served by the factory restaurant.

At nine o'clock, they have a luncheon in the workshop, while their wives and their children take theirs at home.

At two o'clock, all the inhabitants of the same street eat together, in their *republican restaurant*, a dinner prepared by one of the *caterers* of the Republic.

And every evening between nine and ten, each family has, in its own home, a supper prepared by the women of the household.

At all these meals, the first TOAST is *to the glory of the good Icar, benefactor of the workers*, BENEFACTOR OF THE FAMILIES, BENEFACTOR OF THE CITIZENS.

The supper consists mostly of fruits, cakes and sweets. But the *common dinner*, which is taken in superb halls elegantly decorated, and which contain from a thousand to two thousand people, surpasses by its magnificence anything you may be able to imagine. The best restaurants and cafés of Paris are nothing, in my opinion, compared with the restaurants of the Republic. You may not believe me when I tell you that, apart from the abundance and the delicacy of the meals, apart from the decorations with flowers and many other things, a delicious music charms the ear while the sense of smell enjoys delicious perfumes.

When the young people get married, they do not need to spend their dowry in a bad marriage feast and ruin in advance their future children; the dinners which the husband finds in the wife's restaurant, the wife in the husband's, and the two families in the home of each other, replace the most beautiful dinners of other countries.

And yet you must realize that these common meals present a great economy compared with separate meals and can therefore afford better fare.

You will also realize that this community of meals among workers and neighbours has other great advantages, particularly that of inducing the masses to fraternize and also to simplify the housework for women . . .

You may like to know how the *distribution* of the food is carried out: nothing is more simple: but again you must admire!

Distribution of Food

You know firstly that the Republic is the sole grower and producer of all food and that it gathers and stores it in its innumerable and immense storehouses.

You can easily imagine communal *cellars* like those of Paris and London, great storehouses for flour, bread, meat, fish, vegetables, fruit, etc.

Each republican storehouse has, like any of our bakers or butchers, the *list* of restaurants, workshops, schools, hospitals and families which it must supply, and the quantity which must be sent to each of them.

In the storehouse are to be found the employees, utensils, means of transport, and extremely ingenious instruments necessary to the distribution of food.

Everything having been *prepared in advance* in the storehouse, the provisions for the year, the month or the week and the daily provisions are delivered to the homes in the district served by the storehouse.

The distribution of these is organized in a charming way. I will not tell you of the perfect cleanliness which reigns everywhere as a matter of course, but I will not fail to tell you that each storehouse has a *basket*, a jug, a measure for each family marked with the number of its house and holding its provision of bread, milk, etc; and all these containers are *double*, so that when the full one has been delivered, the empty one can be brought back. Each house has, at its entrance, an *alcove* in which the delivery man finds the empty container and replaces it by a full one. In this way, the delivery, being always made at the same time, and announced by a particular sound, is carried out without disturbing the family and with no loss of time for the delivery man.

You can understand, my dear friend, what an economy of time and what advantages this system of mass distribution possesses.

Besides, everything is perfect in this happy country, inhabited by men who deserve the title of *men*, since, even in the smallest things they always make full use of that sublime reason which Providence has given them for their own happiness.

Clothes

As with food, so it is with the law which regulates everything connected with clothes. A committee has consulted everyone, has examined the clothes worn in every country, has made a *list* of them with their shapes and colours (a magnificent book which every family possesses), has indicated which should be adopted and which must be avoided, and has classified them according to their necessity, utility and pleasure.

Everything that was extravagant and tasteless, has been carefully banned ... not a single shoe or head-dress is manufactured without being first discussed and adopted according to a model-plan.

Everyone possesses the same clothes, so that there is no room either for envy or coquettishness. And yet one should not think that *uniformity* here is not without *variety*; for, on the contrary, it is in the clothes that variety combines most happily with the advantages of uniformity. Not only are the two sexes dressed differently, but each of them changes clothes frequently, according to age and condition, for the differences in clothes always indicate the circumstances and position of the person. Childhood and youth, adolescence and maturity, the condition of celibacy or marriage, or widowhood or re-marriage, the various professions and functions are all indicated by the clothes. All the individuals belonging to the same condition wear the same *uniform*; but a thousand various uniforms correspond to a thousand various conditions.

And the difference between these uniforms consists sometimes in the difference between materials and colours, sometimes in the shape or a distinctive sign.

Consider also that if the material and the shape is the same for all girls of the same age, the colour varies according to their tastes or their suitability, a certain colour being more fitting for blondes and another for brunettes.

Consider also that the same person has a simple and comfortable suit of clothes for *work* and another for the *home*, an elegant *drawing room* suit and another for *public meetings*, and a magnificent one for the *feasts* and *ceremonies*, all of them being different. In such a way the variety in costumes is almost infinite.

The shape of each garment has been fixed in such a manner that it can be manufactured in the most easy, rapid and economic way possible.

Practically all the clothes, hats and shoes are *elastic*, in such a way that they can suit people of different sizes.

They are nearly all done by *machine*, either entirely or in part, and the workers have little to do to finish them.

Nearly all clothes are made in four or five different sizes so that the workers never need to take measurements beforehand.

All the clothes are therefore manufactured in enormous quantities, like the materials, and often at the same time; they are afterwards deposited in immense storehouses where everyone is always sure to find immediately all the objects which he needs and which are due to him according to the law.

I have been talking to you of the *women*: O my dear Camille, how you would love these Icarians, you so courteous and so full of passion, as I am, for this master-piece of the Creator, if you saw how they surround women with attention, respect and homages, how they concentrate all their thoughts, their solicitude and their happiness upon them, how they constantly endeavour to please them and make them happy, how they do all they can to make them more beautiful, though they are already so beautiful naturally, in order to have more pleasure in adoring them! Happy women! Happy men! Happy Icaria! Unhappy France!

Icarian regimentation extends to imaginative and cultural life. All books and works of art must be approved by the republic before they can be published. Shortly after the communist revolution which established the present regime in Icaria all 'harmful' books were burned. So Icarians are protected from 'wrong ideas'. Censorship is presented as a matter of common sense:

The Republic should permit only certain persons to publish a work, just as it permits only pharmacists to prepare drugs ... Liberty is not the right to do anything indiscriminately; it consists only in doing that which does not harm other citizens, and certain songs can be moral poisons as fatal to society as physical poisons.

Oppressive and absurd as all this may sound to us, to the hungry workers of Cabet's France it had a very different ring, as we can tell from the fervour that Icarian ideals inspired in them. The following is a discourse by an Icarian silk-worker of Lyons, apprehended by the police in 1843.

Community! The true promised land where the human family will be able to rest after its hard work. There tears will no longer flow, the vultures will no longer drink our blood. Young men, you will know the joys of family life, you will love your wives, your mothers, your sisters, because misery will no longer come to destroy your noble sentiments. Young virgins will no longer put their virtue up for auction, for egotism and pauperism will no longer open houses of prostitution. Children, you will learn early in life to live as brothers; old men, we will respect you for your wisdom; women, we will render you all the respect you merit. Let us be the apostles of this new faith that will make this earth into a valley of pleasure, hope and love. For such a noble cause, let us pledge today to give all our efforts to advance its reign; if we are faithful to this pledge, our names will shine in posterity, as will those thousands of globes that we illuminate.

Source: Etienne Cabet, *Voyage to Icaria*, quotations taken from the translation in Marie Louise Berneri, *Journey Through Utopia*, Freedom Press, 1982; the Icarian silk-worker's testimony is from Christopher H. Johnson, *Utopian Communism in France. Cabet and the Icarians, 1839–1851*, Cornell University Press, 1974.

The Water Cure

Victorian reformers, faced with pestilential slums and swarms of illiterates, could be excused for believing that if only dirt and ignorance could be overcome, life might be perfect. Henry J. Forrest's *A Dream of Reform* (1848) is one of the most naïve expressions of this illusion. Set two hundred years in the future, it portrays a sparkling, sanitized, crime-free England. A high moral tone is everywhere apparent. Cheerful gentlefolk voluntarily limit their wealth. Healthy, happy artisans flock to public parks, libraries and art exhibitions. At six on a summer morning, all the young men are up playing cricket or reading philosophy. It is water that has brought all this about, as a complacent citizen named Mr Kindly explains, while showing the narrator round the house of a cleansed and grateful bootmaker.

'You will notice that all these houses are light, dry and airy,' observed Kindly to me, stepping out into the garden. 'Good sewers are also provided to carry off every impurity, which are well cleansed every evening by a plentiful supply of fresh water from the river; hard and soft water is also in great abundance, so that no excuse can be made for dirty habits, either in person or dwelling; although, as a general rule, if you supply people with plenty of pure water, they will not fail to make a profitable use of it. Water is the great purifier of everything; and to make a race of people healthy and happy, you must not fail to supply that element in profusion, rather than in a niggardly spirit. We have rivers, canals, ponds, baths, both open and under cover, for each sex, for all weathers, and of every description. We have hard and soft water available for each family, and at all times, so that there is no lack of that great regenerator in our community.'

'It is certainly a most powerful element for working much social comfort,' said I; 'and, as you wisely remark, cannot be too bountifully supplied to a nation.'

Source: Henry J. Forrest, *A Dream of Reform*, 1848.

[238]

The Noble Savage

Charles Dickens (1812–70) published this article in his periodical *Household Words* in June 1853. It was prompted by the performances of a troupe of Zulus, brought over to England by A. T. Caldecott, a merchant from Natal. Consisting of eleven men, one woman and a child, the troupe enacted scenes typical of Zulu daily life, and some Zulu dances, in St George's Gallery, Hyde Park Corner. Dickens was a resolute progressive, and scorned the idea, inherent in much eighteenth-century utopianism, that 'savage' life was superior to civilized. He also resented the fact that philanthropic concern for African natives or American Indians deflected attention from the plight of the poor in London's slums. George Catlin, to whom he refers, had exhibited a group of Ojubwa Indians in London in 1843–4, and had published *Letters on North American Indians* in 1842. The 'Bushmen' were first exhibited in 1847. Dickens's criticisms of Europe in the final paragraphs relate to money-marriages, Napoleon III (proclaimed Emperor of France in 1852), and the mid-Victorian craze for spiritualism and table-rappings.

To come to the point at once, I beg to say that I have not the least belief in the Noble Savage. I consider him a prodigious nuisance, and an enormous superstition. His calling rum fire-water, and me a pale face, wholly fail to reconcile me to him. I don't care what he calls me. I call him a savage, and I call a savage a something highly desirable to be civilized off the face of the earth. I think a mere gent (which I take to be the lowest form of civilization) better than a howling, whistling, clucking, stamping, jumping, tearing savage. It is all one to me, whether he sticks a fishbone through his visage, or bits of trees through the lobes of his ears, or birds' feathers in his head; whether he flattens his hair between two boards, or spreads his nose over the breadth of his face, or drags his lower lip down by great weights, or blackens his teeth, or knocks them out, or paints one cheek red and the other blue, or tattoos himself or oils himself, or rubs his body with fat, or crimps it with knives. Yielding to whichsoever of these agreeable eccentricities, he is a savage – cruel, false, thievish, murderous; addicted more or less to grease, entrails, and beastly customs; a wild animal with the questionable gift of boasting; a conceited, tiresome, bloodthirsty, monotonous humbug.

Yet it is extraordinary to observe how some people will talk about him, as they talk about the good old times; how they will regret his disappearance, in the course of this world's development, from such and such lands where his absence is a blessed relief and an indispens-able preparation for the sowing of the very first seeds of any influence that can exalt humanity; how, even with the evidence of himself before them, they will either be determined to believe, or will suffer themselves to be persuaded into believing, that he is something which their five senses tell them he is not.

There was Mr Catlin, some few years ago, with his Ojibbeway Indians. Mr Catlin was an energetic earnest man, who had lived among more tribes of Indians than I need reckon up here, and who had written a picturesque and glowing book about them. With his party of Indians squatting and spitting on the table before him, or dancing their miserable jigs after their own dreary manner, he called, in all good faith, upon his civilized audience to take notice of their symmetry and grace, their perfect limbs, and the exquisite expression of their pantomime; and his civilized audience, in all good faith, complied and admired. Whereas, as mere animals, they were wretched creatures, very low in the scale and very poorly formed; and as men and women possessing any power of truthful dramatic expression by means of action, they were no better than the chorus at an Italian Opera in England – and would have been worse if such a thing were possible.

Mine are no new views of the noble savage. The greatest writers on natural history found him out long ago. Buffon [Georges Buffon (1707–88), French naturalist] knew what he was, and showed why he is the sulky tyrant that he is to his women, and how it happens (Heaven be praised!) that his race is spare in numbers. For evidence of the quality of his moral nature, pass himself for a moment and refer to his 'faithful dog'. Has he ever improved a dog, or attached a dog, since his nobility first ran wild in woods, and was brought down (at a very long shot) by Pope [Alexander Pope (1688–1744), poet]? Or does the animal that is the friend of man, always degenerate in his low society?

It is not the miserable nature of the noble savage that is the new thing; it is the whimpering over him with maudlin admiration, and the affecting to regret him, and the drawing of any comparison of advantage between the blemishes of civilization and the tenor of his swinish life. There may have been a change now and then in those diseased absurdities, but there is none in him.

Think of the Bushmen. Think of the two men and the two women who have been exhibited about England for some years. Are the majority of persons – who remember the horrid little leader of that party in his festering bundle of hides, with his filth and his antipathy to water, and his straddled legs, and his odious eyes shaded by his brutal hand, and his cry of 'Qu-u-u-u-aaa!' (Bosjesman for something desperately insulting I have no doubt) – conscious of an affectionate yearning towards that noble savage, or is it idiosyncratic in me to abhor, detest, abominate, and abjure him? I have no reserve on this subject, and will frankly state that, setting aside that stage of the entertainment when he counterfeited the death of some creature he had shot, by laying his head on his hand and shaking his left leg – at which time I think it would have been justifiable homicide to slay him – I have never seen that group sleeping, smoking, and expectorating round their brazier, but I have sincerely desired that something might happen to the charcoal smouldering therein, which would cause the immediate suffocation of the whole of the noble strangers.

There is at present a party of Zulu Kaffirs exhibiting at the St George's Gallery, Hyde Park Corner, London. These noble savages are represented in a most agreeable manner; they are seen in an elegant theatre, fitted with appropriate scenery of great beauty, and they are described in a very sensible and unpretending lecture, delivered with a modesty which is quite a pattern to all similar exponents. Though extremely ugly, they are much better shaped than such of their predecessors as I have referred to; and they are rather picturesque to the eye, though far from odoriferous to the nose. What a visitor left to his own interpretings and imaginings might suppose these noblemen to be about, when they give vent to that pantomimic expression which is quite settled to be the natural gift of the noble savage, I cannot possibly conceive; for it is so much too luminous for my personal civilization that it conveys no idea to my mind beyond a general stamping, ramping, and raving, remarkable (as everything in savage life is) for its dire uniformity. But let us – with the interpreter's assistance, of which I for one stand so much in need – see what the noble savage does in Zulu Kaffirland.

The noble savage sets a king to reign over him, to whom he submits his life and limbs without a murmur or question, and whose whole life is passed chin deep in a lake of blood; but who, after killing incessantly, is in his turn killed by his relations and friends, the moment a grey hair appears on his head. All the noble savage's wars with his fellow-savages (and he takes no pleasure in anything else) are wars of extermination – which is the best thing I know of him, and the most comfortable to my mind when I look at him. He has no moral feelings of any kind, sort, or description; and his 'mission' may be summed up as simply diabolical.

The ceremonies with which he faintly diversifies his life are, of course, of a kindred nature. If he wants a wife he appears before the kennel of the gentleman whom he has selected for his father-in-law, attended by a party of male friends of a very strong flavour, who screech and whistle and stamp an offer of so many cows for the young lady's hand. The chosen father-in-law – also supported by a high-flavoured party of male friends – screeches, whistles, and yells (being seated on the ground, he can't stamp) that there never was such a daughter in the market as his daughter, and that he must have six more cows. The son-in-law and his select circle of backers, screech, whistle, stamp, and yell in reply, that they will give three more cows. The father-in-law (an old deluder, overpaid at the beginning) accepts four, and rises to bind the bargain. The whole party, the young lady included, then falling into epileptic convulsions, and screeching, whistling, stamping, and yelling together – and nobody taking any notice of the young lady (whose charms are not to be thought of without a shudder) – the noble savage is considered married, and his friends make demoniacal leaps at him by way of congratulation.

When the noble savage finds himself a little unwell, and mentions the circumstance to his friends, it is immediately perceived that he is under the influence of witchcraft. A learned personage, called an Imyanger or Witch Doctor, is immediately sent for to Nooker the Umtargartie, or smell out the witch. The male inhabitants of the kraal being seated on the ground, the learned doctor, got up like a grizzly bear, appears, and administers a dance of a most terrific nature, during the exhibition of which remedy he incessantly gnashes his teeth, and howls: 'I am the original physician to Nooker the Umtargartie. Yow yow yow! No connexion with any other establishment. Till till till! All other Umtargarties are feigned Umtargarties, Boroo Boroo! but I perceive here a genuine and real Umtargartie, Hoosh Hoosh Hoosh! in whose blood I, the original Imyanger and Nookerer, Blizzerum Boo! will wash these bear's claws of mine. O yow yow yow!' All this time the learned physician is looking out among the attentive faces for some unfortunate man who owes him a cow, or who has given him any small offence, or against whom, without offence, he has conceived a spite. Him he never fails to Nooker as the Umtargartie, and he is instantly killed. In the absence of such an individual, the usual practice is to Nooker the quietest and most gentlemanly person in company. But the nookering is invariably followed on the spot by the butchering.

Some of the noble savages in whom Mr Catlin was so strongly interested, and the diminution of whose numbers, by rum and smallpox, greatly affected him, had a custom not unlike this, though much more appalling and disgusting in its odious details.

The women being at work in the fields hoeing the Indian corn, and the noble savage being asleep in the shade, the chief has sometimes the condescension to come forth and lighten the labour by looking at it. On these occasions he seats himself in his own savage chair, and is attended by his shield-bearer: who holds over his head a shield of cowhide – in shape like an immense mussel shell – fearfully and wonderfully, after the manner of a theatrical supernumerary. But lest the great man should forget his greatness in the contemplation of the humble works of agriculture, there suddenly rushes in a poet, retained for the purpose, called a Praiser. This literary gentleman wears a leopard's head over his own, and a dress of tigers' tails; he has the appearance of having come express on his hind legs from the Zoological Gardens; and he incontinently strikes up the chief's praises, plunging and tearing all the while. There is a frantic wickedness in this brute's manner of worrying the air, and gnashing out 'Oh what a delightful chief he is! O what a delicious quantity of blood he sheds! O how majestically he laps it up! O how charmingly cruel he is! O how he tears the flesh of his enemies and crunches the bones! O how like the tiger and the leopard and the wolf and the bear he is! O, row row row row, how fond I am of him!' – which might tempt the Society of Friends to charge at a hand-gallop into the Swartz-Kop location and exterminate the whole kraal.

When war is afoot among the noble savages – which is always – the chief holds a council to ascertain whether it is the opinion of his brothers and friends in general that the enemy shall be exterminated. On this occasion, after the performance of an Umsebeuza, or war song, – which is exactly like all the other songs – the chief makes a speech to his brothers and friends, arranged in single file. No particular order is observed during the delivery of this address, but every gentleman who finds himself excited by the subject, instead of crying 'Hear, hear!' as is the custom with us, darts from the rank and tramples out the life, or crushes the skull, or mashes the face, or scoops out the eyes, or breaks the limbs, or performs a whirlwind of atrocities on the body, of an imaginary enemy. Several gentlemen becoming thus excited at once, and pounding away without the least regard to the orator, that illustrious person is rather in the position of an orator in an Irish House of Commons. But, several of these scenes of savage life bear a strong generic resemblance to an Irish election, and I think would be extremely well received and understood at Cork.

In all these ceremonies the noble savage holds forth to the utmost possible extent about himself; from which (to turn him to some civilized account) we may learn, I think, that as Egotism is one of the most offensive and contemptible littlenesses a civilized man can exhibit, so it is really incompatible with the interchange of ideas; inasmuch as if we all talked about ourselves we should soon have no listeners, and must be all yelling and screeching at once on our own separate accounts: making society hideous. It is my opinion that if we retained in us anything of the noble savage, we could not get rid of it too soon. But the fact is clearly otherwise. Upon the wife and dowry question, substituting coin for cows, we have assuredly nothing of the Zulu Kaffir left. The endurance of despotism is one great distinguishing mark of a savage always. The improving world has quite got the better of that too. In like manner, Paris is a civilized city, and the Théâtre Français a highly civilized theatre; and we shall never hear, and never have heard in these later days (of course) of the Praiser *there*. No, no, civilized poets have better work to do. As to Nookering Umtargarties, there are no pretended Umtargarties in Europe, and no European Powers to Nooker them; that would be mere spydom, subornation, small malice, superstition, and false pretence. And as to private Umtargarties, are we not in the year eighteen hundred and fifty-three, with spirits rapping at our doors?

To conclude as I began. My position is, that if we have anything to learn from the Noble Savage, it is what to avoid. His virtues are a fable; his happiness is a delusion; his nobility, nonsense. We have no greater justification for being cruel to the miserable object, than for being cruel to a William Shakespeare or an Isaac Newton; but he passes away before an immeasurably better and higher power than ever ran wild in any earthly woods, and the world will be all the better when his place knows him no more.

Source: Charles Dickens, 'The Noble Savage', *Household Words*, 11 June 1853.

The Really Precious Things

John Ruskin (1819–1900) was not only England's greatest art critic, he was also a radical social thinker, vastly learned and fearlessly outspoken, who played a major part in shaping Victorian culture, and, consequently, in inaugurating the modern world. He championed Christian social values and bitterly denounced greed, self-interest and reductive scientism. The following extract is from the third volume of *Modern Painters* (1856).

The great mechanical impulses of the age, of which most of us are so proud, are a mere passing fever, half-speculative, half-childish. People will discover at last that royal roads to anything can no more be laid in iron than they can in dust; that there are, in fact, no royal roads to anywhere worth going to; that if there were, it would that instant cease to be worth going to – I mean, so far as the things to be obtained are in any way estimable in terms of *price*. For there are two classes of precious things in the world: those that God gives us for nothing – sun, air, and life (both mortal life and immortal); and the secondarily precious things which He gives us for a price: these secondarily precious things, worldly wine and milk, can only be bought for definite money; they never can be cheapened. No cheating nor bargaining will ever get a single thing out of nature's 'establishment' at half-price. Do we want to be strong? – we must work. To be hungry? – we must starve. To be happy? – we must be kind. To be wise? – we must look and think. No changing of place at a hundred miles an hour, nor making of stuffs a thousand yards a minute, will make us one whit stronger, happier, or wiser. There was always more in the world than men could see, walked they ever so slowly; they will see it no better for going fast. And they will at last, and soon too, find out that their grand inventions for conquering (as they think) space and time, do, in reality, conquer nothing; for space and time are, in their own essence, unconquerable, and besides did not

want any sort of conquering; they wanted *using*. A fool always wants
to shorten space and time: a wise man wants to lengthen both. A
fool wants to kill space and kill time: a wise man, first to gain them,
then to animate them. Your railroad, when you come to understand
it, is only a device for making the world smaller: and as for being
able to talk from place to place, that is, indeed, well and convenient;
but suppose you have, originally, nothing to say. We shall be obliged
at last to confess, what we should long ago have known, that the
really precious things are thought and sight, not pace. It does a bullet
no good to go fast; and a man, if he be truly a man, no harm to go
slow; for his glory is not at all in going, but in being.

'Well; but railroads and telegraphs are so useful for communicating
knowledge to savage nations.' Yes, if you have any to give them. If
you know nothing *but* railroads, and can communicate nothing but
aqueous vapour and gunpowder – what then? But if you have any
other thing than those to give, then the railroad is of use only because
it communicates that other thing; and the question is – what that
other thing may be. Is it religion? I believe if we had really wanted
to communicate that, we could have done it in less than 1,800 years,
without steam. Most of the good religious communication that I
remember, has been done on foot; and it cannot be easily done faster
than at foot pace. Is it science? But what science – of motion, meat,
and medicine? Well; when you have moved your savage, and dressed
your savage, fed him with white bread, and shown him how to set
a limb – what next? Follow out that question. Suppose every obstacle
overcome; give your savage every advantage of civilization to the
full; suppose that you have put the Red Indian in tight shoes; taught
the Chinese how to make Wedgwood's ware, and to paint it with
colours that will rub off; and persuaded all Hindoo women that it is
more pious to torment their husbands into graves than to burn
themselves at the burial – what next? Gradually, thinking on from
point to point, we shall come to perceive that all true happiness and
nobleness are near us, and yet neglected by us; and that till we have
learned how to be happy and noble we have not much to tell,
even to Red Indians. The delights of horse-racing and hunting, of
assemblies in the night instead of the day, of costly and wearisome
music, of costly and burdensome dress, of chagrined contention for
place or power, or wealth, or the eyes of the multitude; and all the
endless occupation without purpose, and idleness without rest, of

our vulgar world, are not, it seems to me, enjoyments we need be ambitious to communicate. And all real and wholesome enjoyments possible to man have been just as possible to him, since first he was made of the earth, as they are now; and they are possible to him chiefly in peace. To watch the corn grow, and the blossoms set; to draw hard breath over ploughshare or spade; to read, to think, to love, to hope, to pray – these are the things that make men happy; they have always had the power of doing these, they never *will* have power to do more. The world's prosperity or adversity depends upon our knowing and teaching these few things: but upon iron, or glass, or electricity, or steam, in no wise.

And I am Utopian and enthusiastic enough to believe, that the time will come when the world will discover this.

Source: *The Works of John Ruskin*, edited by E. T. Cook and Alexander Wedderburn, George Allen, 1903–12.

A New Nation

The Battle of Gettysburg, between a Southern army under Lee and a Northern under Meade, was fought on 1–3 July 1863. On 19 November, with the American Civil War still raging, President Abraham Lincoln (1809–65) delivered an address at a ceremony to dedicate the cemetery at Gettysburg in which those slain in the battle would be laid to rest. His address was preceded by a two-hour oration by Edward Everett, ex-Professor of Greek and President of Harvard, advance copies of which had been sent to the press. On reading one Lincoln told a friend that his own contribution would be 'short, short, short'. Its brevity surprised the audience, and it was widely considered a failure. The London *Times* reported that 'The ceremony was rendered ludicrous by some of the sallies of that poor President Lincoln . . . Anything more dull and commonplace, it would not be easy to produce.' According to the *Chicago Times*, 'The cheek of every American must tingle with shame as he reads the silly, flat and dish-watery utterance of the man who has to be pointed out to intelligent foreigners as the President of the United States.' Since then, Lincoln's Gettysburg Address has come to be acknowledged as one of the supreme masterpieces of modern oratory. Of its 260 words, it has been noted that 190 are of one syllable.

Four score and seven years ago our fathers brought forth on this continent, a new nation, conceived in Liberty, and dedicated to the proposition that all men are created equal.

Now we are engaged in a great civil war, testing whether that nation, or any nation so conceived and so dedicated, can long endure. We are met on a great battle-field of that war. We have come to dedicate a portion of that field, as a final resting place for those who here gave their lives that that nation might live. It is altogether fitting and proper that we should do this.

But, in a larger sense, we can not dedicate – we can not consecrate – we can not hallow – this ground. The brave men, living and dead, who struggled here, have consecrated it, far above our poor power to add or detract. The world will little note, nor long remember what we say here, but it can never forget what they did here. It is for us the living, rather, to be dedicated here to the unfinished work which they who fought here have thus far so nobly advanced. It is rather for us to be here dedicated to the great task remaining before us – that from these honored dead we take increased devotion to that cause for which they gave the last full measure of devotion – that we here highly resolve that these dead shall not have died in vain – that this nation, under God, shall have a new birth of freedom – and that government of the people, by the people, for the people, shall not perish from the earth.

Source: *Three Lincoln Masterpieces*, edited by Benjamin Barondess, Education Foundation of West Virginia, 1954.

To a Nunnery

Monasticism offers a utopia that combines asceticism (purification of the body) with mysticism (elevation of the mind). It was not a Christian invention. Highly organized monasticism existed in India before the Christian era. Among the Jews, the Essenes in Judaea lived a monastic life. Christian monasticism began with St Anthony in the Egyptian desert in the fourth century. But it was St Benedict (c.500) who introduced the idea of a community bound together for life and obeying rules. In the early Middle Ages, the Benedictine houses were the chief civilizing and educating institutions in Europe. There seem to have been convents for women even earlier than for men. By the end of the fourth century nunneries had spread all over Egypt and to Italy and Africa.

The English poet Gerard Manley Hopkins (1844–89) converted to Roman Catholicism in 1866 and became a Jesuit. He was subject to intense depression, partly through a sense of his own failings as priest and preacher, partly perhaps because of his unacknowledged homosexuality. His most famous poem, *The Wreck of the Deutschland* (rejected by the Jesuit journal *The Month* as too difficult), was about four Franciscan nuns, exiled from Germany by religious laws, and drowned when their ship carrying emigrants to America sank in the mouth of the Thames. His brief poem 'Heaven-Haven', subtitled 'A nun takes the veil', is a supreme expression of the attraction of the monastic ideal. It was written two years before Hopkins became a Catholic.

> I have desired to go
>   Where springs not fail,
> To fields where flies no sharp and sided hail
>   And a few lilies blow.
>
> And I have asked to be
>   Where no storms come,

Where the green swell is in the havens dumb,
And out of the swing of the sea.

Source: *Poems of Gerard Manley Hopkins*, edited by Robert Bridges, Oxford University Press, 1918.

Almost Human

Edward Lear (1812–88) was the cause of laughter in others. But he was sad and lonely himself. The youngest of twenty children, many of whom died young, he was rejected by his mother, and brought up by his sister Ann. When he was four, financial disaster struck the family, and they had to leave their grand house. But Lear's greatest affliction was epilepsy – which he called 'the Demon'. He had his first seizure when he was five or six. The attacks were often violent and frightening, and sometimes recurred several times a day. There was no clinical treatment, and the condition was considered obscurely shameful. It was believed to be brought on by masturbation. Lear himself evidently credited this, and it added guilt to his shame. No one outside the family was ever told of his illness, and the secrecy compounded Lear's loneliness. He yearned for marriage and children, but regarded his epilepsy as an insurmountable obstacle, since his children might inherit the disease. Lear's biographer Vivien Noakes quotes him in 1879, bidding farewell to a family of visitors, and 'wishing as I left them that I had sons or daughters. But it was decreed I was not to be human.' Latent homosexuality was probably another factor in his feeling of isolation, particularly as his men friends tended to find wives. 'Every marriage of people I care about rather seems to leave me on the bleak shore alone,' he wrote. When he was fifty-four he thought of proposing to the much younger daughter of a friend. It seemed, he admitted, an 'intangible myth', yet not to make the attempt 'is to resolve on all the rest of life being passed thus – alone – & year by year getting more weary'. But he seems to have decided that telling her about his epilepsy would be too distressing.

The urge to escape from himself made him a compulsive traveller. He wandered far from the tourist trail through the Mediterranean, Egypt, the Near East, India and Ceylon – painting and sketching as he went and writing brilliantly vivid travel diaries. In the 1860s he fell in love with the island of Corfu – then rarely visited – which he described in his diary as an earthly paradise.

As I lie now, green & flowers everywhere – this is Lotus-eating with a vengeance! – 2 p.m. Lovelier ever! a regular intoxication of beauty! Walked up towards the hill church, & down, down, where terraces of close green sward with large patches of bright yell[ow] gr[een] fern, and sheets of blooming rosy & white asters spread away. Myrtle also. Over head ever the loved olive: far below 'bowery hollows' of green – ever & ever retreating: spotless blue above: glimpses of darker blue sea, & pearly radiant mountain through the transparent foliage. No wonder the olive is undrawn – unknown: so inaccessible = poetical = difficult are its belongings. So bright & glorious is all I now see & feel, it seems to overpay any outlay of pain – time – money! Can I give *no* idea of this Paradise island to others?

Lear did give an 'idea' of Corfu in his paintings. But his nonsense writing reflects even more deeply his aching awareness of beauty, his wistfulness, his longing and isolation. The Dong with the Luminous Nose, who is left on the cruel shore, 'Gazing – gazing for evermore' after the beautiful Jumbly girl with her sky-blue hands and her sea-green hair, or the fortunate Owl and Pussy Cat, replete with mince and quince, happily married and dancing by the light of the moon – these creatures are only too easily recognizable as facets of Lear's hope and despair. The nonsense-language makes them funny, and so offers a way of coping with the sadness. But it also intensifies the pathos. For it reaches beyond ordinary language to a region of unutterable poignancy, a sorrow beyond speaking. Lear himself would break down and weep when reciting the nonsense poems.

'The Jumblies', first published in Lear's *Nonsense Songs* (1870), has several of the regular features of a utopia – the perilous voyage, the land of plenty, an improvement in health and stature ('How tall they've grown!'), a return to the old world. It is also a poem about not taking 'good advice'. The Jumblies ignore the busybodies who foretell disaster. Noakes reads it as rejecting narrowness of outlook, whether imposed by religious dogma or false social conventions. You must dare to be true to your own humanity with all its oddities and faults. Perhaps Lear was thinking of homosexuality as well as epilepsy.

I

They went to sea in a Sieve, they did,
   In a Sieve they went to sea:
In spite of all their friends could say,
On a winter's morn, on a stormy day,
   In a Sieve they went to sea!
And when the Sieve turned round and round,

And every one cried, 'You'll all be drowned!'
They called aloud, 'Our Sieve ain't big,
But we don't care a button! we don't care a fig!
    In a Sieve we'll go to sea!'
        Far and few, far and few,
            Are the lands where the Jumblies live;
        Their heads are green, and their hands are blue,
            And they went to sea in a Sieve.

II

They sailed away in a Sieve, they did,
    In a Sieve they sailed so fast,
With only a beautiful pea-green veil
Tied with a riband by way of a sail,
    To a small tobacco-pipe mast;
And every one said, who saw them go,
'O won't they be soon upset, you know!
For the sky is dark, and the voyage is long,
And happen what may, it's extremely wrong
    In a Sieve to sail so fast!'
        Far and few, far and few,
            Are the lands where the Jumblies live;
        Their heads are green, and their hands are blue,
            And they went to sea in a Sieve.

III

The water it soon came in, it did,
    The water it soon came in;
So to keep them dry, they wrapped their feet
In a pinky paper all folded neat,
    And they fastened it down with a pin.
And they passed the night in a crockery-jar,
And each of them said, 'How wise we are!
Though the sky be dark, and the voyage be long,
Yet we never can think we were rash or wrong,
    While round in our Sieve we spin!'
        Far and few, far and few,
            Are the lands where the Jumblies live;
        Their heads are green, and their hands are blue,
            And they went to sea in a Sieve.

[255]

IV

And all night long they sailed away;
  And when the sun went down,
They whistled and warbled a moony song
To the echoing sound of a coppery gong,
  In the shade of the mountains brown.
'O Timballo! How happy we are,
When we live in a sieve and a crockery-jar,
And all night long in the moonlight pale,
We sail away with a pea-green sail,
  In the shade of the mountains brown!'
    Far and few, far and few,
      Are the lands where the Jumblies live;
    Their heads are green, and their hands are blue,
    And they went to sea in a Sieve.

V

They sailed to the Western Sea, they did,
  To a land all covered with trees,
And they bought an Owl, and a useful Cart,
And a pound of Rice, and a Cranberry Tart,
  And a hive of silvery Bees.
And they bought a Pig, and some green Jack-daws,
And a lovely Monkey with lollipop paws,
And forty bottles of Ring-Bo-Ree,
  And no end of Stilton Cheese.
    Far and few, far and few,
      Are the lands where the Jumblies live;
    Their heads are green, and their hands are blue,
    And they went to sea in a Sieve.

VI

And in twenty years they all came back,
  In twenty years or more,
And every one said, 'How tall they've grown!
For they've been to the Lakes, and the Torrible Zone,
  And the hills of the Chankly Bore';
And they drank their health, and gave them a feast
Of dumplings made of beautiful yeast;
And every one said, 'If we only live,

We too will go to sea in a Sieve –
To the hills of the Chankly Bore!'
Far and few, far and few,
Are the lands where the Jumblies live;
Their heads are green, and their hands are blue,
And they went to sea in a Sieve.

Source: Edward Lear, 'The Jumblies', from *Nonsense Songs, Stories, Botany and Alphabets*, 1870; Lear's diary quoted from Vivien Noakes, *Edward Lear*, William Collins, 1968.

Vril, Father of Bovril

The Coming Race (1871), by Edward Bulwer Lytton (1803–73), describes an advanced species, the Vril-ya, who live deep beneath the surface of the earth. They are larger and more intelligent than humans, and have serene, awesome faces. Their supremacy over other underground races (whom, if opposed, they ruthlessly exterminate) is due to their discovery and development of an 'all-permeating fluid' they call vril – which combines the properties of electricity, death-rays, antibiotics, Intercontinental Ballistic Missiles, and much more. It powers the automata that do all mechanical tasks for the Vril-ya, and fuels both their large-scale 'air-boats' and the convenient inflatable wings, attached to a metal harness, which allow individual Vril-ya to fly and play aerobatic games. Vril also enables adepts to see into and control other minds. More mundanely, it heats Turkish baths and provides the ceaseless piped music and perfumed air-conditioning that are accounted amenities of Vril-ya life. Generally females (called *Gy-ei* in Vril-ya language) are better at manipulating vril than males, being more sensitive. They are also taller, stronger and better at abstract thought, and dominate the shy, weak males much as men do women on earth. The novel's narrator, who finds himself among the Vril-ya after losing his way down a mineshaft, learns their history and witnesses vril's operations.

According to the account I received from Zee, who, as an erudite professor in the College of Sages, had studied such matters more diligently than any other member of my host's family, this fluid is capable of being raised and disciplined into the mightiest agency over all forms of matter, animate or inanimate. It can destroy like the flash of lightning; yet, differently applied, it can replenish or invigorate life, heal, and preserve, and on it they chiefly rely for the cure of disease, or rather for enabling the physical organization to re-establish the due equilibrium of its natural powers, and thereby to cure itself. By this agency they rend way through the most solid substances, and open valleys for culture through the rocks of their subterranean wilderness. From it they extract the light which supplies their lamps, finding it steadier, softer, and healthier then the other inflammable materials they had formerly used.

But the effects of the alleged discovery of the means to direct the more terrible force of vril were chiefly remarkable in their influence upon social polity. As these effects became familiarly known and skilfully administered, war between the vril-discoverers ceased, for they brought the art of destruction to such perfection as to annul all superiority in numbers, discipline, or military skill. The fire lodged in the hollow of a rod directed by the hand of a child could shatter the strongest fortress, or cleave its burning way from the van to the rear of an embattled host . . .

I have spoken so much of the Vril Staff that my reader may expect me to describe it. This I cannot do accurately, for I was never allowed to handle it for fear of some terrible accident occasioned by my ignorance of its use; and I have no doubt that it requires much skill and practice in the exercise of its various powers. It is hollow, and has in the handle several stops, keys, or springs by which its force can be altered, modified, or directed – so that by one process it destroys, by another it heals – by one it can rend the rock, by another disperse the vapour – by one it affects bodies, by another it can exercise a certain influence over minds. It is usually carried in the convenient size of a walking-staff, but it has slides by which it can be lengthened or shortened at will. When used for special purposes, the upper part rests in the hollow of the palm with the fore and middle fingers protruded. I was assured, however, that its power was not equal in all, but proportioned to the amount of certain vril properties in the wearer in affinity, or *rapport* with the purposes to be effected. Some were more potent to destroy, others to heal, &c.; much also depended on the calm and steadiness of volition in the manipulator. They assert that the full exercise of vril power can only be acquired by constitutional temperament – i.e. by hereditarily transmitted organization – and that a female infant of four years old belonging to the Vril-ya races can accomplish feats with the wand placed for the first time in her hand, which a life spent in its practice would not enable the strongest and most skilled mechanician, born out of the pale of the Vril-ya, to achieve. All these wands are not equally complicated; those entrusted to children are much simpler than those borne by sages of either sex, and constructed with a view to the special object in which the children are employed; which, as I have before said, is among the youngest children the most destructive [in Fourier-ist fashion (see p. 208) the Vril-ya entrust all destructive tasks, such as killing wild animals, to children, on the grounds that they enjoy them most]. In the wands of wives and mothers the correlative destroying force is usually abstracted, the healing power fully charged. I wish I could say more in detail of this singular conductor of the vril fluid, but its machinery is as exquisite as its effects are marvellous.

I should say, however, that this people have invented certain tubes by which the vril fluid can be conducted towards the object it is meant to destroy, throughout a distance almost indefinite; at least I put it modestly when I say from 500 to 600 miles. And their mathematical science as applied to such purpose is so nicely accurate, that on the report of some observer in an air-boat, any member of the vril department can estimate unerringly the nature of intervening obstacles, the height to which the projectile instrument should be raised, and the extent to which it should be charged, so as to reduce to ashes within a space of time too short for me to venture to specify it, a capital twice as vast as London.

I went with my host and his daughter Zee over the great public museum, which occupies a wing in the College of Sages, and in which are hoarded, as curious specimens of the ignorant and blundering experiments of ancient times, many contrivances on which we pride ourselves as recent achievements . . . This young Gy [female] was a magnificent specimen of the muscular force to which the females of her country attain. Her features were beautiful, like those of all her race: never in the upper world have I seen a face so grand and so faultless; but her devotion to the severer studies had given to her countenance an expression of abstract thought which rendered it somewhat stern when in repose; and such sternness became formidable when observed in connexion with her ample shoulders and lofty stature. She was tall even for a Gy, and I saw her lift up a cannon as easily as I could lift a pocket-pistol. Zee inspired me with a profound terror – a terror which increased when we came into a department of the museum appropriated to models of contrivances worked by the agency of vril; for here, merely by a certain play of her vril staff, she herself standing at a distance, she put into movement large and weighty substances. She seemed to endow them with intelligence, and to make them comprehend and obey her command. She set complicated pieces of machinery into movement, arrested the movement or continued it, until, within an incredibly short time, various kinds of raw material were reproduced as symmetrical works of art, complete and perfect. Whatever effect mesmerism or electro-biology produces over the nerves and muscles of animated objects, this young Gy produced by the motions of her slender rod over the springs and wheels of lifeless mechanism.

The Vril-ya believe that they are destined to return to the upper world and 'supplant all the inferior races now existing therein' – hence the title of Bulwer Lytton's novel.

The proprietary name of J. Lawson Johnston's concentrated essence of beef, Bovril, invented in 1889, combined vril with *bos*, Latin for ox.

Source: Edward Bulwer Lytton, *The Coming Race*, William Blackwood, 1871.

Sick Criminals

Samuel Butler (1835–1902) was the son of a clergyman and grandson of a bishop. But he lost faith in Christianity, and ridicules its beliefs, and its hypocritical Victorian adherents, in his dystopia *Erewhon* (1872). The Erewhonians attend Musical Banks (i.e. churches), which issue a currency that is in fact totally worthless, though everyone pretends it has far more value than real money. Erewhonian treatment of illness and crime is also singular.

This is what I gathered. That in that country if a man falls into ill health, or catches any disorder, or fails bodily in any way before he is seventy years old, he is tried before a jury of his countrymen, and if convicted is held up to public scorn and sentenced more or less severely as the case may be. There are subdivisions of illnesses into crimes and misdemeanours as with offences amongst ourselves – a man being punished very heavily for serious illness, while failure of eyes or hearing in one over sixty-five who has had good health hitherto is dealt with by fine only, or imprisonment in default of payment. But if a man forges a cheque, or sets his house on fire, or robs with violence from the person, or does any other such things as are criminal in our own country, he is either taken to a hospital, and most carefully tended at the public expense, or if he is in good circumstances, he lets it be known to all his friends that he is indisposed, just as we do when we are ill, and they come and visit him with great solicitude, and inquire with interest how it all came about, what symptoms first showed themselves, and so forth – questions which he will answer with perfect unreserve: for bad conduct, though considered no less deplorable than illness with ourselves, and as unquestionably indicating something seriously wrong with the individual who misbehaves, is nevertheless held to be the result of either pre-natal or post-natal misfortune.

Higgs, the narrator of *Erewhon*, later attends the trial of a man accused of having consumption, who is found guilty, and sentenced to life imprisonment with hard labour. The point of Butler's satire is that punishing criminals, as we do, makes no more sense than the Erewhonian punishment of illness. 'A man,' he argued, 'is the resultant and exponent of all the forces that have been brought to bear upon him, whether before his birth or afterwards. His action at any moment depends solely upon his constitution, and on the intensity and direction of the various agencies to which he is and has been subjected.' From this viewpoint, crime, like illness, is involuntary, so to punish the sick and nurse criminals is as reasonable as to punish criminals and nurse the sick.

Source: Samuel Butler, *Erewhon*, Trubner & Co., 1872.

The Withering State

Karl Marx (1818–83) and Friedrich Engels (1820–95) did not approve of utopias. In *The Communist Manifesto* (1848), utopians are reproved because they ignore the inevitable process of history, and substitute their own fantasies. Marxist history has several phases, all inevitable. In the first phase the bourgeoisie, a dynamic, revolutionary class, put an end to feudalism and unleash the enormous powers of modern industry. This had already happened by 1848. In the second phase, industry produces a new revolutionary class, the proletariat (industrial workers), destined to supplant the bourgeoisie. By 1848 the proletariat had been duly produced. Marx had seen some of them when visiting Lancashire cotton mills with Engels (a wealthy cotton merchant's son). It remained for the proletariat to seize power from the bourgeoisie. Marx explained what would then happen in a document he wrote in May 1875 entitled *Critique of the Gotha Programme of the Social Democratic Party*. This consisted of some ill-tempered jottings on the German SDP's draft manifesto, and it has become one of the sacred texts of Communism. It is the nearest Marx ever came to a utopia.

The transition from Capitalism to Communism cannot, Marx explains, happen all at once.

Between capitalist and communist society lies the period of the revolutionary transformation of the one into the other. There corresponds to this also a political transition period in which the state can be nothing but the revolutionary dictatorship of the proletariat.

This transitional phase may entail some unpleasantness, but a more relaxed and harmonious atmosphere will follow.

In a higher phase of communist society, after the enslaving subordination of individuals under division of labour, and therewith also the antithesis between mental and physical labour, has vanished; after labour, from a mere means of life, has itself become the prime necessity of life; after the productive forces have also increased with the all-round development of the individual, and all the springs of co-operative wealth flow more abundantly – only then can the narrow horizon of bourgeois right be fully left behind and society inscribe on its banners: *from each according to his ability, to each according to his needs.*

At the time of the Russian revolution, Marx's notes on the Gotha programme were excitedly annotated, in their turn, by Lenin (1870–1924), who evidently regarded them as a dependable guide to the future. In his notebook for January to February 1917 (published in *Marxism on the State*), Lenin wrote:

The *'higher'* – 'from each according to his ability, to each according to his needs'. When is this possible? When (1) the antagonism between mental and physical labour has disappeared; (2) labour has become the *prime necessity of life* (NB: the habit of working has become the rule without compulsion!!); (3) the productive forces have grown considerably, etc. It is clear that the *complete* withering away of the state is possible only at this higher stage. This NB.

Following Marx, Lenin criticizes 'utopians' for misunderstanding history and expecting instant change. There will have to be a transitional phase after the Revolution, just as Marx predicted. In this phase there will still be inequality. Those who are more productive will be rewarded accordingly. A bourgeois concept of 'right' reward will persist.

Marx formulates the question and warns us, as it were, that to arrive at a scientific answer one must rely only on firmly established scientific data. The first fact that has been established with complete exactitude by the whole theory of development, by science as a whole – a fact which the utopians forget . . . is that, historically, there must undoubtedly be a special stage or special phase of *transition* from capitalism to communism . . . Every member of society, performing a certain part of socially necessary labour, receives a certificate from society to the effect that he has done such-and-such an amount of work. And with this certificate he draws from the social stock of means of consumption, a corresponding quantity of products. After deduction of the amount of labour that goes to the public fund, every worker, therefore, receives from society as much as he has given it.

Lenin wrote this in *The State and Revolution* (August–September 1917), and in the same work he looks forward to happier times – though when these will arrive is, he admits, indefinite.

The state will be able to wither away completely when society applies the rule: 'From each according to his ability, to each according to his needs', i.e. when people have become so accustomed to observing the fundamental rules of social intercourse and when their labour is so productive that they will voluntarily work *according to their ability*. 'The narrow horizon of bourgeois right' [Marx], which compels one to calculate with the stringency of a Shylock whether he has not worked half an hour more than another, whether he is not getting less pay than another – this narrow horizon will then be left behind. There will then be no need for society to regulate the quantity of products to be distributed to each; each will take freely 'according to his needs'.

From the bourgeois point of view it is easy to declare that such a social order is 'a pure utopia' and to sneer at the Socialists for promising everyone the right to receive from society, without any control of the labour of the individual citizen, any quantity of truffles, automobiles, pianos etc. Even now most bourgeois 'savants' confine themselves to sneering in this way, thereby displaying at once their ignorance and their mercenary defence of capitalism.

Ignorance – for it has never entered the head of any Socialist to 'promise' that the higher phase of the development of communism will arrive; and the great Socialists, in *foreseeing* its arrival, presuppose not the present productivity of labour *and not the present* ordinary run of people . . .

Until the 'higher' phase of communism arrives, the Socialists demand the *strictest* control, by society *and by the state*, of the measure of labour and the measure of consumption; but this control must *start* with the expropriation of the capitalists, with the establishment of workers' control over the capitalists, and must be carried out, not by a state of bureaucrats, but by a state of *armed workers* . . .

At a certain stage in the development of democracy it first rallies the proletariat as the revolutionary class against capitalism, and enables it to crush, smash to atoms, wipe off the face of the earth the bourgeois, even the republican bourgeois, state machine, the standing army, the police and bureaucracy, and to substitute for them a *more* democratic state machine, but a state machine nevertheless, in the shape of the armed masses of the workers who are being transformed into a universal people's militia . . .

From the moment all members of society, or even only the vast majority, have learned to administer the state *themselves*, have taken this business into their own hands, have 'set up' control over the insignificant minority of capitalists, over the gentry who wish to preserve their capitalist habits, and over the workers who have been profoundly corrupted by capitalism – from this moment the need for government begins to disappear altogether. The more complete democracy, the nearer the moment approaches when it becomes unnecessary. The more democratic the 'state' which consists of armed workers and which is 'no longer a state in the proper sense of the word' [Marx] the more rapidly does *the state* begin to wither away altogether.

For when *all* have learned to administer, and actually do administer social production independently, independently keep accounts and exercise control over the idlers, the gentlefolk, the swindlers and similar 'guardians of capitalist traditions', the escape from this national accounting and control will inevitably become so incredibly difficult, such a rare exception, and will probably be accompanied by such swift and severe punishments (for the armed workers are practical men and not sentimental intellectuals, and they will scarcely allow anyone to trifle with them), that very soon the *necessity* of observing the simple, fundamental rules of human intercourse will become a *habit*.

And then the door will be wide open for the transition from the first phase of communist society to its higher phase, and with it the complete withering away of the state . . .

Only communism makes the state absolutely unnecessary, for there is *no one* to be suppressed – 'no one' in the sense of a *class*, in the sense of a systematic struggle against a definite section of the population. We are not utopians, and we do not in the least deny the possibility and the inevitability of excesses on the part of *individual persons*, or the need to suppress *such* excesses. But, in the first place, no special machine, no special apparatus of repression is needed for this; this will be done by the armed people itself, as simply and as readily as any crowd of civilized people, even in modern society, parts two people who are fighting, or interferes to prevent a woman being assaulted. And, secondly, we know that the fundamental social cause of excesses, which consist in violating the rules of social intercourse, is the exploitation of the masses, their want and their poverty. With the removal of this chief cause, excesses will inevitably begin to *wither away*. We do not know how quickly and in what order, but we know that they will wither away. With their withering away, the state will also *wither away*.

Source: Karl Marx, *Critique of the Gotha Programme*, with appendices by Marx, Engels and Lenin, Lawrence & Wishart, 1938.

Good Deaths

The Fixed Period (1881–2) by Anthony Trollope (1815–82) is set in the British colony of Britannula, a breakaway from New Zealand, which has introduced legislation to counter the problem of old age. At the age of sixty-seven and a half (a figure arrived at after much debate) all citizens will be ceremonially 'deposited' in a College, equipped with many alluring luxuries, including a modern crematorium. Exactly twelve months later they will undergo a solemn rite of departure, consisting of the administration of morphine and the opening of their arteries in a warm bath. Despite the attractions of the scheme, some attempts to circumvent it are anticipated, and as a precaution all babies in Britannula now have their dates of birth tattooed on their backs.

The President of Britannula outlines the project's humanitarian and economic justifications in the novel's opening paragraphs. Trollope was sixty-six when he wrote *The Fixed Period*.

I think I must begin my story by explaining in moderate language a few of the manifest advantages which would attend the adoption of the 'Fixed Period' in all countries. Its adoption was the first thing discussed by our young Assembly when we found ourselves alone, and though there were hot disputes on the subject, in none of them was opposition made to the system. I myself at the age of thirty had been elected Speaker of that Parliament. But I was nevertheless able to discuss the merits of the bills in committee, and I did so with some enthusiasm. Thirty years have passed since, and my 'Period' is drawing nigh. But I am still as energetic as ever, and as assured that the doctrine will ultimately prevail over the face of the civilized world, though I will acknowledge that men are not as yet ripe for it.

The 'Fixed Period' has been so far discussed as to make it almost unnecessary for me to explain its tenets, though its advantages may require a few words of argument in a world that is at present dead to its charms. It consists altogether of the abolition of the miseries, weakness and *fainéant* imbecility of old age by the prearranged ceasing to live of those who would otherwise become old. Need I explain to the inhabitants of England, for whom I chiefly write, how extreme are those sufferings, and how great the costliness of that old age which is unable in any degree to supply its own wants? Such old age should not, we Britannulists maintain, be allowed to be. This should be prevented, in the interests both of the young and of those who do become old when obliged to linger on after their 'Period' of work is over. Two mistakes have been made by mankind in reference to their own race; first in allowing the world to be burdened with the continued maintenance of those whose cares should have been made to cease, and whose troubles should be at an end. Does not the Psalmist say the same? – 'If by reason of strength they be four-score years, yet is their strength labour and sorrow.' And the second, in requiring those who remain to live a useless and painful life. Both these errors have come from an ill-judged and a thoughtless tenderness – a tenderness to the young in not calling upon them to provide for the decent and comfortable departure of their progenitors; and a tenderness to the old lest the man, when uninstructed and unconscious of good and evil, should be unwilling to leave the world for which he is not fitted. But is such tenderness better than unpardonable weakness? Statistics have told us that the sufficient sustenance of an old man is more costly than the feeding of a young one – as is also the care, nourishment, and education of the as yet unprofitable child. Statistics also have told us that the unprofitable young and the no less unprofitable old form a third of the population. Let the reader think of the burden with which the labour of the world is thus saddled. To these are to be added all who because of illness cannot work, and because of idleness will not. How are a people to thrive when so weighted? And for what good? As for the children, they are clearly necessary. They have to be nourished in order that they may do good work as their time shall come. But for whose good are the old and effete to be maintained amidst all their troubles and miseries? Had there been anyone in our Parliament capable of showing that they could reasonably desire it, the bill would not have been passed. Though to me the politico-economical view of the subject was always very strong, the relief to be brought to the aged was the one argument to which no reply could be given.

It was put forward by some who opposed the movement that the old themselves would not like it. I never felt sure of that, nor do I now. When the colony had become used to the 'Fixed Period' system, the old would become accustomed as well as the young. It is to be understood that a euthanasia [i.e. a good death] was to be prepared for them – and how many, as men now are, does a euthanasia await? And they would depart with the full respect of all their fellow citizens. To how many does that lot now fall? During the last years of their lives they were to be saved from any of the horrors of poverty. How many now lack the comforts they cannot earn for themselves? And to them there would be no degraded feeling that they were the recipients of charity. They would be prepared for their departure, for the benefit of their country, surrounded by all the comforts to which, at their time of life, they would be susceptible, in a college maintained at the public expense; and each, as he drew nearer to the happy day, would be treated with still increasing honour. I myself had gone most closely into the question of expense and had found that by the use of machinery the college could almost be made self-supporting. But we should save on an average £50 for each man and woman who had departed. When our population should have become a million, presuming that one only in fifty would have reached the desired age, the sum actually saved to the colony would amount to £1,000,000 a year. It would keep us out of debt, make for us our railways, render all our rivers navigable, construct our bridges, and leave us shortly the richest people on God's earth! And this would be effected by a measure doing more good to the aged than to any other class of the community!

Source: Anthony Trollope, *The Fixed Period*, 1881–2.

Women in Power

Popular novelist Walter Besant (1836–1901) was in some respects progressive. He founded the Society of Authors, to protect authors' rights. He cared deeply about social deprivation in London's East End, and was the driving force behind the building of the People's Palace, a sports and cultural complex in Mile End Road. On the subject of women, however, he remained unreformed. His brother Frank was unhappily married to Annie Besant, the Fabian trade-union organizer and advocate of birth control. Perhaps this soured Walter's judgement. At all events his dystopia, *The Revolt of Man* (1882), is rampantly sexist, even by Victorian standards.

It is set in a future England ruled by women. The religion of the Perfect Woman has replaced Christianity and is rigorously enforced. Blasphemy or open disbelief carry the death penalty. The monarchy and the House of Commons have been abolished. All power resides in the British House of Peeresses, who regard themselves as ruling by divine right. Their debates, however, are apt to terminate in tears, shrieks, insults and personal abuse.

Men, meanwhile, are kept in subjection, rather like women in Victorian England. They receive little education, and only poorly paid work is open to them. Married men's property belongs to their wives, and they have to do the housework and look after the babies as well as working. The husband takes the wife's name on marriage. In cases of violence against women, the laws of evidence are weighted against men. A husband can be imprisoned for wife-beating on the sole unsupported charge of his wife. Penalties are severe (e.g., twenty years' penal servitude for allegedly swearing at a woman). Laws prevent men assembling. They work in solitude and at home, or, if they work in groups, a woman is always present to enforce silence. Books from the period of men's domination (Shakespeare, Dickens, etc.) are banned. Men are taught to be bashful, modest and compliant. Elderly peeresses and matriarchs use their social power to force young men into marriage with them. If the men refuse, they are imprisoned.

The rule of women has proved so incompetent that the country faces ruin. The industrial towns have fallen into decay. There has been a return to hand-loom weaving and cottage industry. Factories have been pulled down, machinery destroyed. Overseas trade has virtually ceased. Liverpool is a small town with a few fishing smacks, its docks deserted. The railway system no longer functions.

Alerted by these developments, Dorothy Ingleby, Professor of History at Cambridge University, has come to the conclusion that woman's rule is unnatural. She realizes that men are 'the sex which should command and create', and that 'strength of brain goes with strength of muscle'. In collusion with her husband, the former Bishop of London, she organizes a male revolutionary movement, and they adopt as their leader the young Earl of Chester, the rightful heir to the British throne. In the course of the Earl's re-education Professor Ingleby takes him to the Royal Academy, where the paintings, all by women, expose the deplorable state of British art.

There were a great many altar-pieces in the Sacred Department. In these the Perfect Woman was depicted in every attitude and occupation by which perfection may best be represented. It might have been objected, had any one so far ventured outside the beaten path of criticism, that the Perfect Woman's dress, her mode of dressing her hair, and her ornaments were all of the present year's fashion. 'As if,' said the Professor, the only one who did venture, 'as if no one had any conception of beauty and grace except what fashion orders. Sheep! sheep! we follow like a flock.'

The pictures were mostly allegorical: the Perfect Woman directed Labour – represented by twenty or thirty burly young men with implements of various kinds; this was a very favourite subject. Or she led Man upwards. This was a series of pictures: in the first, Man was a rough rude creature, carrying a club with which he banged something – presumably Brother Man; he gradually improved, until at the end he was depicted as laying at the altar of womanhood flowers, fruit, and wine, from his own husbandry. By this time he had got his beard cut off, and was smooth shaven, save for a pair of curly moustaches; his dress was in the fashion of the day; his eyes were down-dropped in reverential awe; and his expression was delightfully submissive, pious, and *béate*. 'Is it,' asked Lord Chester, 'impossible to be religious without becoming such a creature as *that*?'

Again, the Perfect Woman sat alone, thinking for the good of the world. She had a star above her head; she tried, in the picture, not to look as if she were proud of that star. Or the Perfect Woman sat watching, in the dead of night, in the moonlight, for the good of the world; or the Perfect Woman was revealed to enraptured man rising from the waves, not at all wet, and clothed in the most beautifully fashioned and most expensive modern garments. These two rooms, the Sacred and the Ancient History Departments, were mostly deserted. The principal interest of the Exhibition was in the remaining three-and-twenty, which were devoted to general subjects. Here were sweetnesses of flower and fruit, here were lovely creamy faces of male youth, here were full-length figures of athletes, runners, wrestlers, jumpers, rowers, cricket-players, and others, treated with delicate conventionality, so that the most successful pictures represented man with no more expression in his face than a barber's block, and the strongest young Hercules was figured with tiny hands or fingers like a girl's for slimness, for transparency, and for whiteness, and beautifully small feet; on the other hand, his calves were prodigious.

Music, too, has deteriorated. 'Women have never composed great music,' Professor Ingleby reminds the Earl. The universities are all-female, with the result that (as the professor explains) the hard sciences, which are too difficult for women, have disappeared from the curriculum, to be replaced by bogus 'theoretical' subjects.

'What is their political economy, their moral philosophy, their social science – of which they make so great a boast – compared with the noble scholarship, the science, the speculation of former days? How can I make you understand? There was a time when everything was advanced – by men. Science must advance or fall back. We took from men their education, and science has been forgotten. We cannot now read the old books; we do not understand the old discoveries; we cannot use the tools which they invented, the men of old. Mathematics, chemistry, physical science, geology – all these exist no longer, or else exist in such an elementary form as our ancestors would have been ashamed to acknowledge. Astronomy, which widened the heart, is neglected; medicine has become a thing of books; mechanics are forgotten – '

'But why?'

'Because women, who can receive, cannot create; because at no time has any woman enriched the world with a new idea, a new truth, a new discovery, a new invention; because we have undertaken the impossible.'

[274]

At the end of Besant's novel the men's uprising is successful and male power is restored. Some women regret this, but many, including all the younger ones, are relieved. Under women's rule they had enjoyed a monopoly of the learned professions. But they had found this a dreadful strain, for competition was fierce, and professional women generally could not afford to marry till they were forty.

It took a short time indeed to reconcile them to the change.

No more reading for professions! Hurrah! Did any girl ever really *like* reading law? No more drudgery in an office! Very well. Who would not prefer liberty and seeing the men work?

They gave in with astonishing readiness to the new state of things. They ceased to grumble directly they realized what the change meant for them.

First, no anxiety about study, examinations, and a profession. Next, no responsibilities. Next, unlimited time to look after dress and matters of real importance. Then, no longer having to take things gravely on account of the weaker sex – the men, who now took things merrily – even too merrily. Lastly, whereas no one was formerly allowed to marry unless she could support a husband and family, and then one had to go through all sorts of humiliating conferences with parents and guardians – under the new *régime* every man seemed making love with all his might to every girl. Could anything be more delightful? Was it not infinitely better to be wooed and made love to when one was young, than to woo for one's self when one had already passed her best?

Source: Walter Besant, *The Revolt of Man*, Blackwood, 1882.

Green England

In his novel *After London* (1885) Richard Jefferies (1848–87), naturalist and precursor of the green movement, imagines plants taking over England, and turning it back into a wild paradise, after an unspecified disaster has eliminated most of the human population.

The old men say their fathers told them that soon after the fields were left to themselves a change began to be visible. It became green everywhere in the first spring, after London ended, so that all the country looked alike.

The meadows were green, and so was the rising wheat which had been sown, but which neither had nor would receive any further care. Such arable fields as had not been sown, but where the last stubble had been ploughed up, were overrun with couch-grass, and where the short stubble had not been ploughed, the weeds hid it. So that there was no place which was not more or less green; the footpaths were the greenest of all, for such is the nature of grass where it has once been trodden on, and by-and-by, as the summer came on, the former roads were thinly covered with the grass that had spread out from the margin.

In the autumn, as the meadows were not mown, the grass withered as it stood, falling this way and that, as the wind had blown it; the seeds dropped, and the bennets became a greyish-white, or, where the docks and sorrel were thick, a brownish-red. The wheat, after it had ripened, there being no one to reap it, also remained standing, and was eaten by clouds of sparrows, rooks, and pigeons, which flocked to it and were undisturbed, feasting at their pleasure. As the winter came on, the crops were beaten down by the storms, soaked with the rain, and trodden upon by herds of animals.

Next summer the prostrate straw of the preceding year was concealed by the young green wheat and barley that sprang up from the grain sown by dropping from the ears, and by quantities of docks, thistles, oxeye daisies, and similar plants. This matted mass grew up through the bleached straw. Charlock, too, hid the rotting roots in the fields under a blaze of yellow flower. The young spring meadow-grass could scarcely push its way up through the long dead grass and bennets of the year previous, but docks and thistles, sorrel, wild carrots, and nettles, found no such difficulty.

Footpaths were concealed by the second year, but roads could be traced, though as green as the sward, and were still the best for walking, because the tangled wheat and weeds, and, in the meadows, the long grass, caught the feet of those who tried to pass through. Year by year the original crops of wheat, barley, oats, and beans asserted their presence by shooting up, but in gradually diminished force, as nettles and coarser plants, such as the wild parsnips, spread out into the fields from the ditches and choked them.

Aquatic grasses from the furrows and water-carriers extended in the meadows, and, with the rushes, helped to destroy or take the place of the former sweet herbage. Meanwhile the brambles, which grew very fast, had pushed forward their prickly runners farther and farther from the hedges till they had now reached ten or fifteen yards. The briars had followed, and the hedges had widened to three or four times their first breadth, the fields being equally contracted. Starting from all sides at once, these brambles and briars in the course of about twenty years met in the centre of the largest fields.

Hawthorn bushes sprang up among them, and, protected by the briars and thorns from grazing animals, the suckers of elm-trees rose and flourished. Sapling ashes, oaks, sycamores, and horse-chestnuts, lifted their heads. Of old time the cattle would have eaten off the seed leaves with the grass so soon as they were out of the ground, but now most of the acorns that were dropped by birds, and the keys that were wafted by the wind, twirling as they floated, took root and grew into trees. By this time the brambles and briars had choked up and blocked the former roads, which were as impassable as the fields.

No fields, indeed, remained, for where the ground was dry, the thorns, briars, brambles, and saplings already mentioned filled the space, and these thickets and the young trees had converted most part of the country into an immense forest. Where the ground was naturally moist, and the drains had become choked with willow roots, which, when confined in tubes, grow into a mass like the brush of a fox, sedges and flags and rushes covered it. Thorn bushes were there too, but not so tall; they were hung with lichen. Besides the flags and reeds, vast quantities of the tallest cow-parsnips or 'gicks' rose five or six feet high, and the willow herb with its stout stem, almost as woody as a shrub, filled every approach.

By the thirtieth year there was not one single open place, the hills only excepted, where a man could walk, unless he followed the tracks of wild creatures or cut himself a path.

A great lake covers most of central England. But not all humans have perished. The survivors live in medieval conditions – castles, knights in armour, bows and arrows. Modern science has been forgotten. But there are still cigars (manufactured in Devon) and afternoon tea (though as tea is unavailable, chicory is substituted). Where London formerly stood, there is a vast, stagnant swamp.

There exhales from this oozy mass so fatal a vapour that no animal can endure it. The black water bears a greenish-brown floating scum, which for ever bubbles up from the putrid mud of the bottom. When the wind collects the miasma, and, as it were, presses it together, it becomes visible as a low cloud which hangs over the place. The cloud does not advance beyond the limit of the marsh, seeming to stay there by some constant attraction; and well it is for us that it does not, since at such times when the vapour is thickest, the very wildfowl leave the reeds, and fly from the poison. There are no fishes, neither can eels exist in the mud, nor even newts. It is dead.

The flags and reeds are coated with slime and noisome to the touch; there is one place where even these do not grow, and where there is nothing but an oily liquid, green and rank. It is plain there are no fishes in the water, for herons do not go thither, nor the kingfishers, not one of which approaches the spot. They say the sun is sometimes hidden by the vapour when it is thickest, but I do not see how any can tell this, since they could not enter the cloud, as to breathe it when collected by the wind is immediately fatal. For all the rottenness of a thousand years and of many hundred millions of human beings is there festering under the stagnant water, which has sunk down into and penetrated the earth, and floated up to the surface the contents of the buried cloacae [sewers] . . .

The common people aver that demons reside in these swamps; and, indeed, at night fiery shapes are seen which, to the ignorant, are sufficient confirmation of such tales. The vapour, where it is most dense, takes fire, like the blue flame of spirits, and these flaming clouds float to and fro, and yet do not burn the reeds. The superstitious trace in them the forms of demons and winged fiery serpents, and say that white spectres haunt the margin of the marsh after dusk. In a lesser degree, the same thing has taken place with other ancient cities. It is true that there are not always swamps, but the sites are uninhabitable because of the emanations from the ruins. Therefore they are avoided. Even the spot where a single house has been known to have existed, is avoided by the hunters in the woods.

Source: Richard Jefferies, *After London, or Wild England*, Cassell, 1895.

The Frustration of Smith

W. H. Hudson (1841–1922) was a British naturalist and bird-watcher, whose books helped to foster the back-to-nature movement of the 1920s and 30s. In his novel *A Crystal Age* (1887) a jaunty young man-about-town called Smith, nephew of the MP for Wormwood Scrubs, falls through a hole in the earth and finds himself in a fairly typical late-nineteenth-century utopia – a rural paradise sparsely populated by happy vegetarians in beautiful homespun garments. Smith gradually realizes that he has fallen into the far distant future. These people are the survivors of the human race, which virtually destroyed itself many centuries ago by the reckless pursuit of science. They have no machines apart from hand-looms, simple horse-ploughs, and an advanced type of gramophone. Money is unknown to them, and they are amused that Smith should think he can procure one of their beautiful suits of clothes in exchange for the bits of metal and paper in his purse. They live in stately, widely scattered houses. They have never heard of a city: in their language the word means only a beehive. When Smith describes Victorian London to them, they think him mad. The life of each family is devoted to beautifying its house with works of art – carved wood, stained glass, statuary – and replacing its fabric as it wears out. They regard their houses as eternal, and are appalled by Smith's claim that, where he comes from, people actually build new houses.

Smith settles down happily with his utopians and falls in love with a maiden called Yoletta, whose nice legs were almost the first thing he noticed after his amazing flight through space-time. The affair progresses well. She allows him to hold her hand when she has a thorn in it. Later they go for a walk in the hills, and he chases her sportively through the undergrowth.

She laughed and sat down at my side on the grass.

I caught her hand and held it tight. 'Now you shall not escape and run away again,' said I.

'You may keep my hand,' she replied; 'it has nothing to do up here.'

'May I put it to some useful purpose – may I do what I like with it?'

'Yes, you may'; then she added with a smile, 'There is no thorn in it now.'

I kissed it many times, on the back, the palm, the wrist, and then bestowed a separate caress on each finger-tip.

'Why do you kiss my hand?' she asked.

'Do you not know – can you not guess? Because it is the sweetest thing I can kiss, except one other thing. Shall I tell you?'

'My face? And why do you not kiss that?'

'Oh, may I,' said I, and drawing her to me I kissed her soft cheek. 'May I kiss the other cheek now?' I asked.

She turned it to me, and when I had kissed it, rapturously, I gazed into her eyes, which looked back, bright and unabashed, into mine. 'I think – I think I made a slight mistake, Yoletta,' I said. 'What I meant to ask was, will you let me kiss you where I like – on your chin, for instance, or just where I like.'

'Yes; but you are keeping me too long. Kiss me as many times as you like, and then let us admire the prospect.'

I drew her closer and kissed her mouth, not once nor twice, but clinging to it with all the ardour of passion, as if my lips had become glued to hers.

Suddenly she disengaged herself from me. 'Why do you kiss my mouth in that violent way?' she exclaimed, her eyes sparkling, her cheeks flushed. 'You seem like some hungry animal that wanted to devour me.'

That was, oddly enough, just how I had felt. 'Do you not know, sweetest, why I kiss you in that way? – because I love you.'

'I know you do, Smith. I can understand and appreciate your love without having my lips bruised.'

'And do you love me, Yoletta?'

'Yes, certainly – did you not know that I love you?'

'And is it not sweet to kiss when you love? Do you know what love is, darling? Do you love me a thousand times more than anyone else in the world?'

'How extravagantly you talk!' she replied. 'What strange things you say!'

'Yes, dear, because love is strange – the strangest, sweetest thing in life. It comes only once to the heart, and the one person loved is more than all others. Do you not understand that?'

'Oh no; what do you mean, Smith?'

'Is there any other person dearer to your heart than I am?'

'I love everyone in the house, some more than others. Those that are closely related to me, I love most.'

'Oh, please say no more! You love your people with one kind of love, but me with a different love – is it not so?'

'There is only one kind of love,' said she.

Smith starts to suspect that something is wrong, and there are other things about these people that puzzle him. The young men have no facial hair, and look rather like the young women. The father of the family, an ancient sage called Xandroc, is the only male with a beard. The mother, called Chastel, is regarded as sacred. She lives a secluded, invalid life, and when Smith tells her about marriages and families in the world he has come from, she is offended and incredulous.

'Do not say any more,' she said, with strong displeasure. 'This, I suppose, is another of those strange, grotesque fancies you sometimes give expression to. That all people should be equal, and all women wives and mothers seems to me a very disordered and a very repulsive idea ... The human race would multiply until the fruits of the soil would be insufficient for its support; and earth would be filled with degenerate beings, starved in body and debased in mind – all clinging to an existence utterly without joy.'

It gradually dawns on Smith (and his suspicions are confirmed by an ancient tome he finds in the library) that these people are biologically different from himself. The mother of each family is rather like a queen bee – though far less prolific – in that she alone is able to reproduce. The children are all sterile and passionless. It is this that enables the race to keep its population within bounds, and to eliminate the degeneracy that (as many in the nineteenth century thought) results from promiscuous breeding. The discovery horrifies him, for it means that Yoletta can never be his.

Any fate would have been preferable to the blank desolation which now confronted me. I wished to possess the implacable power of some god or demon, that I might shatter the sacred houses of this later race, and destroy them everlastingly, and repeople the peaceful world with struggling, starving millions, as in the past, so that the beautiful flower of love which had withered in men's hearts might bloom again.

How any mothers and fathers come into being in a sexless race is a question to which Smith – and we – never find the answer. For, in a frenzy of unconsummated passion, he drinks from a mysterious bottle, judging, from its inscription, that it will make him sexless too. In fact it turns him to stone, and he becomes one of the melancholy-looking statues that he has previously noticed around the house. These, we gather, are really the petrified bodies of those who, like Smith, could stand sexual frustration no longer.

Source: W. H. Hudson, *A Crystal Age*, T. Fisher Unwin, 1887.

Bring Back National Service

Edward Bellamy's *Looking Backward, 2000–1887* (1888) has had, some utopologists claim, a greater impact than any other single utopia. In America it became the manifesto of the Nationalist Movement, and instrumental in the emergence of the People's Party. Translated into all major languages, including Russian, Bulgarian and Arabic, it had a widespread influence on political opinion at the outset of the modern era, and inspired scores of imitations.

The son of a Baptist minister in Massachusetts, Bellamy (1850–98) was rejected by West Point (he was already suffering from TB) and instead became a barrister. But he quickly abandoned the law in disgust, and took to journalism and novel-writing – with scant success until *Looking Backward* brought him instant fame. His fascination with military discipline reflects his upbringing in post-Civil War America, and also, perhaps, his lifelong struggle with ill-health. Reacting against nineteenth-century individualism, and particularly the 'mad self-assertion' of Romantics such as Byron and Baudelaire, he preached a Religion of Solidarity. The basic premise was that the self could achieve salvation only by merging with a greater whole – whether a vast human concourse such as an army, or the infinite and eternal.

In *Looking Backward*, a wealthy Bostonian, Julian West, falls into a mesmeric trance in 1887 and awakes in the year 2000. From his host, Dr Leete, he learns that America has been transformed by a bloodless revolution. The Religion of Solidarity, known politically as Nationalism, is now universally accepted. The poverty and degradation bred by nineteenth-century individualistic capitalism are looked back on with horror and incredulity. The nation is now one great business syndicate, absorbing all the previous commerce and industry, and employing all citizens, who share equally in its profit.

At the age of twenty-one everyone, both male and female, must enrol in the 'industrial army'. Their compulsory military service lasts until they are forty-five (or, in the case of women, until they become mothers). Retirement at forty-five is looked forward to as the best time of life, and brings rejuvenation. Many people of average constitution live to eighty-five or ninety.

Though a totally peaceful force (war is extinct), the industrial army is subject to strict military discipline. Recruits serve their first three years as common labourers (doing jobs once regarded as menial, though now they have the dignity of national service). After that they choose, or are allocated to, tasks and 'guilds' according to their natural endowments. For unpopular jobs, reduction in the hours of labour, or the granting of extra honours, ensure volunteers. The value of a man's service to the community fixes his rank in the industrial army. However, everyone, irrespective of rank, seniority, gender, skill or occupation, and whether working or retired, receives exactly the same reward, representing an equal share in the annual national surplus. The philosophy justifying this equal treatment of the talented and the untalented is that 'All men who do their best, do the same'. Those who do not do their best, or who refuse to work, are sentenced to solitary confinement on bread and water until they agree to amend. Such cases are extremely rare, however, because devotion to the ideal of human solidarity and national service inspires the industrial army. The same devotion decrees that the physically and mentally disabled should enjoy exactly the same rights as the fit.

'I should not fail to mention,' resumed the doctor, 'that for those too deficient in mental or bodily strength to be fairly graded with the main body of workers, we have a separate grade, unconnected with the others – a sort of invalid corps, the members of which are provided with a light class of tasks fitted to their strength. All our sick in mind and body, all our deaf and dumb, and lame and blind and crippled, and even our insane, belong to this invalid corps, and bear its insignia. The strongest often do nearly a man's work, the feeblest, of course, nothing; but none who can do anything are willing quite to give up. In their lucid intervals, even our insane are eager to do what they can.'

'That is a pretty idea of the invalid corps,' I said. 'Even a barbarian from the nineteenth century can appreciate that. It is a very graceful way of disguising charity, and must be grateful to the feelings of its recipients.'

'Charity!' repeated Dr Leete. 'Did you suppose that we consider the incapable class we are talking of objects of charity?'

'Why, naturally,' I said, 'inasmuch as they are incapable of self-support.'

But here the doctor took me up quickly.

'Who is capable of self-support?' he demanded. 'There is no such

[285]

thing in a civilized society as self-support. In a state of society so barbarous as not even to know family cooperation, each individual may possibly support himself, though even then for a part of his life only; but from the moment that men begin to live together, and constitute even the rudest sort of society, self-support becomes impossible. As men grow more civilized, and the subdivision of occupations and services is carried out, a complex mutual dependence becomes the universal rule. Every man, however solitary may seem his occupation, is a member of a vast industrial partnership, as large as the nation, as large as humanity. The necessity of mutual dependence should imply the duty and guarantee of mutual support; and that it did not in your day constituted the essential cruelty and unreason of your system.'

'That may all be so,' I replied, 'but it does not touch the case of those who are unable to contribute anything to the product of industry.'

'Surely I told you this morning, at least I thought I did,' replied Dr Leete, 'that the right of a man to maintenance at the nation's table depends on the fact that he is a man, and not on the amount of health and strength he may have, so long as he does his best.'

'You said so,' I answered, 'but I supposed the rule applied only to the workers of different ability. Does it also hold of those who can do nothing at all?'

'Are they not also men?'

'I am to understand, then, that the lame, the blind, the sick, and the impotent, are as well off as the most efficient, and have the same income?'

'Certainly,' was the reply.

'The idea of charity on such a scale,' I answered, 'would have made our most enthusiastic philanthropists gasp.'

'If you had a sick brother at home,' replied Dr Leete, 'unable to work, would you feed him on less dainty food, and lodge and clothe him more poorly, than yourself? More likely far, you would give him the preference; nor would you think of calling it charity. Would not the word, in that connection, fill you with indignation?'

'Of course,' I replied; 'but the cases are not parallel. There is a sense, no doubt, in which all men are brothers; but this general sort of brotherhood is not to be compared, except for rhetorical purposes, to the brotherhood of blood, either as to its sentiment or its obligations.'

'There speaks the nineteenth century!' exclaimed Dr Leete. 'Ah, Mr West, there is no doubt as to the length of time that you slept. If I were to give you, in one sentence, a key to what may seem the mysteries of our civilization as compared with that of your age, I should say that it is the fact that the solidarity of the race and the brotherhood of man, which to you were but fine phrases, are, to our thinking and feeling, ties as real and as vital as physical fraternity.

'But even setting that consideration aside, I do not see why it so surprises you that those who cannot work are conceded the full right to live on the produce of those who can. Even in your day, the duty of military service for the protection of the nation, to which our industrial service corresponds, while obligatory on those able to discharge it, did not operate to deprive of the privileges of citizenship those who were unable. They stayed at home, and were protected by those who fought, and nobody questioned their right to be, or thought less of them. So, now, the requirement of industrial service from those able to render it does not operate to deprive of the privileges of citizenship, which now implies the citizen's maintenance, him who cannot work. The worker is not a citizen because he works, but works because he is a citizen. As you recognize the duty of the strong to fight for the weak, we, now that fighting is gone by, recognize his duty to work for him.

'A solution which leaves an unaccounted-for residuum is no solution at all; and our solution of the problem of human society would have been none at all had it left the lame, the sick, and the blind outside with the beasts, to fare as they might. Better far have left the strong and well unprovided for than these burdened ones, toward whom every heart must yearn, and for whom ease of mind and body should be provided, if for no others. Therefore it is, as I told you this morning, that the title of every man, woman, and child to the means of existence rests on no basis less plain, broad, and simple than the fact that they are fellows of one race – members of one human family. The only coin current is the image of God, and that is good for all we have.

'I think there is no feature of the civilization of your epoch so repugnant to modern ideas as the neglect with which you treated your dependent classes. Even if you had no pity, no feeling of brother-hood, how was it that you did not see that you were robbing the incapable class of their plain right in leaving them unprovided for?'

'I don't quite follow you there,' I said. 'I admit the claim of this class to our pity, but how could they who produced nothing claim a share of the product as a right?'

'How happened it,' was Dr Leete's reply, 'that your workers were able to produce more than so many savages would have done? Was it not wholly on account of the heritage of the past knowledge and achievements of the race, the machinery of society, thousands of years in contriving, found by you ready-made to your hand? How did you come to be possessors of this knowledge and this machinery, which represent nine parts to one contributed by yourself in the value of your product? You inherited it, did you not? And were not these others, these unfortunate and crippled brothers whom you cast out, joint inheritors, co-heirs with you? What did you do with their share? Did you not rob them when you put them off with crusts, who were entitled to sit with the heirs, and did you not add insult to robbery when you called the crusts charity?'

The organization of women, as well as men, into the industrial army means that women are released from domestic slavery. Housework is obsolete. Public laundries and kitchens look after washing and cooking. Cleaning is done by army recruits. Each family is allocated an elegant private room, with waiter-service and exquisite *à la carte* fare, in the local communal dining-house.

The industrial army provides the government as well as the workforce. The General-in-Chief is the President of the United States. He will have passed through all ranks from common labourer, and will have owed his promotion to the excellence of his record as a worker. Beneath him are subsidiary generals, elected not by the members of the army – they have no vote – but by its retired members. The electorate are the over-forty-fives. This means that candidates for promotion are not tempted to canvass the votes of those under their command.

Another major reform is the abolition of money. With it have disappeared the enormous (and, Bellamy argues, enormously wasteful) banking and commercial systems engendered by capitalism. Everyone is issued with a credit card, representing his or her equal share in the nation's annual product. There are no shops. Each district has a luxurious 'sample-store', embellished with fountains, frescoes and statuary, and displaying samples of all available commodities. Purchasers fill in an order-form, and have the value of their purchases deducted from their credit-card total. The goods are delivered to their homes from great central warehouses almost instantaneously through electric 'tubes'.

The credit on credit cards cannot accumulate from year to year. It must be spent or forfeited. At death it reverts to the nation. Consequently the notion of 'saving' has vanished. No one cares for the morrow. 'For the nation guarantees the nurture, education and comfortable maintenance of every citizen from the cradle to the grave'. It follows, too, that there are no longer 'rich' or 'poor'.

One result is that women choose husbands for their natural abilities, not wealth. Sexual selection has noticeably improved the breed. Americans are more physically 'stalwart'. The unmarried are mostly poor specimens no good at their jobs. For, Dr Leete explains, 'the woman must be a courageous one, with a very evil sort of courage, too, whom pity for one of these unfortunates should lead to defy the opinion of her generation so far as to accept him for a husband'.

Crime, which was almost invariably linked to inequalities of property, has largely died out. A fortunate result of this is the disappearance of the legal profession. There remain only a few judges, appointed by the President, who double as barristers. But there is no elaborate legal system for them to administer. They adjudicate in the rare criminal trials that do occur according to 'the plainest and simplest legal maxims'. Most criminals plead guilty anyway, partly because their penalty is doubled if they do not, should they be found guilty, and partly because 'falsehood is so despised among us that few offenders would lie to save themselves'. There are no prisons. Offenders are regarded as victims of atavism (inherited criminal tendencies) and treated – with 'firm but gentle restraint' – in hospital.

Education has played its part in the elimination of crime. Everyone pursues higher education till the age of twenty-one, and this civilizes the 'ignorant and bestial', who used to commit crimes of violence. The least educable are precisely those that are considered most worth educating, as Dr Leete explains in reply to the narrator's sceptical enquiry.

'After all,' I remarked, 'no amount of education can cure natural dullness or make up for original mental deficiencies. Unless the average natural mental capacity of men is much above its level in my day, a high education must be pretty nearly thrown away on a large element of the population. We used to hold that a certain amount of susceptibility to educational influences is required to make a mind worth cultivating, just as a certain natural fertility in soil is required if it is to repay tilling.'

'Ah,' said Dr Leete, 'I am glad you used that illustration, for it is just the one I would have chosen to set forth the modern view of education. You say that land so poor that the product will not repay the labor of tilling is not cultivated. Nevertheless, much land that does not begin to repay tilling by its product was cultivated in your day and is in ours. I refer to gardens, parks, lawns, and, in general, to pieces of land so situated that, were they left to grow up to weeds and briers, they would be eyesores and inconveniences to all about. They are therefore tilled, and though their product is little, there is yet no land that, in a wider sense, better repays cultivation. So it is with the men and women with whom we mingle in the relations of society, whose voices are always in our ears, whose behavior in innumerable ways affects our enjoyment – who are, in fact, as much conditions of our lives as the air we breathe, or any of the physical elements on which we depend. If, indeed, we could not afford to educate everybody, we should choose the coarsest and dullest by nature, rather than the brightest, to receive what education we could give. The naturally refined and intellectual can better dispense with aids to culture than those less fortunate in natural endowments.

'To borrow a phrase which was often used in your day, we should not consider life worth living if we had to be surrounded by a population of ignorant, boorish, coarse, wholly uncultivated men and women, as was the plight of the few educated in your day. Is a man satisfied, merely because he is perfumed himself, to mingle with a malodorous crowd? Could he take more than a very limited satisfaction, even in a palatial apartment, if the windows on all four sides opened into stable yards? And yet just that was the situation of those considered most fortunate as to culture and refinement in your day. I know that the poor and ignorant envied the rich and cultured then; but to us the latter, living as they did, surrounded by squalor and brutishness, seem little better off than the former. The cultured man in your age was like one up to the neck in a nauseous bog solacing himself with a smelling bottle. You see, perhaps, now, how we look at this question of universal high education. No single thing is so important to every man as to have for neighbors intelligent, companionable persons. There is nothing, therefore, which the nation can do for him that will enhance so much his own happiness as to educate his neighbors. When it fails to do so, the value of his own education to him is reduced by half, and many of the tastes he has cultivated are made positive sources of pain.

'To educate some to the highest degree, and leave the mass wholly uncultivated, as you did, made the gap between them almost like that between different natural species, which have no means of communication. What could be more inhuman than this consequence of a partial enjoyment of education! Its universal and equal enjoyment leaves, indeed, the differences between men as to natural endowments as marked as in a state of nature, but the level of the lowest is vastly raised. Brutishness is eliminated. All have some inkling of the humanities, some appreciation of the things of the mind, and an admiration for the still higher culture they have fallen short of. They have become capable of receiving and imparting, in various degrees, but all in some measure, the pleasures and inspirations of a refined social life. The cultured society of the nineteenth century – what did it consist of but here and there a few microscopic oases in a vast, unbroken wilderness? The proportion of individuals capable of intellectual sympathies or refined intercourse, to the mass of their contemporaries, used to be so infinitesimal as to be in any broad view of humanity scarcely worth mentioning. One generation of the world today represents a greater volume of intellectual life than any five centuries ever did before.

Bellamy's faith in education was matched by his confidence in technical progress. Music-by-telephone, to which Dr Leete's daughter Edith introduces Julian West, anticipates radio. Bellamy's (or West's) response that it constitutes 'the limit of human felicity', reminds us how quickly we take for granted pleasures that were the stuff of fantasy for previous generations.

'Come, then, into the music room,' she said, and I followed her into an apartment finished, without hangings, in wood, with a floor of polished wood. I was prepared for new devices in musical instruments, but I saw nothing in the room which by any stretch of imagination could be conceived as such. It was evident that my puzzled appearance was affording intense amusement to Edith.

'Please look at today's music,' she said, handing me a card, 'and tell me what you would prefer. It is now five-o'clock, you will remember.'

The card bore the date 'September 12, 2000,' and contained the largest programme of music I had ever seen. It was as various as it was long, including a most extraordinary range of vocal and instrumental solos, duets, quartets, and various orchestral combinations. I remained bewildered by the prodigious list until Edith's pink finger-tip indicated a particular section of it, where several selections were bracketed, with the words '5 p.m.' against them; then I observed that this prodigious programme was an all day one, divided into twenty-four sections answering to the hours. There were but a few pieces of music in the '5 p.m.' section, and I indicated an organ piece as my preference.

She made me sit down comfortably, and crossing the room, so far as I could see, merely touched one or two screws, and at once the room was filled with the music of a grand organ anthem; filled, not flooded, for, by some means, the volume of melody had been perfectly graduated to the size of the apartment. I listened, scarcely breathing, to the close. Such music so perfectly rendered, I had never expected to hear.

'Grand!' I cried, as the last great wave of sound broke and ebbed away into silence. 'Bach must be at the keys of that organ; but where is the organ?'

'Wait a moment, please,' said Edith; 'I want to have you listen to this waltz before you ask any questions. I think it is perfectly charming,' and as she spoke the sound of violins filled the room with the witchery of summer night. When this had also ceased, she said: 'There is nothing in the least mysterious about the music as you seem to imagine. It is not made by the fairies or genii, but by good, honest, and exceedingly clever human hands, We have simply carried the idea of labour-saving by co-operation into our musical service as into everything else. There are a number of music rooms in the city, perfectly adapted acoustically to the different sorts of music. These halls are connected by telephone with all the houses of the city whose people care to pay the small fee, and there are none, you may be sure, who do not. The corps of musicians attached to each hall is so large that, although no individual performer, or group of performers, has more than a brief part, each day's programme lasts through the twenty-four hours. There are on that card for today, as you will see if you observe closely, distinct programmes of four of these concerts, each of a different order of music from the others, being now simultaneously performed, and any one of the four pieces now going on that you prefer, you can hear merely by pressing the button which will connect your house wire with the hall where it is being rendered. The programmes are so co-ordinated that the pieces at any one time simultaneously proceeding in the different halls usually offer a choice, not only between instrumental and vocal, and between different sorts of instruments: but also between different motives from grave to gay, so that all tastes and moods can be suited.'

'It appears to me, Miss Leete,' I said, 'that if we could have devised an arrangement for providing everybody with music in their homes, perfect in quality, unlimited in quantity, suited to every mood, and beginning and ceasing at will, we should have considered the limit of human felicity already attained, and ceased to strive for further improvements.'

Bellamy believed that mankind was essentially good, and became evil only because of the distorting effect of social institutions. He originally set his novel in the year 3000, but changed it to 2000 because he thought his idea of the 'industrial army' would make possible the realization of his totalitarian dream within a very short time.

Source: Edward Bellamy, *Looking Backward, 2000–1887*, Ticknor & Co., 1888.

A Cure for Wrinkles

New Amazonia (1889), by the English campaigner for women's suffrage, Elizabeth Burgoyne Corbett, is a dream of a feminist future, set in the twenty-fifth century. A destructive war, early in the twentieth century, between the Irish and the French on the one side and the British on the other, led to the virtual extermination of the Irish. In order to repopulate Ireland, the British government decided that Britain's surplus population of women (outnumbering men by three to one) should be resettled there. This plan was spectacularly successful. The narrator wakes up in the year 2472 and finds herself in a women's college in Andersonia (previously Dublin). The women are prodigies of grace, beauty and physical fitness, and at least seven feet tall. They welcome the stranger, dress her in rational yet becoming clothes like their own (loose tunic, divided skirt, shoes and stockings) and take her to the college principal who explains the history and customs of New Amazonia.

Corbett's utopia is in some respects surprisingly illiberal, given her fierce resentment of male oppression. When the colony was originally set up, women 'whose poverty would make them a burden to the rest of the community' were rigorously excluded, as were those who bore 'the slightest trace of disease or malformation'. Strict immigration laws protect the island's welfare facilities from foreign 'loafers and adventurers'. Illegal immigrants perform forced labour to pay the expenses of their stay, and are then deported. Men are allowed to live on the island but they are debarred from government office. Stringent legislation protects public health and controls the birthrate. A 'medical certificate of soundness' has to be produced before anyone can marry. Newborn children are medically examined, and the crippled or malformed are not permitted to live. The insane and the incurably ill are also exterminated, as are criminals who do not respond to remedial treatment. Anyone having more than four children is treated as a felon and deprived of civil rights. As a further check to the birthrate, no one is admitted to state office who has ever been married. Most intelligent women, the principal reports, 'prefer honour and advancement to the mere animal pleasures of marriage and the reproduction of the species'. The narrator enquires whether some intelligent women are not tempted to cheat by having illicit affairs. But the principal explains that the penalties for this are severe. If detected, the women are degraded to the lowest menial status, and the men deprived of all their possessions and banished. As for any illegitimate infants: 'The offspring of vice is not permitted to live. We New Amazonians pride ourselves on being of none but honourable parentage.'

The narrator is surprised that all the women she meets look so young and unwrinkled, and astonished to learn that the principal, who looks about forty, is 114 years old. Amused at her puzzlement, the principal promises to reveal the secret.

Nothing loath, and with my curiosity aroused to the very apex of expectation, I followed my guide into a magnificent building which we had approached. There were many other people entering at the same time, and more careful observation convinced me that none of them looked quite as bright and healthy as the New Amazonians with whom I had hitherto associated.

I looked enquiringly at Principal Grey. She did but smile, and bid me be seated.

'Wait awhile,' she said, 'and you shall witness a miracle.'

Being deprived of the necessity of action for a time, yet fully appreciating the advantages of a welcome rest, I made diligent use of my eyes, and marvelled much at the rugged, chaste grandeur of the building, which Principal Grey told me was the Andersonia Physiological Hall.

There was a marvellous groined roof, supported by equally marvellous granite pillars. The floor was tessellated, the doors of massive clamped oak, and the windows were marvellous dreams of the glass painter's art. The splendid staircase which led from the central hall to the upper storeys was of brilliant white marble, the balusters being of polished red granite, as were also the numerous fluted columns which supported both staircase and ceiling. The whole building was a perfect dream of taste and splendour, but it was the people, after all, who claimed most of my attention.

It seemed to me that those who entered the hall, and passed on to what Principal Grey called the 'Renewing Rooms', were none of them quite so vigorous and brisk as those who passed us on their return. And yet the latter all seemed to have grown unaccountably stouter in one arm, which they carried with almost wooden stiffness and awkwardness.

Of course I looked my inquiries, but for a time my guide and entertainer preferred to tantalize me by refraining from explaining the mystery which puzzled me.

When at last she did condescend to enlighten my ignorance, I could scarcely refrain my incredulity, for it seemed to me that I was now asked to believe the greatest wonder of all. I was told that the primary purpose of this building was to afford facilities for inoculating the aged or debilitated with the nerves of young and vigorous animals, and that this was the explanation of the fact that I had as yet seen no really old-looking people in the New Amazonia.

'We all resort at times to the Physiological Hall for recuperation and rejuvenation,' said my companion, 'and it is to the benefit we derive here that much of our national prosperity is due. The breeding and rearing of the animals required is an expensive branch of State economy, but all expenses are more than counterbalanced by the fees which we willingly pay for each operation. Even apart from the fact that we are individually and collectively enormously benefited by our rejuvenating system, it gives employment to a large number of people and adds considerably to the revenues of the State.'

The system, the principal explains, has been in vogue for the last four hundred years, preliminary experiments having been undertaken in the nineteenth century when the human race was just awakening to 'the benefits and beauties of science'. Invited to try nerve-rejuvenation herself, the narrator demurs, since she assumes that the animals involved suffer 'vivisectional cruelties'. But the principal scolds her for her ignorance of scientific advance, and assures her that the animals come to no harm. They are simply rendered unconscious by means of 'a wonderful ether' called 'Bändiger', invented by a German chemist. Reassured, the narrator consents to the experiment.

I was not reluctant to follow the principal, and I was very agreeably surprised on entering the 'Renewing Room'. My mind's eye had conjured a vision of gory disorder, the central figure of which was the quivering and bleeding body of some unhappy animal, and the prominent accessories some brawny and bare-armed surgeons, whose perspiring brows, blood-stained hands, and callous cruelty of expression would be anything but reassuring to the trembling and expectant human beings waiting to be inoculated.

What I really saw was this: The room to which an attendant conducted us was richly carpeted and furnished with oriental luxuriousness. Every accessory to comfort was there, and several people were either standing talking in animated groups, or lounging on the spacious cushioned chairs and settees. Some were reading, some sipping coffee, some playing with some beautiful dogs, that basked in front of the fire. A few were busy at needlework, but all seemed thoroughly at home. There were several tables laden with prints and papers. A magnificent bookcase occupied one end of the room. The walls were panelled in bird's-eye maple, and decorated with beautiful pictures, all photographed in their natural colours, which stood out as vivid and brilliant as an oil-painting.

The operating surgeons were six in number – four of them being women, two men. They were all handsome, of splendid physique, elegantly dressed, and of dignified, yet gentle and calm demeanour. Not a bit like the ogres my excited fancy had pictured.

In one of the window recesses was a sort of bassinette, in which a large dog lay motionless, and apparently sleeping, with a screen partially hiding him from observation. To this dog the surgeons journeyed before attacking the bared arm of the individual to be operated upon. In an incredibly short time the task of inoculation was performed, the people hardly ceasing their pleasant hum of conversation the while. Then the arm was tightly bandaged, and the patient went on her or his way rejoicing, after paying the necessary fee to an official whose duty it was to receive them in an ante-room.

Presently an electric bell was rung. Two attendants entered the room, pushed the bassinette through a door at one side of the window, and drew an empty one from an opening at the other side. Then one of the dogs was coaxed from the hearth, and given a dainty and appetizing meal, afterwards springing upon the bassinette to enjoy a quiet nap after his good dinner. In another second the 'Bändiger' had done its work, and in a few minutes more some of the dog's nerve force was being transferred to my own arm.

The sensation I experienced was little more than a pin-prick in intensity, but, before I left the building with Principal Grey, I felt ten years young and stronger, and was proportionately elated at my good fortune.

Source: Mrs George Corbett, *New Amazonia: A Foretaste of the Future*, Tower Publishing Co., 1889.

An Ideal Ireland

Edward Joseph Martyn (1859–1923) is best known as the first president of Sinn Fein. He came from a family of wealthy Catholic landowners in Galway. His father died when he was an infant, and his mother sent him to a Jesuit college near Windsor, England. Finding the curriculum unacceptable, he attempted to blow the school up and was nearly expelled. At Oxford he became a devotee of the aesthetic movement. He was still, at this stage in his career, a staunch Unionist, a position reinforced by his lifelong contempt for the common people and hatred of democracy. He was also, and remained, a scrupulously devout Catholic and a misogynist – the result, possibly, of his mother's overbearing ways and his own sexual orientation. It is not clear what converted him to Irish nationalism, but it seems to have been connected with his semi-mystical delight in the Galway countryside and growing dislike of England, which he associated with modern democratic materialism. He met W. B. Yeats in 1896 and collaborated with him in the formation of the Irish Literary Theatre, which he initially helped to finance, with a view to furthering his own unsuccessful career as a dramatist.

Martyn wished to rid Ireland of all traces of the 'unclean world' by restoring the Gaelic language and traditional Celtic art, which he compared to the art and language of classical Greece. Some idea of how he would have restructured Ireland, if given a free hand, can be gleaned from his first book *Morgante the Lesser* (1890). Most of this work is heavy-handed satire, anti-Enlightenment, anti-Protestant, anti-science, anti-Socialist. Martyn reflects opinions shared by other 1890s aesthetes. He despises the newspaper-reading masses, and regards their shallowness as essentially female. Women, he judges, are materialists at heart, which is why men must retain mastery, rejecting women's suffrage and 'similar absurdities'.

The book concludes with a description of a utopia, Agathopolis (Good State). This is an island with no women (how the population reproduces itself is not clear) and no vice. The religion is Roman Catholicism, and the government benevolent despotism – infinitely superior, in Martyn's view, to democracy, which is the rule of the 'ignorant and blind'. The language spoken is Greek. The arts flourish, especially sculpture, because the sculptors gain inspiration from watching the bodies of boys as they exercise, in Greek style. Dramatic art benefits greatly from the absence of actresses ('that most monstrous of all modern importations on the stage'), and of all popular elements such as elaborate scenery and realistic action. Photography (hated by many 1890s aesthetes for its vulgar associations) is regarded as 'brutal barbarism' in Agathopolis.

Martyn's rundown of a day in the life of a typical Agathopolite reveals the austerity of his ideals.

It is the custom for all, as a rule, to rise early in the genial climate of Agathopolis. Everyone must also bathe at least once a day, unless prevented by dangerous illness, since after rectitude of life, there is no quality so much esteemed amongst us as bodily cleanliness. It is then usual for us to hear a Mass, if possible, every morning, in one or other of the churches, after which each betakes himself to his particular study, business, or labour of the day. Our breakfast hour is at noon. Afterwards, anyone who has leisure, or is so disposed, may witness naval or military reviews, or again, athletic contests and feats of horsemanship in the great circus, or he may ride out to hunt in the country during the season, or to attend horse-races on the fine course without the city; one or other of which spectacles and pastimes is sure to be held daily. For every citizen is a horseman; and our breed of horses is the finest in the world. We dine always sometime between six and seven; and this is the great sociable meal whereat most hospitality is dispensed. In the evening, if a man cannot find his friends at home, or is in no humour for literary, philosophical, aesthetic, or other discourse, he may always either witness a dramatic performance in the theatre, which is lit by electricity, and sheltered, if the weather should prove inclement, by a movable roof, or failing that listen to the best and most sublime music faultlessly executed in the concert-hall.

The tendency, common among proponents of monarchy and dictatorship, to appropriate art and culture in order to make political power seem more august, is naïvely evident in Martyn's description of the Agathopolitan dictator's palace.

Equality of social intercourse and intimate friendships are denied necessarily to the dictator, who, on account both of his pre-eminent genius and august rank, must, of course, stand ever alone. His palace, commanding a glorious panorama of the harbour and blue sea, is, in respect of style and furniture, the utmost expression of the country's aesthetic impulse, and may best be described as the highest art combined with extreme austerity. Fair are its halls and galleries of inlaid marbles with exquisite Roman pavements; its central court uncovered to the azure infinity of peace, and adorned with rare flowers, and with sculpture dreamingly beautiful; its stately saloons hung with tapestry and pictures, where wondrous frescoes mass like clouds in the vaulted roofs, and curious figures in Antique or Byzantine mosaic peer out from the gilded architraves. The study and workroom of the great admiral at present in office displays features of special interest and magnificence. The spaces between the book-shelves are decorated in beautiful grounds of terra-cotta. Costly furs lie here and there on the tessellated floor, and are thrown in negligence over classic chairs of ivory. One table is devoted to state business; another to literature in the calm intervals of welcome leisure. An organ and a piano also find a fitting place. Priceless paintings hang on wall or easel; and there is no object of use or ornament which is not in itself a work of art. Then, opening off this gorgeous apartment is the bed-chamber – a prison-like cell with a marble bath and a narrow plank-bed of ebony, over which are laid more furs, while from the windows of both, their solitary lord by day may gaze like an eagle from his eyrie over the sea-washed city with her sounds as of many bees, and by night may strive to penetrate the gold embroidered curtain of heaven to the hoarse chanting of the ocean at the beach.

Source: Edward Joseph Martyn, *Morgante the Lesser. His Notorious Life and Wonderful Deeds*, Swan Sonnenschein and Co., 1890.

Socialism for Aesthetes

Oscar Wilde (1854–1900) knew little about Socialism, but he understood it well enough to know what would infuriate most Socialists. His essay 'The Soul of Man under Socialism' was first published in 1891, and it advocates, if anything, Anarchism rather than Socialism, as Wilde's biographer Richard Ellmann has noted. But Wilde's aim, as always, was to shock people into thinking – an exercise that, he believed, they seldom undertook.

The chief advantage that would result from the establishment of Socialism is, undoubtedly, the fact that Socialism would relieve us from that sordid necessity of living for others which, in the present condition of things, presses so hardly upon almost everybody. In fact, scarcely anyone at all escapes.

Now and then, in the course of the century, a great man of science, like Darwin; a great poet like Keats; a fine critical spirit like M. Renan; a supreme artist like Flaubert, has been able to isolate himself, to keep himself out of reach of the clamorous claims of others, to stand, 'under the shelter of the wall,' as Plato puts it, and so to realize the perfection of what was in him, to his own incomparable gain, and to the incomparable and lasting gain of the whole world. These, however, are exceptions. The majority of people spoil their lives by an unhealthy and exaggerated altruism – are forced, indeed, so to spoil them. They find themselves surrounded by hideous poverty, by hideous ugliness, by hideous starvation. It is inevitable that they should be strongly moved by all this. The emotions of man are stirred more quickly than man's intelligence; and as I pointed out some time ago in an article on the function of criticism, it is much more easy to have sympathy with suffering than it is to have sympathy with thought. Accordingly, with admirable, though misdirected intentions, they very seriously and very sentimentally set themselves to the task of remedying the evils that they see. But their remedies do not cure the disease: they merely prolong it. Indeed, their remedies are part of the disease.

They try to solve the problem of poverty, for instance, by keeping the poor alive; or, in the case of a very advanced school, by amusing the poor.

But this is not a solution; it is an aggravation of the difficulty. The proper aim is to try and reconstruct society on such a basis that poverty will be impossible. And the altruistic virtues have really prevented the carrying out of this aim. Just as the worst slave-owners were those who were kind to their slaves, and so prevented the horror of the system being realized by those who suffered from it, and understood by those who contemplated it, so, in the present state of things in England, the people who do most harm are the people who try to do most good; and at last we have had the spectacle of men who have really studied the problem and know the life – educated men who live in the East End – coming forward and imploring the community to restrain its altruistic impulses of charity, benevolence, and the like. They do so on the ground that such charity degrades and demoralizes. They are perfectly right. Charity creates a multitude of sins.

There is also this to be said. It is immoral to use private property in order to alleviate the horrible evils that result from the institution of private property. It is both immoral and unfair.

Under Socialism all this will, of course, be altered. There will be no people living in fetid dens and fetid rags, and bringing up unhealthy, hunger-pinched children in the midst of impossible and absolutely repulsive surroundings. The security of society will not depend, as it does now, on the state of the weather. If a frost comes we shall not have a hundred thousand men out of work, tramping about the streets in a state of disgusting misery, or whining to their neighbours for alms, or crowding round the doors of loathsome shelters to try and secure a hunch of bread and a night's unclean lodging. Each member of the society will share in the general prosperity and happiness of the society, and if a frost comes no one will practically be anything the worse.

Upon the other hand, Socialism itself will be of value simply because it will lead to Individualism.

Socialism, Communism, or whatever one chooses to call it, by converting private property into public wealth, and substituting cooperation for competition, will restore society to its proper condition of a thoroughly healthy organism, and ensure the material well-being of each member of the community. It will, in fact, give Life its proper basis and its proper environment. But, for the full development of Life to its highest mode of perfection, something more is needed. What is needed is Individualism. If the Socialism is Authoritarian; if there are Governments armed with economic power as they are now with political power; if, in a word, we are to have Industrial Tyrannies, then the last state of man will be worse than the first. At present, in consequence of the existence of private property, a great many people are enabled to develop a certain very limited amount of Individualism. They are either under no necessity to work for their living, or are enabled to choose the sphere of activity that is really congenial to them, and gives them pleasure. These are the poets, the philosophers, the men of science, the men of culture – in a word, the real men, the men who have realized themselves, and in whom all Humanity gains a partial realization. Upon the other hand, there are a great many people who, having no private property of their own, and being always on the brink of sheer starvation, are compelled to do the work of beasts of burden, to do work that is quite uncongenial to them, and to which they are forced by the peremptory, unreasonable, degrading Tyranny of want. These are the poor; and amongst them there is no grace of manner, or charm of speech, or civilization or culture, or refinement in pleasures, or joy of life. From their collective force Humanity gains much in material prosperity. But it is only the material result that it gains, and the man who is poor is in himself absolutely of no importance. He is merely the infinitesimal atom of a force that, so far from regarding him, crushes him: indeed, prefers him crushed, as in that case he is far more obedient.

Of course it might be said that the Individualism generated under conditions of private property is not always, or even as a rule, of a fine or wonderful type, and that the poor, if they have not culture and charm, have still many virtues. Both these statements would be quite true. The possession of private property is very often extremely demoralizing, and that is, of course, one of the reasons why Socialism wants to get rid of the institution. In fact, property is really a nuisance. Some years ago people went about the country saying that property has duties. They said it so often and so tediously that, at last, the Church has begun to say it. One hears it now from every pulpit. It is perfectly true. Property not merely has duties, but has so many duties that its possession to any large extent is a bore. It involves endless claims upon one, endless attention to business, endless bother. If property had simply pleasures, we could stand it; but its duties make it unbearable. In the interest of the rich we must get rid of it. The virtues of the poor may be readily admitted, and are much to be regretted. We are often told that the poor are grateful for charity. Some of them are, no doubt, but the best amongst the poor are never grateful. They are ungrateful, discontented, disobedient, and rebellious. They are quite right to be so. Charity they feel to be a ridiculously inadequate mode of partial restitution, or a sentimental dole, usually accompanied by some impertinent attempt on the part of the sentimentalist to tyrannize over their private lives. Why should they be grateful for the crumbs that fall from the rich man's table? They should be seated at the board, and are beginning to know it. As for being discontented, a man who would not be discontented with such surroundings and such a low mode of life would be a perfect brute. Disobedience, in the eyes of any one who has read history, is man's original virtue. It is through disobedience that progress has been made, through disobedience and through rebellion. Sometimes the poor are praised for being thrifty. But to recommend thrift to the poor is both grotesque and insulting. It is like advising a man who is starving to eat less. For a town or country labourer to practise thrift would be absolutely immoral. Man should not be ready to show that he can live like a badly fed animal. He should decline to live like that, and should either steal or go on the rates, which is considered by many to be a form of stealing. As for begging, it is safer to beg than to take, but it is finer to take than to beg. No: a poor man who is ungrateful, unthrifty, discontented, and rebellious, is probably a real personality, and has much in him. He is at any rate a healthy protest. As for the virtuous poor, one can pity them, of course, but one cannot possibly admire them. They have made private terms with the enemy, and sold their birthright for very bad pottage. They must also be extraordinarily stupid. I can quite understand a man accepting laws that protect private property, and admit of its accumulation, as long as he himself is able under those conditions to realize some form of beautiful and intellectual life. But it is almost incredible to me how a man whose life is marred and made hideous by such laws can possibly acquiesce in their continuance.

However, the explanation is not really difficult to find. It is simply this. Misery and poverty are so absolutely degrading, and exercise such a paralysing effect over the nature of men, that no class is ever really conscious of its own suffering. They have to be told of it by other people, and they often entirely disbelieve them. What is said by great employers of labour against agitators is unquestionably true. Agitators are a set of interfering, meddling people, who come down to some perfectly contented class of the community and sow the seeds of discontent amongst them. That is the reason why agitators are so absolutely necessary. Without them, in our incomplete state, there would be no advance towards civilization. Slavery was put down in America, not in consequence of any action on the part of the slaves, or even any express desire on their part that they should be free. It was put down entirely through the grossly illegal conduct of certain agitators in Boston and elsewhere, who were not slaves themselves, nor owners of slaves, nor had anything to do with the question really. It was, undoubtedly, the Abolitionists who set the torch alight, who began the whole thing. And it is curious to note that from the slaves themselves they received, not merely very little assistance, but hardly any sympathy even: and when at the close of the war the slaves found themselves free, found themselves indeed so absolutely free that they were free to starve, many of them bitterly regretted the new state of things. To the thinker, the most tragic fact in the whole of the French Revolution is not that Marie Antoinette was killed for being a queen, but that the starved peasants of the Vendée voluntarily went out to die for the hideous cause of feudalism.

It is clear, then, that no Authoritarian Socialism will do. For while under the present system a very large number of people can lead lives of a certain amount of freedom and expression and happiness, under an industrial-barrack system, or a system of economic tyranny, nobody would be able to have any such freedom at all. It is to be regretted that a portion of our community should be practically in slavery, but to propose to solve the problem by enslaving the entire community is childish. Every man must be left quite free to choose his own work. No form of compulsion must be exercised over him. If there is, his work will not be good for him, will not be good in itself, and will not be good for others. And by work I simply mean activity of any kind.

I hardly think that any Socialist, nowadays, would seriously propose that an inspector should call every morning at each house to see that each citizen rose up and did manual labour for eight hours. Humanity has got beyond that stage, and reserves such a form of life for the people whom, in a very arbitrary manner, it chooses to call criminals. But I confess that many of the socialistic views that I have come across seem to me to be tainted with ideas of authority, if not of actual compulsion. Of course authority and compulsion are out of the question. All association must be quite voluntary. It is only in voluntary associations that man is fine.

But it may be asked how Individualism, which is now more or less dependent on the existence of private property for its development, will benefit by the abolition of such private property. The answer is very simple. It is true that, under existing conditions, a few men who have had private means of their own, such as Byron, Shelley, Browning, Victor Hugo, Baudelaire, and others, have been able to realize their personality, more or less completely. Not one of these men ever did a single day's work for hire. They were relieved from poverty. They had an immense advantage. The question is whether it would be for the good of Individualism that such an advantage should be taken away. Let us suppose that it is taken away. What happens then to Individualism? How will it benefit?

It will benefit in this way. Under the new conditions Individualism will be far freer, far finer, and far more intensified than it is now. I am not talking of the great imaginatively realized Individualism of such poets as I have mentioned, but of the great actual Individualism latent and potential in mankind generally. For the recognition of private property has really harmed Individualism, and obscured it, by confusing a man with what he possesses. It has led Individualism entirely astray. It has made gain, not growth, its aim. So that man thought that the important thing was to have, and did not know that the important thing is to be. The true perfection of man lies, not in what man has, but in what man is. Private property has crushed true Individualism, and set up an Individualism that is false. It has debarred one part of the community from being individual by starving them. It has debarred the other part of the community from being individual by putting them on the wrong road, and encumbering them. Indeed, so completely has man's personality been absorbed by his possessions that the English law has always treated offences against a man's property with far more severity than offences against his person, and property is still the test of complete citizenship. The industry necessary for the making of money is also very demoralizing. In a community like ours, where property confers immense distinction, social position, honour, respect, titles, and other pleasant things of the kind, man, being naturally ambitious, makes it his aim to accumulate this property, and goes on wearily and tediously accumulating it long after he has got far more than he wants, or can use, or enjoy, or perhaps even know of. Man will kill himself by overwork in order to secure property, and really, considering the enormous advantages that property brings, one is hardly surprised. One's regret is that society should be constructed on such a basis that man has been forced into a groove in which he cannot freely develop what is wonderful, and fascinating, and delightful in him – in which, in fact, he misses the true pleasure and joy of living. He is also, under existing conditions, very insecure. An enormously wealthy merchant may be – often is – every moment of his life at the mercy of things that are not under his control. If the wind blows an extra point or so, or the weather suddenly changes, or some trivial thing happens, his ship may go down, his speculations may go wrong, and he finds himself a poor man, with his social position quite gone. Now, nothing should be able to harm a man except himself. Nothing should be able to rob a man at all. What a man really has, is what is in him. What is outside of him should be a matter of no importance . . .

It will be a marvellous thing – the true personality of man – when we see it. It will grow naturally and simply, flowerlike, or as a tree grows. It will not be at discord. It will never argue or dispute. It will not prove things. It will know everything. And yet it will not busy itself about knowledge. It will have wisdom. Its value will not be measured by material things. It will have nothing. And yet it will have everything, and whatever one takes from it, it will still have, so rich will it be. It will not be always meddling with others, or asking them to be like itself. It will love them because they will be different. And yet while it will not meddle with others, it will help all, as a beautiful thing helps us, by being what it is. The personality of man will be very wonderful. It will be as wonderful as the personality of a child.

In its development it will be assisted by Christianity, if men desire that; but if men do not desire that, it will develop none the less surely. For it will not worry itself about the past, nor care whether things happened or did not happen. Nor will it admit any laws but its own laws; nor any authority but its own authority. Yet it will love those who sought to intensify it, and speak often of them. And of these Christ was one.

'Know thyself!' was written over the portal of the antique world. Over the portal of the new world, 'Be thyself' shall be written. And the message of Christ to man was simply 'Be thyself.' That is the secret of Christ.

When Jesus talks about the poor he simply means personalities, just as when he talks about the rich he simply means people who have not developed their personalities. Jesus moved in a community that allowed the accumulation of private property just as ours does, and the gospel that he preached was, not that in such a community it is an advantage for a man to live on scanty, unwholesome food, to wear ragged, unwholesome clothes, to sleep in horrid, unwholesome dwellings, and a disadvantage for a man to live under healthy, pleasant, and decent conditions. Such a view would have been wrong there and then, and would, of course, be still more wrong now and in England; for as man moves northward the material necessities of life become of more vital importance, and our society is infinitely more complex, and displays far greater extremes of luxury and pauperism than any society of the antique world. What Jesus meant was this. He said to man, 'You have a wonderful personality. Develop it. Be yourself. Don't imagine that your perfection lies in accumulating or possessing external things. Your affection is inside of you. If only you could realize that, you would not want to be rich. Ordinary riches can be stolen from a man. Real riches cannot. In the treasury-house of your soul, there are infinitely precious things, that may not be taken from you. And so, try to so shape your life that external things will not harm you. And try also, to get rid of personal property. It involves sordid preoccupation, endless industry, continual wrong. Personal property hinders Individualism at every step.' It is to be noted that Jesus never says that impoverished people are necessarily good, or wealthy people necessarily bad. That would not have been true. Wealthy people are, as a class, better than impoverished people, more moral, more intellectual, more well-behaved. There is only one class in the community that thinks more about money than the rich, and that is the poor. The poor can think of nothing else. That is the misery of being poor. What Jesus does say, is that man reaches his perfection, not through what he has, not even through what he does, but entirely through what he is. And so the wealthy young man who comes to Jesus is represented as a thoroughly good citizen, who has broken none of the laws of his state, none of the commandments of his religion. He is quite respectable, in the ordinary sense of that extraordinary word. Jesus says to him, 'You should give up private property. It hinders you from realizing your perfection. It is a drag upon you. It is a burden. Your personality does not need it. It is within you, and not outside of you, that you will find what you really are, and what you really want.' To his own friends he says the same thing. He tells them to be themselves, and not to be always worrying about other things. What do other things matter? Man is complete in himself. When they go into the world, the world will disagree with them. That is inevitable. The world hates Individualism. But that is not to trouble them. They are to be calm and self-centred. If a man takes their cloak, they are to give him their coat, just to show that material things are of no importance. If people abuse them, they are not to answer back. What does it signify? The things people say of a man do not alter a man. He is what he is. Public opinion is of no value whatsoever. Even if people employ actual violence, they are not to be violent in turn. That would be to fall to the same low level. After all, even in prison, a man can be quite free. His soul can be free. His personality can be untroubled. He can be at peace. And, above all things, they are not to interfere with other people or judge them in any way. Personality is a very mysterious thing. A man cannot always be estimated by what he does. He may keep the law, and yet be worthless. He may break the law, and yet be fine. He may be bad, without ever doing anything bad. He may commit a sin against society, and yet realize through that sin his true perfection . . .

Yes, there are suggestive things in Individualism. Socialism annihilates family life, for instance. With the abolition of private property, marriage in its present form must disappear. This is part of the programme. Individualism accepts this and makes it fine. It converts the abolition of legal restraint into a form of freedom that will help the full development of personality, and make the love of man and woman more wonderful, more beautiful, and more ennobling. Jesus knew this. He rejected the claims of family life, although they existed in his day and community in a very marked form. 'Who is my mother? Who are my brothers?' he said, when he was told that they wished to speak to him. When one of his followers asked leave to go and bury his father, 'Let the dead bury the dead,' was his terrible answer. He would allow no claim whatsoever to be made on personality.

And so he who would lead a Christlike life is he who is perfectly and absolutely himself. He may be a great poet, or a great man of science, or a young student at a University, or one who watches sheep upon a moor; or a maker of dramas, like Shakespeare, or a thinker about God, like Spinoza; or a child who plays in a garden, or a fisherman who throws his net into the sea. It does not matter what he is, as long as he realizes the perfection of the soul that is within him. All imitation in morals and in life is wrong . . .

Individualism, then, is what through Socialism we are to attain. As a natural result the State must give up all idea of government. It must give it up because, as a wise man once said many centuries before Christ, there is such a thing as leaving mankind alone; there is no such thing as governing mankind. All modes of government are failures. Despotism is unjust to everybody, including the despot, who was probably made for better things. Oligarchies are unjust to the many, and ochlocracies are unjust to the few. High hopes were once formed of democracy; but democracy means simply the bludgeoning of the people by the people for the people. It has been found out. I must say that it was high time, for all authority is quite degrading. It degrades those who exercise it, and degrades those over whom it is exercised. When it is violently, grossly, and cruelly used, it produces a good effect, by creating, or at any rate bringing out, the spirit of revolt and Individualism that is to kill it. When it is used with a certain amount of kindness, and accompanied by prizes and rewards, it is dreadfully demoralizing. People, in that case, are less conscious of the horrible pressure that is being put on them, and so go through their lives in a sort of coarse comfort, like petted animals, without ever realizing that they are probably thinking other people's thoughts, living by other people's standards, wearing practically what one may

call other people's second-hand clothes, and never being themselves
for a single moment. 'He who would be free,' says a fine thinker,
'must not conform.' And authority, by bribing people to conform,
produces a very gross kind of over-fed barbarism amongst us.

With authority, punishment will pass away. This will be a great
gain – a gain, in fact, of incalculable value. As one reads history, not
in the expurgated editions written for schoolboys and passmen, but in
the original authorities of each time, one is absolutely sickened, not
by the crimes that the wicked have committed, but by the punishments that the good have inflicted; and a community is infinitely
more brutalized by the habitual employment of punishment than it
is by the occasional occurrence of crime. It obviously follows that
the more punishment is inflicted the more crime is produced, and
most modern legislation has clearly recognized this, and has made it
its task to diminish punishment as far as it thinks it can. Wherever
it has really diminished it, the results have always been extremely
good. The less punishment, the less crime. When there is no punishment at all, crime will either cease to exist, or, if it occurs, will be
treated by physicians as a very distressing form of dementia, to
be cured by care and kindness. For what are called criminals nowadays are not criminals at all. Starvation, and not sin, is the parent
of modern crime. That indeed is the reason why our criminals are,
as a class, so absolutely uninteresting from any psychological point
of view. They are not marvellous Macbeths and terrible Vautrins.
They are merely what ordinary respectable, commonplace people
would be if they had not got enough to eat. When private property
is abolished there will be no necessity for crime, no demand for it;
it will cease to exist. Of course all crimes are not crimes against
property, though such are the crimes that the English law, valuing
what a man has more than what a man is, punishes with the harshest
and most horrible severity (if we except the crime of murder, and
regard death as worse than penal servitude, a point on which our
criminals, I believe, disagree). But though a crime may not be against
property, it may spring from the misery and rage and depression
produced by our wrong system of property-holding, and so, when
that system is abolished, will disappear. When each member of the
community has sufficient for his wants, and is not interfered with by
his neighbour, it will not be an object of any interest to him to
interfere with any one else. Jealousy, which is an extraordinary source

of crime in modern life, is an emotion closely bound up with our conceptions of property, and under Socialism and Individualism will die out. It is remarkable that in communistic tribes jealousy is entirely unknown.

Now as the State is not to govern, it may be asked what the State is to do. The State is to be a voluntary manufacturer and distributor of necessary commodities. The State is to make what is useful. The individual is to make what is beautiful. And as I have mentioned the word labour, I cannot help saying that a great deal of nonsense is being written and talked nowadays about the dignity of manual labour. There is nothing necessarily dignified about manual labour at all, and most of it is absolutely degrading. It is mentally and morally injurious to man to do anything in which he does not find pleasure, and many forms of labour are quite pleasureless activities, and should be regarded as such. To sweep a slushy crossing for eight hours on a day when the east wind is blowing is a disgusting occupation. To sweep it with mental, moral, or physical dignity seems to me to be impossible. To sweep it with joy would be appalling. Man is made for something better than disturbing dirt. All work of that kind should be done by a machine.

And I have no doubt that it will be so. Up to the present, man has been, to a certain extent, the slave of machinery, and there is something tragic in the fact that as soon as man had invented a machine to do his work he began to starve. This, however, is, of course, the result of our property system and our system of competition. One man owns a machine which does the work of five hundred men. Five hundred men are, in consequence, thrown out of employment, and, having no work to do, become hungry and take to thieving. The one man secures the produce of the machine and keeps it, and has five hundred times as much as he should have, and probably, which is of much more importance, a great deal more than he really wants. Were that machine the property of all, everybody would benefit by it. It would be an immense advantage to the community. All unintellectual labour, all monotonous, dull labour, all labour that deals with dreadful things, and involves unpleasant conditions, must be done by machinery. Machinery must work for us in coal mines, and do all sanitary services, and be the stoker of steamers, and clean the streets, and run messages on wet days, and do anything that is tedious or distressing. At present machinery competes against man. Under

[313]

proper conditions machinery will serve man. There is no doubt at all that this is the future of machinery; and just as trees grow while the country gentleman is asleep, so while Humanity will be amusing itself, or enjoying cultivated leisure – which, and not labour, is the aim of man – or making beautiful things, or reading beautiful things, or simply contemplating the world with admiration and delight, machinery will be doing all the necessary and unpleasant work. The fact is, that civilization requires slaves. The Greeks were quite right there. Unless there are slaves to do the ugly, horrible, uninteresting work, culture and contemplation become almost impossible. Human slavery is wrong, insecure, and demoralizing. On mechanical slavery, on the slavery of the machine, the future of the world depends. And when scientific men are no longer called upon to go down to a depressing East End and distribute bad cocoa and worse blankets to starving people, they will have delightful leisure in which to devise wonderful and marvellous things for their own joy and the joy of everyone else. There will be great storages of force for every city, and for every house if required, and this force man will convert into heat, light, or motion, according to his needs. Is this Utopian? A map of the world that does not include Utopia is not worth even glancing at, for it leaves out the one country at which Humanity is always landing. And when Humanity lands there, it looks out, and, seeing a better country, sets sail. Progress is the realization of Utopias.

Source: Oscar Wilde, 'The Soul of Man under Socialism', *Fortnightly Review* XLIX, 1891; *The Soul of Man*, 1895.

Going Nowhere

The cynical view that rich kids are the likeliest to become Socialist revolutionaries is powerfully borne out by William Morris (1834–96). For an advocate of classless equality, he had a remarkably privileged life. The son of a wealthy stockbroker, he was educated at Marlborough College and Oxford University. Afflicted by the 'ugliness' of the modern world, he became a passionate advocate of old-style handicrafts, and a foe of the machine-made. He founded, in 1861, a highly prosperous company for the manufacture of stained glass, textiles, wallpapers and other costly furnishings, which included Queen Victoria among its clients.

In 1884 he helped to organize the Socialist League, dedicated to destroying class distinction and advancing 'revolutionary international Socialism'. He hoped England would return to 'that primitive Communism which preceded civilization', but he also wanted workers to have a life of 'refinement and education' like himself. His utopia, *News from Nowhere*, was published in the League's journal *The Commonweal* in 1890. It draws upon a rosy vision of the Middle Ages, derived partly from Sir Walter Scott's Waverley novels (all of which Morris had read by the time he was seven).

In Morris's Middle Ages, such inconveniences as feudalism, plague and famine have no place. The narrator in *News from Nowhere* awakes some hundreds of years in the future, to find himself back in the fourteenth century – or in a Morrisite version of it. The inhabitants are polite, jolly, friendly people, with musical laughter and prettily embroidered clothes. They love folk festivals, handicrafts and haymaking. The women are lightly clad and affectionate, and enjoy waiting on and cooking for the men. Old ideas of female emancipation have long been forgotten. The narrator learns that an armed revolution, followed by civil war between capital and labour, took place in the 1950s. When it was over, the survivors decided to regress to a pre-industrial culture. The cities of the industrial Midlands were pulled down, along with London's sprawling suburbs, and the railway system was destroyed. Meadow and woodland now flourish where buildings once stood. Commerce and money no longer exist. In shops, goods are given away. Work is pleasurable and voluntary. People gather in 'banded workshops' to make beautiful objects for everyday use. There are no politics and no government – beyond local 'motes' or meetings, held to discover the will of the majority.

Many critics have pointed out the impracticalities of Morris's scheme. It ignores virtually every basic factor of social and economic reality. All crucial issues are left vague. The narrator reveals, almost in an aside, that the utopians have 'immensely improved machinery', and a 'force' superior to steam-power, for tasks that it would be irksome to do by hand. But how these are generated and maintained is unclear. The population has not increased since the late nineteenth century, yet there is no mention of birth control or other checks. Everyone enjoys robust health without, apparently, medical knowledge, surgery or drugs. Morris's defenders reply that these flaws are immaterial, since the work is self-confessedly a dream. Yet it was published in an official political paper, and displays, in its inadequacies, the confusion and hypocrisy that have dogged the course of English Socialism.

News from Nowhere was Morris's riposte to Bellamy's *Looking Backward* (p. 284). 'I wouldn't care,' sneered Morris, 'to live in such a Cockney paradise as he imagines.' It was not only Bellamy's trust in technology that Morris despised, but also his yen for regimentation. In Morris's utopia, freedom prevails. There is no legal system or penal code. Even murder carries no penalty, the argument being that it brings its own retribution: 'In a society where there is no punishment to evade, no law to triumph over, remorse will certainly follow transgression.' Marriage and divorce, too, are matters of 'simple inclination', following the pattern laid down in Morris's Manifesto of the Socialist League. Partners come together or separate as they wish, without the rest of the community interfering. There is also freedom from what we regard as education – as the narrator learns from his companion, Dick, while they ride through the woodland that has replaced Kensington.

It was exceedingly pleasant in the dappled shadow, for the day was growing as hot as need be, and the coolness and shade soothed my excited mind into a condition of dreamy pleasure, so that I felt as if I should like to go on for ever through that balmy freshness. My companion seemed to share in my feelings, and let the horse go slower and slower as he sat inhaling the green forest scents, chief amongst which was the smell of the trodden bracken near the way-side.

Romantic as this Kensington wood was, however, it was not lonely. We came on many groups both coming and going, or wandering in the edges of the wood. Amongst these were many children from six to eight years old up to sixteen or seventeen. They seemed to me to be especially fine specimens of their race, and were clearly enjoying themselves to the utmost; some of them were hanging about little tents pitched on the greensward, and by some of these fires were burning, with pots hanging over them gipsy fashion. Dick explained to me that there were scattered houses in the forest, and indeed we caught a glimpse of one or two. He said they were mostly quite small, such as used to be called cottages when there were slaves in the land, but they were pleasant enough and fitting for the wood.

'They must be pretty well stocked with children,' said I, pointing to the many youngsters about the way.

'O,' said he, 'these children do not all come from the near houses, the woodland houses, but from the countryside generally. They often make up parties, and come to play in the woods for weeks together in summer-time, living in tents, as you see. We rather encourage them to it; they learn to do things for themselves, and get to notice the wild creatures; and, you see, the less they stew inside houses the better for them. Indeed, I must tell you that many grown people will go to live in the forests through the summer; though they for the most part go to the bigger ones, like Windsor, or the Forest of Dean, or the northern wastes. Apart from the other pleasures of it, it gives them a little rough work, which I am sorry to say is getting somewhat scarce for these last fifty years.'

He broke off, and then said, 'I tell you all this, because I see that if I talk I must be answering questions, which you are thinking, even if you are not speaking them out; but my kinsman will tell you more about it.'

I saw that I was likely to get out of my depth again, and so merely for the sake of tiding over an awkwardness and to say something, I said:

'Well, the youngsters here will be all the fresher for school when the summer gets over and they have to go back again.'

'School?' he said; 'yes, what do you mean by that word? I don't see how it can have anything to do with children. We talk, indeed, of a school of herring, and a school of painting, and in the former sense we might talk of a school of children – but otherwise,' said he, laughing, 'I must own myself beaten.'

Hang it! thought I, I can't open my mouth without digging up some new complexity. I wouldn't try to set my friend right in his etymology; and I thought I had best say nothing about the boy-farms which I had been used to call schools, as I saw pretty clearly that they had disappeared; and so I said after a little fumbling, 'I was using the word in the sense of a system of education.'

'Education?' said he, meditatively, 'I know enough Latin to know that the word must come from *educere*, to lead out; and I have heard it used; but I have never met anybody who could give me a clear explanation of what it means.'

You may imagine how my new friends fell in my esteem when I heard this frank avowal; and I said, rather contemptuously, 'Well, education means a system of teaching young people.'

'Why not old people also?' said he with a twinkle in his eye. 'But,' he went on, 'I can assure you our children learn, whether they go through a "system of teaching" or not. Why, you will not find one of these children about here, boy or girl, who cannot swim, and every one of them has been used to tumbling about the little forest ponies – there's one of them now! They all of them know how to cook; the bigger lads can mow; many can thatch and do odd jobs at carpentering; or they know how to keep shop. I can tell you they know plenty of things.'

'Yes, but their mental education, the teaching of their minds,' said I, kindly translating my phrase.

'Guest,' said he, 'perhaps you have not learned to do these things I have been speaking about; and if that's the case, don't run away with the idea that it doesn't take some skill to do them, and doesn't give plenty of work for one's mind: you would change your opinion if you saw a Dorsetshire lad thatching, for instance. But, however, I understand you to be speaking of book-learning; and as to that, it is a simple affair. Most children, seeing books lying about, manage to read by the time they are four years old; though I am told it has not always been so. As to writing, we do not encourage them to scrawl too early (though scrawl a little they will), because it gets them into a habit of ugly writing; and what's the use of a lot of ugly writing being done, when rough printing can be done so easily. You understand that handsome writing we like, and many people will write their books out when they make them, or get them written; I mean books of which only a few copies are needed – poems, and such like, you know. However, I am wandering from my lambs; but you must excuse me, for I am interested in this matter of writing, being myself a fair writer.'

'Well,' said I, 'about the children; when they know how to read and write, don't they learn something else – languages, for instance?'

'Of course,' he said; 'sometimes even before they can read, they can talk French, which is the nearest language talked on the other side of the water; and they soon get to know German also, which is talked by a huge number of communes and colleges on the mainland. These are the principal languages we speak in these islands, along with English or Welsh, or Irish, which is another form of Welsh; and children pick them up very quickly, because their elders all know them; and besides our guests from oversea often bring their children with them, and the little ones get together, and rub their speech into one another.'

'And the older languages?' said I.

'O yes,' said he, 'they mostly learn Latin and Greek along with the modern ones, when they do anything more than merely pick up the latter.'

'And history?' said I; 'how do you teach history?'

'Well,' said he, 'when a person can read, of course he reads what he likes to; and he can easily get some one to tell him what are the best books to read on such or such a subject, or to explain what he doesn't understand in the books when he is reading them.'

'Well,' said I, 'what else do they learn? I suppose they don't all learn history?'

'No, no,' said he; 'some don't care about it; in fact, I don't think many do. I have heard my great-grandfather say that it is mostly in periods of turmoil and strife and confusion that people care much about history; and you know,' said my friend, with an amiable smile, 'we are not like that now. No; many people study facts about the make of things and the matters of cause and effect, so that knowledge increases on us, if that be good; and some, as you heard about friend Bob yonder, will spend time over mathematics. 'Tis no use forcing people's tastes.'

Said I: 'But you don't mean that children learn all these things?'

Said he: 'That depends on what you mean by children; and also you must remember how much they differ. As a rule, they don't do much reading, except for a few story-books, till they are about fifteen years old; we don't encourage early bookishness, though you will find some children who *will* take to books very early; which perhaps is not good for them; but it's no use thwarting them; and very often it doesn't last long with them, and they find their level before they are twenty years old. You see, children are mostly given to imitating their elders, and when they see most people about them engaged in genuinely amusing work, like house-building and street-paving, and gardening, and the like, that is what they want to be doing; so I don't think we need fear having too many book-learned men.'

Source: William Morris, *News from Nowhere*, Reeves and Turner, 1891.

Suicide on Tap

The American novelist and social reformer Ignatius Donnelly (1831–1901) was a leading advocate of the theory that Bacon wrote Shakespeare's plays (and also Marlowe's plays and Montaigne's *Essays*). More creditably he was a liberal politician and Congressman, who edited a weekly, *Anti-Monopolist*, attacking bankers and financiers, and helped to found the Populist Party in 1892. His utopia *Caesar's Column* (1891) was a best-seller, translated into several languages. Set in New York in 1988, it depicts an overcrowded world with enormous gulfs between rich and poor, ruled by corrupt, tyrannical businessmen, mainly Jewish. In the course of the novel a workers' organization called The Brotherhood of Destruction, armed with airships and poison-gas bombs, carries out its pledge to exterminate most of the human race, so that it may establish a 'purer and better state of society'. The civilized world is reduced to rubble, the few survivors starve or devour one another, wild beasts roam the streets, and the Swiss narrator and his friends depart to set up a happy republic in Uganda.

At the start of the novel New York is described as a city of heartless luxury and despair. Suicide has become a social problem because the numbers drowning themselves in rivers and reservoirs tend to pollute the water supply, and those who attempt to shoot, stab or poison themselves often linger distressingly for hours before expiring. To counter this evil, a new facility is introduced.

In all the public squares or parks they have erected handsome houses, beautifully furnished, with baths and bed-rooms. If a man has decided to die, he goes there. He is first photographed; then his name, if he sees fit to give it, is recorded, with his residence; and his directions are taken as to the disposition of his body. There are tables at which he can write his farewell letters to his friends. A doctor explains to him the nature and effect of the different poisons, and he selects the kind he prefers. He is expected to bring with him the clothes in which he intends to be cremated. He swallows a little pill, lies down upon a bed, or, if he prefers it, in his coffin; pleasant music is played for him; he goes to sleep, and wakes up on the other side of the great line. Every day hundreds of people, men and women, perish in this way; and they are borne off to the great furnaces for the dead, and consumed. The authorities assert that it is a marked improvement over the old-fashioned methods; but to my mind it is a shocking combination of impiety and mock-philanthropy. The truth is, that, in this vast, over-crowded city, man is a drug – a superfluity – and I think many men and women end their lives out of an overwhelming sense of their own insignificance – in other words, from a mere weariness of feeling that they are nothing, they become nothing.

Source: Ignatius Donnelly, *Caesar's Column: A Story of the Twentieth Century*, Sampson Low, Marston & Co., 1891.

Utopian Menopause

Elizabeth Wolstenholme (1834–1918), feminist and suffragette, was the author of one of the earliest sex-education books for children, *The Human Flower* (1892). In her utopian poem *Woman Free* (1893) she deplores the 'aeons of wrong' during which women have been the victims of men's lust and cruelty, but looks forward to a time of moral and scientific enlightenment, already dawning. The poem develops the theory that menstruation, far from being a natural occurrence, is an inherited disease traceable to the brutal rapes suffered by women in prehistory. With the aid of science, new-age women will eliminate this physical disadvantage.

> For carnal servitude left cruel stain,
> And galls that fester from the fleshly chain;
> Unhealed the scars of man's distempered greed,
> The wounds of blind injustice still they bleed;
> Recurrent suffering lets her not forget
> The aimless payments of a dismal debt –
> Survival from dim age of man's abuse
> Of functions immature, profaned by savage use.
>
> Her girlhood's helpless years through cycles long
> Had been a martyrdom of sexual wrong,
> For little strength or choice might child oppose
> To shield herself from force of sensual foes;
> Impending motherhood might win no rest
> Or refuge sacred from the satyr quest;
> Unripe maternity, untimely birth,
> The woman's constant dole in those dark days of earth.
>
> Action repeated tends to rhythmic course,
> And thus the mischief, due at first to force,
> Brought cumulative sequence to the race,

Till habit bred hereditary trace;
On woman falls that heritage of woe,
And e'en the virgin feels its dastard blow –
For, long ere fit to wield maternal cares,
Abnormal fruits of birth her guiltless body bears.

Misread by man, this sign of his misdeed
Was held as symbol of her nubile need,
And on through history's length her tender age
Has still been victim to his adult rage;
He, by his text, with irony serene,
Banned her resultant 'manner' as 'unclean';
The censure base upon himself recoils,
Yet leaves the woman wan and cumbered in his toils.

Vicarious punishment for manhood's crime
Takes grievous toll of all her active prime;
The hap, in educated woman's fate,
Is instinct with antipathy and hate;
Reason confirming tells, no honest claim
Could ever cause such gust of inward shame,
Nor act of normal wont might man blaspheme
To make of Nature's need a vile opprobrious theme.

Thoughts like to these are breathings of the truth
To whoso ponders deep the tale of ruth;
The futile mannish pleas that would explain
The purport of her periodic pain,
All bear unconscious witness to the wrong
In blindness born, in error fostered long –
The spurious function growing with the years,
Till almost natural use the morbid mode appears.

Grievous the hurt to women, which to right
Is instant duty of our stronger sight;
From off her weary shoulders, bruised and worn,
To lift the cross in longtime misery borne;
Until, reintegrate in frame and mind,
A speedy restitution she shall find,
From every trammel of man's mastery freed,
Nor held by his behest from fullest life and deed.

And soon may pass her suffering, for the ill
By man begot, lies subject to our skill;
All human malady may be allayed
With human forethought, human action's aid;
Ours then the fault, since, given in our hand
Is power the evil hazard to command;
For Nature, kindly wise our woes to shape,
In every pang of pain both prompts and points escape.

So woman shall her own redemption gain,
Instructed by the sting of bootless pain;
With Nature ever helpful to retrieve
The injury we heedlessly achieve,
For seed of act, by recent woman sown,
Already guerdon rich in hope is shown –
Such faculty her new-found presence decks,
The sage physician, she, and saviour of her sex.

With purer phase of life proves woman less
The burden of the wasting weariness;
And thus, in rank refined or rude have grown
Maidens in whom the weakness was not known;
Hale woman and true mother they have been,
Yet never have the noisome habit seen:
Not to neglectful man to greatly care
How such immunity all womanhood might share.

Her intellect alert the harm shall heal,
And ways of wholesomeness and strength reveal;
The saving truth she wins with studious thought
More swiftly to her daughter shall be taught –
How body still is supple unto mind
By dint of soul is fleshly form inclined,
And woman's will shall work of man atone,
The deed his darkness wrought be by her light undone.

No longer drilled deformity to nurse,
And woo, when slow to appear, the absent curse,
Her counter-effort, helped by Nature's grace,
Shall quell the 'custom's' last abhorrent trace;
Its morbid usurpation shall refute –

No more to woman natural than to brute –
A needless noyance with a baseless claim,
The lingering mark of man's unthinking guilt and shame.

Wolstenholme's 32-page poem is followed by 190 pages of notes, drawn from medical, sociological and feminist publications. To support the claim in the tenth stanza quoted above she observes: 'The writer has had detailed personal experiences of perfect health and maternity being co-existent with little or no appearance of the menses in the case of women whose names, if published, would be indubitable guarantee for their accuracy and veracity.'

Source: Ellis Ethelmer [Elizabeth Wolstenholme], *Woman Free*, The Women's Emancipation Union, 1893.

The Law of the Jungle

Many would cite Rudyard Kipling (1865–1936) as the greatest English short-story writer. In *The Jungle Book* (1894) and *The Second Jungle Book* (1895) he creates another world with its own unwritten laws, ceremonies, codes and hierarchies, and makes it instantly credible – more credible, arguably, than any other utopia ever written. It is, of course, impossible as well as credible, which is a further testimony to Kipling's art. The story of the little waif Mowgli, loved and fostered by a big motherly animal, had a deep personal attraction for Kipling, since his own childhood had been bitter and lonely. He was born in India, but his parents left him, at the age of six, with a foster family in Southsea, whom he hated and despised.

The Jungle Books have been read as an allegory of imperialism – the man child dominates the 'lesser breeds' naturally, by virtue of his superior intelligence. This, however, is to oversimplify. The stories bring out the animals' superiority to Mowgli as much as his power over them. That he survives at all is due to their mercy and courage. The dream of the natural man, free of civilization's sterile, cramping routines, is a utopian motif at the centre of the stories, and it is a dream that depends on man acquiring the keen senses and pure physical being of the animal. The Law of the Jungle, by which the animals live, is not mere catch-as-catch-can social Darwinism. It embodies chivalry, loyalty and sportsmanship as well as the rigours of a natural law. In these respects it may be seen as a conscious improvement on what Kipling knew to be the faulty system of British imperial administration. The story that follows, 'Mowgli's Brothers', was the first of the series. Kipling wrote it in 1892 when he was living in Vermont and his wife, Carrie, was expecting their first child.

> Now Chil the Kite brings home the night
>   That Mang the Bat sets free –
> The herds are shut in byre and hut
>   For loosed till dawn are we.
> This is the hour of pride and power,

Talon and tusk and claw.
Oh hear the call! – Good hunting all
That keep the Jungle Law!
Night-Song in the Jungle

It was seven o'clock of a very warm evening in the Seeonee hills when Father Wolf woke up from his day's rest, scratched himself, yawned, and spread out his paws one after the other to get rid of the sleepy feeling in their tips. Mother Wolf lay with her big gray nose dropped across her four tumbling, squealing cubs, and the moon shone into the mouth of the cave where they all lived. 'Augrh!' said Father Wolf, 'it is time to hunt again'; and he was going to spring down hill when a little shadow with a bushy tail crossed the threshold and whined: 'Good luck go with you, O Chief of the Wolves; and good luck and strong white teeth go with the noble children, that they may never forget the hungry in this world.'

It was the jackal – Tabaqui, the Dish-licker – and the wolves of India despise Tabaqui because he runs about making mischief, and telling tales, and eating rags and pieces of leather from the village rubbish-heaps. But they are afraid of him too, because Tabaqui, more than anyone else in the jungle, is apt to go mad, and then he forgets that he was ever afraid of anyone, and runs through the forest biting everything in his way. Even the tiger runs and hides when little Tabaqui goes mad, for madness is the most disgraceful thing that can overtake a wild creature. We call it hydrophobia, but they call it *dewanee* – the madness – and run.

'Enter, then, and look,' said Father Wolf, stiffly; 'but there is no food here.'

'For a wolf, no,' said Tabaqui; 'but for so mean a person as myself a dry bone is a good feast. Who are we, the Gidur-log [the jackal people], to pick and choose?' He scuttled to the back of the cave, where he found the bone of a buck with some meat on it, and sat cracking the end merrily.

'All thanks for this good meal,' he said, licking his lips. 'How beautiful are the noble children! How large are their eyes! And so young too! Indeed, indeed, I might have remembered that the children of kings are men from the beginning.'

Now, Tabaqui knew as well as anyone else that there is nothing so unlucky as to compliment children to their faces; and it pleased him to see Mother and Father Wolf look uncomfortable.

Tabaqui sat still, rejoicing in the mischief that he had made, and then he said spitefully:

'Shere Khan, the Big One, has shifted his hunting-grounds. He will hunt among these hills for the next moon, so he has told me.'

Shere Khan was the tiger who lived near the Waingunga River, twenty miles away.

'He has no right!' Father Wolf began angrily – 'By the Law of the Jungle he has no right to change his quarters without due warning. He will frighten every head of game within ten miles, and I – I have to kill for two, these days.'

'His mother did not call him Lungri [the Lame One] for nothing,' said Mother Wolf, quietly. 'He has been lame in one foot from his birth. That is why he has only killed cattle. Now the villagers of the Waingunga are angry with him, and he has come here to make *our* villagers angry. They will scour the jungle for him when he is far away, and we and our children must run when the grass is set alight. Indeed, we are very grateful to Shere Khan!'

'Shall I tell him of your gratitude?' said Tabaqui.

'Out!' snapped Father Wolf. 'Out and hunt with thy master. Thou hast done harm enough for one night.'

'I go,' said Tabaqui, quietly. 'Ye can hear Shere Khan below in the thickets. I might have saved myself the message.'

Father Wolf listened, and below in the valley that ran down to a little river, he heard the dry, angry, snarly, singsong whine of a tiger who has caught nothing and does not care if all the jungle knows it.

'The fool!' said Father Wolf. 'To begin a night's work with that noise! Does he think that our buck are like his fat Waingunga bullocks?'

'H'sh. It is neither bullock nor buck he hunts tonight,' said Mother Wolf. 'It is Man.' The whine had changed to a sort of humming purr that seemed to come from every quarter of the compass. It was the noise that bewilders woodcutters and gipsies sleeping in the open, and makes them run sometimes into the very mouth of the tiger.

'Man!' said Father Wolf, showing all his white teeth. 'Faugh! Are there not enough beetles and frogs in the tanks that he must eat Man, and on our ground too!'

The Law of the Jungle, which never orders anything without a reason, forbids every beast to eat Man except when he is killing to show his children how to kill, and then he must hunt outside the hunting-grounds of his pack or tribe. The real reason for this is that man-killing means, sooner or later, the arrival of white men on elephants, with guns, and hundreds of brown men with gongs and rockets and torches. Then everybody in the jungle suffers. The reason the beasts give among themselves is that Man is the weakest and most defenceless of all living things, and it is unsportsmanlike to touch him. They say too – and it is true – that man-eaters become mangy, and lose their teeth.

The purr grew louder, and ended in the full-throated 'Aaarh!' of the tiger's charge.

Then there was a howl – an untigerish howl – from Shere Khan. 'He has missed,' said Mother Wolf. 'What is it?'

Father Wolf ran out a few paces and heard Shere Khan muttering and mumbling savagely, as he tumbled about in the scrub.

'The fool has had no more sense than to jump at a woodcutters' camp-fire, and has burned his feet,' said Father Wolf, with a grunt. 'Tabaqui is with him.'

'Something is coming uphill,' said Mother Wolf, twitching one ear. 'Get ready.'

The bushes rustled a little in the thicket, and Father Wolf dropped with his haunches under him, ready for his leap. Then, if you had been watching, you would have seen the most wonderful thing in the world – the wolf checked in mid-spring. He made his bound before he saw what it was he was jumping at, and then he tried to stop himself. The result was that he shot up straight into the air for four or five feet, landing almost where he left ground.

'Man!' he snapped. 'A man's cub. Look!'

Directly in front of him, holding on by a low branch, stood a naked brown baby who could just walk – as soft and as dimpled a little atom as ever came to a wolf's cave at night. He looked up into Father Wolf's face, and laughed.

'Is that a man's cub?' said Mother Wolf. 'I have never seen one. Bring it here.'

A wolf accustomed to moving his own cubs can, if necessary, mouth an egg without breaking it, and though Father Wolf's jaws closed right on the child's back not a tooth even scratched the skin, as he laid it down among the cubs.

[330]

'How little! How naked, and – how bold!' said Mother Wolf, softly. The baby was pushing his way between the cubs to get close to the warm hide. 'Ahai! He is taking his meal with the others. And so this is a man's cub. Now, was there ever a wolf that could boast of a man's cub among her children?'

'I have heard now and again of such a thing, but never in our Pack or in my time,' said Father Wolf. 'He is altogether without hair, and I could kill him with a touch of my foot. But see, he looks up and is not afraid.'

The moonlight was blocked out of the mouth of the cave, for Shere Khan's great square head and shoulders were thrust into the entrance. Tabaqui, behind him, was squeaking: 'My lord, my lord, it went in here!'

'Shere Khan does us great honour,' said Father Wolf, but his eyes were very angry. 'What does Shere Khan need?'

'My quarry. A man's cub went this way,' said Shere Khan. 'Its parents have run off. Give it to me.'

Shere Khan had jumped at a woodcutters' camp-fire, as Father Wolf had said, and was furious from the pain of his burned feet. But Father Wolf knew that the mouth of the cave was too narrow for a tiger to come in by. Even where he was, Shere Khan's shoulders and fore paws were cramped for want of room, as a man's would be if he tried to fight in a barrel.

'The Wolves are a free people,' said Father Wolf. 'They take orders from the Head of the Pack, and not from any striped cattle-killer. The man's cub is ours – to kill if we choose.'

'Ye choose and ye do not choose! What talk is this of choosing? By the bull that I killed, am I to stand nosing into your dog's den for my fair dues? It is I, Shere Khan, who speak!'

The tiger's roar filled the cave with thunder. Mother Wolf shook herself clear of the cubs and sprang forward, her eyes, like two green moons in the darkness, facing the blazing eyes of Shere Khan.

'And it is I, Raksha [The Demon], who answer. The man's cub is mine, Lungri – mine to me! He shall not be killed. He shall live to run with the Pack and to hunt with the Pack; and in the end, look you, hunter of little naked cubs – frog-eater – fish-killer – he shall hunt *thee*! Now get hence, or by the Sambhur that I killed (*I* eat no starved cattle), back thou goest to thy mother, burned beast of the jungle, lamer than ever thou camest into the world! Go!'

[331]

Father Wolf looked on amazed. He had almost forgotten the days when he won Mother Wolf in fair fight from five other wolves, when she ran in the Pack and was not called The Demon for compliment's sake. Shere Khan might have faced Father Wolf, but he could not stand up against Mother Wolf, for he knew that where he was she had all the advantage of the ground, and would fight to the death. So he backed out of the cave-mouth growling, and when he was clear he shouted:

'Each dog barks in his own yard! We will see what the Pack will say to this fostering of man-cubs. The cub is mine, and to my teeth he will come in the end, O bush-tailed thieves!'

Mother Wolf threw herself down panting among the cubs, and Father Wolf said to her gravely:

'Shere Khan speaks this much truth. The cub must be shown to the Pack. Wilt thou still keep him, Mother?'

'Keep him!' she gasped. 'He came naked, by night, alone and very hungry; yet he was not afraid! Look, he has pushed one of my babes to one side already. And that lame butcher would have killed him and would have run off to the Waingunga while the villagers here hunted through all our lairs in revenge! Keep him? Assuredly I will keep him. Lie still, little frog. O thou Mowgli – for Mowgli the Frog I will call thee – the time will come when thou wilt hunt Shere Khan as he has hunted thee.'

'But what will our Pack say?' said Father Wolf.

The Law of the Jungle lays down very clearly that any wolf may, when he marries, withdraw from the Pack he belongs to; but as soon as his cubs are old enough to stand on their feet he must bring them to the Pack Council, which is generally held once a month at full moon, in order that the other wolves may identify them. After that inspection the cubs are free to run where they please, and until they have killed their first buck no excuse is accepted if a grown wolf of the Pack kills one of them. The punishment is death where the murderer can be found; and if you think for a minute you will see that this must be so.

Father Wolf waited till his cubs could run a little, and then on the night of the Pack Meeting took them and Mowgli and Mother Wolf to the Council Rock – a hilltop covered with stones and boulders where a hundred wolves could hide. Akela, the great gray Lone Wolf, who led all the Pack by strength and cunning, lay out at full length on his rock, and below him sat forty or more wolves of every size and colour, from badger-coloured veterans who could handle a buck alone, to young black three-year-olds who thought they could. The Lone Wolf had led them for a year now. He had fallen twice into a wolf-trap in his youth, and once he had been beaten and left for dead; so he knew the manners and customs of men. There was very little talking at the rock. The cubs tumbled over each other in the centre of the circle where their mothers and fathers sat, and now and again a senior wolf would go quietly up to a cub, look at him carefully, and return to his place on noiseless feet. Sometimes a mother would push her cub far out into the moonlight, to be sure that he had not been overlooked. Akela from his rock would cry: 'Ye know the Law – ye know the Law. Look well, O Wolves!' and the anxious mothers would take up the call: 'Look – look well, O Wolves!'

At last – and Mother Wolf's neck-bristles lifted as the time came – Father Wolf pushed 'Mowgli the Frog', as they called him, into the centre, where he sat laughing and playing with some pebbles that glistened in the moonlight.

Akela never raised his head from his paws, but went on with the monotonous cry: 'Look well!' A muffled roar came up from behind the rocks – the voice of Shere Khan crying: 'The cub is mine. Give him to me. What have the Free People to do with a man's cub?' Akela never even twitched his ears: all he said was: 'Look well, O Wolves! What have the Free People to do with the orders of any save the Free People? Look well!'

There was a chorus of deep growls, and a young wolf in his fourth year flung back Shere Khan's question to Akela: 'What have the Free People to do with a man's cub?' Now the Law of the Jungle lays down that if there is any dispute as to the right of a cub to be accepted by the Pack, he must be spoken for by at least two members of the Pack who are not his father and mother.

'Who speaks for this cub?' said Akela. 'Among the Free People who speaks?' There was no answer, and Mother Wolf got ready for what she knew would be her last fight, if things came to fighting.

Then the only other creature who is allowed at the Pack Council – Baloo, the sleepy brown bear who teaches the wolf cubs the Law of the Jungle: old Baloo, who can come and go where he pleases because he eats only nuts and roots and honey – rose up on his hind quarters and grunted.

'The man's cub – the man's cub?' he said. '*I* speak for the man's cub. There is no harm in a man's cub. I have no gift of words, but I speak the truth. Let him run with the Pack, and be entered with the others. I myself will teach him.'

'We need yet another,' said Akela. 'Baloo has spoken, and he is our teacher for the young cubs. Who speaks beside Baloo?'

A black shadow dropped down into the circle. It was Bagheera the Black Panther, inky black all over, but with the panther markings showing up in certain lights like the pattern of watered silk. Everybody knew Bagheera, and nobody cared to cross his path; for he was as cunning as Tabaqui, as bold as the wild buffalo, and as reckless as the wounded elephant. But he had a voice as soft as wild honey dripping from a tree, and a skin softer than down.

'O Akela, and ye the Free People,' he purred, 'I have no right in your assembly; but the Law of the Jungle says that if there is a doubt which is not a killing matter in regard to a new cub, the life of that cub may be bought at a price. And the Law does not say who may or may not pay that price. Am I right?'

'Good! good!' said the young wolves, who are always hungry. 'Listen to Bagheera. The cub can be bought for a price. It is the Law.'

'Knowing that I have no right to speak here, I ask your leave.'

'Speak then,' cried twenty voices.

'To kill a naked cub is shame. Besides, he may make better sport for you when he is grown. Baloo has spoken in his behalf. Now to Baloo's word I will add one bull, and a fat one, newly killed, not half a mile from here, if ye will accept the man's cub according to the Law. Is it difficult?'

There was a clamour of scores of voices, saying: 'What matter? He will die in the winter rains. He will scorch in the sun. What harm can a naked frog do us? Let him run with the Pack. Where is the bull, Bagheera? Let him be accepted.' And then came Akela's deep bay, crying: 'Look well – look well, O Wolves!'

Mowgli was still deeply interested in the pebbles, and he did not notice when the wolves came and looked at him one by one. At last they all went down the hill for the dead bull, and only Akela, Bagheera, Baloo, and Mowgli's own wolves were left. Shere Khan roared still in the night, for he was very angry that Mowgli had not been handed over to him.

'Ay, roar well,' said Bagheera, under his whiskers; 'for the time comes when this naked thing will make thee roar to another tune, or I know nothing of man.'

'It was well done,' said Akela. 'Men and their cubs are very wise. He may be a help in time.'

'Truly, a help in time of need; for none can hope to lead the Pack for ever,' said Bagheera.

Akela said nothing. He was thinking of the time that comes to every leader of every pack when his strength goes from him and he gets feebler and feebler, till at last he is killed by the wolves and a new leader comes up – to be killed in his turn.

'Take him away,' he said to Father Wolf, 'and train him as befits one of the Free People.'

And that is how Mowgli was entered into the Seeonee wolfpack for the price of a bull and on Baloo's good word.

Now you must be content to skip ten or eleven whole years, and only guess at all the wonderful life that Mowgli led among the wolves, because if it were written out it would fill ever so many books. He grew up with the cubs, though they, of course, were grown wolves almost before he was a child, and Father Wolf taught him his business, and the meaning of things in the jungle, till every rustle in the grass, every breath of the warm night air, every note of the owls above his head, every scratch of a bat's claws as it roosted for a while in a tree, and every splash of every little fish jumping in a pool, meant just as much to him as the work of his office means to a business man. When he was not learning he sat out in the sun and slept, and ate and went to sleep again; when he felt dirty or hot he swam in the forest pools; and when he wanted honey (Baloo told him that honey and nuts were just as pleasant to eat as raw meat) he climbed up for it, and that Bagheera showed him how to do. Bagheera would lie out on a branch and call, 'Come along, Little Brother,' and at first Mowgli would cling like the sloth, but afterward he would fling himself through the branches almost as boldly as the gray ape. He took his place at the Council Rock, too, when the Pack met, and there he discovered that if he stared hard at any wolf, the wolf would be forced to drop his eyes, and so he used to stare for fun. At other times he would pick the long thorns out of the pads of his friends, for wolves suffer terribly from thorns and burs in their coats. He would go down the hillside into the cultivated lands by night, and look very curiously at the villagers in their huts, but he had a mistrust of men because Bagheera showed him a square box with a drop-gate so cunningly hidden in the jungle that he nearly walked into it, and told him that it was a trap. He loved better than anything else to go with Bagheera into the dark warm heart of the forest, to sleep all through the drowsy day, and at night see how Bagheera did his killing. Bagheera killed right and left as he felt hungry, and so did Mowgli – with one exception. As soon as he was old enough to understand things, Bagheera told him that he must never touch cattle because he had been bought into the Pack at the price of a bull's life. 'All the jungle is thine,' said Bagheera, 'and thou canst kill everything that thou art strong enough to kill; but for the sake of the bull that bought thee thou must never kill or eat any cattle young or old. That is the Law of the Jungle.' Mowgli obeyed faithfully.

And he grew and grew strong as a boy must grow who does not know that he is learning any lessons, and who has nothing in the world to think of except things to eat.

Mother Wolf told him once or twice that Shere Khan was not a creature to be trusted, and that some day he must kill Shere Khan; but though a young wolf would have remembered that advice every hour, Mowgli forgot it because he was only a boy – though he would have called himself a wolf if he had been able to speak in any human tongue.

Shere Khan was always crossing his path in the jungle, for as Akela grew older and feebler the lame tiger had come to be great friends with the younger wolves of the Pack, who followed him for scraps, a thing Akela would never have allowed if he had dared to push his authority to the proper bounds. Then Shere Khan would flatter them and wonder that such fine young hunters were content to be led by a dying wolf and a man's cub. 'They tell me,' Shere Khan would say, 'that at Council ye dare not look him between the eyes'; and the young wolves would growl and bristle.

Bagheera, who had eyes and ears everywhere, knew something of this, and once or twice he told Mowgli in so many words that Shere Khan would kill him some day; and Mowgli would laugh and answer:

'I have the Pack and I have thee; and Baloo, though he is so lazy, might strike a blow or two for my sake. Why should I be afraid?'

It was one very warm day that a new notion came to Bagheera – born of something that he had heard. Perhaps Sahi the Porcupine had told him; but he said to Mowgli when they were deep in the jungle, as the boy lay with his head on Bagheera's beautiful black skin: 'Little Brother, how often have I told thee that Shere Khan is thy enemy?'

'As many times as there are nuts on that palm,' said Mowgli, who, naturally, could not count. 'What of it? I am sleepy, Bagheera, and Shere Khan is all long tail and loud talk – like Mor the Peacock.'

'But this is no time for sleeping. Baloo knows it; I know it; the Pack know it; and even the foolish, foolish deer know. Tabaqui had told thee, too.'

'Ho! ho!' said Mowgli. 'Tabaqui came to me not long ago with some rude talk that I was a naked man's cub and not fit to dig pig-nuts; but I caught Tabaqui by the tail and swung him twice against a palm-tree to teach him better manners.'

'That was foolishness; for though Tabaqui is a mischief-maker, he would have told thee of something that concerned thee closely. Open those eyes, Little Brother. Shere Khan dare not kill thee in the jungle; but remember, Akela is very old, and soon the day comes when he cannot kill his buck, and then he will be leader no more. Many of the wolves that looked thee over when thou wast brought to the Council first are old too, and the young wolves believe, as Shere Khan has taught them, that a man-cub has no place with the Pack. In a little time thou wilt be a man.'

'And what is a man that he should not run with his brothers?' said Mowgli. 'I was born in the jungle. I have obeyed the Law of the Jungle, and there is no wolf of ours from whose paws I have not pulled a thorn. Surely they are my brothers!'

Bagheera stretched himself at full length and half shut his eyes. 'Little Brother,' said he, 'feel under my jaw.'

Mowgli put up his strong brown hand, and just under Bagheera's silky chin, where the giant rolling muscles were all hid by the glossy hair, he came upon a little bald spot.

'There is no one in the jungle that knows that I, Bagheera, carry that mark – the mark of the collar; and yet, Little Brother, I was born among men, and it was among men that my mother died – in the cages of the King's Palace at Oodeypore. It was because of this that I paid the price for thee at the Council when thou wast a little naked cub. Yes, I too was born among men. I had never seen the jungle. They fed me behind bars from an iron pan till one night I felt that I was Bagheera – the Panther – and no man's plaything, and I broke the silly lock with one blow of my paw and came away; and because I had learned the ways of men, I became more terrible in the jungle than Shere Khan. Is it not so?'

'Yes,' said Mowgli; 'all the jungle fear Bagheera – all except Mowgli.'

'Oh, *thou* art a man's cub,' said the Black Panther, very tenderly; 'and even as I returned to my jungle, so thou must go back to men at last – to the men who are thy brothers – if thou art not killed in the Council.'

'But why – but why should any wish to kill me?' said Mowgli.

'Look at me,' said Bagheera; and Mowgli looked at him steadily between the eyes. The big panther turned his head away in half a minute.

'*That* is why,' he said, shifting his paw on the leaves. 'Not even I can look thee between the eyes, and I was born among men, and I love thee, Little Brother. The others they hate thee because their eyes cannot meet thine; because thou art wise; because thou hast pulled out thorns from their feet – because thou art a man.'

'I did not know these things,' said Mowgli, sullenly; and he frowned under his heavy black eyebrows.

'What is the Law of the Jungle? Strike first and then give tongue. By thy very carelessness they know that thou art a man. But be wise. It is in my heart that when Akela misses his next kill – and at each hunt it costs him more to pin the buck – the Pack will turn against him and against thee. They will hold a jungle Council at the Rock, and then – and then – I have it!' said Bagheera, leaping up. 'Go thou down quickly to the men's huts in the valley, and take some of the Red Flower which they grow there, so that when the time comes thou mayest have even a stronger friend than I or Baloo or those of the Pack that love thee. Get the Red Flower.'

By Red Flower Bagheera meant fire, only no creature in the jungle will call fire by its proper name. Every beast lives in deadly fear of it, and invents a hundred ways of describing it.

'The Red Flower?' said Mowgli. 'That grows outside their huts in the twilight. I will get some.'

'There speaks the man's cub,' said Bagheera, proudly. 'Remember that it grows in little pots. Get one swiftly, and keep it by thee for time of need.'

'Good!' said Mowgli. 'I go. But art thou sure, O my Bagheera' – he slipped his arm round the splendid neck, and looked deep into the big eyes – 'art thou sure that all this is Shere Khan's doing?'

'By the Broken Lock that freed me, I am sure, Little Brother.'

'Then, by the Bull that bought me, I will pay Shere Khan full tale for this, and it may be a little over,' said Mowgli; and he bounded away.

'That is a man. That is all a man,' said Bagheera to himself, lying down again. 'Oh, Shere Khan, never was a blacker hunting than that frog-hunt of thine ten years ago!'

Mowgli was far and far through the forest, running hard, and his heart was hot in him. He came to the cave as the evening mist rose, and drew breath, and looked down the valley. The cubs were out, but Mother Wolf, at the back of the cave, knew by his breathing that something was troubling her frog.

'What is it, Son?' she said.

'Some bat's chatter of Shere Khan,' he called back. 'I hunt among the ploughed fields tonight'; and he plunged downward through the bushes, to the stream at the bottom of the valley. There he checked, for he heard the yell of the Pack hunting, heard the bellow of a hunted Sambhur, and the snort as the buck turned at bay. Then there were wicked, bitter howls from the young wolves: 'Akela! Akela! Let the Lone Wolf show his strength. Room for the leader of the Pack! Spring, Akela!'

The Lone Wolf must have sprung and missed his hold, for Mowgli heard the snap of his teeth and then a yelp as the Sambhur knocked him over with his fore foot.

He did not wait for anything more, but dashed on; and the yells grew fainter behind him as he ran into the crop-lands where the villagers lived.

'Bagheera spoke truth,' he panted, as he nestled down in some cattle-fodder by the window of a hut. 'Tomorrow is one day both for Akela and for me.'

Then he pressed his face close to the window and watched the fire on the hearth. He saw the husbandman's wife get up and feed it in the night with black lumps; and when the morning came and mists were all white and cold, he saw the man's child pick up a wicker pot plastered inside with earth, fill it with lumps of red-hot charcoal, put it under his blanket, and go out to tend the cows in the byre.

'Is that all?' said Mowgli. 'If a cub can do it, there is nothing to fear'; so he strode round the corner and met the boy, took the pot from his hand, and disappeared into the mist while the boy howled with fear.

'They are very like me,' said Mowgli, blowing into the pot, as he had seen the woman do. 'This thing will die if I do not give it things to eat'; and he dropped twigs and dried bark on the red stuff. Half-way up the hill he met Bagheera with the morning dew shining like moonstones on his coat.

'Akela has missed,' said the Panther. 'They would have killed him last night, but they needed thee also. They were looking for thee on the hill.'

'I was among the ploughed lands. I am ready. See!' Mowgli held up the fire-pot.

'Good! Now, I have seen men thrust a dry branch into that stuff, and presently the Red Flower blossomed at the end of it. Art thou not afraid?'

'No. Why should I fear? I remember now – if it is not a dream – how, before I was a Wolf, I lay beside the Red Flower, and it was warm and pleasant.'

All that day Mowgli sat in the cave tending his fire-pot and dipping dry branches into it to see how they looked. He found a branch that satisfied him, and in the evening when Tabaqui came to the cave and told him rudely enough that he was wanted at the Council Rock, he laughed till Tabaqui ran away. Then Mowgli went to the Council, still laughing.

Akela the Lone Wolf lay by the side of his rock as a sign that the leadership of the Pack was open, and Shere Khan with his following of scrap-fed wolves walked to and fro openly being flattered. Bagheera lay close to Mowgli, and the fire-pot was between Mowgli's knees. When they were all gathered together, Shere Khan began to speak – a thing he would never have dared to do when Akela was in his prime.

[340]

'He has no right,' whispered Bagheera. 'Say so. He is a dog's son. He will be frightened.'

Mowgli sprang to his feet. 'Free People,' he cried, 'does Shere Khan lead the Pack? What has a tiger to do with our leadership?'

'Seeing that the leadership is yet open, and being asked to speak – ' Shere Khan began.

'By whom?' said Mowgli. 'Are we *all* jackals, to fawn on this cattle-butcher? The leadership of the Pack is with the Pack alone.'

There were yells of 'Silence, thou man's cub!' 'Let him speak. He has kept our Law'; and at last the seniors of the Pack thundered: 'Let the Dead Wolf speak.' When a leader of the Pack has missed his kill, he is called the Dead Wolf as long as he lives, which is not long.

Akela raised his old head wearily:

'Free People, and ye too, jackals of Shere Khan, for twelve seasons I have led ye to and from the kill, and in all that time not one has been trapped or maimed. Now I have missed my kill. Ye know how that plot was made. Ye know how ye brought me up to an untried buck to make my weakness known. It was cleverly done. Your right is to kill me here on the Council Rock, now. Therefore, I ask, who comes to make an end of the Lone Wolf? For it is my right, by the Law of the Jungle, that ye come one by one.'

There was a long hush, for no single wolf cared to fight Akela to the death. Then Shere Khan roared: 'Bah! what have we to do with this toothless fool? He is doomed to die! It is the man-cub who has lived too long. Free People, he was my meat from the first. Give him to me. I am weary of this man-wolf folly. He has troubled the jungle for ten seasons. Give me the man-cub, or I will hunt here always, and not give you one bone. He is a man, a man's child, and from the marrow of my bones I hate him!'

Then more than half the Pack yelled: 'A man! a man! What has a man to do with us? Let him go to his own place.'

'And turn all the people of the villages against us?' clamoured Shere Khan. 'No; give him to me. He is a man, and none of us can look him between the eyes.'

Akela lifted his head again, and said: 'He has eaten our food. He has slept with us. He has driven game for us. He has broken no word of the Law of the Jungle.'

'Also, I paid for him with a bull when he was accepted. The worth of a bull is little, but Bagheera's honour is something that he will perhaps fight for,' said Bagheera, in his gentlest voice.

'A bull paid ten years ago!' the Pack snarled. 'What do we care for bones ten years old?'

'Or for a pledge?' said Bagheera, his white teeth bared under his lip. 'Well are ye called the Free People!'

'No man's cub can run with the people of the jungle,' howled Shere Khan. 'Give him to me!'

'He is our brother in all but blood,' Akela went on; 'and ye would kill him here! In truth, I have lived too long. Some of ye are eaters of cattle, and of others I have heard that, under Shere Khan's teaching, ye go by dark night and snatch children from the villager's door-step. Therefore I know ye to be cowards, and it is to cowards I speak. It is certain that I must die, and my life is of no worth, or I would offer that in the man-cub's place. But for the sake of the Honour of the Pack – a little matter that by being without a leader ye have forgotten – I promise that if ye let the man-cub go to his own place, I will not, when my time comes to die, bare one tooth against ye. I will die without fighting. That will at least save the Pack three lives. More I cannot do; but if ye will, I can save ye the shame that comes of killing a brother against whom there is no fault – a brother spoken for and bought into the Pack according to the Law of the Jungle.'

'He is a man – a man – a man!' snarled the Pack; and most of the wolves began to gather round Shere Khan, whose tail was beginning to switch.

'Now the business is in thy hands,' said Bagheera to Mowgli. 'We can do no more except fight.'

Mowgli stood upright – the fire-pot in his hands. Then he stretched out his arms, and yawned in the face of the Council; but he was furious with rage and sorrow, for, wolf-like, the wolves had never told him how they hated him. 'Listen you!' he cried. 'There is no need for this dog's jabber. Ye have told me so often tonight that I am a man (and indeed I would have been a wolf with you to my life's end), that I feel your words are true. So I do not call ye my brothers any more, but *sag* [dogs], as a man should. What ye will do, and what ye will not do, is not yours to say. That matter is with *me*; and that we may see the matter more plainly, I, the man, have brought here a little of the Red Flower which ye, dogs, fear.'

He flung the fire-pot on the ground, and some of the red coals lit a tuft of dried moss that flared up, as all the Council drew back in terror before the leaping flames.

Mowgli thrust his dead branch into the fire till the twigs lit and crackled, and whirled it above his head among the cowering wolves.

'Thou art the master,' said Bagheera, in an undertone. 'Save Akela from the death. He was ever thy friend.'

Akela, the grim old wolf who had never asked for mercy in his life, gave one piteous look at Mowgli as the boy stood all naked, his long black hair tossing over his shoulders in the light of the blazing branch that made the shadows jump and quiver.

'Good!' said Mowgli, staring round slowly. 'I see that ye are dogs. I go from you to my own people – if they be my own people. The Jungle is shut to me, and I must forget your talk and your companionship; but I will be more merciful than ye are. Because I was all but your brother in blood, I promise that when I am a man among men I will not betray ye to men as ye have betrayed me.' He kicked the fire with his foot, and the sparks flew up. 'There shall be no war between any of us in the Pack. But here is a debt to pay before I go.' He strode forward to where Shere Khan sat blinking stupidly at the flames, and caught him by the tuft on his chin. Bagheera followed in case of accidents. 'Up, dog!' Mowgli cried. 'Up, when a man speaks, or I will set that coat ablaze!'

Shere Khan's ears lay flat back on his head, and he shut his eyes, for the blazing branch was very near.

'This cattle-killer said he would kill me in the Council because he had not killed me when I was a cub. Thus and thus, then, do we beat dogs when we are men. Stir a whisker, Lungri, and I ram the Red Flower down thy gullet!' He beat Shere Khan over the head with the branch, and the tiger whimpered and whined in an agony of fear.

'Pah! Singed jungle-cat – go now! But remember when next I come to the Council Rock, as a man should come, it will be with Shere Khan's hide on my head. For the rest, Akela goes free to live as he pleases. Ye will *not* kill him, because that is not my will. Nor do I think that ye will sit here any longer, lolling out your tongues as though ye were somebodies, instead of dogs whom I drive out – thus! Go!' The fire was burning furiously at the end of the branch, and Mowgli struck right and left round the circle, and the wolves ran howling with the sparks burning their fur. At last there were only Akela, Bagheera, and perhaps ten wolves that had taken Mowgli's part. Then something began to hurt Mowgli inside him, as he had never been hurt in his life before, and he caught his breath and sobbed, and the tears ran down his face.

'What is it? What is it?' he said. 'I do not wish to leave the jungle, and I do not know what this is. Am I dying, Bagheera?'

'No, Little Brother. That is only tears such as men use,' said Bagheera. 'Now I know thou art a man, and a man's cub no longer. The Jungle is shut indeed to thee henceforward. Let them fall, Mowgli. They are only tears.' So Mowgli sat and cried as though his heart would break; and he had never cried in all his life before.

'Now,' he said, 'I will go to men. But first I must say farewell to my mother'; and he went to the cave where she lived with Father Wolf, and he cried on her coat, while the four cubs howled miserably.

'Ye will not forget me?' said Mowgli.

'Never while we can follow a trail,' said the cubs. 'Come to the foot of the hill when thou art a man, and we will talk to thee; and we will come into the crop-lands to play with thee by night.'

'Come soon!' said Father Wolf. 'Oh, wise little frog, come again soon; for we be old, thy mother and I.'

'Come soon,' said Mother Wolf, 'little naked son of mine; for, listen, child of man, I loved thee more than ever I loved my cubs.'

'I will surely come,' said Mowgli; 'and when I come it will be to lay out Shere Khan's hide upon the Council Rock. Do not forget me! Tell them in the jungle never to forget me!'

The dawn was beginning to break when Mowgli went down the hillside alone, to meet those mysterious things that are called men.

Source: Rudyard Kipling, *The Jungle Book*, 1894.

Garden Cities

Ebenezer Howard (1850–1928) started work at fifteen in a stockbroker's office. But he became interested in social reform, inspired by Bellamy's *Looking Backward* (see p. 284). During the 1880s he wrote *Tomorrow: A Peaceful Path to Reform* which, in place of the fiery schemes of Marxists, Communists and Socialists, offered a practical vision of happy home-owners breathing country air but surrounded by urban amenities. Published in 1898, the book was enormously popular, and launched the garden-city movement, which was to influence city-planning world-wide.

Howard's idea was that each garden city should be a self-sufficient community, not a dormitory suburb. It would be built on a greenfield site, and owned by a private corporation which would raise money for the initial site purchase, and lease plots to prospective home-owners. The optimum population would be 32,000. Garden cities would form clusters, joined by road and rail, but with open country and farmland (green belts) between them. All the revenue would come from the rents paid by householders. Howard presents elaborate calculations to demonstrate that these will be sufficient to pay off the loan needed for the original site purchase, to construct and maintain all municipal buildings (as well covering the running costs of the schools, museums and libraries), and to leave a large surplus for old-age pensions and accident and health insurance.

Each city will require a 6,000-acre site. The city itself will occupy only 1,000 acres of this, and will be circular in design, measuring about three-quarters of a mile from centre to circumference. Six 'magnificent boulevards' will radiate from the centre, each 120ft wide. In the centre will be a circular space of five and a half acres, 'laid out as a beautiful and well-watered garden'. Surrounding this will be a ring of public buildings, each in its own grounds (town hall, concert and lecture halls, theatre, library, museum, picture gallery, hospital). Next, also forming a ring round the centre, will come a 145-acre open space (Central Park), easily accessible from every house in the city.

Howard proceeds to take his reader on a guided tour of the as-yet-unbuilt city.

Running all round the Central Park (except where it is intersected by the boulevards) is a wide glass arcade called the Crystal Palace, opening onto the park. This building is in wet weather one of the favourite resorts of the people, whilst the knowledge that its bright shelter is ever close at hand tempts people into Central Park even in the most doubtful of weathers. Here manufactured goods are exposed for sale, and here most of that class of shopping which requires the joy of deliberation and selection is done. The space enclosed by the Crystal Palace is, however, a good deal larger than is required for these purposes, and a considerable part of it is used as a Winter Garden – the whole forming a permanent exhibition of a most attractive character, whilst its circular form brings it near to every dweller in the town – the furthest removed inhabitant being within 600 yards.

Passing out of the Crystal Palace on our way to the outer ring of the town, we cross Fifth Avenue – lined, as are all the roads of the town, with trees – fronting which, and looking onto the Crystal Palace, we find a ring of very excellently built houses, each standing in its own ample grounds; and as we continue our walk we observe that the houses are for the most part built either in concentric rings, facing the various avenues (as the circular roads are called), or fronting the boulevards and roads, which all converge to the centre of the town . . .

Of the 32,000 inhabitants, Howard explains, 30,000 live in the city, 2,000 in the surrounding agricultural estate. The city has 5,500 building lots, averaging 20 × 130ft, and none smaller than 20 × 100ft.

Noticing the very varied architecture and design which the houses and groups of houses display – some having common gardens and co-operative kitchens – we learn that the general observance of street line or harmonious departure from it are the chief points as to house-building over which the municipal authorities exercise control, for, though proper sanitary arrangements are strictly enforced, the fullest measure of individual taste and preference is encouraged.

Walking still toward the outskirts of the town, we come upon the 'Grand Avenue'. This avenue is fully entitled to the name it bears, for it is 420 feet wide, and forming a belt of green upwards of three miles long, divides that part of the town which lies outside Central Park into two belts. It really constitutes an additional park of 115 acres – a park which is within 240 yards of the furthest removed inhabitant. In this splendid avenue six sites, each of four acres, are occupied by public schools and their surrounding play-grounds and gardens, while other sites are reserved for churches, of such denomination as the religious beliefs of the people may determine, to be erected and maintained out of the funds of the worshippers and their friends . . .

On the outer ring of the town are factories, warehouses, dairies, markets, coal yards, timber yards etc., all fronting on the circle railway, which encompasses the whole town, and which has sidings connecting it with a main line of railway which passes through the estate . . . The smoke fiend is kept well within bounds in Garden City; for all machinery is driven by electric energy . . .

The refuse [i.e. sewage] of the town is utilized on the agricultural portions of the estate, which are held by various individuals in large farms, small holdings, allotments, cow pastures etc.

Agricultural production, Howard envisages, will be greatly increased by this 'well-devised system of sewage disposal'. The image he uses for his design is one of organic growth: 'A town, like a flower, or a tree, or an animal, should, at each stage of its growth, possess unity, symmetry, completeness.' It is an important aspect of the plan that every breadwinner will live within easy walking distance of his work. No publicly owned housing will be provided for the working class, but Howard reckons that they will be able to form building societies or borrow money to build their own homes (six-roomed cottages, with gardens) from co-operative societies, friendly societies or trade unions. Police costs will be low, because citizens 'for the most part will be of the law-abiding class'.

An elected Board of Management, with both men and women members, will be in central control. They will decide which shops should be allowed in the city, with a view to preventing 'the absurd and wasteful multiplication of shops' and also guarding against monopoly. Citizens, too, will be socially responsible. They will not (Howard trusts) buy from shopkeepers who treat their employees harshly or sell goods produced by sweated labour. 'In Garden City there will be a splendid opportunity for the public conscience to express itself.' The Board of Management will also decide whether to allow pubs. Howard's opinion is that it will be unwise to ban the sale of alcohol altogether, as this would exclude 'the very large and increasing class of moderate drinkers'. He presents his scheme not just as a matter of bricks and mortar, but as a spiritual mission for modern man.

Among the greatest needs of man and of society today, as at all times, are these: A worthy aim and opportunity to realize it; work and ends worth working for. All that a man is, and all that he may become, is summed up in his aspirations, and this is no less true of society than of the individual. The end I now venture to set before the people of this country and of other countries is no less 'noble and adequate' than this, that they should forthwith gird themselves to the task of building up clusters of beautiful home-towns, each zoned by gardens, for those who now dwell in crowded, slum-infested cities.

Two garden cities were founded in Howard's lifetime, Letchworth (1903) and Welwyn Garden City (1920), both in Hertfordshire.

Source: Ebenezer Howard, *Garden Cities of Tomorrow*, Swan Sonnenschein & Co., 1902.

Young Man Goes East

For many people utopia was when they were young, and 'Youth' by Joseph Conrad expresses this. But it also contains two other, less common, versions of utopia – the British merchant marine and the mysterious East. Conrad (born Jozef Teodor Konrad Nalecz Korzeniowski in Poland in 1857) sailed the world's oceans for 20 years before he became a writer. He gained his British Master Mariner's certificate and British nationality in 1886. Britain was, at that time, the most powerful nation on earth, and for Conrad British seamanship had deep moral and aesthetic significance. The comradeship of a British ship's crew, with its traditions of reliability, efficiency, courage and fairness, became for him one of the few positives in a hostile or indifferent universe. It represented a little ideal commonwealth of modest, unsung heroes, braving the destructive powers of nature.

The incident described in 'Youth' was based on a real-life experience, which took place early in 1882 when Conrad was serving as second mate on a barque called the *Palestine* (in the story she becomes the *Judea*). The speaker in 'Youth' is called Marlow. He tells his drinking companions (a company director, an accountant, a lawyer, and the narrator) how on his first voyage to the East, twenty-two years before, the ship's cargo of coal caught fire as she was sailing through the Indian Ocean bound for Bangkok.

'The captain called us into the cabin. He had a chart spread on the table, and looked unhappy. He said, "The coast of West Australia is near, but I mean to proceed to our destination. It is the hurricane month, too; but we will just keep her head for Bankok, and fight the fire. No more putting back anywhere, if we all get roasted. We will try first to stifle this 'ere damned combustion by want of air."

'We tried. We battened down everything, and still she smoked. The smoke kept coming out through imperceptible crevices; it forced itself through bulkheads and covers; it oozed here and there and everywhere in slender threads, in an invisible film, in an incomprehensible manner. It made its way into the cabin, into the forecastle; it poisoned the sheltered places on the deck, it could be sniffed as high as the mainyard. It was clear that if the smoke came out the air came in. This was disheartening. This combustion refused to be stifled.

'We resolved to try water, and took the hatches off. Enormous volumes of smoke, whitish, yellowish, thick, greasy, misty, choking, ascended as high as the trucks. All hands cleared out aft. Then the poisonous cloud blew away, and we went back to work in a smoke that was no thicker now than that of an ordinary factory chimney.

'We rigged the force-pump, got the hose along, and by-and-by it burst. Well, it was as old as the ship – a prehistoric hose, and past repair. Then we pumped with the feeble head-pump, drew water with buckets, and in this way managed in time to pour lots of Indian Ocean into the main hatch. The bright stream flashed in sunshine, fell into a layer of white crawling smoke, and vanished on the black surface of coal. Steam ascended mingling with the smoke. We poured salt water as into a barrel without a bottom. It was our fate to pump in that ship, to pump out of her, to pump into her; and after keeping water out of her to save ourselves from being drowned, we frantically poured water into her to save ourselves from being burnt.

'And she crawled on, do or die, in the serene weather. The sky was a miracle of purity, a miracle of azure. The sea was polished, was blue, was pellucid, was sparkling like a precious stone, extending on all sides, all round to the horizon – as if the whole terrestrial globe had been one jewel, one colossal sapphire, a single gem fashioned into a planet. And on the lustre of the great calm waters the *Judea* glided imperceptibly, enveloped in languid and unclean vapours, in a lazy cloud that drifted to leeward, light and slow; a pestiferous cloud defiling the splendour of sea and sky.

'All this time of course we saw no fire. The cargo smouldered at the bottom somewhere. Once Mahon [the first mate], as we were working side by side, said to me with a queer smile: "Now, if she only would spring a tidy leak – like that time when we first left the Channel – it would put a stopper on this fire. Wouldn't it?" I remarked irrelevantly, "Do you remember the rats?" [Rats had been seen leaving the ship before it sailed.]

'We fought the fire and sailed the ship too as carefully as though nothing had been the matter. The steward cooked and attended on us. Of the other twelve men, eight worked while four rested. Everyone took his turn, captain included. There was equality, and if not exactly fraternity, then a deal of good feeling. Sometimes a man, as he dashed a bucketful of water down the hatchway, would yell out, "Hurrah for Bankok!" and the rest laughed. But generally we were taciturn and serious – and thirsty. Oh! how thirsty! And we had to be careful with the water. Strict allowance. The ship smoked, the sun blazed . . . Pass the bottle.

'We tried everything. We even made an attempt to dig down to the fire. No good, of course. No man could remain more than a minute below. Mahon, who went first, fainted there, and the man who went to fetch him out did likewise. We lugged them out on deck. Then I leaped down to show how easily it could be done. They had learned wisdom by that time, and contented themselves by fishing for me with a chain-hook tied to a broom-handle, I believe. I did not offer to go and fetch up my shovel, which was left down below.

'Things began to look bad. We put the long-boat into the water. The second boat was ready to swing out. We had also another, a 14-foot thing, on davits aft, where it was quite safe.

'Then, behold, the smoke suddenly decreased. We redoubled our efforts to flood the bottom of the ship. In two days there was no smoke at all. Everybody was on the broad grin. This was on a Friday. On Saturday no work, but sailing the ship of course, was done. The men washed their clothes and their faces for the first time in a fortnight, and had a special dinner given them. They spoke of spontaneous combustion with contempt, and implied *they* were the boys to put out combustions. Somehow we all felt as though we each had inherited a large fortune. But a beastly smell of burning hung about the ship. Captain Beard had hollow eyes and sunken cheeks. I had never noticed so much before how twisted and bowed he was. He and Mahon prowled soberly about hatches and ventilators, sniffing. It struck me suddenly poor Mahon was a very, very old chap. As to me, I was as pleased and proud as though I had helped to win a great naval battle. O! Youth!

'The night was fine. In the morning a homeward-bound ship passed us hull down – the first we had seen for months; but we were nearing the land at last, Java Head being about 190 miles off, and nearly due north.

'Next day it was my watch on deck from eight to twelve. At breakfast the captain observed, "It's wonderful how that smell hangs about the cabin." About ten, the mate being on the poop, I stepped down on the main-deck for a moment. The carpenter's bench stood abaft the mainmast: I leaned against it sucking at my pipe, and the carpenter, a young chap, came to talk to me. He remarked, "I think we have done very well, haven't we?" and then I perceived with annoyance the fool was trying to tilt the bench. I said curtly, "Don't, Chips," and immediately became aware of a queer sensation, of an absurd delusion – I seemed somehow to be in the air. I heard all round me like a pent-up breath released – as if a thousand giants simultaneously had said Phoo! – and felt a dull concussion which made my ribs ache suddenly. No doubt about it – I was in the air, and my body was describing a short parabola. But short as it was, I had the time to think several thoughts in, as far as I can remember, the following order: "This can't be the carpenter – What is it? – Some accident – Submarine volcano? – Coals, gas! – By Jove! we are being blown up – Everybody's dead – I am falling into the after-hatch – I see fire in it."

'The coal-dust suspended in the air of the hold had glowed dull-red at the moment of the explosion. In the twinkling of an eye, in an infinitesimal fraction of a second since the first tilt of the bench, I was sprawling full length on the cargo. I picked myself up and scrambled out. It was quick like a rebound. The deck was a wilderness of smashed timber, lying crosswise like trees in a wood after a hurricane; an immense curtain of soiled rags waved gently before me – it was the mainsail blown to strips. I thought, The masts will be toppling over directly; and to get out of the way bolted on all-fours towards the poop-ladder. The first person I saw was Mahon, with eyes like saucers, his mouth open, and the long white hair standing straight on end round his head like a silver halo. He was just about to go down when the sight of the main-deck stirring, heaving up, and changing into splinters before his eyes, petrified him on the top step. I stared at him in unbelief, and he stared at me with a queer kind of shocked curiosity. I did not know that I had no hair, no eyebrows, no eyelashes, that my young moustache was burnt off, that my face was black, one cheek laid open, my nose cut, and my chin bleeding. I had lost my cap, one of my slippers, and my shirt was torn to rags. Of all this I was not aware. I was amazed to see the ship still afloat, the poop-deck whole – and, most of all, to see anybody alive. Also the peace of the sky and the serenity of the sea were distinctly surprising. I suppose I expected to see them convulsed with horror . . . Pass the bottle.

'There was a voice hailing the ship from somewhere – in the air, in the sky – I couldn't tell. Presently I saw the captain – and he was mad. He asked me eagerly, "Where's the cabin-table?" and to hear such a question was a frightful shock. I had just been blown up, you understand, and vibrated with that experience – I wasn't quite sure whether I was alive. Mahon began to stamp with both feet and yelled at him, "Good God! don't you see the deck's blown out of her?" I found my voice, and stammered out as if conscious of some gross neglect of duty, "I don't know where the cabin-table is." It was like an absurd dream.

'Do you know what he wanted next? Well, he wanted to trim the yards. Very placidly, and as if lost in thought, he insisted on having the foreyard squared. "I don't know if there's anybody alive," said Mahon, almost tearfully. "Surely," he said, gently, "there will be enough left to square the foreyard."

'The old chap, it seems, was in his own berth winding up the chronometers, when the shock sent him spinning. Immediately it occurred to him – as he said afterwards – that the ship had struck something, and ran out into the cabin. There, he saw, the cabin-table had vanished somewhere. The deck being blown up, it had fallen down into the lazarette of course. Where we had our breakfast that morning he saw only a great hole in the floor. This appeared to him so awfully mysterious, and impressed him so immensely, that what he saw and heard after he got on deck were mere trifles in comparison. And, mark, he noticed directly the wheel deserted and his barque off her course – and his only thought was to get that miserable, stripped, undecked, smouldering shell of a ship back again with her head pointing at her port of destination. Bankok! That's what he was after. I tell you this quiet, bowed, bandy-legged, almost deformed little man was immense in the singleness of his idea and in his placid ignorance of our agitation. He motioned us forward with a commanding gesture, and went to take the wheel himself.

'Yes; that was the first thing we did – trim the yards of that wreck! No one was killed, or even disabled, but everyone was more or less hurt. You should have seen them! Some were in rags, with black faces, like coal-heavers, like sweeps, and had bullet heads that seemed closely cropped, but were in fact singed to the skin. Others, of the

watch below, awakened by being shot out from their collapsing
bunks, shivered incessantly, and kept on groaning even as we went
about our work. But they all worked. That crew of Liverpool hard
cases had in them the right stuff. It's my experience they always have.
It is the sea that gives it – the vastness, the loneliness surrounding
their dark stolid souls. Ah! Well! we stumbled, we crept, we fell, we
barked our shins on the wreckage, we hauled. The masts stood, but
we did not know how much they might be charred down below. It
was nearly calm, but a long swell ran from the west and made
her roll. They might go at any moment. We looked at them with
apprehension. One could not foresee which way they would fall.

'Then we retreated aft and looked about us. The deck was a
tangle of planks on edge, of planks on end, of splinters, of ruined
woodwork. The masts rose from that chaos like big trees above a
matted undergrowth. The interstices of that mass of wreckage were
full of something whitish, sluggish, stirring – of something that was
like a greasy fog. The smoke of the invisible fire was coming up
again, was trailing, like a poisonous thick mist in some valley choked
with dead wood. Already lazy wisps were beginning to curl upwards
amongst the mass of splinters. Here and there a piece of timber, stuck
upright, resembled a post. Half of a fife-rail had been shot through
the foresail, and the sky made a patch of glorious blue in the ignobly
soiled canvas. A portion of several boards holding together had fallen
across the rail, and one end protruded overboard, like a gangway
leading upon nothing, like a gangway leading over the deep sea,
leading to death – as if inviting us to walk the plank at once and be
done with our ridiculous troubles. And still the air, the sky – a ghost,
something invisible was hailing the ship.

'Someone had the sense to look over, and there was the helmsman,
who had impulsively jumped overboard, anxious to come back. He
yelled and swam lustily like a merman, keeping up with the ship. We
threw him a rope, and presently he stood amongst us streaming with
water and very crestfallen. The captain had surrendered the wheel,
and apart, elbow on rail and chin in hand, gazed at the sea wistfully.
We asked ourselves, What next? I thought, Now, this is something
like. This is great. I wonder what will happen. O youth!

'Suddenly Mahon sighted a steamer far astern. Captain Beard said,
"We may do something with her yet." We hoisted two flags, which
said in the international language of the sea, "On fire. Want

immediate assistance." The steamer grew bigger rapidly, and by-and-by spoke with two flags on her foremast, "I am coming to your assistance."

'In half an hour she was abreast, to windward, within hail, and rolling slightly, with her engines stopped. We lost our composure, and yelled all together with excitement, "We've been blown up." A man in a white helmet, on the bridge, cried, "Yes! All right! all right!" and he nodded his head, and smiled, and made soothing motions with his hand as though at a lot of frightened children. One of the boats dropped in the water, and walked towards us upon the sea with her long oars. Four Calashes pulled a swinging stroke. This was my first sight of Malay seamen. I've known them since, but what struck me then was their unconcern: they came alongside, and even the bowman standing up and holding to our main-chains with the boat-hook did not deign to lift his head for a glance. I thought people who had been blown up deserved more attention.

'A little man, dry like a chip and agile like a monkey, clambered up. It was the mate of the steamer. He gave one look, and cried, "O boys – you had better quit."

'We were silent. He talked apart with the captain for a time – seemed to argue with him. Then they went away together to the steamer.

'When our skipper came back we learned that the steamer was the *Somerville*, Captain Nash, from West Australia to Singapore *via* Batavia with mails, and that the agreement was she should tow us to Anjer or Batavia, if possible, where we could extinguish the fire by scuttling, and then proceed on our voyage – to Bankok! The old man seemed excited. "We will do it yet," he said to Mahon, fiercely. He shook his fist at the sky. Nobody else said a word.

'At noon the steamer began to tow. She went ahead slim and high, and what was left of the *Judea* followed at the end of seventy fathom of tow-rope – followed her swiftly like a cloud of smoke with mast-heads protruding above. We went aloft to furl the sails. We coughed on the yards, and were careful about the bunts. Do you see the lot of us there, putting a neat furl on the sails of that ship doomed to arrive nowhere? There was not a man who didn't think that at any moment the masts would topple over. From aloft we could not see the ship for smoke, and they worked carefully, passing the gaskets with even turns. "Harbour furl – aloft there!" cried Mahon from below.

'You understand this? I don't think one of those chaps expected to get down in the usual way. When we did I heard them saying to each other, "Well, I thought we would come down overboard, in a lump – sticks and all – blame me if I didn't." "That's what I was thinking to myself," would answer wearily another battered and bandaged scarecrow. And, mind, these were men without the drilled-in habit of obedience. To an onlooker they would be a lot of profane scallywags without a redeeming point. What made them do it – what made them obey me when I, thinking consciously how fine it was, made them drop the bunt of the foresail twice to try and do it better? What? They had no professional reputation – no examples, no praise. It wasn't a sense of duty; they all knew well enough how to shirk, and laze, and dodge – when they had a mind to it – and mostly they had. Was it the two pounds ten a-month that sent them there? They didn't think their pay half good enough. No; it was something in them, something inborn and subtle and everlasting. I don't say positively that the crew of a French or German merchantman wouldn't have done it, but I doubt whether it would have been done in the same way. There was a completeness in it, something solid like a principle, and masterful like an instinct – a disclosure of something secret – of that hidden something, that gift of good or evil that makes racial difference, that shapes the fate of nations.

'It was that night at ten that, for the first time since we had been fighting it, we saw the fire. The speed of the towing had fanned the smouldering destruction. A blue gleam appeared forward, shining below the wreck of the deck. It wavered in patches, it seemed to stir and creep like the light of a glow-worm. I saw it first, and told Mahon. "Then the game's up," he said. "We had better stop this towing, or she will burst out suddenly fore and aft before we can clear out." We set up a yell; rang bells to attract their attention; they towed on. At last Mahon and I had to crawl forward and cut the rope with an axe. There was no time to cast off the lashings. Red tongues could be seen licking the wilderness of splinters under our feet as we made our way back to the poop.

'Of course they very soon found out in the steamer that the rope was gone. She gave a loud blast of her whistle, her lights were seen sweeping in a wide circle, she came up ranging close along-side, and stopped. We were all in a tight group on the poop looking at her. Every man had saved a little bundle or a bag. Suddenly a conical flame with a twisted top shot up forward and threw upon the black sea a circle of light, with the two vessels side by side and heaving gently in its centre. Captain Beard had been sitting on the gratings still and mute for hours, but now he rose slowly and advanced in front of us, to the mizzen-shrouds. Captain Nash hailed: "Come along! Look sharp. I have mail-bags on board. I will take you and your boats to Singapore."

' "Thank you! No!" said our skipper. "We must see the last of the ship."

' "I can't stand by any longer," shouted the other. "Mails – you know."

' "Ay! ay! We are all right."

' "Very well! I'll report you in Singapore . . . Good-bye!"

'He waved his hand. Our men dropped their bundles quietly. The steamer moved ahead, and passing out of the circle of light, vanished at once from our sight, dazzled by the fire which burned fiercely. And then I knew that I would see the East first as commander of a small boat. I thought it fine; and the fidelity to the old ship was fine. We should see the last of her. Oh, the glamour of youth! Oh, the fire of it, more dazzling than the flames of the burning ship, throwing a magic light on the wide earth, leaping audaciously to the sky, presently to be quenched by time, more cruel, more pitiless, more bitter than the sea – and like the flames of the burning ship surrounded by an impenetrable night.'

'The old man warned us in his gentle and inflexible way that it was part of our duty to save for the underwriters as much as we could of the ship's gear. Accordingly we went to work aft, while she blazed forward to give us plenty of light. We lugged out a lot of rubbish. What didn't we save? An old barometer fixed with an absurd quantity of screws nearly cost me my life: a sudden rush of smoke came upon me, and I just got away in time. There were various stores, bolts of canvas, coils of rope; the poop looked like a marine bazaar, and the boats were lumbered to the gunwales. One would have thought the old man wanted to take as much as he could of his first command with him. He was very, very quiet, but off his balance evidently. Would you believe it? He wanted to take a length of old stream-cable and a kedge-anchor with him in the long-boat. We said, "Ay, ay, sir," deferentially, and on the quiet let the things slip overboard. The heavy medicine-chest went that way, two bags of green coffee, tins of paint – fancy, paint! – a whole lot of things. Then I was ordered with two hands into the boats to make a stowage and get them ready against the time it would be proper for us to leave the ship.

'We put everything straight, stepped the long-boat's mast for our skipper, who was to take charge of her, and I was not sorry to sit down for a moment. My face felt raw, every limb ached as if broken, I was aware of all my ribs, and would have sworn to a twist in the backbone. The boats, fast astern, lay in a deep shadow, and all around I could see the circle of the sea lighted by the fire. A gigantic flame arose forward straight and clear. It flared fierce, with noises like the whirr of wings, with rumbles as of thunder. There were cracks, detonations, and from the cone of flame the sparks flew upwards, as man is born to trouble, to leaky ships, and to ships that burn.

'What bothered me was that the ship, lying broadside to the swell and to such wind as there was – a mere breath – the boats would not keep astern where they were safe, but persisted, in a pig-headed way boats have, in getting under the counter and then swinging along-side. They were knocking about dangerously and coming near the flame, while the ship rolled on them, and, of course, there was always the danger of the masts going over the side at any moment. I and my two boat-keepers kept them off as best we could, with oars and boat-hooks; but to be constantly at it became exasperating, since there was no reason why we should not leave at once. We could not see those on board, nor could we imagine what caused the delay. The boat-keepers were swearing feebly, and I had not only my share of the work but also had to keep at it two men who showed a constant inclination to lay themselves down and let things slide.

'At last I hailed, "On deck there," and someone looked over. "We're ready here," I said. The head disappeared, and very soon popped up again. "The captain says, All right, sir, and to keep the boats well clear of the ship."

'Half an hour passed. Suddenly there was a frightful racket, rattle, clanking of chain, hiss of water, and millions of sparks flew up into the shivering column of smoke that stood leaning slightly above the ship. The cat-heads had burned away, and the two red-hot anchors had gone to the bottom, tearing out after them two hundred fathom of red-hot chain. The ship trembled, the mass of flame swayed as if ready to collapse, and the fore top-gallant-mast fell. It darted down like an arrow of fire, shot under, and instantly leaping up within an oar's-length of the boats, floated quietly, very black on the luminous sea. I hailed the deck again. After some time a man in an unexpectedly cheerful but also muffled tone, as though he had been trying to speak with his mouth shut, informed me, "Coming directly, sir," and vanished. For a long time I heard nothing but the whirr and roar of the fire. There were also whistling sounds. The boats jumped, tugged at the painters, ran at each other playfully, knocked their sides together, or, do what we would, swung in a bunch against the ship's side. I couldn't stand it any longer, and swarming up a rope, clambered aboard over the stern.

'It was as bright as day. Coming up like this, the sheet of fire facing me was a terrifying sight, and the heat seemed hardly bearable at first. On a settee cushion dragged out of the cabin Captain Beard, his legs drawn up and one arm under his head, slept with the light playing on him. Do you know what the rest were busy about? They were sitting on deck right aft, round an open case, eating bread and cheese and drinking bottled stout.

'On the background of flames twisting in fierce tongues above their heads they seemed at home like salamanders, and looked like a band of desperate pirates. The fire sparkled in the whites of their eyes, gleamed on patches of white skin seen through the torn shirts. Each had the marks as of a battle about him – bandaged heads, tied-up arms, a strip of dirty rag round a knee – and each man had a bottle between his legs and a chunk of cheese in his hand. Mahon got up. With his handsome and disreputable head, his hooked profile, his long white beard, and with an uncorked bottle in his hand, he resembled one of those reckless sea-robbers of old making merry amidst violence and disaster. "The last meal on board," he explained solemnly. "We had nothing to eat all day, and it was no use leaving all this." He flourished the bottle and indicated the sleeping skipper. "He said he couldn't swallow anything, so I got him to lie down," he went on; and as I stared, "I don't know whether you are aware, young fellow, the man had no sleep to speak of for days – and there will be dam' little sleep in the boats." "There will be no boats by-

and-by if you fool about much longer," I said, indignantly. I walked up to the skipper and shook him by the shoulder. At last he opened his eyes, but did not move. "Time to leave her, sir," I said quietly.

'He got up painfully, looked at the flames, at the sea sparkling round the ship, and black, black as ink farther away; he looked at the stars shining dim through a thin veil of smoke in a sky black, black as Erebus.

' "Youngest first," he said.

'And the ordinary seaman, wiping his mouth with the back of his hand, got up, clambered over the taffrail, and vanished. Others followed. One, on the point of going over, stopped short to drain his bottle, and with a great swing of his arm flung it at the fire. "Take this!" he cried.

'The skipper lingered disconsolately, and we left him to commune alone for a while with his first command. Then I went up again and brought him away at last. It was time. The ironwork on the poop was hot to the touch.

'Then the painter of the long-boat was cut, and the three boats, tied together, drifted clear of the ship. It was just sixteen hours after the explosion when we abandoned her. Mahon had charge of the second boat, and I had the smallest – the 14-foot thing. The long-boat would have taken the lot of us; but the skipper said we must save as much property as we could – for the underwriters – and so I got my first command. I had two men with me, a bag of biscuits, a few tins of meat, and a breaker of water. I was ordered to keep close to the long-boat, that in case of bad weather we might be taken into her.

'And do you know what I thought? I thought I would part company as soon as I could. I wanted to have my first command all to myself. I wasn't going to sail in a squadron if there were a chance for independent cruising. I would make land by myself. I would beat the other boats. Youth! All youth! The silly, charming, beautiful youth.

'But we did not make a start at once. We must see the last of the ship. And so the boats drifted about that night, heaving and setting on the swell. The men dozed, waked, sighed, groaned. I looked at the burning ship.

'Between the darkness of earth and heaven she was burning fiercely upon a disc of purple sea shot by the blood-red play of gleams; upon a disc of water glittering and sinister. A high, clear flame, an immense and lonely flame, ascended from the ocean, and from its summit the black smoke poured continuously at the sky. She burned furiously; mournful and imposing like a funeral pile kindled in the night, surrounded by the sea, watched over by the stars. A magnificent death had come like a grace, like a gift, like a reward to that old ship at the end of her laborious days. The surrender of her weary ghost to the keeping of stars and sea was stirring like the sight of a glorious triumph. The masts fell just before daybreak, and for a moment there was a burst and turmoil of sparks that seemed to fill with flying fire the night patient and watchful, the vast night lying silent upon the sea. At daylight she was only a charred shell, floating still under a cloud of smoke and bearing a glowing mass of coal within.

'Then the oars were got out, and the boats forming in a line moved round her remains as if in procession – the long-boat leading. As we pulled across her stern a slim dart of fire shot out viciously at us, and suddenly she went down, head first, in a great hiss of steam. The unconsumed stern was the last to sink; but the paint had gone, had cracked, had peeled off, and there were no letters, there was no word, no stubborn device that was like her soul, to flash at the rising sun her creed and her name.

'We made our way north. A breeze sprang up, and about noon all the boats came together for the last time. I had no mast or sail in mine, but I made a mast out of a spare oar and hoisted a boat-awning for a sail, with a boat-hook for a yard. She was certainly over-masted, but I had the satisfaction of knowing that with the wind aft I could beat the other two. I had to wait for them.

Then we all had a look at the captain's chart, and, after a sociable meal of hard bread and water, got our last instructions. These were simple: steer north, and keep together as much as possible. "Be careful with that jury-rig, Marlow," said the captain; and Mahon, as I sailed proudly past his boat, wrinkled his curved nose and hailed, "You will sail that ship of yours under water, if you don't look out, young fellow." He was a malicious old man – and may the deep sea where he sleeps now rock him gently, rock him tenderly to the end of time!

'Before sunset a thick rain-squall passed over the two boats, which were far astern, and that was the last I saw of them for a time. Next day I sat steering my cockle-shell – my first command – with nothing but water and sky around me. I did sight in the afternoon the upper sails of a ship far away, but said nothing, and my men did not notice her. You see I was afraid she might be homeward bound, and I had no mind to turn back from the portals of the East. I was steering for Java – another blessed name – like Bankok, you know. I steered many days.

'I need not tell you what it is to be knocking about in an open boat. I remember nights and days of calm, when we pulled, we pulled, and the boat seemed to stand still, as if bewitched within the circle of the sea horizon. I remember the heat, the deluge of rain-squalls that kept us baling for dear life (but filled our water-cask), and I remember sixteen hours on end with a mouth dry as a cinder and a steering-oar over the stern to keep my first command head on to a breaking sea. I did not know how good a man I was till then. I remember the drawn faces, the dejected figures of my two men, and I remember my youth and the feeling that will never come back any more – the feeling that I could last for ever, outlast the sea, the earth, and all men; the deceitful feeling that lures us on to joys, to perils, to love, to vain effort – to death; the triumphant conviction of strength, the heat of life in the handful of dust, the glow in the heart that with every year grows dim, grows cold, grows small, and expires – and expires, too soon, too soon – before life itself.

'And this is how I see the East. I have seen its secret places and have looked into its very soul; but now I see it always from a small boat, a high outline of mountains, blue and afar in the morning; like faint mist at noon; a jagged wall of purple at sunset. I have the feel of the oar in my hand, the vision of a scorching blue sea in my eyes. And I see a bay, a wide bay, smooth as glass and polished like ice, shimmering in the dark. A red light burns far off upon the gloom of the land, and the night is soft and warm. We drag at the oars with aching arms, and suddenly a puff of wind, a puff faint and tepid and laden with strange odours of blossoms, of aromatic wood, comes out of the still night – the first sigh of the East on my face. That I can never forget. It was impalpable and enslaving, like a charm, like a whispered promise of mysterious delight.

'We had been pulling this finishing spell for eleven hours. Two pulled, and he whose turn it was to rest sat at the tiller. We had made out the red light in that bay and steered for it, guessing it must mark some small coasting port. We passed two vessels, outlandish and high-sterned, sleeping at anchor, and, approaching the light, now very dim, ran the boat's nose against the end of a jutting wharf. We were blind with fatigue. My men dropped the oars and fell off the thwarts as if dead. I made fast to a pile. A current rippled softly. The scented obscurity of the shore was grouped into vast masses, a density of colossal clumps of vegetation, probably – mute and fantastic shapes. And at their foot the semicircle of a beach gleamed faintly, like an illusion. There was not a light, not a stir, not a sound. The mysterious East faced me, perfumed like a flower, silent like death, dark like a grave.

'And I sat weary beyond expression, exulting like a conqueror, sleepless and entranced as if before a profound, a fateful enigma.

'A splashing of oars, a measured dip reverberating on the level of water, intensified by the silence of the shore into loud claps, made me jump up. A boat, a European boat, was coming in. I invoked the name of the dead; I hailed: *Judea* ahoy! A thin shout answered.

'It was the captain. I had beaten the flagship by three hours, and I was glad to hear the old man's voice again, tremulous and tired. "Is it you, Marlow?" "Mind the end of that jetty, sir," I cried.

'He approached cautiously, and brought up with the deep-sea lead-line which we had saved – for the underwriters. I eased my painter and fell alongside. He sat, a broken figure at the stern, wet with dew, his hands clasped in his lap. His men were asleep already. "I had a terrible time of it," he murmured. "Mahon is behind – not very far." We conversed in whispers, in low whispers, as if afraid to wake up the land. Guns, thunder, earthquakes would not have awakened the men just then.

'Looking round as we talked, I saw away at sea a bright light travelling in the night. "There's a steamer passing the bay," I said. She was not passing, she was entering, and she even came close and anchored. "I wish," said the old man, "you would find out whether she is English. Perhaps they could give us a passage somewhere." He seemed nervously anxious. So by dint of punching and kicking I started one of my men into a state of somnambulism, and giving him an oar, took another and pulled towards the lights of the steamer.

'There was a murmur of voices in her, metallic hollow clangs of the engine-room, footsteps on the deck. Her ports shone, round like dilated eyes. Shapes moved about, and there was a shadowy man high up on the bridge. He heard my oars.

'And then, before I could open my lips, the East spoke to me, but it was in a Western voice. A torrent of words was poured into the enigmatical, the fateful silence; outlandish, angry words, mixed with words and even whole sentences of good English, less strange but even more surprising. The voice swore and cursed violently; it riddled the solemn peace of the bay by a volley of abuse. It began by calling me Pig, and from that went crescendo into unmentionable adjectives – in English. The man up there raged aloud in two languages, and with a sincerity in his fury that almost convinced me I had, in some way, sinned against the harmony of the universe. I could hardly see him, but began to think he would work himself into a fit.

'Suddenly he ceased, and I could hear him snorting and blowing like a porpoise. I said –

' "What steamer is this, pray?"

' "Eh? What's this? And who are you?"

' "Castaway crew of an English barque burnt at sea. We came here tonight. I am the second mate. The captain is in the long-boat, and wishes to know if you would give us a passage somewhere."

' "Oh, my goodness! I say . . . This is the *Celestial* from Singapore on her return trip. I'll arrange with your captain in the morning, . . . and, I say, . . . did you hear me just now?"

' "I should think the whole bay heard you."

' "I thought you were a shore-boat. Now, look here – this infernal lazy scoundrel of a caretaker has gone to sleep again – curse him. The light is out, and I nearly ran foul of the end of this damned jetty. This is the third time he plays me this trick. Now, I ask you, can anybody stand this kind of thing? It's enough to drive a man out of his mind. I'll report him . . . I'll get the Assistant Resident to give him the sack, by . . .! See – there's no light. It's out, isn't it? I take you to witness the light's out. There should be a light, you know. A red light on the – "

' "There was a light," I said, mildly.

' "But it's out, man! What's the use of talking like this? You can see for yourself it's out – don't you? If you had to take a valuable steamer along this God-forsaken coast you would want a light, too. I'll kick him from end to end of his miserable wharf. You'll see if I don't. I will – "

' "So I may tell my captain you'll take us?" I broke in.

' "Yes, I'll take you. Good-night," he said, brusquely.

'I pulled back, made fast again to the jetty, and then went to sleep at last. I had faced the silence of the East. I had heard some of its language. But when I opened my eyes again the silence was as complete as though it had never been broken. I was lying in a flood of light, and the sky had never looked so far, so high, before. I opened my eyes and lay without moving.

'And then I saw the men of the East – they were looking at me. The whole length of the jetty was full of people. I saw brown, bronze, yellow faces, the black eyes, the glitter, the colour of an Eastern crowd. And all these beings stared without a murmur, without a sigh, without a movement. They stared down at the boats, at the sleeping men who at night had come to them from the sea. Nothing moved. The fronds of palms stood still against the sky. Not a branch stirred along the shore, and the brown roofs of hidden houses peeped through the green foliage, through the big leaves that hung shining and still like leaves forged of heavy metal. This was the East of the ancient navigators, so old, so mysterious, resplendent and sombre, living and unchanged, full of danger and promise. And these were the men. I sat up suddenly. A wave of movement passed through the crowd from end to end, passed along the heads, swayed the bodies, ran along the jetty like a ripple on the water, like a breath of wind on a field – and all was still again. I see it now – the wide sweep of the bay, the glittering sands, the wealth of green infinite and varied, the sea blue like the sea of a dream, the crowd of attentive faces, the blaze of vivid colour – the water reflecting it all, the curve of the shore, the jetty, the high-sterned outlandish craft floating still, and the three boats with the tired men from the West sleeping, unconscious of the land and the people and of the violence of sunshine. They slept thrown across the thwarts, curled on bottom-boards, in the careless attitudes of death. The head of the old skipper, leaning back in the stern of the long-boat, had fallen on his breast, and he looked as though he would never wake. Farther out old Mahon's face was upturned to the sky, with the long white beard spread out on his breast, as though he had been shot where he sat at the tiller; and a man, all in a heap in the bows of the boat, slept with both arms embracing the stem-head and with his cheek laid on the gunwale. The East looked at them without a sound.

[365]

'I have known its fascination since; I have seen the mysterious shores, the still water, the lands of brown nations, where a stealthy Nemesis lies in wait, pursues, overtakes so many of the conquering race, who are proud of their wisdom, of their knowledge, of their strength. But for me all the East is contained in that vision of my youth. It is all in that moment when I opened my young eyes on it. I came upon it from a tussle with the sea – and I was young – and I saw it looking at me. And this is all that is left of it! Only a moment; a moment of strength, of romance, of glamour – of youth! ... A flick of sunshine upon a strange shore, the time to remember, the time for a sigh, and – good-bye! – Night – Good-bye ...!'

He drank.

'Ah! The good old time – the good old time. Youth and the sea. Glamour and the sea! The good, strong sea, the salt, bitter sea, that could whisper to you and roar at you and knock your breath out of you.'

He drank again.

'By all that's wonderful it is the sea, I believe, the sea itself – or is it youth alone? Who can tell? But you here – you all had something out of life: money, love – whatever one gets on shore – and, tell me, wasn't that the best time, that time when we were young at sea; young and had nothing, on the sea that gives nothing, except hard knocks – and sometimes a chance to feel your strength – that only – what you all regret?'

And we all nodded at him: the man of finance, the man of accounts, the man of law, we all nodded at him over the polished table that like a still sheet of brown water reflected our faces, lined, wrinkled; our faces marked by toil, by deceptions, by success, by love; our weary eyes looking still, looking always, looking anxiously for something out of life, that while it is expected is already gone – has passed unseen, in a sigh, in a flash – together with the youth, with the strength, with the romance of illusions.

Source: Joseph Conrad, 'Youth, a Narrative', *Blackwood's Magazine*, September 1898.

Eliminating the Unfit

H. G. Wells (1866–1946), son of a failed shopkeeper and a domestic servant, became a prolific inventor of utopias and dystopias. He was a serious political thinker, as well as an imaginative artist, and he truly wanted to change the world.

In his first book *The Time Machine* (1895) a time-traveller arrives in the year 802,701, and finds that the modern division between capital and labour has evolved two distinct races, the childlike, pleasure-loving Eloi, who play in the sunlight, and the fearsome Morlocks, descendants of the labouring classes, who live underground and eat the Eloi.

Strict class-division also characterizes the Selenites (moon-dwellers), discovered by two astronauts from earth in Wells's *The First Men in the Moon* (1901). Inhabiting the labyrinthine lunar interior, the Selenites are ant-like in their social organization. In addition to males and females, they have neuters, employed as soldiers and workers (who, when not working, are put into a drugged sleep, on the grounds that they are incapable of using leisure profitably). Young Selenites undergo surgical adaptation to fit them for their future employments. Some have tiny heads and huge bodies, whereas scholars have vast, distended brains, containing whole libraries of information, and are carried about in tubs like 'wobbling jellies of knowledge'. Government is autocratic. When one of the astronauts tries to explain democracy to the Grand Lunar, the moon's supremo, his attendants have to spray his brain to prevent it overheating.

A grimmer vision inspires Wells's *When the Sleeper Wakes* (1899), which portrays a world rendered nightmarish by overpopulation. Humanity is crammed into massive, multi-storeyed, glassed-roofed cities. Forests of windmills supply energy. In the treeless, depopulated countryside vast fields of carrots and swedes are mechanically sprayed with deodorized sewage. There are no rivers. Fresh water is scarce, and for most ordinary purposes salt water is pumped along huge aqueducts. Literacy has virtually died out. 'Phonographs' and videos have replaced books. The brutalized, semi-articulate working class spend their whole lives in the dark underworld of the cities' lower strata.

As time went on, fear of overpopulation came to dominate Wells's utopian thought. The Catholic church, with its opposition to birth control, was, he once said, the most evil thing on earth. Social Darwinism, which meant the elimination of weaklings, criminals and other 'unfit' types, also became a leading principle. He considered world government vital too, since it would make war obsolete. To replace democracy, which inevitably pandered to patriotism, he favoured rule by a voluntary, non-hereditary class of austere, selfless, scientifically educated people, variously called 'new Cromwellians' or 'Samurai'.

The most chilling formulation of his utopian hopes came in *Anticipations* (1901), which looks forward to a Wellsian world-state or 'New Republic' in the year 2000. The book confronts the problem of Europe's 'vicious, helpless and pauper masses' (also called 'People of the Abyss'), and of the non-European peoples who, Wells believes, will not be able to keep pace with Europe's technological advance. Both these sections of the population must, he decides, be phased out. The nation that 'most resolutely picks over, educates, sterilizes, exports or poisons its People of the Abyss' will gain ascendancy. Equally, the 'swarms of black and brown, and dirty-white, and yellow people', who do not meet the needs of the new efficiency, 'will have to go'. It is 'their portion to die out and disappear'. Wells's wording here suggests gradual decline rather than actual genocide. However, *Anticipations* makes it clear that the 'unfit' will, in some cases, be exterminated.

It has become apparent that whole masses of human population are, as a whole, inferior in their claim upon the future, to other masses, that they cannot be given opportunities or trusted with power as the superior peoples are trusted, that their characteristic weaknesses are contagious and detrimental in the civilizing fabric, and that their range of incapacity tempts and demoralizes the strong. To give them equality is to sink to their level, to protect and cherish them is to be swamped in their fecundity . . .

The ethical system of these men of the New Republic, the ethical system which will dominate the world state, will be shaped primarily to favour the procreation of what is fine and efficient and beautiful in humanity – beautiful and strong bodies, clear and powerful minds, and a growing body of knowledge – and to check the procreation of base and servile types, of fear-driven and cowardly souls, of all that is mean and ugly and bestial in the souls, bodies, or habits of men. To do the latter is to do the former; the two things are inseparable. And the method that nature has followed hitherto in the shaping of the world, whereby weakness was prevented from propagating weakness, and cowardice and feebleness were saved from the accomplishment of their desires, the method that has only one alternative, the method that must in some cases still be called in to the help of man, is death. In the new vision death is no inexplicable horror, no pointless terminal terror to the miseries of life, it is the end of all the pain of life, the end of the bitterness of failure, the merciful obliteration of weak and silly and pointless things . . .

The new ethics will hold life to be a privilege and a responsibility, not a sort of night refuge for base spirits out of the void; and the alternative in right conduct between living fully, beautifully, and efficiently will be to die. For a multitude of contemptible and silly creatures, fear-driven and helpless and useless, unhappy or hatefully happy in the midst of squalid dishonour, feeble, ugly, inefficient, born of unrestrained lusts, and increasing and multiplying through sheer incontinence and stupidity, the men of the New Republic will have little pity and less benevolence. To make life convenient for the breeding of such people will seem to them not the most virtuous and amiable thing in the world, as it is held to be now, but an exceedingly abominable proceeding. Procreation is an avoidable thing for sane persons of even the most furious passions, and the men of the New Republic will hold that the procreation of children who, by the circumstances of their parentage, *must* be diseased bodily or mentally – I do not think it will be difficult for the medical science of the coming time to define such circumstances – is absolutely the most loathsome of all conceivable sins. They will hold, I anticipate, that a certain portion of the population – the small minority, for example, afflicted with indisputably transmissible diseases, with transmissible mental disorders, with such hideous incurable habits of mind as the craving for intoxication – exists only on sufferance, out of pity and patience, and on the understanding that they do not propagate; and I do not foresee any reason to suppose that they will hesitate to kill when that sufferance is abused. And I imagine also the plea and proof that a grave criminal is also insane will be regarded by them not as a reason for mercy, but as an added reason for death. I do not see how they can think otherwise on the principles they will profess.

The men of the New Republic will not be squeamish, either, in facing or inflicting death, because they will have a fuller sense of the

[369]

possibilities of life than we possess. They will have an ideal that will make killing worth the while; like Abraham, they will have the faith to kill, and they will have no superstitions about death. They will naturally regard the modest suicide of incurably melancholy, or diseased or helpless persons as a high and courageous act of duty rather than a crime. And since they will regard, as indeed all men raised above a brutish level do regard, a very long term of imprisonment as infinitely worse than death, as being, indeed, death with a living misery added to its natural terror, they will, I conceive, where the whole tenor of a man's actions, and not simply some incidental or impulsive action, seems to prove him unfitted for free life in the world, consider him carefully, and condemn him, and remove him from being. All such killing will be done with an opiate, for death is too grave a thing to be made painful or dreadful, and used as a deterrent from crime. If deterrent punishments are used at all in the code of the future, the deterrent will neither be death, nor mutilation of the body, nor mutilation of the life by imprisonment, nor any horrible things like that, but good scientifically caused pain, that will leave nothing but a memory. Yet even the memory of overwhelming pain is a sort of mutilation of the soul. The idea that only those who are fit to live freely in an orderly world-state should be permitted to live, is entirely against the use of deterrent punishments at all. Against outrageous conduct to children or women, perhaps, or for very cowardly or brutal assaults of any sort, the men of the future may consider pain a salutary remedy, at least during the ages of transition while the brute is still at large. But since most acts of this sort done under conditions that neither torture nor exasperate, point to an essential vileness in the perpetrator, I am inclined to think that even in these cases the men of the coming time will be far less disposed to torture than to kill. They will have another aspect to consider. The conscious infliction of pain *for the sake of the pain* is against the better nature of man, and it is unsafe and demoralizing for anyone to undertake this duty. To kill under the seemly conditions science will afford is a far less offensive thing. The rulers of the future will grudge making good people into jailers, warders, punishment-dealers, nurses, and attendants on the bad. People who cannot live happily and freely in the world without spoiling the lives of others are better out of it. That is a current sentiment even today, but the men of the New Republic will have the courage of their opinions.

Wells's new sexual morality, outlined in *Anticipations* and *Mankind in the Making* (1903), lays it down that in utopia mere sexual intercourse, without procreation, will be considered no more culpable than a game of golf. 'Reckless parentage', on the other hand, will be severely discouraged. No one will be allowed to become a parent unless he or she is in employment, free of debt, over twenty-one (twenty-six for a man), healthy, without a criminal record, and able to meet minimum standards of intelligence and education. Those who reproduce in defiance of these regulations will be sterilized. The authorities will fix acceptable standards of clothing, cleanliness and nutrition for all children, and if these are not met the child will be taken away and reared by the state *at the parents' expense*. Should the parents fail in their payments, they will be put in celibate labour colonies (to prevent breeding) until their debt is fully discharged.

Wells's most comprehensive vision of perfection was *A Modern Utopia* (1905). Two hikers in the Swiss Alps find themselves in a parallel world, identical in geography to our own, but conducted on Wellsian principles. There is world-government, and English is the universal language. Earned income is accepted as an index of a person's social worth. To be moneyless is 'clear evidence of unworthiness'. So the ability to pay for privileges is regarded as a reasonable way to ration them. The state insists on every citizen being properly housed, nourished and clothed. Crowded or dirty houses are pulled down. The unemployed are forced into work by the state and paid a minimum wage. Idiots, drunkards, drug addicts, thieves, cheats and violent criminals are secluded on islands patrolled by guards, and sexually segregated to prevent reproduction. The nerve-centre of this unprecedented experiment in social control is an enormous card-index, housed in Paris, and kept up to date by an army of workers, day and night, containing the personal records of every inhabitant of the globe. 'Such a record is inevitable if a Modern Utopia is to be achieved,' wrote Wells. He did not foresee that the computer would make it perfectly possible.

In later works Wells tended to portray the destruction of earth's surplus millions by man-made or natural catastrophe as a needful prelude to the establishment of utopia. *The World Set Free* (1914) predicts atomic fission and nuclear war, followed by famine, plague and cholera, which wipe out most of the world's population. The spokesman for the survivors, a Russian called Marcus Karenin, decides that Armageddon was 'necessary', and that in future woman must be controlled to prevent excessive breeding. Fortunately, Karenin observes, genetic engineering will make it possible to determine the sex of children: 'If woman is too much for us we'll reduce her to a minority, and if we do not like any type of men or women, we'll have no more of it.'

Wells's wish to have fewer people was not just negative. He was among the first to notice that the world's bulging populations were destroying animal species and their habitats. He deserves recognition as a founder of green politics. In *The Shape of Things to Come* (1933) he looks forward to a time when mankind (much reduced in size by various plagues and cataclysms) will live in a 'world garden'. Biological research will produce many new plant varieties. Animal species will be preserved in vast wild areas, closed to humans. The world's population will be kept below the safety level of two billion. Some demographers still regard this as the ideal number of humans for the earth to sustain. In fact, between 1985 and 1990 the world's population grew by about 1.7 million a week. The current population estimate for 2025 is 8.6 billion.

Source: H. G. Wells, *Anticipations of the Reaction of Mechanical and Scientific Progress upon Human Life and Thought*, Chapman & Hall, 1901.

Progressing to the Higher Life

John Macmillan Brown (1846–1935) was a Scots literary academic who became Chancellor of the University of New Zealand. His two utopias, *Riallaro, or the Archipelago of Exiles* (1897) and *Limanora: The Island of Progress* (1903), tell of an ideal civilization developed by the Limanorans, who combine spectacular technological advances with sensational spiritual powers. Their religion is science, their ideal, progress to a 'higher' form of being.

All that is bestial, regressive or irrational, they have systematically eliminated. No animals are allowed on their island, for their presence would mean 'the daily obtrusion of offensive sights that would either shock or degrade'. Their food is made in laboratories: food-plants and agriculture have become obsolete. Greed and selfishness are unknown to them. So is sexual pleasure. Those selected to breed, on eugenic grounds, are motivated in their embraces by will-power, intellect, and service to the race. There are few births, and few deaths. The old idea of mass-produced mankind is abhorred. Each child is reared with microscopic attention to its physical and spiritual well-being and carefully segregated from all other children, because Limanorans have observed that children encourage regressive savagery in each other. Medical science, combining spare-part surgery with exquisite sensitivity to the magnetic and electrical forces of the universe, allows Limanorans to live for centuries. But if they choose to die, euthanasia is available, and regarded as a 'holy duty', since death of the body means advance for the 'higher energy' and 'truer self'. It is carried out by an electric 'petrifier' which instantly turns the moribund Limanoran into a lifelike effigy constructed of irelium (a much-prized and versatile metal).

Many years ago the Limanorans exiled to other islands in their archipelago all those who suffered from 'major vices' (lechers, liars, socialists, political orators, etc.). Since then their minds and bodies have become so refined that they resemble, in many respects, the conventional notion of angels. They can dematerialize, fly, and communicate by 'will-telegraph' (a form of extra-sensory perception). Their super-subtle bodies absorb electric energy from space. They have X-ray vision and can watch thoughts and moods forming

[373]

in each other's brains. Instead of books, they have 'electrograms of the author's thoughts as they developed and shaped themselves'.

By combining aspects of psychoanalysis with brain surgery they have made the workings of the human mind accessible not only to observation but to manipulation. Using 'psychometers' they can 'measure the growth of soul in a child', and a young Limanoran who exhibits a moral failing, such as deceit, enters an 'ethical sanatorium' to undergo electrical-magnetic therapy on his or her 'diseased tissues'. In a sleeping patient they can stimulate and observe dreams, and so compile a complete psychobiography (or 'dream-confession'). Understanding the physical basis of desire, appetite and other psychological phenomena, they can develop parts of the brain in infants for specific functions in later life, and carry out extensive adaptation of the unborn embryo.

They knew the exact stage at which any new organ or function appeared, for they had first of all studied the moulding of embryos in animals; and afterwards, by the aid of their new photographic and microscopic apparatus that revealed the minutest detail of any part or movement within the living human body, they were able to study the effect of changes in exercise or diet or mode of life upon the development of the human embryo. Nothing was neglected to make the knowledge complete and scientific, nothing that might help to turn the science of embryology into a creative art. The invention of instruments which could take the senses of the investigators close to any internal item of the living system had made an era in the history of physiology, and cancelled the necessity of anatomy as its hand-maid. The most microscopic change in the structure of any tissue in the innermost part of the body became patent to the eye or the ear or the electric sense of research. Embryology had thus become almost an exact science; even the physiological side of it had attained to such exactitude as to make it practically an art. The medical elders could investigate the health of the embryo and guide its development as well as in the case of the full-grown child.

They were thus able to formulate a complete art for the moulding of the unborn to the purpose the elders indicated as best for the future of the race.

Limanorans have no formal religion. This is partly because when they had exiled all those with major vices they found there were no ministers of religion left. Also, believing in the constant progress of spiritual understanding, they realize that any idea of God they could formulate would soon become obsolete. Further, they have made preliminary contact with 'ethereal beings living in infinite space' and plan to extend this communication with other, higher forms of life. They do not believe in philanthropy towards their disadvantaged fellow-mortals, because it hinders the upward progress of the race.

It soon came to be acknowledged that intercourse with inferior civilizations, even for the purpose of raising them, lowered the moral standard of the missionaries, whilst failing in its original motive. Much of the philanthropy that began at home was found to be no less obstructive and immoral. It fed and clothed the poor and improvident, and thus helped to slay and bury the only habit that could save them out of their slough, the habit of measuring every step they took, and seeing whither it led; and it helped to perpetuate the evil; for the ready yet limited supplies combined with the improvidence to make them breed like the lower animals, and the race of paupers and unprogressive was inordinately multiplied. The same feeble and immoral philanthropy opposed all attempts to stop the multiplication of the diseased and semi-criminal, and had to increase the armies of doctors and guardians of the peace every generation. It did well to nurse the feeble in mind and body, and to reduce the penalties under which heredity had placed them; but it failed to see that it was doing endless evil by letting them penalize an increasing posterity with their own punishment. Not till it was branded as the worst of immoralities was such philanthropy ended.

In lieu of philanthropy, the Limanorans have developed a potent weapon for improving the lot of mankind in the form of an electric sterilizer, which puts it in their power to carry out a programme of selective birth-control.

By this and this alone was the snail-pace advance of mankind likely to be quickened. Without more rapid elimination of the unfit than was afforded by natural selection, sexual selection, and the accidents of surroundings, there was little hope of wise propagation of the human race. The blunders and defects and maladies of every new century were treasured up by heredity in the tissues of mankind along with any feeble tendency to advance that might appear. The struggle was a losing one in spite of the development of science and

Deep-Frozen Genius

The French sociologist and criminologist Gabriel Tarde (1843–1904) emphasized the role of the individual in society. All progress, he taught, came through invention and subsequent imitation, and about one person in a hundred was inventive. His utopia, published in English the year after Tarde's death as *Underground Man*, relates the obliteration of most of the human race by the sudden cooling of the sun towards the end of the twentieth-fifth century. In northern countries, whole populations freeze to death. Panic-stricken refugees head for the tropics, but are buried in gigantic snowdrifts. The cold splits the walls of houses, admitting blasts of air that kill the inhabitants on the spot. A few intrepid survivors make their way underground. There they learn to harness the energy of the earth's molten core, and develop sophisticated tunnelling techniques. As the labyrinth of subterranean settlements spreads, a new civilization establishes itself, more refined than the old. The natural world of animals and plants no longer exists. The environment is so warm that the 'neo-troglodytes' do not need clothes, though women sometimes wear diaphanous fabrics spun out of metal or asbestos. Food supply is no problem, for there are vast herds of dead farm animals on the earth's surface, preserved as if in a giant refrigerator. Though underground life might seem claustrophobic, it holds, Tarde's narrator explains, opportunity for adventure:

Our universe can offer boundless excursions under the Atlantic and Pacific Oceans frozen to their very lowest depths. Venturesome explorers, I was going to say discoverers, have in every direction and in the easiest imaginable fashion honeycombed these immense ice-caps with endless passages much in the same way as the termites, according to our palaeontologists, bored through the floors of our fathers. We extend at will these fantastic galleries of crystal, which, wherever they cross one another, form so many crystal palaces, by casting on the walls a ray of intense heat which makes them melt. We take good care to drain the water due to the liquefaction into one of those bottomless pits which here and there yawn hideously beneath our feet. Thanks to this method and the improvements it has undergone we have succeeded in cutting, hewing and carving the solidified sea-water. We are able to glide through it, to manoeuvre in it, to course through it on skates or velocipedes with an ease and agility that are always admired in spite of our being accustomed to it. The severe cold of these regions is scarcely tempered by millions of electric lamps which are mirrored in the emerald-green icicles with their velvet-like tints and renders a permanent stay impossible. It would even prevent us crossing them if, by good luck, the earliest pioneers had not discovered in them crowds of seals which had been caught while still alive by the freezing of the waters in which they remain imprisoned. Their carefully prepared skins have furnished us with warm clothing. Nothing is more curious than thus suddenly to catch sight of, as it were through a mysterious glass case, one of these huge marine animals, sometimes a whale, a shark or a devil fish, and that star-like flora which carpets the seas. Though appearing crystallized in its transparent prison, in its Elysium of pure brine, it has lost none of its secret charm, that was quite unknown to our ancestors. Idealized by its very lack of motion, immortalized by its death, it dimly shines here and there with gleams of pearl and mother of pearl in the twilight of the depths below, to the right, the left, beneath the feet or above the head of the solitary skater who roams with his lamp on his forehead in pursuit of the unknown.

Since the earth's inner energy reserves, and the almost limitless supply of frozen food, meet all practical needs, humanity, in its underground existence, has turned to the arts. Aestheticism dominates the new culture, as utilitarianism did the old. The tunnels and underground chambers are decorated with exquisite graffiti. To be human is to be artistically creative.

Man in becoming a town dweller has become really human. From the time that all sorts of trees and beasts, of flowers and insects no longer interpose between men, and all sorts of vulgar wants no longer hinder the progress of the truly human faculties, everyone seems to be born well-bred, just as everyone is born a sculptor or musician, philosopher or poet.

Artistic genius is the only kind of superiority recognized. The underground world is a 'geniocratic' republic. With a view to producing more geniuses, and to avoid overtaxing resources, population growth is strictly controlled. Nothing amazes the new people more, when they search through the records of above-ground humanity, than to find that unregulated childbirth was allowed in the old world.

Is it possible that after manufacturing the rubbish heaps of law with which our libraries are lumbered up, they precisely omitted to regulate the only matter considered worthy today of regulation? Can we conceive that it could ever have been permissible to the first comer without due authorization to expose society to the arrival of a new hungry and wailing member – above all at a time when it was not possible to kill a partridge without a game licence, or to import a sack of corn without paying duty? Wiser and more far-sighted, we degrade, and in case of a second offence we condemn to be thrown into a lake of petroleum, whoever allows himself to infringe our constitutional law on this point, or rather we should say, should allow himself, for the force of public opinion has got the better of the crime and has rendered our penalties unnecessary. We sometimes, nay very often, see lovers who go mad from love and die in consequence. Others courageously get themselves hoisted by a lift to the gaping mouth of an extinct volcano and reach the outer air which in a moment freezes them to death. They have scarcely time to regard the azure sky – a magnificent spectacle, so they say – and the twilight hues of the still dying sun or the vast and unstudied disorder of the stars; then locked in each other's arms they fall dead upon the ice! The summit of their favourite volcano is completely crowned with their corpses which are admirably preserved always in twos, stark and livid, a living image still of love and agony, of despair and frenzy, but more often of ecstatic repose.

But what is unheard of and unexampled in our day is for a woman in love to abandon herself to her lover before the latter has under her inspiration produced a masterpiece which is adjudged and proclaimed as such by his rivals. For here we have the indispensable condition to which legitimate marriage is subordinated. The right to have children is the monopoly and supreme recompense of genius. It is besides a powerful lever for the uplifting and exaltation of the race.

Source: Gabriel Tarde, *Underground Man*, translated by Cloudesley Brereton, Duckworth, 1905.

Fish Heaven

Not many writers have tried to imagine utopias for other creatures besides humans. But the English poet Rupert Brooke (1887–1915) does so in his poem 'Heaven'. This satirizes St John's vision of the Christian heaven in Revelation: 21 (compare the biblical 'and there was no more sea' with Brooke's last line).

Fish (fly-replete, in depth of June,
Dawdling away their wat'ry noon)
Ponder deep wisdom, dark or clear,
Each secret fishy hope or fear.
Fish say, they have their Stream and Pond;
But is there anything Beyond?
This life cannot be All, they swear,
For how unpleasant, if it were!
One may not doubt that, somehow, Good
Shall come of Water and of Mud;
And, sure, the reverent eye must see
A Purpose in Liquidity.
We darkly know, by Faith we cry,
The future is not Wholly Dry.
Mud unto mud! – Death eddies near –
Not here the appointed End, not here!
But somewhere, beyond Space and Time,
Is wetter water, slimier slime!
And there (they trust) there swimmeth One
Who swam ere rivers were begun,
Immense, of fishy form and mind,
Squamous, omnipotent, and kind;
And under that Almighty Fin,
The littlest fish may enter in.

Oh! never fly conceals a hook,
Fish say, in the Eternal Brook,
But more than mundane weeds are there,
And mud, celestially fair;
Fat caterpillars drift around,
And Paradisal grubs are found;
Unfading moths, immortal flies,
And the worm that never dies.
And in that Heaven of all their wish,
There shall be no more land, say fish.

Source: *Rupert Brooke: The Complete Poems*, Sidgwick & Jackson, 1932.

Virgin Births

Pioneer American feminist Charlotte Perkins Gilman (1860–1935) had an unhappy childhood, her father deserting her mother soon after her birth. She studied art, and earned her living designing greetings cards and teaching. Her marriage to a fellow artist ended in divorce after severe post-natal depression. The sinister, semi-autobiographical story 'The Yellow Wallpaper' (1892), Gilman's masterpiece, tells something of her psychological troubles. She became a lecturer and writer, publishing a succession of books on the rights of women and socialism. Suffering from inoperable cancer, she committed suicide in 1935, leaving a note which explained: 'When all usefulness is over, when one is assured of unavoidable and imminent death, it is the simplest of human rights to choose a quick and easy death in place of a slow and horrible one . . . I have preferred chloroform to cancer.'

Published in 1915 in Gilman's monthly *The Forerunner*, her novel *Herland* describes an all-woman utopia, situated in a remote mountain region. Three young American explorers, Terry, Jeff and Van (the narrator) come upon this forgotten land. They find a race of calm, dignified, athletic, rational women, who seem beautiful yet strangely sexless, lacking the charms and the fragility that the young men have been culturally conditioned to associate with femininity. The women easily overpower the intruders when they try to escape, but treat them kindly and teach them their language.

They tell them that the men of their nation were wiped out in a catastrophe two thousand years ago. Soon after, one woman found she was capable of virgin birth. Her five daughters had the same power, and so had theirs. Thus a race of parthenogenic women evolved, a sisterhood, without social classes or competitiveness.

Motherhood is the dominant note of the whole culture, and children are the prime consideration. But children are not regarded as belonging to one mother. The whole race mothers them. There are no such things as private 'homes' or 'families'. Children have given-names, but no surnames. After the first year they are tended mainly by expert educationalists, who draw on the culture's profound understanding of child psychology. Children's literature is highly developed (though adult Herland literature, lacking any sex motive, strikes the young Americans as rather 'flat'). Sixteen hundred years have been spent developing educational games, which teach the children citizenship without their realizing they are being taught. Thanks to this early conditioning, war, greed and hatred are unknown in Herland. Herland babies never cry.

However, the fivefold increase of the population in each generation soon posed problems, which the women faced rationally and effectively:

When a population multiplies by five every thirty years it soon reaches the limits of a country, especially a small one like this. They very soon eliminated all the grazing cattle – sheep were the last to go, I believe. Also, they worked out a system of intensive agriculture surpassing anything I ever heard of, with the very forests all reset with fruit- or nut-bearing trees.

Do what they would, however, there soon came a time when they were confronted with the problem of 'the pressure of population' in an acute form. There was really crowding, and with it, unavoidably, a decline in standards.

And how did those women meet it?

Not by a 'struggle for existence' which would result in an ever-lasting writhing mass of underbred people trying to get ahead of one another – some few on top, temporarily, many constantly crushed out underneath, a hopeless substratum of paupers and degenerates, and no serenity or peace for anyone, no possibility for really noble qualities among the people at large.

Neither did they start off on predatory excursions to get more land from somebody else, or to get more food from somebody else, to maintain their struggling mass.

Not at all. They sat down in council together and thought it out. Very clear, strong thinkers they were. They said: 'With our best endeavors this country will support about so many people, with the standard of peace, comfort, health, beauty, and progress we demand. Very well. That is all the people we will make.'

It was found that if a woman concentrated hard on other things, such as physical labour, at the time when she would normally conceive, conception could be averted. Employing this technique, Herland adopted a policy of 'negative eugenics'. Mothers agreed to restrict themselves to one child each. In order 'to breed out, where possible, the lowest types', girls showing 'bad qualities' were persuaded to renounce motherhood altogether. By these means the population of Herland (area 10,000 square miles) has been stabilized at three million. Disease is virtually unknown. It is six hundred years since Herland produced a criminal.

Though they grow some grain, forest culture is the great Herland skill, because trees give the highest yield per acre. The country's entire forest area has been replaced by food-yielding trees. All waste is recycled:

All the scraps and leavings of their food, plant waste from lumber work or textile industry, all the solid matter from the sewage, properly treated and combined – everything which came from the earth went back into it.

Metalled roads and fast electric cars have been developed, but do not impinge much. Herlanders live in close harmony with the forest. Their cities of rose-coloured stone lie among groves and gardens, 'like a broken rosary of pink coral'. The national diet is vegan and teetotal, based on nuts, berries, grains, and a drink 'like cocoa'. On this, as on other subjects, the explorers' explanation of Western ways arouses dismay and consternation among the Herlanders.

'Have you no cattle – sheep – horses?' I drew some rough outlines of these beasts and showed them to her.

'We had, in the very old days, these,' said Somel, and sketched with swift sure touches a sort of sheep or llama, 'and these' – dogs, of two or three kinds, 'and that' – pointing to my absurd but recognizable horse.

'What became of them?' asked Jeff.

'We do not want them anymore. They took up too much room – we need all our land to feed our people. It is such a little country, you know.'

'Whatever do you do without milk?' Terry demanded incredulously.

'*Milk?* We have milk in abundance – our own.'

'But – but – I mean for cooking – for grown people,' Terry blundered, while they looked amazed and a shade displeased.

Jeff came to the rescue. 'We keep cattle for their milk, as well as for their meat,' he explained. 'Cow's milk is a staple article of diet. There is a great milk industry – to collect and distribute it.'

Still they looked puzzled. I pointed to my outline of a cow. 'The farmer milks the cow,' I said, and sketched a milk pail, the stool, and in pantomime showed the man milking. 'Then it is carried to the city and distributed by milkmen – everybody has it at the door in the morning.'

'Has the cow no child?' asked Somel earnestly.

'Oh, yes, of course, a calf, that is.'

'Is there milk for the calf and you, too?'

It took some time to make clear to those three sweet-faced women the process which robs the cow of her calf, and the calf of its true food; and the talk led us into a further discussion of the meat business. They heard it out, looking very white, and presently begged to be excused.

Herland religion is a kind of maternal pantheism, with a mother goddess. There is no domineering paternal god, no hell, no after-life punishments, indeed, no after-life, as Van finds when he questions Ellador (with whom he has fallen in love) about metaphysics.

'And the life everlasting? What does your religion teach about eternity?'

'Nothing,' said Ellador. 'What is eternity?'

What indeed? I tried, for the first time in my life, to get a real hold on the idea.

'It is – never stopping.'

'Never stopping?' She looked puzzled.

'Yes, life, going on forever.'

'Oh – we see that, of course. Life does go on forever, all about us.'

'But eternal life goes on *without dying*.'

'The same person?'

'Yes, the same person, unending, immortal.' I was pleased to think that I had something to teach from our religion, which theirs had never promulgated.

'Here?' asked Ellador. 'Never to die – here?' I could see her practical mind heaping up the people, and hurriedly reassured her.

'Oh no, indeed, not here – hereafter. We must die here, of course, but then we "enter into eternal life." The soul lives forever.'

'How do you know?' she inquired.

'I won't attempt to prove it to you,' I hastily continued. 'Let us assume it to be so. How does this idea strike you?'

Again she smiled at me, that adorable, dimpling, tender, mischievous, motherly smile of hers. 'Shall I be quite, quite honest?'

'You couldn't be anything else,' I said, half gladly and half a little sorry. The transparent honesty of these women was a never-ending astonishment to me.

'It seems to me a singularly foolish idea,' she said calmly. 'And if true, most disagreeable.'

Also incomprehensible to Herlanders are Western notions of sex. Though Ellador and Van wed, the idea of having sexual intercourse just for pleasure, when there is no intention of begetting a child, is abhorrent to her. 'You mean,' she asks him incredulously, 'that with you – love between men and women expresses itself in that way – without regard to motherhood? . . . It seems so against nature . . . None of the creatures we know do that. Do other animals – in your country?' Forced to admit they do not, Van eventually reconciles himself to a largely sexless union: 'I found that much, very much, of what I honestly supposed to be a physiological necessity was a psychological necessity – or so believed.' Terry, the most macho of the Americans, also marries a Herlander (Alima), and encountering similar resistance tries to take his 'marital rights' by force. He is overpowered, anaesthetized, put on trial, and banished.

Source: Charlotte Perkins Gilman, *Herland*, with an introduction by Ann J. Lane, The Women's Press, 1979.

A Surgical Cure for Imagination

Yevgeny Zamyatin's *We* (written in 1920, but banned in Soviet Russia, and first published in 1924, in an English translation) is perhaps the greatest of all dystopias. It inspired two other masterpieces, Huxley's *Brave New World* (see p. 447) and Orwell's *Nineteen Eighty-Four* (see p. 432). Often read as a satire on Stalinist totalitarianism, it in fact preceded Stalin's rise to power. It is set in The One State, where the inhabitants have numbers, not names, and all live by the same rigid timetable. Buildings and furniture are made of glass, so that nothing is concealed from the eyes of the ever-present Guardians (government spies). Elegantly camouflaged membranes, placed along the streets, record all conversations carried on out of doors. Glass walls surround the city, excluding the anarchic, fecund world of nature. Within, all traces of natural life have been eradicated. The food consumed is a chemical derivative of naphtha. State-controlled promiscuity has replaced love and marriage. The *Lex Sexualis* states that 'every number has the right of availability, as a sexual product, to any other number'. Each number is issued with a book of pink tickets, entitling him or her, on appointed Sexual Days, to sex with any other number. It is permissible for blinds to be lowered for fifteen minutes during intercourse. All infringements of regulations must be reported to the Operational Division, where suspects are interrogated and asphyxiated under the Gas Bell Glass. The Benefactor, the supreme ruler of The One State, is a gigantic, hieratic figure, who personally carries out executions by means of The Machine, an electrical device that reduces the body to 'a puddle of chemically pure water'.

The story centres on a mathematician, D-503, inventor of the Integral, a space-ship designed to spread The One State throughout the solar system. His robot-like obedience to The One State's rational dictates is disturbed when he is seduced by, and falls in love with, a strange alluring woman, E-330. She belongs to a secret dissident organization, Mephis, which plans to blow up the Glass Wall and bring back Nature. Opportunely, in the face of this danger, The One State's scientists discover that they can eradicate human imagination – a breakthrough announced on the front page of *The Gazette of The One State*.

REJOICE!

For henceforth you are perfect! Up to this day your own offspring, your various mechanisms, were of greater perfection than ourselves.

IN WHAT WAY?

Every spark of a dynamo is a spark of purest reason; every thrust of a piston is an immaculate syllogism. But then, does not the same inerrable reason dwell within you as well?

The philosophy of cranes, presses and pumps is as finished and clear as a circle drawn with a pair of compasses. But then, is your philosophy any less circular?

The beauty of a mechanism lies in that which is undeviating and exact, as in a pendulum, as in rhythm. But then you, who have been nurtured on the Taylor System* from your very childhood – have you not become as exact as pendulums?

There is, however, one point of difference:

MECHANISMS HAVE NO FANTASY!

Did you ever see a wool-gathering, senselessly dreamy smile spread over the physiognomy of a pump cylinder while it was working? Did you ever hear any cranes tossing restlessly in bed and sighing of nights, during the hours appointed for rest?

YOU NEVER DID!

And yet the Guardians have more and more often (well may you blush!) seen these smiles and heard these sighs among you. And (you may well hide your eyes!) the historians of The One State are tendering their resignation so that they may be spared having to chronicle sundry ignominious occurrences.

However, you are not to blame for these things – you are sick. And the name of your sickness is

FANTASY!

Fantasy is a worm whose boring leaves black furrows on your brows. Fantasy is a fever which drives you on to further and further

---

* Frederick Taylor (1856–1915), American industrial efficiency expert and inventor of time-and-motion study whose ideas lay behind Ford's revolutionary mass-production methods.

flight, even though this *further* point may begin where happiness ends. Fantasy is the last barricade on the road to happiness.

And yet,

REJOICE!

That barricade has been dynamited.

The road lies clear ahead.

The location of the Centre of Fantasy is the latest discovery of science in The One State. This Centre is a miserable little cerebral node in the region of the Bridge of Varoli. A triple cauterization of this node with X-rays, and you are cured of Fantasy –

PERMANENTLY!

You are perfect; you are on a par with machines; the road to one hundred per cent happiness lies clear ahead. Hasten, then, all of you, young and old – hasten to submit yourselves to the Grand Operation! Hasten to the auditoria, where the Grand Operation is now being carried on!

All hail to the Grand Operation!

All hail to the Benefactor!

Soon, all numbers are commanded to undergo Fantasiectomy, on pain of death, and though D-503 tries to escape, he is operated on. It is a complete success. Freed at last from the bewildering urges of his imagination, he betrays Mephis to the Bureau of Guardians, and sits happily beside the Benefactor to watch E-330 and her associates tortured under the Gas Bell Glass, prior to execution by The Machine.

Source: Yevgeny Zamyatin, We, translated by Bernard Guilbert Guerney, with an introduction by Michael Glenny, Penguin, 1970.

Sailing to Byzantium

W. B. Yeats (1865–1939) was a poet of other worlds. He filled his early poems with myths and visions – sensuous, sleepy, magical – which escape from the brutal reality of the everyday. The idea for 'The Lake Isle of Innisfree' came to him one day in 1890, when he was standing 'very homesick' before a shop window that displayed a little fountain. 'I began to remember lake water. From that sudden remembrance came my poem *Innisfree*.'

I will arise and go now, and go to Innisfree,
And a small cabin build there, of clay and wattles made:
Nine bean-rows will I have there, a hive for the honey-bee,
And live alone in the bee-loud glade.

And I shall have some peace there, for peace comes dropping slow,
Dropping from the veils of the morning to where the cricket sings;
There midnight's all a glimmer, and noon a purple glow,
And evening full of the linnet's wings.

I will arise and go now, for always night and day
I hear lake water lapping with low sounds by the shore;
While I stand on the roadway, or on the pavements grey,
I hear it in the deep heart's core.

That *Innisfree* should have become his most popular poem caused the later Yeats some displeasure. He regarded it as sentimental, and went on to develop a tougher, more complex poetry. In this he was aided by spirits. Four years after his marriage in 1917 his wife found that she could contact the spirit world through 'automatic writing' and 'automatic speech'. Yeats spent seven years studying the messages she relayed, and published the results in *A Vision* (1925). Essentially, the secret that the spirits communicated was that the key to all reality is the number 28, which corresponds to the phases of the moon. Thus history divides itself into cycles of about two thousand years, each of twenty-eight phases. There are also twenty-eight incarnations each man must live through, and twenty-eight possible psychological types (or, rather, twenty-six, since life is impossible in phase 1 and phase 15, the dark and the full moon). *A Vision* elaborates upon these basic truths with much care and ingenuity. One of the benefits of the spirits' revelations was that they proved Yeats's liking for Byzantine art to be supernaturally correct. His calculations revealed that Byzantine civilization under the emperor Justinian (AD 527–65) occurred almost exactly half-way along the first thousand-year sub-cycle of our present historical cycle, just as the Renaissance occurred half-way along the second.

I think if I could be given a month of Antiquity and leave to spend it where I chose, I would spend it in Byzantium a little before Justinian opened St Sophia and closed the Academy of Plato. I think I could find in some little wine-shop some philosophical worker in mosaic who could answer all my questions, the supernatural descending nearer to him than to Plotinus even, for the pride of his delicate skill would make what was an instrument of power to princes and clerics, a murderous madness in the mob, show as a lovely flexible presence like that of a perfect human body.

I think that in early Byzantium, maybe never before or since in recorded history, religious, aesthetic and practical life were one, that architect and artificers – though not, it may be, poets, for language had been the instrument of controversy and must have grown abstract – spoke to the multitude and the few alike. The painter, the mosaic worker, the worker in gold and silver, the illuminator of sacred books, were almost impersonal, almost perhaps without the consciousness of individual design, absorbed in their subject-matter and that the vision of a whole people. They could copy out of old Gospel books those pictures that seemed as sacred as the text, and yet weave all into a vast design, the work of many that seemed the work of one, that made building, picture, pattern, metal-work of rail and lamp, seem but a single image; and this vision, this proclamation of their invisible master, had the Greek nobility, Satan always the still half-divine Serpent, never the horned scarecrow of the didactic Middle Ages.

The ascetic, called in Alexandria 'God's Athlete', has taken the place of those Greek athletes whose statues have been melted or broken up or stand deserted in the midst of cornfields, but all about him is an incredible splendour like that which we see pass under our closed eyelids as we lie between sleep and waking, no representation of a living world but the dream of a somnambulist. Even the drilled pupil of the eye, when the drill is in the hand of some Byzantine worker in ivory, undergoes a somnambulistic change, for its deep shadow among the faint lines of the tablet, its mechanical circle, where all else is rhythmical and flowing, give to Saint or Angel a look of some great bird staring at miracle. Could any visionary of those days, passing through the Church named with so un-theological a grace 'The Holy Wisdom', can even a visionary of today wandering among the mosaics at Ravenne or in Sicily, fail to recognize some one image seen under his closed eyelids? To me it seems that He, who among the first Christian communities was little but a ghostly exorcist, had in His assent to a full Divinity made possible this sinking-in upon a supernatural splendour, these walls with their little glimmering cubes of blue and green and gold.

Sources: W. B. Yeats, *The Rose* in *Poems*, Fisher Unwin, 1893; *A Vision*, 1925.

Samoan Fibs

American anthropologist Margaret Mead (1901–78) spent nine months in Samoa in 1925–6. The book that resulted, *Coming of Age in Samoa: A Psychological Study of Primitive Youth for Western Civilisation* (1929), outsold any anthropology book before or since, and had an enormous influence on both the academic establishment and popular thought. Throughout the 1920s there had been fierce dispute over whether human personality is formed by nature (genetic inheritance) or nurture (culture and environment). Following the lead of Francis Galton (1822–1911), the founder of eugenics, the 'nature' brigade recommended eliminating the 'unfit' by encouraging higher types to breed and, where necessary, sterilizing undesirables – a measure adopted in Nazi Germany with the introduction of a Eugenic Sterilization Law in 1933. In reaction, champions of 'nurture' insisted that personality was entirely a cultural product and owed nothing to heredity. Their leader was Mead's professor, Franz Boas.

Mead's book seemed to provide objective proof of Boas's beliefs. Having lived among female adolescents in Samoa, she was able to report that they were quite free from the emotional stresses and rebellious urges that affected their American counterparts. This was traceable, she argued, to the free-and-easy society in which they had been brought up. The Samoans were, in Mead's account, a remarkably casual and relaxed people. Family tensions were almost unknown, for there were no strong emotional ties between children and parents. The whole community was a kind of extended family, and children could, if they wished, wander off and live with other couples. They were almost never punished, and competitiveness was discouraged. In the society at large, there was little emphasis on rank. The happy-go-lucky Samoan life-style found no place for male aggression, homicide or warfare – or for strict sexual morality. Adolescent girls were allowed to be promiscuous before marriage, and they took full advantage of their liberty. Hence their happy, casual approach to womanhood, and hence, too, the extreme rarity of rape among young Samoans.

The second chapter of Mead's book, entitled 'A Day in Samoa', affectionately evokes this idyll.

The life of the day begins at dawn, or if the moon has shown until daylight, the shouts of the young men may be heard before dawn from the hillside. Uneasy in the night, populous with ghosts, they shout lustily to one another as they hasten with their work. As the dawn begins to fall among the soft brown roofs and the slender palm trees stand out against a colourless, gleaming sea, lovers slip home from trysts beneath the palm trees or in the shadow of beached canoes, that the light may find each sleeper in his appointed place. Cocks crow, negligently, and a shrill-voiced bird cries from the bread-fruit trees. The insistent roar of the reef seems muted to an undertone for the sounds of a waking village. Babies cry, a few short wails before sleepy mothers give them the breast. Restless little children roll out of their sheets and wander drowsily down to the beach to freshen their faces in the sea. Boys, bent upon an early fishing, start collecting their tackle and go to rouse their more laggard companions. Fires are lit, here and there, the white smoke hardly visible against the paleness of the dawn. The whole village, sheeted and frowsy, stirs, rubs its eyes, and stumbles towards the beach. 'Talofa!' 'Talofa!' 'Will the journey start today?' 'Is it bonito fishing your lordship is going?' Girls stop to giggle over some young ne'er-do-well who escaped during the night from an angry father's pursuit and to venture a shrewd guess that the daughter knew more about his presence than she told. The boy who is taunted by another, who has succeeded him in his sweetheart's favour, grapples with his rival, his foot slipping in the wet sand. From the other end of the village comes a long drawn-out, piercing wail. A messenger has just brought word of the death of some relative in another village. Half-clad, unhurried women, with babies at their breasts, or astride their hips, pause in their tale of Losa's outraged departure from her father's house to the greater kindness in the home of her uncle, to wonder who is dead. Poor relatives whisper their requests to rich relatives, men make plans to set a fish trap together, a woman begs a bit of yellow dye from a kinswoman, and through the village sounds the rhythmic tattoo which calls the young men together. They gather from all parts of the village, digging sticks in hand, ready to start inland to the plantation. The older men set off upon their more lonely occupations, and each household, reassembled under its peaked roof, settles down to the routine of the morning. Little children, too hungry to wait for the late breakfast, beg lumps of cold taro which they munch greedily. Women carry piles of washing to the sea or to the spring at the far end of the village, or set off inland after weaving materials. The older girls go fishing on the reef, or perhaps set themselves to weaving a new set of Venetian blinds.

In the houses, where the pebbly floors have been swept bare with a stiff long-handled broom, the women great with child and the nursing mothers, sit and gossip with one another. Old men sit apart, unceasingly twisting palm husk on their bare thighs and muttering old tales under their breath. The carpenters begin work on the new house, while the owner bustles about trying to keep them in a good humour. Families who will cook today are hard at work; the taro, yams and bananas have already been brought from inland; the children are scuttling back and forth, fetching sea water, or leaves to stuff the pig. As the sun rises higher in the sky, the shadows deepen under the thatched roofs, the sand is burning to the touch, the hibiscus flowers wilt on the hedges, and little children bid the smaller ones, 'Come out of the sun.' Those whose excursions have been short return to the village, the women with strings of crimson jelly fish, or baskets of shell fish, the men with cocoanuts, carried in baskets slung on a shoulder pole. The women and children eat their breakfasts, just hot from the oven, if this is cook day, and the young men work swiftly in the midday heat, preparing the noon feast for their elders.

It is high noon. The sand burns the feet of the little children, who leave their palm leaf balls and their pin-wheels of frangipani blossoms to wither in the sun, as they creep into the shade of the houses. The women who must go abroad carry great banana leaves as sun-shades or wind wet cloths about their heads. Lowering a few blinds against the slanting sun, all who are left in the village wrap their heads in sheets and go to sleep. Only a few adventurous children may slip away for a swim in the shadow of a high rock, some industrious woman continue with her weaving, or a close little group of women bend anxiously over a woman in labour. The village is dazzling and dead; any sound seems oddly loud and out of place. Words have to cut through the solid heat slowly. And then the sun gradually sinks over the sea.

A second time, the sleeping people stir, roused perhaps by the cry of 'a boat', resounding through the village. The fishermen beach their canoes, weary and spent from the heat, in spite of the slaked lime on their heads, with which they have sought to cool their brains and redden their hair. The brightly coloured fishes are spread out on the floor, or piled in front of the houses until the women pour water over them to free them from taboo. Regretfully, the young fishermen separate out the 'Taboo fish', which must be sent to the chief, or proudly they pack the little palm-leaf baskets with offerings of fish to take to their sweethearts. Men come home from the bush, grimy and heavy laden, shouting as they come, greeted in a sonorous rising cadence by those who have remained at home. They gather in the guest house for their evening kava drinking. The soft clapping of hands, the high-pitched intoning of the talking chief who serves the kava echoes through the village. Girls gather flowers to weave into necklaces; children, lusty from their naps and bound to no particular task, play circular games in the half shade of the late afternoon. Finally the sun sets, in a flame which stretches from the mountain behind to the horizon on the sea, the last bather comes up from the beach, children straggle home, dark little figures etched against the sky; lights shine in the houses, and each household gathers for its evening meal. The suitor humbly presents his offering, the children have been summoned from their noisy play, perhaps there is an honoured guest who must be served first, after the soft, barbaric singing of Christian hymns and the brief and graceful evening prayer. In front of a house at the end of the village, a father cries out the birth of a son. In some family circles a face is missing, in others little runaways have found a haven! Again quiet settles upon the village, as first the head of the household, then the women and children, and last of all the patient boys, eat their supper.

After supper the old people and the little children are bundled off to bed. If the young people have guests the front of the house is yielded to them. For day is the time for the councils of old men and the labours of youth, and night is the time for lighter things. Two kinsmen, or a chief and his councillor, sit and gossip over the day's events or make plans for the morrow. Outside a crier goes through the village announcing that the communal breadfruit pit will be opened in the morning, or that the village will make a great fish trap. If it is moonlight, groups of young men, women by twos and threes, wander through the village, and crowds of children hunt for land crabs or chase each other among the breadfruit trees. Half the village may go fishing by torchlight and the curving reef will gleam with wavering lights and echo with shouts of triumph or disappointment, teasing words or smothered cries of outraged modesty. Or a group of youths may dance for the pleasure of some visiting maiden. Many of those who have retired to sleep, drawn by the merry music, will wrap their sheets about them and set out to find the dancing. A white-clad, ghostly throng will gather in a circle about the gaily lit house, a circle from which every now and then a few will detach themselves and wander away among the trees. Sometimes sleep will not descend upon the village until long past midnight; then at last there is only the mellow thunder of the reef and the whisper of lovers, as the village rests until dawn.

Besides greatly enhancing the prestige of cultural determinism in academic circles, Mead's book also chimed with the free-love movement of the 1920s. Sleeping around, it seemed, was healthful, natural and good for your psychological stability.

On the strength of *Coming of Age in Samoa*, Mead gained recognition as one of the outstanding American women of her time. She herself predicted that her monograph 'would stand forever for the edification and enjoyment of future generations . . . like the lovers on Keats's Grecian Urn'. In the years following its publication, discrepancies between her account of Samoan society and others' were sometimes remarked on. But it was not until the New Zealand-born anthropologist Derek Freeman undertook a thorough investigation of Mead's work (an investigation that included six years' fieldwork in the Samoan archipelago) that the full extent of her misinformation came to light. Freeman was able to show that, on nearly every issue she touched on, Mead's account was preposterously at variance with the facts of Samoan life. Far from being casual and unaggressive, the history of the Samoans revealed them as unusually warlike. Bloody battles between communities were a traditional feature. Warriors were admired. Social conventions were based on a rigorous system of rank and dominance, which bred an intense and pervasive competitiveness, bitter rivalries, and acts of violence. The homicide rate was high. Sexual mores were strict. The cult of premarital virginity was carried to a greater extreme than in almost any other culture known to anthropology. Child-rearing was severe and punitive, occasioning rebellious, aggressive and hysterical behaviour – and suicide – among teenagers. The delinquency rate among adolescent girls was very high, and rape was twice as frequent as in the USA.

The question of how Mead could have got things so wrong puzzled Freeman. But in 1987 he met one of the young Samoan women (now aged eighty-six) who had been among her original informants. She explained that the whole thing had been a prank. Embarrassed by Mead's questions about their sex lives, they had fed her a completely spurious account of the society in which they lived: 'We just fibbed and fibbed.'

Sources: Margaret Mead, *Coming of Age in Samoa*, Cape, 1929; Derek Freeman, *Margaret Mead and the Heretic: The Making and Unmaking of an Anthropological Myth*, Penguin, 1996.

Imaginary Etruscans

D. H. Lawrence (1885–1930) yearned for a utopia, and planned one. It was to be called Rananim. 'I want to gather together about twenty souls,' he wrote in 1915, 'and sail away from this world of war and squalor and find a little colony where there shall be no money but a sort of communism as far as necessaries of life go, and some real decency.' After consideration, however, he decided that none of his friends would make suitable utopians. His letters, in the years that followed, record his disappointment with each successive sample of humanity he encountered.

He finally lost patience with England ('a banquet of vomit') in 1919, and moved to Taormina in Sicily. This seemed attractive at first, but within a year he was wishing that red-hot lava would rain down and engulf it. The Orient beckoned, and he sailed to Ceylon, where he found 'the silly dark people' and their 'hideous little Buddha temples like decked-up pigsties' deeply offensive. Australia, his next landfall, also disappointed. It was apparent within weeks that the Australians were 'almost imbecile'. So he left for the South Sea Islands. A brief inspection was enough to inform him that the inhabitants were brown and soft and smelled of coconut oil, and he did not prolong his visit. By September 1922 he had reached America, which he realized almost immediately, and with dismay, was a continent of 'tight iron-clanking little wills'. He fled to Taos, New Mexico, hoping to share the deep ancient wisdom of the Indians. But they turned out to be utterly devoid of the 'inside life-throb' he was looking for.

There remained the Etruscans. Their advantage, from Lawrence's viewpoint, was that they were dead, and almost nothing was known about them. Consequently they could be reinvented as utopians. In April 1927 he visited several Etruscan sites in northern Italy – Cerveteri, Tarquinia, Vulci and Volterra – inspecting the burial urns and the tomb-paintings of dancing, feasting and hunting. He decided that the Etruscans had possessed a 'phallic consciousness', contrasting with the mental or spiritual consciousness of later Western culture, and that they had been ruled by natural aristocrats who had access to secret knowledge from which the 'plebs' were debarred. Both these aspects attracted him very much. So, evidently, did the Etruscans' determination to turn death into something joyful and lifelike. For Lawrence was dying of TB, and had little more than two years to live. His travel-book, *Etruscan Places* (published posthumously in 1932) contains some of his most intense and rapturous writing.

The Etruscans built their cities, whenever possible, on a long narrow plateau or headland above the surrounding country, and they liked to have a rocky cliff for their base, as in Cerveteri. Round the summit of this cliff, this headland, went the enclosure wall, sometimes miles of the great cincture. And within the walls they liked to have one inner high place, the arx, the citadel. Then outside they liked to have a sharp dip or ravine, with a parallel hill opposite. And on the parallel hill opposite they liked to have their city of the dead, the necropolis. So they could stand on their ramparts and look over the hollow where the stream flowed among its bushes, across from the city of life, gay with its painted houses and temples, to the near-at-hand city of their dear dead, pleasant with its smooth walks and stone symbols, and painted fronts . . .

There is a queer stillness and a curious peaceful repose about the Etruscan places I have been to, quite different from the weirdness of Celtic places, the slightly repellent feeling of Rome and the old Campagna, and the rather horrible feeling of the great pyramid places in Mexico, Teotihuacan and Cholula, and Mitla in the south; or the amiably idolatrous Buddha places in Ceylon. There is a stillness and a softness in these great grassy mounds with their ancient stone girdles, and down the central walk there lingers still a kind of homeli-ness and happiness . . .

And death, to the Etruscan, was a pleasant continuance of life, with jewels and wine and flutes playing for the dance. It was neither an ecstasy of bliss, a heaven, nor a purgatory of torment. It was just a natural continuance of the fullness of life. Everything was in terms of life, of living . . .

The big phallic stones that, it is said, probably stood on top of the tumuli, are sometimes carved very beautifully, sometimes with inscriptions. The scientists call them *cippus, cippi*. But surely the cippus is a truncated column used usually as a gravestone: a column quite squat, often square, having been cut across, truncated, to repre-sent maybe a life cut short. Some of the little phallic stones are like this – truncated. But others are tall, huge and decorated, and with the double cone that is surely phallic. And little inserted phallic stones are not cut short.

By the doorway of some tombs there is a carved stone house, or a stone imitation chest with sloping lids like the two sides of the roof of an oblong house. The guide-boy, who works on the railway and is no profound scholar, mutters that every woman's tomb had one of these stone houses or chests over it – over the doorway, he says – and every man's tomb had one of the phallic stones, or lingams. But since the great tombs were family tombs, perhaps they had both.

The stone house, as the boy calls it, suggests the Noah's Ark without the boat part: the Noah's Ark box we had as children, full of animals. And that is what it is, the Ark, the *arx*, the womb. The womb of all the world, that brought forth all the creatures. The womb, the ark, where life retreats in the last refuge. The womb, the ark of the covenant, in which lies the mystery of eternal life, the manna and the mysteries. There it is, standing displaced outside the doorway of Etruscan tombs at Cerveteri.

And perhaps in the insistence on these two symbols, in the Etruscan world, we can see the reason for the utter destruction and annihilation of the Etruscan consciousness. The new world wanted to rid itself of these fatal, dominant symbols of the old world, the old physical world. The Etruscan consciousness was rooted quite blithely in these symbols, the phallus and the arx. So the whole consciousness, the whole Etruscan pulse and rhythm, must be wiped out.

Now we see again, under the blue heavens where the larks are singing in the hot April sky, why the Romans called the Etruscans vicious. Even in their palmy days the Romans were not exactly saints. But they thought they ought to be. They hated the phallus and the ark, because they wanted empire and dominion and, above all, riches: social gain. You cannot dance gaily to the double flute and at the same time conquer nations or rake in large sums of money. *Delenda est Cartago*. To the greedy man, everybody that is in the way of his greed is vice incarnate. . . .

Myself, I like to think of the little wooden temples of the early Greeks and of the Etruscans: small, dainty, fragile, and evanescent as flowers. We have reached the stage when we are weary of huge stone erections, and we begin to realize that it is better to keep life fluid and changing than to try to hold it fast down in heavy monuments. Burdens on the face of the earth are man's ponderous erections.

The Etruscans made small temples, like little houses with pointed roofs, entirely of wood. But then, outside, they had friezes and cornices and crests of terra-cotta, so that the upper part of the temple would seem almost made of earthenware, terra-cotta plaques fitted neatly, and alive with freely modelled painted figures in relief, gay dancing creatures, rows of ducks, round faces like the sun, and faces grinning and putting out a big tongue, all vivid and fresh and unimposing. The whole thing small and dainty in proportion, and fresh, somehow charming instead of impressive. There seems to have been in the Etruscan instinct a real desire to preserve the natural humour of life. And that is a task surely more worthy, and even much more difficult in the long run, than conquering the world or sacrificing the self or saving the immortal soul.

Why has mankind had such a craving to be imposed upon? Why this lust after imposing creeds, imposing deeds, imposing buildings, imposing language, imposing works of art? The thing becomes an imposition and a weariness at last. Give us things that are alive and flexible, which won't last too long and become an obstruction and a weariness. Even Michelangelo becomes at last a lump and a burden and a bore. It is so hard to see past him . . .

It is all a question of sensitiveness. Brute force and overbearing may make a terrific effect. But in the end, that which lives lives by delicate sensitiveness. If it were a question of brute force, not a single human baby would survive for a fortnight. It is the grass of the field, most frail of all things, that supports all life all the time. But for the green grass, no empire would rise, no man would eat bread: for grain is grass; and Hercules or Napoleon or Henry Ford would alike be denied existence.

Brute force crushes many plants. Yet the plants rise again. The Pyramids will not last a moment compared with the daisy. And before Buddha or Jesus spoke the nightingale sang, and long after the words of Jesus and Buddha are gone into oblivion the nightingale still will sing. Because it is neither preaching nor teaching nor commanding nor urging. It is just singing. And in the beginning was not a Word, but a chirrup.

Because a fool kills a nightingale with a stone, is he therefore greater than the nightingale? Because the Roman took the life out of the Etruscan, was he therefore greater than the Etruscan? Not he! Rome fell, and the Roman phenomenon with it. Italy today is far more Etruscan in its pulse than Roman; and will always be so. The Etruscan element is like the grass of the field and the sprouting of corn, in Italy: it will always be so . . .

The guide's lamp begins to flare up, and we find ourselves in a little chamber in the rock, just a small, bare little cell of a room that some anchorite might have lived in. It is so small and bare and familiar, quite unlike the rather splendid spacious tombs at Cerveteri.

But the lamp flares bright, we get used to the change of light, and see the paintings on the little walls. It is the Tomb of Hunting and Fishing, so called from the pictures on the walls, and it is supposed to date from the sixth century BC. It is very badly damaged, pieces of the wall have fallen away, damp has eaten into the colours, nothing seems to be left. Yet in the dimness we perceive flights of birds flying through the haze, with the draught of life still in their wings. And as we take heart and look closer we see the little room is frescoed all round with hazy sky and sea, with birds flying and fishes leaping, and little men hunting, fishing, rowing in boats. The lower part of the wall is all a blue-green of sea with a silhouette surface that ripples all round the room. From the sea rises a tall rock, off which a naked man, shadowy but still distinct, is beautifully and cleanly diving into the sea, while a companion climbs up the rock after him, and on the water a boat waits with rested oars in it, three men watching the diver, the middle man standing up naked, holding out his arms. Meanwhile a great dolphin leaps behind the boat, a flight of birds soars upwards to pass the rock, in the clear air. Above all, from the bands of colour that border the wall at the top hang the regular loops of garlands, garlands of flowers and leaves and buds and berries, garlands which belong to maidens and to women, and which represent the flowery circle of the female life and sex. The top border of the wall is formed of horizontal stripes or ribands of colour that go all round the room, red and black and dull gold and blue and primrose, and these are the colours that occur invariably. Men are nearly always painted a darkish red, which is the colour of many Italians when they go naked in the sun, as the Etruscans went. Women are coloured paler, because women did not go naked in the sun.

At the end of the room, where there is a recess in the wall, is painted another rock rising from the sea, and on it a man with a sling is taking aim at the birds which rise scattering this way and that. A boat with a big paddle oar is holding off from the rock, a naked man amidships is giving a queer salute to the slinger, a man kneels over the bows with his back to the others, and is letting down a net. The prow of the boat has a beautifully painted eye, so the vessel shall see where it is going. In Syracuse you will see many a two-eyed boat today come swimming in to quay. One dolphin is diving down into the sea, one is leaping out. The birds fly, and the garlands hang from the border.

It is all small and gay and quick with life, spontaneous as only young life can be. If only it were not so much damaged, one would be happy, because here is the real Etruscan liveliness and naturalness. It is not impressive or grand. But if you are content with just a sense of the quick ripple of life, then here it is . . .

The underworld of the Etruscans was a gay place. While the living feasted out of doors, at the tomb of the dead, the dead himself feasted in like manner, with a lady to offer him garlands and slaves to bring him wine, away in the underworld. For the life on earth was so good, the life below could but be a continuance of it.

This profound belief in life, acceptance of life, seems characteristic of the Etruscans. It is still vivid in the painted tombs. There is a certain dance and glamour in all the movements, even in those of the naked slave men. They are by no means downtrodden menials, let later Romans say what they will. The slaves in the tombs are surging with full life . . .

On the end wall is a gentle little banquet scene, the bearded man softly touching the woman with him under the chin, a slave-boy standing childishly behind, and an alert dog under the couch. The *kylix*, or wine-bowl, that the man holds is surely the biggest on record; exaggerated, no doubt, to show the very special importance of the feast. Rather gentle and lovely is the way he touches the woman under the chin, with a delicate caress. That again is one of the charms of the Etruscan paintings: they really have the sense of touch; the people and the creatures are all really in touch. It is one of the rarest qualities, in life as well as in art. There is plenty of pawing and laying hold, but no real touch. In pictures especially, the people may be in contact, embracing or laying hands on one another. But there is no soft flow of touch. The touch does not come from the middle of the human being. It is merely a contact of surfaces, and a juxtaposition of objects. This is what makes so many of the great masters boring, in spite of all their clever composition. Here, in this faded Etruscan painting, there is a quiet flow of touch that unites the man and the woman on the couch, the timid boy behind, the dog that lifts his nose, even the very garlands that hang from the wall . . .

There is a haunting quality in the Etruscan representations. Those leopards with their long tongues hanging out: those flowing hippo-campi; those cringing spotted deer, struck in flank and neck; they get into the imagination, and will not go out. And we see the wavy edge of the sea, the dolphins curving over, the diver going down clean, the little man climbing up the rock after him so eagerly. Then the men with beards who recline on the banqueting beds: how they hold up the mysterious egg! And the women with the conical head-dress, how strangely they lean forward, with caresses we no longer know! The naked slaves joyfully stoop to the wine-jars. Their nakedness is its own clothing, more easy than drapery. The curves of their limbs show pure pleasure in life, a pleasure that goes deeper still in the limbs of the dancers, in the big, long hands thrown out and dancing to the very ends of the fingers, a dance that surges from within, like a current in the sea. It is as if the current of some strong different life swept through them, different from our shallow current today: as if they drew their vitality from different depths that we are denied.

Yet in a few centuries they lost their vitality. The Romans took the life out of them. It seems as if the power of resistance to life, self-assertion, and overbearing, such as the Romans knew: a power which must needs be moral, or carry morality with it, as a cloak for its inner ugliness: would always succeed in destroying the natural flowering of life. And yet there still are a few wild flowers and creatures.

The natural flowering of life! It is not so easy for human beings as it sounds. Behind all the Etruscan liveliness was a religion of life, which the chief men were seriously responsible for. Behind all the dancing was a vision, and even a science of life, a conception of the universe and man's place in the universe which made men live to the depth of their capacity.

To the Etruscan all was alive; the whole universe lived; and the business of man was himself to live amid it all. He had to draw life into himself, out of the wandering huge vitalities of the world. The

[405]

cosmos was alive, like a vast creature. The whole thing breathed and stirred. Evaporation went up like breath from the nostrils of a whale, steaming up. The sky received it in its blue bosom, breathed it in and pondered on it and transmuted it, before breathing it out again. Inside the earth were fires like the heat in the hot red liver of a beast. Out of the fissures of the earth came breaths of other breathing, vapours direct from the living physical underearth, exhalations carrying inspiration. The whole thing was alive, and had a great soul, or *anima*: and in spite of one great soul, there were myriad roving, lesser souls: every man, every creature and tree and lake and mountain and stream, was animate, had its own peculiar consciousness. And has it today.

Source: D. H. Lawrence, *Etruscan Places*, Martin Secker, 1932.

Shangri-La

James Hilton's *Lost Horizon* (1933) embodies one of the great, recurrent myths of the West – the fantasy of an exquisite but slightly sinister oriental paradise. Hilton (1900–1954) was a journalist, the son of a Lancashire schoolmaster, and ended up as a Hollywood scriptwriter. Like *Goodbye, Mr Chips*, which he published the following year, *Lost Horizon* was a runaway best-seller. It owed its popularity in part to the war-clouds that hung over 1930s Europe. A character in the book confidently predicts the coming apocalypse – fleets of aircraft unloading death upon the world's great cities; the monuments of culture being razed in one vast chaos. With these horrors in prospect, readers understandably clung to the fiction of a remote sanctuary where civilization would be preserved. Shangri-La, the name Hilton invented for his utopia, has become part of the language.

The events of the novel are retold at second and third hand, so the story is swathed in mists of uncertainty and surmise. Like Shangri-La itself, it shimmers, distant and irrecoverable. It begins with the hijacking of an aircraft. Four passengers – a woman missionary, an American financier, a young English diplomat, and a First World War veteran called Conway – are awaiting take-off on an airfield in northwest India when an unknown pilot enters, and flies them off across trackless mountain wastes. When they try to intervene he threatens them with a revolver. At last they crash-land in an upland valley in Tibet. The pilot, they find, is dead. But a curious reception-party consisting of Tibetan porters and a stately, enigmatic Chinese elder, borne in a litter, comes to meet them across the snow. An arduous trek and hair-raising climb bring them to their first glimpse of the lamasery (Buddhist monastery) of Shangri-La.

To Conway, seeing it first, it might have been a vision fluttering out of that solitary rhythm in which lack of oxygen had encompassed all his faculties. It was, indeed, a strange and almost incredible sight. A group of coloured pavilions clung to the mountainside with none of the grim deliberation of a Rhineland castle, but rather with the chance delicacy of flower-petals impaled upon a crag. It was superb and exquisite. An austere emotion carried the eye upward from milk-blue roofs to the grey rock bastion above, tremendous as the Wetterhorn above Grindelwald. Beyond that, in a dazzling pyramid, soared the snow-slopes of Karakal. It might well be, Conway thought, the most terrifying mountain-scape in the world, and he imagined the immense stress of snow and glacier against which the rock functioned as a gigantic retaining wall. Some day, perhaps, the whole mountain would split, and a half of Karakal's icy splendour come toppling into the valley. He wondered if the slightness of the risk combined with its fearfulness might even be found agreeably stimulating.

Hardly less an enticement was the downward prospect, for the mountain wall continued to drop, nearly perpendicularly, into a cleft that could only have been the result of some cataclysm in the far past. The floor of the valley, hazily distant, welcomed the eye with greenness; sheltered from winds, and surveyed rather than dominated by the lamasery, it looked to Conway a delightfully favoured place, though if it were inhabited its community must be completely isolated by the lofty and sheerly unscalable ranges on the farther side. Only to the lamasery did there appear to be any climbable egress at all.

The travellers are graciously welcomed and waited on. Shangri-La, they find, combines the latest American sanitation and central heating with exquisite oriental antiquities and priceless artworks. The luxurious fresh fruits and wines come from the fertile valley, which the lamasery overlooks, and of which they are given a conducted tour.

When at last they reached the lower levels of forest and foot-hill the supreme good fortune of the lamasery was everywhere to be realized. For the valley was nothing less than an enclosed paradise of amazing fertility, in which the vertical difference of a few thousand feet spanned the whole gulf between temperate and tropical. Crops of unusual diversity grew in profusion and contiguity, with not an inch of ground untended. The whole cultivated area stretched for perhaps a dozen miles, varying in width from one to five, and, though narrow, it had the luck to take sunlight at the hottest part of the day. The atmosphere, indeed, was pleasantly warm even out of the sun, though the little rivulets that watered the soil were ice-cold from the snows.

Conway felt again, as he gazed up at the stupendous mountain wall, that there was a superb and exquisite peril in the scene; but for some chance-placed barrier, the whole valley would clearly have been a lake, nourished continually from the glacial heights around it. Instead of which, a few streams dribbled through to fill reservoirs and irrigate fields and plantations with a disciplined conscientiousness worthy of a sanitary engineer. The whole design was almost uncannily fortunate, so long as the structure of the frame remained unmoved by earthquake or landslide.

But even such vaguely future fears could only enhance the total loveliness of the present. Once again Conway was captivated, and by the same qualities of charm and ingenuity that had made his years in China happier than others. The vast encircling *massif* made perfect contrast with the tiny lawns and weedless gardens, the painted tea-houses by the stream, and the frivolously toy-like houses. The inhabitants seemed to him a very successful blend of Chinese and Tibetan; they were cleaner and handsomer than the average of either race, and looked to have suffered little from the inevitable inbreeding of such a small society. They smiled and laughed as they passed the chaired strangers, and had a friendly word for Chang [the guide] they were good-humoured and mildly inquisitive, courteous and care-free, busy at innumerable jobs but not in any apparent hurry over them. Altogether Conway thought them one of the pleasantest communities he had ever seen . . .

Conway is granted the unusual privilege of an interview with the Head Lama, an aged man, who tells him the history of the lamasery. In 1719, he recounts, four Capuchin friars set out from Peking to search for traces of Nestorian Christianity in Tibet. Three of them died, but the fourth, named Perrault, stumbled on Shangri-La, then in a semi-derelict state. He supervised the rebuilding of it, and took up residence there himself in 1734, when he was fifty-three years old. He studied Buddhism, practised yoga, and became addicted to a narcotic berry called *tangatse*, favoured in those parts. For some reason, whether it had to do with the mountain air or the yoga or the berry, or all three, he went on living far past the normal human span. Over the years other lost travellers reached the lamasery, adopted the same regimen, and achieved unusual longevity. A pupil of Chopin's, and a young curate who knew the Brontës at Haworth, are, the Head Lama assures Conway, still living in the lamasery. He reveals finally that he is himself Shangri-La's rebuilder Perrault, now some two hundred and fifty years old.

In succeeding interviews the Head Lama sets before Conway the advantages he and his companions would enjoy if they remained at Shangri-La. He assures him, from experience, that grief for loved ones left behind in the old life never lasts for more than five years, whereas the compensations are literally out-of-this-world.

'Now let me begin by sketching for you a very agreeable picture. You are still, I should say, a youngish man by the world's standards; your life, as people say, lies ahead of you; in the normal course you might expect twenty or thirty years of only slightly and gradually diminishing activity. By no means a cheerless prospect, and I can hardly expect you to see it as I do – as a slender, breathless, and far too frantic interlude. The first quarter-century of your life was doubtless lived under the cloud of being too young for things, while the last quarter-century would normally be shadowed by the still darker cloud of being too old for them; and between those two clouds, what small and narrow sunlight illumines a human lifetime! But you, it may be, are destined to be more fortunate, since by the standards of Shangri-La your sunlit years have scarcely yet begun. It will happen, perhaps, that decades hence you will feel no older than you are today – you may preserve . . . a long and wondrous youth. But that, believe me, is only an early and superficial phase. There will come a time when you will age like others, though far more slowly, and into a condition infinitely nobler; at eighty you may still climb to the pass with a young man's gait, but at twice that age you must not expect the whole marvel to have persisted. We are not workers of miracles; we have made no conquest of death, or even of decay. All we have done and can sometimes do is to slacken the *tempo* of this brief interval that is called life. We do this by methods which are as simple here as they are impossible elsewhere; but make no mistake; the end awaits us all.

'Yet it is, nevertheless, a prospect of much charm that I unfold for you – long tranquillities during which you will observe a sunset as men in the outer world hear the striking of a clock, and with far less care. The years will come and go, and you will pass from fleshly enjoyments into austerer but no less satisfying realms; you may lose the keenness of muscle and appetite, but there will be gain to match your loss; you will achieve calmness and profundity, ripeness and wisdom and the clear enchantment of memory. And, most precious of all, you will have Time – that rare and lovely gift that your Western countries have lost the more they have pursued it. Think for a moment. You will have time to read – never again will you skim pages to save minutes, or avoid some study lest it prove too engrossing. You have also a taste for music – here, then, are your scores and instruments, with Time, unruffled and unmeasured, to give you their richest savour. And you are also, we will say, a man of good fellowship – does it not charm you to think of wise and serene friendships, a long and kindly traffic of the mind from which death may not call you away with his customary hurry? Or, if it is solitude that you prefer, could you not employ our pavilions to enrich the gentleness of lonely thoughts? . . .

'Chang, I believe, explained to you our principle of moderation, and one of the things in which we are always moderate is activity. I myself, for instance, have been able to learn ten languages; the ten might have been twenty had I worked immoderately. But I did not. And it is the same in other directions; you will find us neither profligate nor ascetic. Until we reach an age when care is advisable, we gladly accept the pleasures of the table, while – for the benefit of our younger colleagues – the women of the valley have happily applied the principle of moderation to their own chastity. All things considered, I feel sure you will get used to our ways without much effort.'

Conway learns, finally, that he and his companions did not come to Shangri-La by chance. The mysterious hijacker was a member of the lamasery, sent out to bring new recruits to the community. Further, they will not be allowed to leave, for the lamas fear the peace of Shangri-La would be shattered if anyone took news of them to the outside world.

Source: James Hilton, *Lost Horizon*, Macmillan, 1933.

Women in Cages

Written when the storm-clouds were gathering over Europe, Katharine Burdekin's *Swastika Night* (1937) reflects – and must have done its bit to increase – the panic and misinformation rife in the immediate pre-war phase. A feminist and anti-militarist, Burdekin (1896–1963) assumes a Nazi victory, and describes a Nazi-dominated twenty-sixth century. Hitler is worshipped as divine. He was not born, it is believed, but 'exploded' from the head of God the Thunderer, who made the world. Christians are few and despised, eking out a marginal, vagabond existence. Most books have been destroyed. Illiteracy is common, and officially encouraged. History has been suppressed. Almost no one knows, for example, that the British once had an empire.

As in many feminist dystopias, women are depicted as the chief victims, subjected to the virtually boundless cruelty of the male. By comparison, little is made of the fate of the Jews, though it is mentioned in passing that they have been exterminated. In the Nazi empire of the Year of the Lord Hitler 720, men alone are regarded as human. Women are categorized as soulless animals. Herded into 'cages' (squalid hutted compounds) they are at the disposal of any man who wishes to use them. Their heads are shaved and they wear dirty-brown uniforms. All memories of the time when women were considered beautiful have been expunged, because the power beauty gave them over men was considered an insult to manhood. Boy children are taken away from their mothers at eighteen months and reared by men. No one, except the verminous Christians, lives in families any more. To show sexual preference for one woman rather than another is deemed unmanly. There must be no love, the Nazi ethos decrees, only lust and the desire to beget sons. The holy Hitler creed, recited by all males in Hitler churches and chapels, is relentlessly military: 'I believe in pride, in courage, in violence, in brutality, in bloodshed, in ruthlessness, and all other soldierly and heroic virtues.'

In fact Nazi ideology encouraged the health and welfare of women, provided they were racially 'pure'. Maternity benefits and other measures to promote the well-being of mother and child were introduced. Nazi propaganda minister Joseph Goebbels, in a 1934 speech, stressed that though the

National Socialist movement was in its nature masculine, it looked to woman with her 'inner fullness and inner eagerness' to give life its colour. Burdekin's misleading account of Nazi thought seems to be derived from the woman-hating fulminations of the Viennese Otto Weininger in his book *Sex and Character* (1903).

In Burdekin's novel a wise old patrician German called von Hess, a Knight of the Nazi Order, possesses, from his forebears, a knowledge of history. He knows that women were once beautiful and honoured, and is able to explain, to those with whom he shares his secret knowledge, why and how they changed.

'They acquiesced in the Reduction of Women, which was a deliberate thing deliberately planned by German men. Women will always be exactly what men want them to be. They have no will, no character, and no souls, they are only a reflection of men. So nothing that they are or can become is ever their fault or their virtue. If men want them to be beautiful they will be beautiful. If men want them to appear to have wills and characters they will develop something that looks like a will and a character though it is really only a sham. If men want them to have an appearance of perfect freedom, even an appearance of masculine power, they will develop a simulacrum of those things. But what men cannot do, never have been able to do, is to *stop* this blind submission and cause the women to ignore them and disobey them. It's the tragedy of the human race.'

Asked what women did, when faced with the Reduction programme, von Hess replies:

'What they always do. Once they were convinced that men really wanted them to be animals and ugly and completely submissive and give up their boy children for ever at the age of one year, they threw themselves into the new pattern with a conscious enthusiasm that knew no bounds. They shaved their heads till they bled, they rejoiced in their hideous uniforms as a young Knight might rejoice in his Robe of Ceremony, they pulled out their front teeth until they were forbidden for reasons of health, and they gave up their baby sons with the same heroism with which they had been used to giving their grown sons to the war.'

Once every three months, women are herded into a Hitler church (though

[413]

they are allowed only into its outer precincts) for religious indoctrination. In the following scene, von Hess officiates at one of these sessions. A disturbing fact, to which only high-ranking Nazis have access, is that fewer and fewer female children are being born. It is as if women are subconsciously refusing to perpetuate their own despised gender. Consequently the whole future of Hitlerdom is threatened. This thought preoccupies the Knight as he prepares to address the assembled women.

The Knight knew, what no other man knew, and what no woman ever dreamed of in the most fantastic efforts of her small and cloudy imagination, that women had once been as beautiful and desirable as boys, and that they had once been *loved*. What blasphemy, he thought, curling his lips a little. To love a woman, in the German mind, would be equal to loving a worm, or a Christian. Women like these. Hairless, with naked shaven scalps, the wretched ill-balance of their feminine forms outlined by their tight bifurcated clothes – that horrible meek bowed way they had of walking and standing, head low, stomach out, buttocks bulging behind – no grace, no beauty, no uprightness, all those were male qualities. If a woman dared to stand like a man she would be beaten.

'I wonder,' thought the old Knight, 'that we didn't make them walk on all fours all the time, and have each baby-girl's brain extracted at the age of six months. Well, they've beaten us. They've destroyed us by doing what we told them, and now unless the Thunderer can throw the whole mass of Germans out of his head we're coming to an inglorious end.' With this blasphemy, a crowning one, the Knight finished his private meditation.

'Women, be quiet,' he began, frowning at them as a matter of form. 'Do not disturb the sacred air of this holy male place with your feminine squeakings and wailings. What have you to cry for? Are you not blessed above all female animals in being allowed to be the mothers of *men*?'

He paused. In dreary little scattered whispers came the formal response: 'Yes, Lord. Yes, Lord. We are blessed.' But a renewed burst of weeping followed as the women wondered where were the men they had borne. He is twelve now – he is twenty-five and Rudi twenty-one – if Hans is still alive he's seventy this summer, with a white beard like the Knight. But this last thought was in the mind of a very old and incredibly repulsive hag, far too old to cry.

The Knight went on with his homily. It was always of necessity much the same. There were so few things one could talk to women about. They had hardly more understanding than a really intelligent dog, and besides nearly everything was too sacred for them to hear. Anything that had to do with men's lives was banned, and naturally it was impossible to read to them, out of the Hitler Bible, the stories of the heroic deeds of the Lord and His friends. Such matters, even at long distance and second-hand, were far too holy to be spoken of into unclean ears. The most important thing was to get it firmly fixed in the heads of the younger women that they must not mind being raped. Naturally the Knight did not call it this, there was no such crime as rape except in connection with children under age. And this, as the Knight knew, was less, far less for the sake of the little girls than for the sake of the race. Very young girls if just adolescent might bear puny babies as the result of rape. Over sixteen, women's bodies were well-grown and womanly, that danger was past, and as rape implies will and choice and a spirit of rejection on the part of women there could be no such crime.

'It is not for you to say, "I shall have this man or that man," ' he told them, 'or "I am not ready" or "it is not convenient" or to put any womanish whim in opposition to a man's will. It is for a man to say, if he wishes, "This is my woman till I am tired of her." If then another man wants her, still she is not to oppose him; he is a man; for a woman to oppose any man (except a Christian) on any point, is blasphemous and most supremely wicked.'

The Knight coughed, and made a pause, an impressive one, to allow this to sink in.

'She may tell the man who temporarily owns her about what has happened, and there her responsibility ends. The rest is Men's Business, not on any account to be meddled with by females. And for you girls,' he rolled his mild eye towards the sixteen- and seventeen-year-olds, 'be submissive and humble and rejoice to do man's will, for whatever you may think in your empty brains at moments it is *always* your will too, and be fruitful and bear strong daughters.'

The women instantly stopped crying, except three or four who were not even half listening. They all gaped at him. The shock of being told to bear strong daughters was equal to a half-stunning blow on each little shaven bristly head. They couldn't believe their ears. The Knight couldn't believe his, either. He had been used for so many years to thinking one thing and saying another; his whole life was such a complicated pattern of secrecy and deceit that he could not credit himself with at last making such a crashing mistake. It was true that it was vital women should bear more daughters, true that every German of the literate knightly class had nightmare dreams of the extinction of the sacred race, but it was a truth that must not be spoken freely, above all not spoken to the women themselves. All they knew was that in their particular Women's Quarters was born a remarkable number of young males, but not that the condition was general. If they once knew that the *Knights*, and even der Fuehrer, wanted girl-children to be born in large quantities; that every fresh statistical paper with its terribly disproportionate male births caused groanings and anxieties and endless secret conferences – if the women once realized all this, what could stop them developing a small thin thread of self-respect? If a woman could rejoice publicly in the birth of a girl Hitlerdom would start to crumble. Some did, he knew, rejoice secretly, for the girls at least could not be taken away from them, but these were only the more shrinking, the more cowardly, the more animal-motherly kind of women. For, even where all were shrinking, cowardly and animal, yet some managed to shrink more than others and fail even in the little unnatural and human feeling allowed them, the leave to be so passionately proud of a male child, that not even the pain of losing him outweighed it. But whatever women might think and feel in private, in public there was no rejoicing whatever at the birth of a female. It was a disgraceful event, a calamitous accident which might of course happen to any woman but did not happen to the best women, and as for a woman who had nothing but daughters she was only one half step higher than that lifelong hopeless useless burden on Hitler Society, the woman who bore no children at all. 'Yet actually,' thought the Knight, pinching his moustache and stroking his nearly white beard, and looking mildly down at his stunned flock, 'a woman who had ten daughters and wasted no time whatever on sons would be, at this juncture, a howling success.' Meanwhile he had made a howling error. 'It's age,' he thought; 'I'm losing grip. One can walk on ledges at twenty, where one would fall over at seventy.' But he was in no hurry to cover up his error with words. He knew silence is alarming to women. So he was silent, looking at them, and they went on gaping. But at last they began to shuffle uncomfortably.

'Something is troubling you?' he asked them, as politely as if they had been men, or even Knights. His courteous manner terrified them. They shrank away from him like a wind-blown field of corn.

'No, Lord, no,' they whispered. One, a little bolder, or possibly more hysterically frightened than the rest, gasped out, 'Lord, we thought you said – '

'What did you think I said?' asked the Knight, still in that very polite way.

All but one woman knew then that they had misheard. They had actually thought, with appalling and yet quite typical feminine stupidity, that he had told them to bear strong daughters. It was all a dreadful blasphemous mistake. He had, of course, said 'Sons.' '*Sohnen.*' The word was like the deep tolling of an enormous bell. The Knight was thinking it hard, vigorously, like the man pulling on the bell-rope. The women felt so deeply guilty that they even blushed, all but one. They recommenced crying. All was as it had been before. The Knight coughed, and resumed his discourse. But afterwards, when he had thankfully dismissed them, and signalled with a little bell for the Nazi outside to unlock the door and let them out and drive them back to their cage, there was a certain amount of astonishingly bright chatter.

'Shut up,' said the Nazi gruffly. This waiting on the Women's Worship was a tedious and humiliating duty. He kicked at one or two of them as if they had been tiresome puppies, not savagely, just irritably. The women scuttled out of his way and were quiet for a moment, but presently they began again: 'How *could* we have thought – did you, I did, but of course it wasn't – *I* didn't, I don't know what you're talking about – but I did *think* he said – yes, well – oh, how could anyone *think* such a thing?'

But old Marta, hobbling very slowly on two sticks, said, 'He told you you were to bear strong daughters.'

Perhaps she was so old she was no longer a woman at all, and therefore out of reach of all womanly feelings of shame and humility. She was not free, but perhaps by mere age had passed out of reach of psychic subjection. She was not a man, no, but not a woman either, something more like an old incredibly ugly tree. Not human, but not female. At any rate the Knight's hypnotism had rebounded from her. But all the other women despised her. Ugly as they were they could see she was uglier. A revolting dirty old woman, speaking an awful toothless German – she *said* she had had sons – a hundred years ago – but no one knew.

'He never said that – *never*. We only thought it. He said we were to have *sons*. Of course. Sons. *Sons*. Marta, do you hear?'

'I'm not deaf,' said Marta. It was a fact, she had every unpleasant attribute of old age except deafness – and senility. 'He said you were to bear daughters – *strong* daughters.'

'It's a lie. Why *should* he say such a thing?'

'I don't know. It doesn't matter. That was what he said.'

They jeered at her and left her to hobble along by herself, quite convinced and completely uninterested. As convinced of the Knight's words as she was that the hard thing that occasionally poked her in the back was the herding Nazi's thick cane, and as uninterested as she was in his stick or in him or in anything in the world except food (of which she got very little) and the faint memory of Hans, her first child. The Knight would have found himself in a certain amount of sympathy with her, had he been in psychic contact. Marta's cynicism was as deep, no, far deeper than his own, though arrived at in an entirely different way.

Source: Murray Constantine [Katharine Burdekin], *Swastika Night*, Gollancz, 1937.

Christ Takes Over

Published in England in 1939, Newman Watts's *The Man Who Did Not Sin* cannot have brought much comfort to those awaiting the outbreak of the Second World War. It predicted that the whole of southern England would be wiped out by enemy bombs and gas. But a lone survivor, Cecil Mackay, would awake 225 years in the future, having prudently put himself to sleep in a bomb-proof capsule. In Watts's novel, Cecil finds himself in a New Age, which, he learns, began on 7 February 1960, with the second coming of Christ. At the time the world was in the grip of a wicked dictator, but Christ and his angelic host descended from the clouds and took over the enemy's tanks, armoured cars, and other weaponry. The Redeemer now rules the world from his headquarters in Jerusalem, appearing annually on TV. Under his personal reign, many reforms have been effected. Each family has a smallholding and grows its own food, Hebrew is the universal language, women wear simple sari-type dresses and no cosmetics. Although Christ has limitless supernatural power, and could bring about any change without help, he still requires mankind to make an effort. In this respect, things are much as they were – though with Christ actually on earth, his failure to put things right simply by using his omnipotence is even more glaring than when he was in heaven. This awkward mixture of divine omnipotence and old-fashioned human work can be observed in the account of Christ's reforms given to Cecil by Miss Violet Montgomery of the British Museum.

'The first great popular move which raised the hopes of despairing and baffled humanity was an order to smash up all implements of war and consign all the shells, bombs, guns and cannon to the bottom of the sea. This act of iconoclasm was taken up enthusiastically by the people of all nations. Millions of tons of explosives were shipped into the Atlantic and Pacific Oceans and thrown overboard. Armament factories were razed to the ground. Warships, tanks, armoured cars, were scrapped. All war memorials and statues of soldiers and other military and naval heroes were cast down and in one great, glad celebration war was outlawed by a world-wide elimination of the means of warfare. War offices and ministries were abandoned, and a reign of world peace proclaimed.'

'And do you mean to say there has never been a war of any kind since?'

'No. There was a revolt in Russia, and thousands of misguided Russian atheists who looked upon this new regime as merely a reversion to the superstitions of religion marched on the Holy Land, but they were scattered by a hailstorm which rained on them persistently all the while they were on the march and got heavier the nearer they got to the Holy Land. The storm ceased as soon as they had fully decided to give up the rebellion.'

'Is that the way Christ is able to subdue His enemies?'

'Yes, very largely. He has complete control over the heavens and can use natural forces to remind forgetful humanity of His absolute power. War, as the world had known it, was abolished at last. The reign of peace had begun.'

'What next?'

'The next item of reform was not so easy to bring about or to make popular. It was the overthrow of all secret societies, trusts, monopolies and vested interests in the political, social and commercial realms. Secret societies were very reluctant to be classed among the earth's curses, but individual members gave the secrets away and the lodges broke up in confusion. A reconstruction of the world's commerce also brought a speedy end to "the powers that be" in the way of business trusts and monopolies.'

'I suppose the Labour world assisted in that reform?'

'Yes, it did, and the working class soon realized that here was a world Ruler with wisdom and power enough to reconstruct the world's economics on lines which would insure to all men an equal share in the world's goods. The working class, however, didn't like the next reform.'

'What was that?'

'The suppression of wasteful and useless elements of life. The production and sale of all alcoholic drinks, tobacco in all its forms, drugs, cosmetics, immoral and low-grade literature and films, etc., were forbidden, and the governments were given instructions to see that all these things were stopped at the source. This reform was accompanied by a publicity campaign by radio and press, educating the people into the facts of the situation. "The world," declared the new World-Emperor, "could not recover its prosperity nor face the tremendous tasks of the future unless all useless and wasteful elements were eliminated." No man had a right to luxuries while there were any who were without necessities. Moreover, no luxuries were to be allowed if indulgence in them had any harmful effect on body or mind or character. This was a law which millions tried to avoid. Those who were fond of their pipe soon found tobacco unobtainable. Others did contrive for a time to indulge in some of the coarser pleasures of the old world by various deceptions and subterfuges, but in the course of a century the habits of the people have so completely changed that few of the old vices are to be found nowadays.'

'I should have thought that world prosperity would have allowed a reasonable and legitimate return of some of these harmless pleasures.'

'The tastes of the people have in the meantime so radically changed that a return to tobacco smoking, cocktail drinking, lipstick, hair waving and drug taking is neither desired nor permitted.

'The next great task was the reconstruction of the economic, industrial and cultural life of the whole world. The idea of democratic rule was entirely thrown overboard. All rule was vested in the new World-Emperor. No monarch of the past reigned with such complete authority and power as Christ, our present King.'

'Do the people have no say in the government at all?'

'No. Why should they want it when an all-wise, omnipotent and benevolent Ruler is on the throne? Christ can be absolutely depended on to reign in righteousness. He does no wrong. He is the Man who could not sin.'

'What happened to science?'

'Nothing but good. It was rescued entirely from its materialistic atmosphere and, what was nearly as important, from immoral and destructive uses. An age was ushered in when no advance in scientific knowledge would be used for evil purposes. Furthermore, tremendous progress was made in the harnessing of natural forces for man's good. You have seen one or two in the vast improvements in our radio services, our air transport and our educational programme. If the century ending in 1960 was noted for its rapid strides in scientific knowledge and development, it was nothing in comparison with the first half-century of the new age.

'Two other things you must have noticed – one is the splendid physique of all the people you see about, which is the result of medical research and also the different food eaten, very little of it being cooked.'

'Yes, I must admit the type of physical perfection on the earth today has amazed me more than anything. I suppose it is the change in the conditions of life which has enabled people to live such lengthy lives, like yourself, for instance.'

'Yes, that is so. Deaths declined very rapidly indeed. But the old folk died off, some because they could not adapt themselves to the new world morally, and some because their bodies were so far affected by bad living in the old world that death had too great a hold on them before the new conditions of life could repair the damage done.'

Source: Newman Watts, *The Man Who Did Not Sin*, Henry E. Walter, 1939.

Hitler's Russian Garden

Adolf Hitler (1889–1945) has a unique place in the history of utopianism. He can be seen as the culmination of the great utopian tradition that starts with Plato, and he terminated that tradition. After the holocaust, utopianism could never be the same.

Hitler was anxious to raise the cultural level and improve the living conditions of the German people, as he makes clear in his autobiography *Mein Kampf* (1924). Like many intellectuals of his day and ours, he deplores the 'poison' spread among the masses by 'gutter journalism' and 'cinema bilge'. He advocates high art, admiring the culture of Greece and Rome, and scathingly contrasting it with American materialism, based on cars, clothes, and refrigerators. Germany must, he decides, have more opera houses, theatres, and museums. 'The only things that exist are the works of human genius.' The young must be reared on Shakespeare, Mozart, Rembrandt, and their like, not 'smutty literature, artistic tripe, theatrical banalities'. For the debasement of the press and popular literature he blames the controlling influence of Jews. The Jew is a 'moral pestilence worse than the Black Death', and 'must clear out of Europe'. If they refuse to go voluntarily, 'I see no other solution but extermination'.

He does not envisage that his reforms can be carried out democratically. Democracy means rule by 'the crowd of simpletons' who believe what they read in the newspapers. It is 'the breeding ground in which the bacilli of the Marxist world pest can grow and spread'. Dictatorship, rule by the strong, will replace democracy. This 'aristocratic principle' is 'a fundamental law of nature'. In the new Germany the State will control the press and other media with 'ruthless determination'.

Ruthlessness will, indeed, be the keynote of the new ethic. Christianity is 'the heaviest blow that ever struck humanity', and Communism is its child. Humanitarianism amounts to no more than 'fatuous timidity', and it will melt away in the competition for living-space that the earth's bulging populations will face in the future. 'No one can doubt that this world will one day be the scene of dreadful struggles for existence on the part of mankind.' In these struggles, the ruthless and the fittest will survive.

[423]

A vital component of fitness, in Hitler's view, is racial purity. Aryans are the highest breed, 'the highest image of God among His creatures'. Art and science have been 'almost exclusively the product of the Aryan creative power'. If the Aryan race disappears, 'human culture will vanish and the world will become a desert'. For the Aryan to mingle with lesser breeds, and adulterate the strain, would be 'a sin against the will of the Eternal Creator'. Cross-breeds are inevitably inferior, and in a world composed of 'mongrels and negroids' all ideals of human beauty would be lost. Inferior races do not merit education. To train a negro, 'a being who is only an anthropoid by birth', to become a doctor or lawyer, would be an 'act of criminal insanity'.

For the good of the Aryan race, too, it must be made impossible for 'defective people' to propagate. All incurables must be 'mercilessly isolated'. It is the 'iron law of nature' that the 'weak, diseased and wavering' should die out. For the same reason, the emphasis in German schools will be on physical education. Boxing and gymnastics will be esteemed more than academic education, which makes for degeneracy.

Hitler was a pioneer of the green movement, lamenting the 'unlimited and injurious industrialization' that had scarred the German countryside and weakened the agricultural class. The landscape, he declared, should not be ruined by electric cables, funicular railways or needless road-building. It was not the town-dweller but the sturdy peasant that formed the 'solid backbone of a nation'. In conquered territories, German soldier-peasants will be given fully equipped farms on condition they marry countrywomen, not townees. The Führer's enthusiasm for the simple, natural life was accompanied by ardent vegetarianism. He advocated a diet of raw fruit and vegetables, and suspected that cooked and chemically processed foods caused cancer. 'There's one thing I can predict to eaters of meat, that the world of the future will be vegetarian.'

It was the Ukraine that Hitler destined to be the site of his utopia – 'the territory on which one day our German peasants will be able to bring forth and nourish their sturdy sons'. Its conquest and annexation by Germany were, he explained, no more than natural justice, for it was clearly wrong that 'amorphous masses which contribute nothing to civilization' should occupy the rich soil of the Ukraine, while 'higher people' went short of living-space. The 'ridiculous hundred million Slavs' who occupied it would not be wiped out, but simply 'isolated in their own pigsties', without health-care, hygiene facilities, vaccination or education. 'The least of our stable lads must be superior to any native.'

In his table-talk, discreetly recorded by party officials under the direction of Martin Bormann, Hitler enjoyed planning the colonization of the Ukraine that would follow the conquest of Russia by German armies.

We'll take away its character of an Asiatic steppe, we'll Europeanize it. With this object we have undertaken the construction of roads that will lead to the southernmost point of the Crimea and to the Caucasus. These roads will be studded along their whole length by German towns, and around these towns our colonists will settle... In a hundred years the country will be one of the loveliest gardens in the world... We shan't settle in the Russian towns, and will let them fall to pieces without intervening... The Slav people are not destined to live a cleanly life. They know it, and we would be wrong to persuade them of the contrary... The Crimea will give us its citrus fruits, cotton and rubber (100,000 acres of plantation would be enough to ensure our independence)... The Black Sea will be for us a sea whose wealth our fishermen will never exhaust. Thanks to the cultivation of the Soya bean, we'll increase our livestock. We'll win from that soil several times as much as the Ukrainian peasant is winning at present... We shall get between ten and twelve million tons of grain annually. I think we ought to build spaghetti factories on the spot; all the prerequisites are there... We shall become the most self-supporting state, in every respect, including cotton, in the world. The only thing we shall not have will be a coffee plantation – but we'll find a coffee-growing colony somewhere or other! Timber we shall have in abundance, iron in limitless quantity, the greatest manganese ore mines in the world, oil – we shall swim in it! And to handle it all, the whole strength of the entire German manpower! By God! how right the peasant is to put his trust solely in the earth.

Sources: Adolf Hitler, *Mein Kampf*, translated by James Murphy, Hurst & Blackett, 1939; *Hitler's Table-Talk*, 1941–44, translated by Norman Cameron and R. H. Stevens, with an introduction by H. R. Trevor-Roper, Weidenfeld & Nicolson, 1953.

On Not Licking Your Lollipop

US psychologist B. F. Skinner (1904–90) was a leading exponent of Behaviourism, the dominant psychological theory in the interwar period, which regarded all behaviour, in humans and animals, as a response to stimuli. This held out hope of almost infinite behavioural engineering, since if the stimuli were changed, behaviour would change too. Skinner had remarkable success with laboratory animals, training pigeons to play table tennis. His utopia *Walden Two* (1948) caused a furore – the *New York Times* called it 'appalling' – because it was seen, correctly, to fly in the face of human freedom.

Set in contemporary America, *Walden Two*, unlike Thoreau's *Walden*, does not entirely reject the modern world. The community Skinner describes has light industry, and many labour-saving gadgets (e.g., transparent trays in the dining-room, so you can see both sides are clean without turning the tray over). But the simple life is preferred. The thousand inhabitants live in buildings of rammed earth, and avoid unnecessary possessions. There are no servants, leisure class, or money. Everyone works a four-hour day, which must include some menial work. In return, all goods and services are free. The family is (as in Plato's *Republic*) virtually eliminated. Communal living replaces private houses, releasing women from domestic labour. Husbands and wives have separate rooms, which makes them happier and better adjusted. Children are reared communally ('Home is not the place to raise children'), and regard all adults as their parents. In time it is hoped that all breeding will be by artificial insemination. People will marry as they wish, but have children according to a genetic plan.

These social changes have become possible only through widespread psychological change. In Walden Two, fear, hate, rage and jealousy are unknown. Competitiveness has vanished, along with heroes, hero-worship, the cult of leadership and the idea of personal triumph. There are no boxing, wrestling or team games, and no memorials to the 'great' dead. Exceptional achievement is not admired, because it exposes the unexceptional achievement of others. Politics and world affairs arouse no interest. Government of the commune is happily left to an unelected Board of Planners (six men and six women) who serve for ten years.

In the following passage Frazier, the founder of the commune, explains to some visitors (Castle, Rogers, Barbara and the narrator Professor Burris) the techniques of behavioural engineering that have yielded these desirable results.

'We found a few suggestions worth following in the practices of the clinical psychologist. We undertook to build a tolerance for annoying experiences. The sunshine of midday is extremely painful if you come from a dark room, but take it in easy stages and you can avoid pain altogether. The analogy can be misleading, but in much the same way it's possible to build a tolerance to painful or distasteful stimuli, or to frustration, or to situations which arouse fear, anger or rage. Society and nature throw these annoyances at the individual with no regard for the development of tolerances. Some achieve tolerances, most fail. Where would the science of immunization be if it followed a schedule of accidental dosages?

'Take the principle of "Get thee behind me, Satan," for example,' Frazier continued. 'It's a special case of self-control by altering the environment. Subclass A3, I believe. We give each child a lollipop which has been dipped in powdered sugar so that a single touch of the tongue can be detected. We tell him he may eat the lollipop later in the day, provided it hasn't already been licked. Since the child is only three or four, it is a fairly diff–'

'Three or four!' Castle exclaimed.

'All our ethical training is completed by the age of six,' said Frazier quietly. 'A simple principle like putting temptation out of sight would be acquired before four. But at such an early age the problem of not licking the lollipop isn't easy. Now, what would you do, Mr Castle, in a similar situation?'

'Put the lollipop out of sight as quickly as possible.'

'Exactly. I can see you've been well trained. Or perhaps you discovered the principle for yourself. We're in favor of original inquiry wherever possible, but in this case we have a more important goal and we don't hesitate to give verbal help. First of all, the children are urged to examine their own behavior while looking at the lollipops. This helps them to recognize the need for self-control. Then the lollipops are concealed, and the children are asked to notice any gain in happiness or any reduction in tension. Then a strong distraction is arranged – say, an interesting game. Later the children are reminded of the candy and encouraged to examine their reaction. The value of the distraction is generally obvious. Well, need I go on? When the experiment is repeated a day or so later, the children all run with the lollipops to their lockers and do exactly what Mr Castle would do – a sufficient indication of the success of our training.'

'I wish to report an objective observation of my reaction to your story,' said Castle, controlling his voice with great precision. 'I find myself revolted by this display of sadistic tyranny.'

'I don't wish to deny you the exercise of an emotion which you seem to find enjoyable,' said Frazier. 'So let me go on. Concealing a tempting but forbidden object is a crude solution. For one thing, it's not always feasible. We want a sort of psychological concealment – covering up the candy by paying no attention. In a later experiment the children wear their lollipops like crucifixes for a few hours.'

> ' "Instead of the cross, the lollipop,
>   About my neck was hung," '

said Castle.

'I wish somebody had taught me that, though,' said Rodge, with a glance at Barbara.

'Don't we all?' said Frazier. 'Some of us learn control, more or less by accident. The rest of us go all our lives not even understanding how it is possible, and blaming our failure on being born the wrong way.'

'How do you build up a tolerance to an annoying situation?' I said.

'Oh, for example, by having the children "take" a more and more painful shock, or drink cocoa with less and less sugar in it until a bitter concoction can be savored without a bitter face.'

'But jealousy or envy – you can't administer them in graded doses,' I said.

'And why not? Remember, we control the social environment, too, at this age. That's why we get our ethical training in early. Take this case. A group of children arrive home after a long walk tired and hungry. They're expecting supper; they find, instead, that it's time for a lesson in self-control: they must stand for five minutes in front of steaming bowls of soup.

'The assignment is accepted like a problem in arithmetic. Any groaning or complaining is a wrong answer. Instead, the children begin at once to work upon themselves to avoid any unhappiness during the delay. One of them may make a joke of it. We encourage a sense of humor as a good way of not taking an annoyance seriously. The joke won't be much, according to adult standards – perhaps the child will simply pretend to empty the bowl of soup into his upturned mouth. Another may start a song with many verses. The rest join in at once, for they've learned that it's a good way to make time pass.'

Frazier glanced uneasily at Castle, who was not to be appeased.

'That also strikes you as a form of torture, Mr Castle?' he asked.

'I'd rather be put on the rack,' said Castle.

'Then you have by no means had the thorough training I supposed. You can't imagine how lightly the children take such an experience. It's a rather severe biological frustration, for the children are tired and hungry and they must stand and look at food; but it's passed off as lightly as a five-minute delay at curtain time. We regard it as a fairly elementary test. Much more difficult problems follow.'

'I suspected as much,' muttered Castle.

'In a later stage we forbid all social devices. No songs, no jokes – merely silence. Each child is forced back upon his own resources – a very important step.'

'I should think so,' I said. 'And how do you know it's successful? You might produce a lot of silently resentful children. It's certainly a dangerous stage.'

'It is, and we follow each child carefully. If he hasn't picked up the necessary techniques, we start back a little. A still more advanced stage' – Frazier glanced again at Castle, who stirred uneasily – 'brings me to my point. When it's time to sit down to the soup, the children count off – heads and tails. Then a coin is tossed and if it comes up heads, the "heads" sit down and eat. The "tails" remain standing for another five minutes.'

Castle groaned.

'And you call that envy?' I asked.

'Perhaps not exactly,' said Frazier. 'At least there's seldom any aggression against the lucky ones. The emotion, if any, is directed against Lady Luck herself, against the toss of the coin. That, in itself, is a lesson worth learning, for it's the only direction in which emotion has a surviving chance to be useful. And resentment toward things in general, while perhaps just as silly as personal aggression, is more easily controlled. Its expression is not socially objectionable.' . . .

'May you not inadvertently teach your children some of the very emotions you're trying to eliminate?' I said. 'What's the effect, for example, of finding the anticipation of a warm supper suddenly thwarted? Doesn't that eventually lead to feelings of uncertainty, or even anxiety?'

'It might. We had to discover how often our lessons could be safely administered. But all our schedules are worked out experimentally. We watch for undesired consequences just as any scientist watches for disrupting factors in his experiments.

'After all, it's a simple and sensible program,' he went on in a tone of appeasement. 'We set up a system of gradually increasing annoyances and frustrations against a background of complete serenity. An easy environment is made more and more difficult as the children acquire the capacity to adjust.' . . .

Castle grew black.

'But what do your children get out of it?' he insisted, apparently trying to press some vague advantage in Frazier's anger.

'What do they get out of it!' exclaimed Frazier, his eyes flashing with a sort of helpless contempt. His lips curled and he dropped his head to look at his fingers, which were crushing a few blades of grass.

'They must get happiness and freedom and strength,' I said, putting myself in a ridiculous position in attempting to make peace.

'They don't sound happy or free to me, standing in front of bowls of Forbidden Soup,' said Castle, answering me parenthetically while continuing to stare at Frazier.

'If I must spell it out,' Frazier began with a deep sigh, 'what they get is escape from the petty emotions which eat the heart out of the unprepared. They get the satisfaction of pleasant and profitable social relations on a scale almost undreamed of in the world at large. They get immeasurably increased efficiency, because they can stick to a job without suffering the aches and pains which soon beset most of us. They get new horizons, for they are spared the emotions characteristic of frustration and failure. They get – ' His eyes searched the branches of the trees. 'Is that enough?' he said at last.

'And the community must gain their loyalty,' I said, 'when they discover the fears and jealousies and diffidences in the world at large.'

'I'm glad you put it that way,' said Frazier. 'You might have said that they must feel superior to the miserable products of our public schools. But we're at pains to keep any feeling of superiority or contempt under control, too. Having suffered most acutely from it myself, I put the subject first on our agenda. We carefully avoid any joy in a personal triumph which means the personal failure of somebody else. We take no pleasure in the sophistical, the disputative, the dialectical.' He threw a vicious glance at Castle. 'We don't use the motive of domination, because we are always thinking of the whole group. We could motivate a few geniuses that way – it was certainly my own motivation – but we'd sacrifice some of the happiness of everyone else. Triumph over nature and over oneself, yes. But over others, never.'

'You've taken the mainspring out of the watch,' said Castle flatly.

'That's an experimental question, Mr Castle, and you have the wrong answer.'

Source: B. F. Skinner, *Walden Two*, Macmillan, 1969.

The Worst Thing

Life in *Nineteen Eighty-Four* (1949) by George Orwell (1903–50) is based on three models: Stalinist Russia, wartime London, where Orwell worked in the BBC's propaganda department, and St Cyprian's prep school, Eastbourne, as described in Orwell's autobiographical essay 'Such, Such Were the Joys'. Each of these contributes its own measure of cruelty, oppression and squalor to Orwell's nightmare.

The world of *Nineteen Eighty-Four* is divided into three totalitarian super-states: Oceania, Eurasia, and Eastasia. Oceania, which includes the Americas and Britain (renamed Airstrip One), is ruled by the Party. Its head, Big Brother, never appears in public, but his portrait, with the caption *Big Brother is Watching You*, is on every wall and hoarding. Surveillance is the responsibility of the Thought Police. In every flat there are telescreens, which cannot be switched off. They transmit and receive simultaneously, and are sensitive enough to pick up even changes in heartbeat. Out of doors there are hidden cameras and microphones. Children, under the aegis of the Spies youth organization, are expected to keep watch for thoughtcrime (i.e., any deviation from the principles of 'Ingsoc' or English Socialism) in parents or teachers.

It is Party policy that warfare between Oceania and one of the other superstates should be perpetual. This is not because any principles are involved (the other superstates have similar totalitarian regimes to Oceania's), but because war conveniently destroys the products of human labour, which might otherwise be used to make the masses too comfortable and hence, in the long run, too intelligent. The masses comprise eighty-five per cent of the population, and are called the proles. They live in filth and ignorance. As they are politically inert, the Party does not bother to monitor their doings. But it controls their thought by distributing propaganda, cheap fiction and pornography, collectively designated prolefeed. Continual war fever is stimulated by the daily Two Minutes Hate on the telescreen, and by special Hate Weeks offering popular spectacles such as the public execution of defectors and prisoners of war.

Four great Ministries dominate London: the Ministry of Peace is the war ministry; the Ministry of Truth fabricates propaganda; the Ministry of Love is where suspected dissidents are tortured; and the Ministry of Plenty keeps the population close to starvation by strict rationing.

Winston Smith, the book's central character, works in the department of the Ministry of Truth responsible for falsifying the past. The Party has rewritten history, and continues to adjust it to keep step with shifts in Party policy. Dissidents who are 'vaporized' (executed) become 'unpersons' and all trace of them must be removed from the written records. This feature of Orwell's dystopia reflects his indignation at Russian Communist doctoring of truth during the Spanish Civil War, in which he fought on the Republican side with the POUM Anarchist militia. Another distinctive feature of *Nineteen Eighty-Four* is Newspeak, the official language of Ingsoc, the principles of which are explained to Winston by Syme, who works on the Newspeak Dictionary.

'How is the Dictionary getting on?' said Winston, raising his voice to overcome the noise.

'Slowly,' said Syme. 'I'm on the adjectives. It's fascinating.'

He had brightened up immediately at the mention of Newspeak. He pushed his pannikin aside, took up his hunk of bread in one delicate hand and his cheese in the other, and leaned across the table so as to be able to speak without shouting.

'The Eleventh Edition is the definitive edition,' he said. 'We're getting the language into its final shape – the shape it's going to have when nobody speaks anything else. When we've finished with it, people like you will have to learn it all over again. You think, I dare say, that our chief job is inventing new words. But not a bit of it! We're destroying words – scores of them, hundreds of them, every day. We're cutting the language down to the bone. The Eleventh Edition won't contain a single word that will become obsolete before the year 2050.'

He bit hungrily into his bread and swallowed a couple of mouthfuls, then continued speaking, with a sort of pedant's passion. His thin dark face had become animated, his eyes had lost their mocking expression and grown almost dreamy.

'It's a beautiful thing, the destruction of words. Of course the great wastage is in the verbs and adjectives, but there are hundreds of nouns that can be got rid of as well. It isn't only the synonyms; there are also the antonyms. After all, what justification is there for a word which is simply the opposite of some other word? A word contains its opposite in itself. Take "good", for instance. If you have a word like "good", what need is there for a word like "bad"? "Ungood" will do just as well – better, because it's an exact opposite, which the other is not. Or again, if you want a stronger version of "good", what sense is there in having a whole string of vague useless words like "excellent" and "splendid" and all the rest of them? "Plusgood" covers the meaning; or "doubleplusgood" if you want something stronger still. Of course we use those forms already, but in the final version of Newspeak there'll be nothing else. In the end the whole notion of goodness and badness will be covered by only six words – in reality, only one word. Don't you see the beauty of that, Winston? It was BB's idea originally, of course,' he added as an afterthought.

A sort of vapid eagerness flitted across Winston's face at the mention of Big Brother. Nevertheless Syme immediately detected a certain lack of enthusiasm.

'You haven't a real appreciation of Newspeak, Winston,' he said almost sadly. 'Even when you write it you're still thinking in Old-speak. I've read some of those pieces that you write in *The Times* occasionally. They're good enough, but they're translations. In your heart you'd prefer to stick to Oldspeak, with all its vagueness and its useless shades of meaning. You don't grasp the beauty of the destruction of words. Do you know that Newspeak is the only language in the world whose vocabulary gets smaller every year?'

Winston did know that, of course. He smiled, sympathetically he hoped, not trusting himself to speak. Syme bit off another fragment of the dark-coloured bread, chewed it briefly, and went on:

'Don't you see that the whole aim of Newspeak is to narrow the range of thought? In the end we shall make thoughtcrime literally impossible, because there will be no words in which to express it. Every concept that can ever be needed, will be expressed by exactly *one* word, with its meaning rigidly defined and all its subsidiary meanings rubbed out and forgotten. Already, in the Eleventh Edition, we're not far from that point. But the process will still be continuing long after you and I are dead. Every year fewer and fewer words, and the range of consciousness always a little smaller. Even now, of course, there's no reason or excuse for committing thoughtcrime. It's merely a question of self-discipline, reality-control. But in the end there won't be any need even for that. The Revolution will be complete when the language is perfect. Newspeak is Ingsoc and Ingsoc is Newspeak,' he added with a sort of mystical satisfaction. 'Has it ever occurred to you, Winston, that by the year 2050, at the very latest, not a single human being will be alive who could understand such a conversation as we are having now?'

Winston has only vague memories of the past. To remember it, as opposed to the official record, would, in any case, be thoughtcrime. But he cherishes a vision of the English countryside (dear to Orwell), and this recurs in his dreams, contrasting cruelly with the waking reality.

Suddenly he was standing on short springy turf, on a summer evening when the slanting rays of the sun gilded the ground. The landscape that he was looking at recurred so often in his dreams that he was never fully certain whether or not he had seen it in the real world. In his waking thoughts he called it the Golden Country. It was an old, rabbit-bitten pasture, with a foot-track wandering across it and a molehill here and there. In the ragged hedge on the opposite side of the field the boughs of the elm trees were swaying very faintly in the breeze, their leaves just stirring in dense masses like women's hair. Somewhere near at hand, though out of sight, there was a clear, slow-moving stream where dace were swimming in the pools under the willow trees.

The girl with dark hair was coming towards them across the field. With what seemed a single movement she tore off her clothes and flung them disdainfully aside. Her body was white and smooth, but it aroused no desire in him, indeed he barely looked at it. What overwhelmed him in that instant was admiration for the gesture with which she had thrown her clothes aside. With its grace and careless-ness it seemed to annihilate a whole culture, a whole system of thought, as though Big Brother and the Party and the Thought Police could all be swept into nothingness by a single splendid movement of the arm. That too was a gesture belonging to the ancient time. Winston woke up with the word 'Shakespeare' on his lips.

The telescreen was giving forth an ear-splitting whistle which con-tinued on the same note for thirty seconds. It was nought seven fifteen, getting-up time for office workers. Winston wrenched his body out of bed – naked, for a member of the Outer Party received only 3,000 clothing coupons annually, and a suit of pyjamas was 600 – and seized a dingy singlet and a pair of shorts that were lying across a chair. The Physical Jerks would begin in three minutes. The next moment he was doubled up by a violent coughing fit which nearly always attacked him soon after waking up. It emptied his lungs so completely that he could only begin breathing again by lying on his back and taking a series of deep gasps. His veins had swelled with the effort of the cough, and the varicose ulcer had started itching.

'Thirty to forty group!' yapped a piercing female voice. 'Thirty to forty group! Take your places, please. Thirties to forties!'

Winston sprang to attention in front of the telescreen, upon which the image of a youngish woman, scrawny but muscular, dressed in tunic and gym-shoes, had already appeared.

'Arms bending and stretching!' she rapped out. 'Take your time by me. *One*, two, three, four! *One*, two, three, four! Come on, comrades, put a bit of life into it! *One*, two, three, four! *One*, two, three, four! . . .'

The pain of the coughing fit had not quite driven out of Winston's mind the impression made by his dream, and the rhythmic movements of the exercise restored it somewhat. As he mechanically shot his arms back and forth, wearing on his face the look of grim enjoyment which was considered proper during the Physical Jerks, he was struggling to think his way backward into the dim period of his early childhood. It was extraordinarily difficult. Beyond the late 'fifties everything faded. When there were no external records that you could refer to, even the outline of your own life lost its sharpness. You remembered huge events which had quite probably not happened, you remembered the detail of incidents without being able to recapture their atmosphere, and there were long blank periods to which you could assign nothing. Everything had been different then. Even the names of countries, and their shapes on the map, had been different. Airstrip One, for instance, had not been so called in those days: it had been called England or Britain, though London, he felt fairly certain, had always been called London.

The plot of Orwell's novel hinges on Winston's secret love affair with Julia, who also works in the Ministry of Truth. Though outwardly conformist, and a member of the Junior Anti-Sex League, she hates the Party and all its ideas. The lovers rent a room in a prole district, where they can meet unobserved – as they think. But their every movement is in fact observed by

[436]

the Thought Police. It is an Inner Party member, O'Brien, whom they have trusted, believing he shares their dissident views, who eventually supervises their arrest and torture. Under torture Winston breaks down completely, confessing to countless crimes at O'Brien's suggestion. He does not, however, betray Julia – or not until O'Brien, who has studied him carefully, and knows his most secret fears, takes him to the dreaded Room 101. Here he is strapped upright in a chair, so tightly that he cannot even move his head.

The door opened again. A guard came in, carrying something made of wire, a box or basket of some kind. He set it down on the further table. Because of the position in which O'Brien was standing, Winston could not see what the thing was.

'The worst thing in the world,' said O'Brien, 'varies from individual to individual. It may be burial alive, or death by fire, or by drowning, or by impalement, or fifty other deaths. There are cases where it is some quite trivial thing, not even fatal.'

He had moved a little to one side, so that Winston had a better view of the thing on the table. It was an oblong wire cage with a handle on top for carrying it by. Fixed to the front of it was something that looked like a fencing mask, with the concave side outwards. Although it was three or four metres away from him, he could see that the cage was divided lengthways into two compartments, and that there was some kind of creature in each. They were rats.

'In your case,' said O'Brien, 'the worst thing in the world happens to be rats.'

A sort of premonitory tremor, a fear of he was not certain what, had passed through Winston as soon as he caught his first glimpse of the cage. But at this moment the meaning of the mask-like attachment in front of it suddenly sank into him. His bowels seemed to turn to water.

'You can't do that!' he cried out in a high cracked voice. 'You couldn't, you couldn't! It's impossible.'

'Do you remember,' said O'Brien, 'the moment of panic that used to occur in your dreams? There was a wall of blackness in front of you, and a roaring sound in your ears. There was something terrible on the other side of the wall. You knew that you knew what it was, but you dared not drag it into the open. It was the rats that were on the other side of the wall.'

'O'Brien!' said Winston, making an effort to control his voice. 'You know this is not necessary. What is it that you want me to do?'

O'Brien made no direct answer. When he spoke it was in the schoolmasterish manner that he sometimes affected. He looked thoughtfully into the distance, as though he were addressing an audience somewhere behind Winston's back.

'By itself,' he said, 'pain is not always enough. There are occasions when a human being will stand out against pain, even to the point of death. But for everyone there is something unendurable – something that cannot be contemplated. Courage and cowardice are not involved. If you are falling from a height it is not cowardly to clutch at a rope. If you have come up from deep water it is not cowardly to fill your lungs with air. It is merely an instinct which cannot be destroyed. It is the same with the rats. For you, they are unendurable. They are a form of pressure that you cannot withstand, even if you wished to. You will do what is required of you.'

'But what is it, what is it? How can I do it if I don't know what it is?'

O'Brien picked up the cage and brought it across to the nearer table. He set it down carefully on the baize cloth. Winston could hear the blood singing in his ears. He had the feeling of sitting in utter loneliness. He was in the middle of a great empty plain, a flat desert drenched with sunlight, across which all sounds came to him out of immense distances. Yet the cage with the rats was not two metres away from him. They were enormous rats. They were at the age when a rat's muzzle grows blunt and fierce and his fur brown instead of grey.

'The rat,' said O'Brien, still addressing his invisible audience, 'although a rodent, is carnivorous. You are aware of that. You will have heard of the things that happen in the poor quarters of this town. In some streets a woman dare not leave her baby alone in the house, even for five minutes. The rats are certain to attack it. Within quite a small time they will strip it to the bones. They also attack sick or dying people. They show astonishing intelligence in knowing when a human being is helpless.'

There was an outburst of squeals from the cage. It seemed to reach Winston from far away. The rats were fighting; they were trying to get at each other through the partition. He heard also a deep groan of despair. That, too, seemed to come from outside himself.

O'Brien picked up the cage, and, as he did so, pressed something in it. There was a sharp click. Winston made a frantic effort to tear himself loose from the chair. It was hopeless; every part of him, even his head, was held immovably. O'Brien moved the cage nearer. It was less than a metre from Winston's face.

'I have pressed the first lever,' said O'Brien. 'You understand the construction of this cage. The mask will fit over your head, leaving no exit. When I press this other lever, the door of the cage will slide up. These starving brutes will shoot out of it like bullets. Have you ever seen a rat leap through the air? They will leap on to your face and bore straight into it. Sometimes they attack the eyes first. Sometimes they burrow through the cheeks and devour the tongue.'

The cage was nearer; it was closing in. Winston heard a succession of shrill cries which appeared to be occurring in the air above his head. But he fought furiously against his panic. To think, to think, even with a split second left – to think was the only hope. Suddenly the foul musty odour of the brutes struck his nostrils. There was a violent convulsion of nausea inside him, and he almost lost conscious-ness. Everything had gone black. For an instant he was insane, a screaming animal. Yet he came out of the blackness clutching an idea. There was one and only one way to save himself. He must interpose another human being, the *body* of another human being, between himself and the rats.

The circle of the mask was large enough now to shut out the vision of anything else. The wire door was a couple of hand-spans from his face. The rats knew what was coming now. One of them was leaping up and down, the other, an old scaly grandfather of the sewers, stood up, with his pink hands against the bars, and fiercely sniffed the air. Winston could see the whiskers and the yellow teeth. Again the black panic took hold of him. He was blind, helpless, mindless.

'It was a common punishment in Imperial China,' said O'Brien as didactically as ever.

The mask was closing on his face. The wire brushed his cheek. And then – no, it was not relief, only hope, a tiny fragment of hope. Too late, perhaps too late. But he had suddenly understood that in the whole world there was just *one* person to whom he could transfer his punishment – *one* body that he could thrust between himself and the rats. And he was shouting frantically, over and over.

'Do it to Julia! Do it to Julia! Not me! Julia! I don't care what you do to her. Tear her face off, strip her to the bones. Not me! Julia! Not me!'

Source: George Orwell, *Nineteen Eighty-Four*, Secker & Warburg, 1949.

Men or Machines?

Kurt Vonnegut (b.1922) served in the US Air Force in the Second World War, was captured by the Germans, and survived the fire-bombing of Dresden in February 1945. His first novel, *Player Piano* (1952), has become a classic of dystopian fiction. It foretells what many commentators now see as the harmful social consequences of automation and computerization.

Set in Ilium, New York, in the aftermath of the Third World War, the novel depicts a rigidly stratified society. The élite of technocrats, engineers and scientists live in a fortified enclave that occupies one-third of the city. A further third is inhabited by machines and computers, which do most of the work. The remaining third, known as Homestead, houses the unemployed – that is, the majority of the population. They are amply supplied with material goods by the indefatigable machines, but have no hope or aims. They exhibit the symptoms that have become familiar in Western societies in the late twentieth century – breakdown of family life, organized vice, juvenile crime, alcoholism, drug abuse, and high divorce and suicide rates. The able-bodied unemployed are enlisted either in the Army or in the Reclamation and Reconstruction Corps (known as the Recks and Wrecks) which undertakes menial tasks like road repair.

The social system is impeccably and rigorously meritocratic. Everyone carries a computer-readable card which records a complete personal profile from smallpox vaccination to IQ, together with educational record and job qualifications. Computers regularly sift through these details, and anyone who is found to be doing a job that can now be done by machine joins the unemployed.

Among the élite, concern about the degradation of the common people grows. A secret resistance-group forms, calling itself the Ghost Shirt Society (after a nineteenth-century American Indian protest-movement against white domination). The manifesto of this group declares that:

Men, by their nature, seemingly, cannot be happy unless engaged in enterprises that make them feel useful. They must, therefore, be returned to participation in such enterprises.

[441]

I hold, and the members of the Ghost Shirt Society hold:

That there must be virtue in imperfection, for Man is imperfect, and Man is a creation of God.

That there must be virtue in frailty, for Man is frail, and Man is a creation of God.

That there must be virtue in inefficiency, for Man is inefficient, and Man is a creation of God.

That there must be virtue in brilliance followed by stupidity, for Man is alternately brilliant and stupid, and Man is a creation of God.

You perhaps disagree with the antique and vain notion of Man's being a creation of God.

But I find it a far more defensible belief than the one implicit in intemperate faith in lawless technological progress – namely, that man is on earth to create more durable and efficient images of himself, and hence, to eliminate any justification at all for his own continued existence.

The signatory of this manifesto is Dr Paul Proteus, a disillusioned engineer, once manager of the whole Ilium industrial complex. Among other rebel-leaders are Dr Francis Finnerty, who, like Proteus, was once a pioneer of automation in Ilium, the Reverend James Lasher, Protestant minister and social scientist, Professor Ludwig von Neumann, another social scientist, and Bud Calhoun, a brilliant engineer who lost his job because he helped to make machines that could replace him.

Under their leadership, simultaneous armed rebellions break out in many US cities. Most are suppressed by the military. But in Ilium the rebels are partly successful. Hysterical mobs embark on an orgy of machine-breaking and looting, despite their leaders' efforts at restraint, and occupy the city – though it is surrounded by government forces.

The twist in the novel's ending sharply registers the limits of Vonnegut's optimism for mankind. On the morning after the rising the leaders tour the city in a hijacked State Department limousine.

As the sun arose over Ilium, and the embers of the town seemed gray in the light of the eternal fire ninety-three million miles away, the State Department limousine, flying a ghost shirt from its radio antenna, crept through the streets.

Bodies lay everywhere, in grotesque attitudes of violent death, but manifesting the miracle of life in a snore, a mutter, the flight of a bubble from the lips.

In the early light, the town seemed an enormous jewel box, lined with the black and gray velvet of fly-ash, and filled with millions of twinkling treasures: bits of air conditioners, amplidynes, analyzers, arc welders, batteries, belts, billers, bookkeeping machines, bottlers, canners, capacitors, circuitbreakers, clocks, coin boxes, calorimeters, colorimeters, computers, condensers, conduits, controls, converters, conveyers, cryostats, counters, cutouts, densitometers, detectors, dust precipitators, dishwashers, dispensers, dynamometers, dynamotors, electrodes, electronic tubes, exciters, fans, filers, filters, frequency changers, furnaces, fuses, gages, garbage disposers, gears, generators, heat exchangers, insulators, lamps, loudspeakers, magnets, mass spectrometers, motor generators, motors, noisemeters, oscillographs, panelboards, personnel machines, photoelectric cells, potentiometers, pushbuttons, radios, radiation detectors, reactors, recorders, rectifiers, reducers, regulators, relays, remote controls, resistors, rheostats, selsyns, servos, solenoids, sorters, spectrophotometers, spectroscopes, springs, starters, strain-gages, switchboards, switches, tape recorders, tachometers, telemeters, television sets, television cameras, testers, thermocouples, thermostats, timers, toasters, torquemeters, traffic controls, transistors, transducers, transformers, turbines, vacuum cleaners, vacuum gages, vacuum tubes, venders, vibration meters, viscosimeters, water heaters, wheels, X-ray spectrogoniometers, zymometers . . .

At the wheel of the limousine was Doctor Edward Francis Finnerty. Beside him was Doctor Paul Proteus. In the back seat were the Reverend James J. Lasher and Professor Ludwig von Neumann . . .

The brains of the Ghost Shirt Society were touring the strongpoints on the frontiers of their Utopia. And everywhere they found the same things: abandoned weapons, abandoned posts, mounds of expended ammunition, and riddled machinery.

The four had come to an exciting decision: during the six months of blockade threatened by the authorities, they would make the ruins a laboratory, a demonstration of how well and happily men could live with virtually no machines. They saw now the common man's wisdom in wrecking practically everything. That *was* the way to do it, and the hell with moderation!

[443]

'All right, so we'll heat our water and cook our food and light and warm our homes with wood fires,' said Lasher.

'And walk wherever we're going,' said Finnerty.

'And read books instead of watching television,' said von Neumann. 'The Renaissance comes to upstate New York! We'll rediscover the two greatest wonders of the world, the human mind and hand.'

'No quarter asked, no quarter given,' said Paul as they contemplated the entire furnishings of an M-11 house, dragged into a vacant lot and hacked to bits.

'This is like the Indians' massacre of Custer and his men,' said Lasher reflectively. 'The Little Bighorn. One isolated victory against an irresistible tide. More and more whites where Custer came from; more and more machines where these came from. But we may win yet. Well! What is that noise? Somebody awake?'

A faint hubbub came from around a corner, from where the railroad station had been, where it still was after a fashion. Finnerty turned the corner for a better look at the celebrators.

In the station's waiting room, carnage was everywhere. The terrazzo floor, depicting an earlier slaughter of Iliumites by Oneida Indians, was strewn with the guts and internal secretions of the automatic ticket vendor, the automatic nylon vendor, the automatic coffee vendor, the automatic newspaper vendor, the automatic toothbrush vendor, the automatic shoeshine machine, the automatic photo studio, the automatic baggage checker, the automatic insurance salesman . . .

But around one machine a group had gathered. The people were crowding one another excitedly, as though a great wonder were in their midst.

Paul and Finnerty left the car to examine the mystery, and saw that the center of attention was an Orange-O machine. Orange-O, Paul recalled, was something of a *cause célèbre*, for no one in the whole country, apparently, could stomach the stuff – no one save Doctor Francis Eldgrin Gelhorne, National Industrial, Commercial, Communications, Foodstuffs, and Resources Director. As a monument to him Orange-O machines stood shoulder-to-shoulder with the rest, though the coin-box collectors never found anything in the machines but stale Orange-O.

But now the excretor of the blended wood pulp, dye, water, and orange-type flavoring was as popular as a nymphomaniac at an American Legion convention.

'OK, now let's try anotha' nickel in her an' see how she does,' said a familiar voice from behind the machine – the voice of Bud Calhoun.

'*Clunkle*' went the coin, and then a whir, and a gurgle.

The crowd was overjoyed.

'Filled the cup almost to the top that time; and she's nice and cold now, too,' called the man by the machine's spout.

'But the light behind the Orange-O sign didn't light up,' said a woman. 'Supposed to.'

'We'll fix that, won't we, Bud?' said another voice from behind the machine. 'You people get me about three feet of that red wire hanging out of the shoeshine machine, and somebody let me borrow their penknife a second.' The speaker stood up and stretched, and smiled contentedly, and Paul recognized him: the tall, middle-aged, ruddy-faced man who'd fixed Paul's car with the sweatband of his hat long ago.

The man had been desperately unhappy then. Now he was proud and smiling because his hands were busy doing what they liked to do best, Paul supposed – replacing men like himself with machines. He hooked up the lamp behind the Orange-O sign. 'There we are.'

Bud Calhoun bolted on the back. 'Now try her.'

The people applauded and lined up, eager for their Orange-O. The first man up emptied his cup, and went immediately to the end of the line for seconds.

'Now, let's have a look at this li'l ol' ticket seller,' said Bud. 'Oh, oh. Got it right through the microphone.'

'I knew we'd be able to use the telephone out in the street for something,' said the ruddy man. 'I'll go get it.'

The crowd, filled with Orange-O, was drifting over to encourage them in their new enterprise.

When Paul and Finnerty returned to the limousine, they found Lasher and von Neumann looking extremely glum, engaged in conversation with a bright-looking teenager.

'Have you seen an eight-horsepower electric motor lying around anywhere?' said the youngster. 'One that isn't busted up too bad?'

Lasher shook his head.

'Well, I just have to keep looking, I guess,' said the youngster, picking up a cardboard carton jammed with gears, tubes, switches,

[445]

and other odd parts. 'This place is a gold mine, all right, but it's tough finding exactly what you need.'

'I imagine,' said Lasher.

'Yep, if I had a decent little motor to go with what I got,' said the youngster excitedly. 'I'll betcha anything I could make a gadget that'd play the drums like nothing you ever heard before. See, you take a selsyn, and – '

'Proteus! Finnerty!' said Lasher irritably. 'What's been keeping you?'

The four disillusioned leaders drive to the city's outskirts and surrender to the authorities.

Source: Kurt Vonnegut, *Player Piano*, Macmillan, 1953.

Huxley's Hell and Heaven

When Aldous Huxley (1894–1963) first visited America in the 1920s, he saw the future and hated it. The Eton-educated scion of one of England's foremost intellectual families, he was repelled by what seemed to him the shallowness of American consumerism and mass culture. They represented 'a radical alteration (for the worse) of established standards'. His classic dystopia *Brave New World* (1932), based on his American experience, depicts a World State dedicated to the happiness of the masses. Those things that Huxley's social class valued most – literature, high art, selfless dedication to an ideal – have been scrapped. They stir the passions and engage the mind too deeply to be compatible with happiness. Christianity has been discarded for the same reason. So has freedom. All babies are produced in test-tubes in state hatcheries. Natural childbirth is obsolete: to mention it is considered indecent. In this way, the deep ties and potential unhappiness of family life have been superseded. Further, by varying the supply of oxygen to the embryos, the hatcheries produce five grades of human being, Alphas, Betas, Gammas, Deltas and semi-moronic Epsilons. The lowest three grades are cloned from single eggs, producing standard men and women in uniform batches. So everyone is adapted to the kind of employment for which he or she is destined. The unhappiness of frustrated ambition is a thing of the past.

Life, outside of working hours, is given up to mind-numbing pleasure. Sexual promiscuity is universal, even among small children, and eagerly encouraged by the State, which teaches that 'Everyone belongs to everyone else', and supplies free contraceptives. Instant escape from reality is supplied by the 'feelies' (movies which arouse all the senses, through electrodes implanted in cinema-seat armrests) and soma, a euphoric, pleasantly hallucinogenic drug, which everyone takes.

Huxley certainly meant his dystopia to be abhorrent. Yet it has positive features. In *Brave New World*, medical science has eliminated virtually all diseases, together with the debilitating effects of old age. There is no pain, no hunger, no want. Even the reduction of the mass of mankind to docile automata might seem, to an intellectual aristocrat like Huxley, no bad thing.

He did not favour universal education, declaring that it merely swelled the ranks of the 'new stupid'. *Brave New World*, then, can be read as an ambivalent text, dystopian from one angle, utopian from another.

When, in his final novel *Island* (1962), Huxley portrayed a utopia, it had several features in common with *Brave New World* – though in other respects it was glaringly different. Pala, the island of the title, is a tropical paradise, peopled by beautiful, lightly clad natives. They choose to remain secluded from the modern world, shunning industrialization and consumerism. They are guided by reason and ecological concern, believing that 'we shall be permitted to live on this planet only for as long as we treat all nature with compassion and intelligence'. Like the Brave New Worlders, they have no time for religions and dogmas, such as Christianity, which renounce the world or deny its value. Inspired, rather, by 'Buddhism shot through with Tantra', they strive for a higher awareness of earthly life and the life of the senses.

In pursuit of this they use a drug (the equivalent of *Brave New World*'s soma), called variously 'the *moksha*-medicine', 'the reality-revealer', and 'the truth-and-beauty pill', which they extract from toadstools. Four hundred milligrams of *moksha* allow you to glimpse the world as it looks to someone who has been 'liberated from the bondage of the ego'. The most ordinary things, and the most trivial events, are seen as jewels and miracles. Will Farnaby, the narrator of *Island*, discovers this when he takes *moksha* for the first time.

The fountain of forms, the coloured orbs in their conscious arrays and purposefully changing lattices gave place to a static composition of uprights and diagonals, of flat planes and curving cylinders, all carved out of some material that looked like living agate, and all emerging from a matrix of living and pulsating mother-of-pearl. Like a blind man newly healed and confronted for the first time by the mystery of light and colour, he stared in uncomprehending astonishment. And then, at the end of another twenty timeless bars of the Fourth Brandenburg, a bubble of explanation rose into consciousness. He was looking, Will suddenly perceived, at a small square table, and beyond the table at a rocking-chair, and beyond the rocking-chair at a blank wall of whitewashed plaster. The explanation was reassuring; for in the eternity that he had experienced between the opening of his eyes and the emergent knowledge of what he was looking at, the mystery confronting him had deepened from inexplicable beauty to a consummation of shining alienness that filled him, as he looked, with a kind of metaphysical terror. Well, this terrifying mystery consisted of nothing but two pieces of furniture and an expanse of wall. The fear was allayed, but the wonder only increased. How was it possible that things so familiar and common-place could be *this*? Obviously it wasn't possible; and yet there it was, there it was.

His attention shifted from the geometrical constructions in brown agate to their pearly background. Its name he knew, was 'wall'; but in experienced fact it was a living process, a continuing series of transubstantiations from plaster and whitewash into the stuff of a supernatural body – into a god-flesh that kept modulating, as he looked at it, from glory to glory. Out of what the word-bubbles had tried to explain away as mere calcimine, some shaping spirit was evoking an endless succession of the most delicately discriminated hues, at once faint and intense, that emerged out of latency and went flushing across the god-body's divinely radiant skin. Wonderful, wonderful! And there must be other miracles, new worlds to conquer and be conquered by. He turned his head to the left and there (appropriate words had bubbled up almost immediately) was the large marble-topped table at which they had eaten their supper. And now, thick and fast, more bubbles began to rise. This breathing apocalypse called 'table' might be thought of as a picture by some mystical Cubist, some inspired Juan Gris with the soul of Traherne and a gift for painting miracles with conscious gems and the changing moods of water-lily petals.

Turning his head a little further to the left he was startled by a blaze of jewellery. And what strange jewellery! Narrow slabs of emerald and topaz, of ruby and sapphire and lapis lazuli, blazing away, row above row, like so many bricks in a wall of the New Jerusalem. Then – at the end, not in the beginning – came the word. In the beginning were the jewels, the stained glass windows, the walls of paradise. It was only now, at long last, that the word 'book-case' presented itself for consideration.

Huxley was here drawing on his own experience of mescalin, as recounted in *The Doors of Perception* (1954). He took the drug for the first time in Los Angeles in 1953, and was overwhelmed by its effects. Even the creases in a pair of trousers became 'a labyrinth of endlessly significant complexity'. He developed the theory that evolution had narrowed mankind's sensory perceptions to what was strictly necessary in the struggle for survival. 'The function of the brain and nervous system and sense organs is in the main *eliminative*.' Mescalin, and similar hallucinogens, could reverse this process, and re-open the doors of perception, presenting not a transformation of reality but the true reality – in accord with William Blake's dictum that 'If the doors of perception were cleansed everything would appear to man as it is, infinite.' Huxley recommended mescalin and lysergic acid as 'drugs of unique distinction', which should be exploited for the visionary experiences they afforded. Widespread dependence on mind-changing drugs was, he argued, inevitable.

That humanity at large will ever be able to dispense with Artificial Paradises seems very unlikely. Most men and women lead lives at the worst so painful, at the best so monotonous, poor and limited that the urge to escape, the longing to transcend themselves if only for a few moments, is and has always been one of the principal appetites of the soul.

Drug-dependence is the most striking similarity between *Brave New World* and Huxley's utopia, Pala. But there are others. Sexual promiscuity is the rule in both cultures. The Palanese have no bodily shame, and believe in free love. Fidelity between couples is not expected. Love-making starts in the mid-teens. Boys who prove backward are seduced by more energetic girls, or by older women who teach 'special techniques'. Homosexuality is equally accepted, however: 'one kind of love doesn't exclude the other'. The aim is to make every man, woman and child free and happy.

Contraceptives are distributed by the government. The postman delivers a thirty-night supply at the start of each month. But the Palanese mostly prefer to practise *Maithuna* ('the yoga of love'), which means the deliberate avoidance of orgasm during intercourse. They find that this technique gives them a special awareness of the self and the other, making profane love sacred. Through it they regain the Freudian childhood paradise, when sexuality was not concentrated in the genitals but diffused through the whole organism.

Though the Palanese, unlike the Brave New Worlders, still practise natural childbirth, they are similarly suspicious of family ties. The mother–child relationship is not particularly close or enduring. Every child has a Mutual Adoption Club (MAC) of about twenty assorted couples that it can transfer to to get away from its own family. Further, as in *Brave New World*, the kind of child produced is not left wholly to chance – as Will discovers in conversation with a Palanese couple, Shanta and Vijaya, who are expecting their third child.

'Four years ago,' Shanta explained, 'we produced a pair of twins who are the living image of Vijaya. This time we thought it would be fun to have a complete change. We decided to enrich the family with an entirely new physique and temperament. Did you ever hear of Gobind Singh?'

'Vijaya has just been showing me his painting in your meditation room.'

'Well, that's the man we chose for Rama's father.'

'But I understood he was dead.'

Shanta nodded. 'But his soul goes marching along.'

'What do you mean?'

'DF and AI.'

'DF and AI?'

'Deep Freeze and Artificial Insemination.'

'Oh, I see.'

'Actually,' said Vijaya, 'we developed the techniques of AI about twenty years before you did. But of course we couldn't do much with it until we had electric power and reliable refrigerators. We got those in the late twenties. Since when we've been using AI in a big way.'

'So you see,' Shanta chimed in, 'my baby might grow up to be a painter – that is, if that kind of talent is inherited. And even if it isn't, he'll be a lot more endomorphic and viscerotonic than his brothers or either of his parents. Which is going to be very interesting and educative for everybody concerned.'

'Do many people go in for this kind of thing?' Will asked.

'More and more. In fact I'd say that practically all the couples who decide to have a third child now go in for AI. So do quite a lot of those who mean to stop at number two. Take my family, for example. There's been some diabetes among my father's people; so they thought it best – he and my mother – to have both their children by AI' . . .

'So you're improving the race.'

'Very definitely. Give us another century, and our average IQ will be up to a hundred and fifteen.'

As this suggests, the Palanese are not ignorant of modern science. But they choose to develop only those branches of it that they consider beneficial. Their agricultural research has yielded new strains of rice, maize, millet and breadfruit, and better breeds of cattle and chickens. A Palanese elder explains the economy to Will:

'Lenin used to say that electricity plus socialism equals communism. Our equations are rather different. Electricity minus heavy industry plus birth control equals democracy and plenty. Electricity plus heavy industry minus birth control equals misery, totalitarianism and war.'

'Incidentally,' Will asked, 'who owns all this? Are you capitalists or state socialists?'

'Neither. Most of the time we're cooperators. Palanese agriculture has always been an affair of terracing and irrigation. But terracing and irrigation call for pooled efforts and friendly agreements. Cut throat competition isn't compatible with rice-growing in a mountainous country. Our people found it quite easy to pass from mutual aid in a village community to streamlined cooperative techniques for buying and selling and profit-sharing and financing.' . . .

'You seem to have solved your economic problems pretty successfully.'

'Solving them wasn't difficult. To begin with, we never allowed ourselves to produce more children than we could feed, clothe, house, and educate into something like full humanity. Not being over-populated, we have plenty. But although we have plenty, we've managed to resist the temptation that the West has now succumbed to – the temptation to over-consume. We don't give ourselves coronaries by guzzling six times as much saturated fat as we need. We don't hypnotize ourselves into believing that two television sets will make us twice as happy as one television set. And finally we don't spend a quarter of the gross national product preparing for World War III or even World War's baby brother, Local War MMMCCXXXIII. Armaments, universal debt, and planned obsolescence – those are the three pillars of Western prosperity. If war, waste, and money-lenders were abolished, you'd collapse. And while you people are over-consuming, the rest of the world sinks more and more deeply into chronic disaster. Ignorance, militarism, and breeding, these three – and the greatest of these is breeding. No hope, not the slightest possibility, of solving the economic problem until *that's* under control. As population rushes up, prosperity goes down.' He traced the descending curve with an outstretched finger. 'And as prosperity goes down, discontent and rebellion' (the forefinger moved up again), 'political ruthlessness and one-party rule, nationalism and bellicosity begin to rise. Another ten or fifteen years of uninhibited breeding, and the whole world, from China to Peru via Africa and the Middle East, will be fairly crawling with Great Leaders, all dedicated to the suppression of freedom, all armed to the teeth by Russia or America or, better still, by both at once, all waving flags, all screaming for *Lebensraum*.'

'What about Pala?' Will asked. 'Will *you* be blessed with a Great Leader ten years from now?'

'Not if we can help it,' Dr Robert answered. 'We've always done everything possible to make it very difficult for a Great Leader to arise.' . . .

'Tell me how you do it,' he said.

'Well, to begin with we don't fight wars or prepare for them. Consequently we have no need for conscription, or military hier-archies, or a unified command. Then there's our economic system: it doesn't permit anybody to become more than four or five times as rich as the average. That means that we don't have any captains of industry or omnipotent financiers. Better still, we have no omnipotent politicians or bureaucrats. Pala's a federation of self-governing units, geographical units, professional units, economic units – so there's plenty of scope for small-scale initiative and democratic leaders, but no place for any kind of dictator at the head of a centralized govern-ment. Another point: we have no established church, and our religion stresses immediate experience and deplores belief in unverifiable dogmas and the emotions which that belief inspires. So we're pre-served from the plagues of popery on the one hand and fundamentalist revivalism on the other. And along with transcen-dental experience we systematically cultivate scepticism. Discouraging children from taking words too seriously, teaching them to analyse whatever they hear or read – this is an integral part of the school curriculum. Result: the eloquent rabble-rouser, like Hitler or our neighbour across the Strait, Colonel Dipa, just doesn't have a chance here in Pala.'

Colonel Dipa is a military dictator who plans to take over Pala, force it into the modern world, and exploit its oil resources. At the end of *Island* he succeeds in doing so – a conclusion that reflects Huxley's pessimism about the future.

Sources: Aldous Huxley, *Brave New World*, Chatto & Windus, 1932; *The Doors of Perception*, Chatto & Windus, 1954; *Island*, Chatto & Windus, 1962.

Disneyland at Christmas

The American novelist E. L. Doctorow (b.1931) based his novel *The Book of Daniel* (1971) on the Rosenberg case. Julius and Ethel Rosenberg were American Communists, found guilty of passing atomic secrets to Russia in 1951, and executed in the electric chair at Sing Sing in 1953. The novel depicts the Communist-phobia of Cold War America, and introduces, in its closing pages, a dystopian view of Disneyland as an epitome of middle-American culture.

This famous amusement park is shaped like a womb. It is situated in a flatland of servicing motels, restaurants, gas stations, bowling alleys and other places of fun, and abuts on its own giant parking lot. A mono-rail darts along its periphery, in a loop that carries to the Disneyland Hotel. A replica nineteenth-century railroad line, the Sante Fé and Disneyland, complete with stations, conductors, steam engine and surrey type cars, delineates its circumference. Within the park itself five major amusement areas are laid out on different themes: the American West, called Frontierland; current technology, which is called Tomorrowland; nursery literature, called Fantasyland; and Adventureland, which proposes colonialist exploration of wild jungles of big game and native villages. Customers are invited to explore each area and its delights according to their whim. In the centre of the park, where all the areas converge, there is a plaza; and the fifth thematic area, an avenue called Main Street USA, a romantic rendering of small-town living at the turn of the century, leads like the birth canal from the plaza to the entrance to the park.

As in all amusement parks the featured experience is the ride, or trip. The notability of Disneyland is its elaboration of this simple pleasure. You will not find the ordinary roller coaster or Ferris wheel except disguised as a bobsled ride down a plastic Matterhorn, or a 'people mover'. In toy submarines with real hatches, the customer experiences a simulated dive underwater, as bubbles rise past the portholes and rubber fish wag their tails. The submarines are said to be nuclear and bear the names of ships of the American nuclear fleet. Disneyland invites the customer not merely to experience the controlled thrills of a carny ride, but to participate in mythic rituals of the culture. Your boat ride is a Mississippi sternwheeler. Your pony ride is a string of pack mules going over the mountains to where the gold is. The value of the experience is not the ride itself but its vicariousness.

Two problems arise in the customer's efforts to fulfil Disneyland's expectations of him. The first is that for some reason while the machinery of the rides is impressively real – that is to say, technologically perfect and historically accurate – the simulated plant and animal and geological surroundings are unreal. When you take the jungle river cruise the plants and animals on the banks betray their plastic being and electronic motivation. The rocks of the painted desert or grand canyon cannot sustain the illusion of even the least sophisticated. The second difficulty is that Disneyland is usually swarming with people. People are all over the place in Disneyland. Thus the customers on the Mark Twain Mississippi steamboat look into the hills and see the customers on the mule pack train looking down at them. There is a constant feedback of human multiplicity, one's own efforts of vicarious participation constantly thwarted by the mirror of others' eyes.

Within the thematic unities of Disneyland, there are numbers of references, usually in the form of rides, exhibits or stores, to figures or works of our literary heritage. Some of these are Alice in Wonderland (Mad Hatter's Teacup Ride), Peter Pan (Peter Pan Flight), Life on the Mississippi (Mark Twain Riverboat), Wind in the Willows (Mr Toad's Wild Ride), Swiss Family Robinson (Swiss Family Tree House), and Tom Sawyer (Tom Sawyer's Island Rafts). In addition there are implications of proprietary relationships with various figures of history, myth and legend such as King Arthur, Sleeping Beauty, Snow White, Casey Jones, Mike Fink, Jean Lafitte, and Abraham Lincoln. It is hard to find a pattern in the selection of these particular figures. Most of them have passed through a previous process of film or film animation and are made to recall the preemptive powers of the Disney organization with regard to Western culture. But beyond that no principle of selection is obvious. It is interesting to note, however, that Walt Disney's early achievements in his original medium, the animated cartoon, employed animal characters of his own devising. The animated cartoon itself, except for Disney's subsequent climb into the respectability of public domain literature, came to express the collective unconsciousness of the community of the American Naïve. A study today of the products of the animated cartoon industry of the twenties, thirties and forties would yield the following theology: 1. People are animals. 2. The body is mortal and subject to incredible pain. 3. Life is antagonistic to the living. 4. The flesh can be sawed, crushed, frozen, stretched, burned, bombed, and plucked for music. 5. The dumb are abused by the smart and the smart destroyed by their own cunning. 6. The small are tortured by the large and the large destroyed by their own momentum. 7. We are able to walk on air, but only as long as our illusion supports us. It is possible to interpret the Disney organization's relentless programme of adaptation of literature, myth and legend, as an attempt to escape these dark and rowdy conclusions of the genre – in the same way a tenement kid from the Lower East Side might have grown up with the ambition of building himself a mansion on Fifth Avenue. Yet, ironically, many of the stories and characters chosen by Disney for their cultural respectability are just as dark and just as rowdy. The original *Alice in Wonderland* is a symbolic and surreal work by a benign deviate genius. Mark Twain was an atheist and a pornographer, and his great work, *Huckleberry Finn*, is a nightmare of childhood in confrontation with American social reality. In this light it is possible to understand the aesthetics of cartoon adaptation as totalitarian in nature.

It it is clear that few of the children who ride in the Mad Hatter's Teacup have read or even will read *Alice*, let alone the works of Mark Twain. Most of them will only know Alice's story through the Disney film, if at all. And that suggests a separation of two ontological degrees between the Disneyland customer and the cultural artifacts he is presumed upon to treasure in his visit. The Mad Hatter's Teacup Ride is emblematic of the Disney animated film, which is itself a drastic revision in form and content of a subtle dreamwork created out of the English language. And even to an adult who dimly remembers reading the original *Alice*, and whose complicated response to this powerfully symbolic work has long since been incorporated into the psychic constructs of his life, what

[457]

is being offered does not suggest the resonance of the original work, but is only a sentimental compression of something that is itself already a lie.

We find this radical process of reduction occurring too with regard to the nature of historical reality. The life and life-style of slave-trading America on the Mississippi River in the nineteenth century is compressed into a technologically faithful steamboat ride of five or ten minutes on an HO-scale river. The intermediary between us and this actual historical experience, the writer Mark Twain, author of *Life on the Mississippi*, is now no more than the name of the boat. Piracy on the high seas, a hundred and fifty years of harassment of European mercantile exploration and trade, becomes a moving diorama of all the scenes and situations of the pirate movies made by Hollywood in the thirties and forties. When the customer is invited then to buy, say, a pirate hat in one of the many junk shops on the premises, the Pavlovian process of symbolic transference to the final consumer moment may be said to be complete.

The ideal Disneyland patron may be said to be one who responds to a process of symbolic manipulation that offers him his culminating and quintessential sentiment at the moment of a purchase.

The following corporations offer shows and exhibits at Disneyland: Monsanto Chemical Co., Bell Telephone, General Electric, and Coca-Cola. Other visible corporate representation includes McDonnell Aircraft, Goodyear, Carnation Milk, Sunkist, Eastman Kodak, Upjohn Pharmaceuticals, Insurance Company of North America, United Air Lines, and Bank of America.

Obviously there are political implications. What Disneyland proposes is a technique of abbreviated shorthand culture for the masses, a mindless thrill, like an electric shock, that insists at the same time on the recipient's rich psychic relation to his country's history and language and literature. In a forthcoming time of highly governed masses in an overpopulated world, this technique may be extremely useful both as a substitute for education and, eventually, as a substitute for experience. One cannot tour Disneyland today without noticing its real achievement, which is the handling of crowds. Coupled open vans, pulled by tractors, collect customers at various points of the parking areas and pour them out at the entrance to the park. The park seems built to absorb infinite numbers of customers in its finite space by virtue of the simultaneous appeal of numbers of attractions at the same time, including not only the fixed rides and exhibits and restaurants and shops but special parades and flag raising and lowering ceremonies, band concerts, and the like. (At Christmas time Main Street residents in period dress sing Christmas carols at the foot of a large odourless evergreen whose rubberized needles spring to the touch.) In front of the larger attractions are mazes of pens, designed to hold great numbers of people waiting to board, or to mount or to enter. Guards, attendants, guides, and other personnel, including macrocephalic Disney costume characters, are present in abundance. Plain-clothes security personnel appear in any large gathering with walkie-talkies. The problems of mass ingress and egress seem to have been solved here to a degree that would light admiration in the eyes of an SS transport officer.

Source: E. L. Doctorow, *The Book of Daniel*, Pan, 1973.

Describing Venice

In *Invisible Cities* (1972) by Italo Calvino (1923–87), Marco Polo tells Kubla Khan that 'Cities, like dreams, are made of desires and fears.' The traveller can never see the foreign as it is, only as it differs from what is familiar. 'Elsewhere is a negative mirror.' This is true, too, of imaginary cities. When the emperor asks Marco why, among all the fantastic cities he has described, he has never described his native Venice, he replies that he has been describing it all along. These and other speculations about the nature of utopias can be glimpsed behind all the cities Marco invents. Here are three.

Now I will tell how Octavia, the spider-web city, is made. There is a precipice between two steep mountains: the city is over the void, bound to the two crests with ropes and chains and catwalks. You walk on the little wooden ties, careful not to set your foot in the open spaces, or you cling to the hempen strands. Below there is nothing for hundreds and hundreds of feet: a few clouds glide past; farther down you can glimpse the chasm's bed.

This is the foundation of the city: a net which serves as passage and as support. All the rest, instead of rising up, is hung below: rope ladders, hammocks, houses made like sacks, clothes hangers, terraces like gondolas, skins of water, gas jets, spits, baskets on strings, dumb-waiters, showers, trapezes and rings for children's games, cable cars, chandeliers, pots with trailing plants.

Suspended over the abyss, the life of Octavia's inhabitants is less uncertain than in other cities. They know the net will last only so long . . .

After a seven days' march through woodland, the traveler directed toward Baucis cannot see the city and yet he has arrived. The slender stilts that rise from the ground at a great distance from one another and are lost above the clouds support the city. You climb them with ladders. On the ground the inhabitants rarely show themselves: having already everything they need up there, they prefer not to come down. Nothing of the city touches the earth except those long flamingo legs on which it rests and, when the days are sunny, a pierced, angular shadow that falls on the foliage.

There are three hypotheses about the inhabitants of Baucis: that they hate the earth; that they respect it so much they avoid all contact; that they love it as it was before they existed and with spyglasses and telescopes aimed downward they never tire of examining it, leaf by leaf, stone by stone, ant by ant, contemplating with fascination their own absence . . .

A sibyl, questioned about Marozia's fate, said: 'I see two cities: one of the rat, one of the swallow.'

This was the interpretation of the oracle: today Marozia is a city where all run through leaden passages like packs of rats who tear from one another's teeth the leftovers which fall from the teeth of the most voracious ones; but a new century is about to begin in which all the inhabitants of Marozia will fly like swallows in the summer sky, calling one another as in a game, showing off, their wings still, as they swoop, clearing the air of mosquitos and gnats.

'It is time for the century of the rat to end and the century of the swallow to begin,' the more determined said. In fact, already beneath the grim and petty rattish dominion, you could sense, among the less obvious people a pondering, the preparation of a swallowlike flight, heading for the transparent air with a deft flick of the tail, then tracing with their wings' blade the curve of an opening horizon.

I have come back to Marozia after many years: for some time the sibyl's prophecy is considered to have come true; the old century is dead and buried, the new is at its climax. The city has surely changed, and perhaps for the better. But the wings I have seen moving about are those of suspicious umbrellas under which heavy eyelids are lowered; there are people who believe they are flying, but it is already an achievement if they can get off the ground flapping their batlike overcoats.

It also happens that, if you move along Marozia's compact walls, when you least expect it, you see a crack open and a different city appear. Then, an instant later, it has already vanished. Perhaps everything lies in knowing what words to speak, what actions to perform, and in what order and rhythm; or else someone's gaze, answer, gesture is enough; it is enough for someone to do something for the sheer pleasure of doing it, and for his pleasure to become the pleasure of others: at that moment, all spaces change, all heights, distances; the city is transfigured, becomes crystalline, transparent as a dragonfly. But everything must happen as if by chance, without attaching too much importance to it, without insisting that you are performing a decisive operation, remembering clearly that any moment the old Marozia will return and solder its ceiling of stone, cobwebs and mold over all heads.

Was the oracle mistaken? Not necessarily. I interpret it in this way: Marozia consists of two cities, the rat's and the swallow's; both change with time, but their relationship does not change; the second is the one about to free itself from the first.

Source: Italo Calvino, *Invisible Cities*, translated by William Weaver, Secker & Warburg, 1974.

Space Potatoes

In 1929 the Irish physicist J. D. Bernal (1901–71) published a book called *The World, the Flesh and the Devil: An Inquiry into the Future of the Three Enemies of the Rational Soul*. It anticipates much science fiction, though Bernal intended it as a serious scientific forecast. By 'the World' he meant planet Earth's inorganic constraints (harsh terrain, climate, food shortage). Mankind would overcome these, he prophesied, by building space colonies. 'The Flesh' (ageing and deteriorating organs and brains) would be overcome by advanced artificial spare-parts surgery. 'Transformed' human beings would consist of a human brain, kept alive in a cylinder, electrically linked to improved sense organs (an organ for detecting wireless frequencies, eyes for seeing infrared and ultraviolet light and X-rays, ears for supersonics). In place of the present body-structure, the transformed human's brain would control artificial motor-organs – antenna, jaw, limb – of great power and delicacy, rather like those of an extremely refined lobster. This surgically transformed human being must, Bernal admitted, seem strange and monstrous to us at present. But it would allow mankind immortality. For brains could be linked up electrically to communicate without language, and this would allow the creation of a 'multiple individual', consisting of many brains with shared thought and memory. As a single brain became too old to preserve (after maybe a thousand years) newer brains could take its place in the 'compound mind'. This would solve the third of mankind's great problems – 'the Devil' – by which Bernal meant current individual human psychology with its destructive desires and inner confusions. Corporate personalities would form greater and greater complexes until there was only one intelligence world-wide.

In fact, Bernal speculates, only ten per cent of humanity (the scientists) will opt to become 'transformed'. They will constitute a new, superior species, leaving behind the majority who are too stupid or too stubborn to change. The ignorant masses will ignore the scientific 'fanatics' who choose to distort their bodies and blow themselves into space. But these scientific experts will inevitably become the rulers of the future. Psychological discoveries will allow them to direct the masses into harmless occupations, where they remain perfectly docile under the appearance of freedom. Alternatively, there may not be room for both types in the same world. Then the better-organized 'transformed' humans will be obliged to reduce the numbers of the masses, until they are no longer inconvenienced by them. Or perhaps, Bernal suggests, untransformed man may be left in possession of the earth. Transformed man will live in space colonies, eventually spreading over 'most of the sidereal universe', and the earth will become a human zoo – so intelligently managed that its inhabitants never suspect they exist merely for observation and experiment by transformed space-dwellers.

In 1972 the English physicist and advocate of space-colonization Freeman J. Dyson (b.1923) gave a lecture in Bernal's honour, updating his scientific utopia. Dyson soft-pedals the idea of 'transformed' human beings – though he observes that the discovery of the molecular structure of DNA opens the way to genetic surgery, and the removal of certain human types – transformations Bernal never imagined when he wrote his book. In other respects Dyson outdoes even Bernal in the ingenuity and courage of his imagining.

Leaving aside genetic surgery applied to humans, I foresee that the coming century will place in our hands two other forms of biological technology which are less dangerous but still revolutionary enough to transform the conditions of our existence. I count these new technologies as powerful allies in the attack on Bernal's three enemies. I give them the names 'biological engineering' and 'self-reproducing machinery'. Biological engineering means the artificial synthesis of living organisms designed to fulfil human purposes. Self-reproducing machinery means the imitation of the function and reproduction of a living organism with non-living materials, a computer-program imitating the function of DNA and a miniature factory imitating the functions of protein molecules. After we have attained a complete understanding of the principles of organization and development of a simple multicellular organism, both of these avenues of technological exploitation should be open to us.

I would expect the earliest and least controversial triumphs of biological engineering to be extensions of the art of industrial fermentation. When we are able to produce micro-organisms equipped with enzyme-systems tailored to our own design, we can use such organisms to perform chemical operations with far greater delicacy and economy than present industrial practices allow. For example, oil refineries would contain a variety of bugs designed to metabolize crude petroleum into the precise hydrocarbon stereo-isomers which are needed for various purposes. One tank would contain the n-octane bug, another the benzene bug, and so on. All the bugs would contain enzymes metabolizing sulphur into elemental form, so that pollution of the atmosphere by sulphurous gases would be completely controlled. The management and operation of such fermentation-tanks on a vast scale would not be easy, but the economic and social rewards are so great that I am confident we shall learn how to do it. After we have mastered the biological oil-refinery, more important applications of the same principles will follow. We shall have factories producing specific foodstuffs biologically from cheap raw materials, and sewage-treatment plants converting our wastes efficiently into usable solids and pure water. To perform these operations we shall need an armamentarium of many species of micro-organisms trained to ingest and excrete the appropriate chemicals. And we shall design into the metabolism of these organisms the essential property of self-liquidation, so that when deprived of food they disappear by cannibalizing one another. They will not, like the bacteria that feed upon our sewage in today's technology, leave their rotting carcasses behind to make a sludge only slightly less noxious than the mess they have eaten.

If these expectations are fulfilled, the advent of biological technology will help enormously in the establishment of patterns of industrial development with which human beings can live in health and comfort. Oil-refineries need not stink. Rivers need not be sewers. However, there are many environmental problems which the use of artificial organisms in enclosed tanks will not touch. For example, the fouling of the environment by mining and by abandoned automobiles will not be reduced by building cleaner factories. The second step in biological engineering, after the enclosed biological factory, is to let artificial organisms loose into the environment. This is admittedly a more dangerous and problematical step than the first. The second step should be taken only when we have a deep understanding of its ecological consequences. Nevertheless the advantages which artificial organisms offer in the environmental domain are so great that we are unlikely to forgo their use for ever.

The two great functions which artificial organisms promise to perform for us when let loose upon the earth are mining and scavenging. The beauty of a natural landscape undisturbed by man is largely due to the fact that the natural organisms in a balanced ecology are excellent miners and scavengers. Mining is mostly done by plants and micro-organisms extracting minerals from water, air and soil. For example, it has been recently discovered that organisms in the ground mine ammonia and carbon monoxide from air with high efficiency. To the scavengers we owe the fact that a natural forest is not piled as high with dead birds as one of our junk-yards with dead cars. Many of the worst offences of human beings against natural beauty are due to our incompetence in mining and scavenging. Natural organisms know how to mine and scavenge effectively in a natural environment. In a man-made environment, neither they nor we know how to do it. But there is no reason why we should not be able to design artificial organisms that are adaptable enough to collect our raw materials and to dispose of our refuse in an environment that is a careful mixture of natural and artificial.

A simple example of a problem that an artificial organism could solve is the eutrophication of lakes. At present many lakes are being ruined by excessive growth of algae feeding on high levels of nitrogen and phosphorus in the water. The damage could be stopped by an organism that could convert nitrogen to molecular form or phosphorus to an insoluble solid. Alternatively and preferably, an organism could be designed to divert the nitrogen and phosphorus into a food-chain culminating in some species of palatable fish. To control and harvest the mineral resources of the lake in this way will in the long run be more feasible than to maintain artificially a state of 'natural' barrenness.

The artificial mining organisms would not operate in the style of human miners. Many of them would be designed to mine the ocean. For example, oysters might extract gold from sea-water and secrete golden pearls. A less poetic but more practical possibility is the artificial coral that builds a reef rich in copper or magnesium. Other mining organisms would burrow like earthworms into mud and clay, concentrating in their bodies the ores of aluminium or tin or iron, and excreting the ores in some manner convenient for human harvesting. Almost every raw material necessary for our existence can be mined from ocean, air or clay, without digging deep into the earth. Where conventional mining is necessary, artificial organisms can still be useful for digesting and purifying the ore.

Not much imagination is needed to foresee the effectiveness of artificial organisms as scavengers. A suitable micro-organism could convert the dangerous organic mercury in our rivers and lakes to a harmless insoluble solid. We could make good use of an organism with a consuming appetite for polyvinyl chloride and similar plastic materials which now litter beaches all over the earth. Conceivably we may produce an animal specifically designed for chewing up dead automobiles. But one may hope that the automobile in its present form will become extinct before it needs to be incorporated into an artificial food-chain. A more serious and permanent role for scavenging organisms is the removal of trace quantities of radioactivity from the environment. The three most hazardous radioactive elements produced in fission reactors are strontium, caesium and plutonium. These elements have long half-lives and will inevitably be released in small quantities so long as mankind uses nuclear fission as an energy source. The long-term hazard of nuclear energy would be notably reduced if we had organisms designed to gobble up these three elements from water or soil and to convert them into indigestible form. Fortunately, none of these three elements is essential to our body chemistry, and it therefore does us no harm if they are made indigestible.

I have spoken about the two first steps of biological engineering. The first will transform our industry, and the second will transform our earth-bound ecology. It is now time to speak of the third step, which is the colonization of space. I believe in fact that biological engineering is the essential tool which will make Bernal's dream of the expansion of mankind in space a practical possibility.

First I have to clear away a few popular misconceptions about space as a habitat. It is generally considered that planets are important. Except for Earth, they are not. Mars is waterless, and the others are for various reasons basically inhospitable to man. It is generally considered that beyond the Sun's family of planets there is absolute emptiness extending for light years until you come to another star. In fact it is likely that the space around the Solar System is populated by huge numbers of comets, small worlds a few miles in diameter, rich in water and other chemicals essential to life. We see one of these comets only when it happens to suffer a random perturbation of its orbit which sends it plunging close to the Sun. It seems that roughly one comet per year is captured into the region near the Sun, where it eventually evaporates and disintegrates. If we assume that the supply of distant comets is sufficient to sustain this process over the thousands of millions of years that the Solar System has existed, then the total population of comets loosely attached to the sun must be numbered in the thousands of millions. The combined surface area of these comets is then a thousand or ten thousand times that of the Earth. I conclude from these facts that comets, not planets, are the major potential habitat of life in space. If it were true that other stars have as many comets as the Sun, it then would follow that comets pervade our entire galaxy. We have no evidence either supporting or contradicting this hypothesis. If true, it implies that our galaxy is a much friendlier place for interstellar travellers than it is popularly supposed to be. The average distance between habitable oases in the desert of space is not measured in light-years, but is of the order of a light-day or less.

I propose to you then an optimistic view of the galaxy as an abode of life. Countless millions of comets are out there, amply supplied with water, carbon and nitrogen, the basic constituents of living cells. We see when they fall close to the Sun that they contain all the common elements necessary to our existence. They lack only two essential requirements for human settlement, namely warmth and air. And now biological engineering will come to our rescue. We shall learn to grow trees on comets.

To make a tree grow in airless space by the light of a distant Sun is basically a problem of redesigning the skin of its leaves. In every organism the skin is the crucial part which must be most delicately tailored to the demands of the environment. The skin of a leaf in space must satisfy four requirements. It must be opaque to far-ultraviolet radiation to protect the vital tissues from radiation damage. It must be impervious to water. It must transmit visible light to the organs of photosynthesis. It must have extremely low emissivity for far-infrared radiation, so that it can limit loss of heat and keep itself from freezing. A tree whose leaves possess such a skin should be able to take root and flourish upon any comet as near to the Sun as the orbits of Jupiter and Saturn. Farther out than Saturn the sunlight is too feeble to keep a simple leaf warm, but trees can grow at far greater distances if they provide themselves with compound leaves. A compound leaf would consist of a photosynthetic part which is able to keep itself warm, together with a convex mirror part which itself remains cold but focuses concentrated sunlight upon the photosynthetic part. It should be possible to programme the genetic instructions of a tree to produce such leaves and orient them correctly toward the Sun. Many existing plants possess structures more complicated than this.

Once leaves can be made to function in space, the remaining parts of a tree, trunk, branches, and roots, do not present any great problems. The branches must not freeze, and therefore the bark must be a superior heat-insulator. The roots will penetrate and gradually melt the frozen interior of the comet, and the tree will build its substance from the materials which the roots find there. The oxygen which the leaves manufacture must not be exhaled into space; instead it will be transported down to the roots and released into the regions where men live and take their ease among the tree-trunks. One question still remains. How high can a tree on a comet grow? The answer is surprising. On any celestial body whose diameter is of the order of ten miles or less, the force of gravity is so weak that a tree can grow infinitely high. Ordinary wood is strong enough to lift its own weight to an arbitrary distance from the centre of gravity. This means that from a comet of ten-mile diameter trees can grow out for hundreds of miles, collecting the energy of sunlight from an area thousands of miles as large as the area of the comet itself. Seen from far away the comet will look like a small potato sprouting an immense growth of stems and foliage. When man comes to live on the comets, he will find himself returning to the arboreal existence of his ancestors.

We shall bring to the comets not only trees but a great variety of other flora and fauna to create for ourselves an environment as beautiful as ever existed on Earth. Perhaps we shall teach our plants to make seeds which will sail out across the ocean of space to propagate life upon comets still unvisited by man. Perhaps we shall start a wave of life which will spread from comet to comet without end until we have achieved the greening of the galaxy. That may be an end or a beginning, as Bernal said, but from here it is out of sight.

In parallel with our exploitation of biological engineering, we may achieve an equally profound industrial revolution by following the alternative route of self-reproducing machinery. Self-reproducing machines are devices which have the multiplying and self-organizing capabilities of living organisms but are built of metal and computers instead of protoplasm and brains. It was the mathematician John von Neumann who first demonstrated that self-reproducing machines are theoretically possible and sketched the logical principles underlying their construction. The basic components of a self-reproducing machine are precisely analogous to those of a living cell. The separation of function between genetic material (DNA) and enzymatic machinery (protein) in a cell corresponds exactly to the separation between software (computer programs) and hardware (machine tools) in a self-reproducing machine.

I assume that in the next century, partly imitating the processes of life, and partly improving on them, we shall learn to build self-reproducing machines programmed to multiply, differentiate and coordinate their activities as skilfully as the cells of a higher organism such as a bird. After we have constructed a single egg-machine and supplied it with the appropriate computer-program, the egg and its progeny will grow into an industrial complex capable of performing economic tasks of arbitrary magnitude. It can build cities, plant gardens, construct electric power-generating facilities, launch spaceships or raise chickens. The overall programmes and their execution will always remain under human control.

The effects of such a powerful and versatile technology on human affairs are not easy to foresee. Unwisely used, it offers a rapid road to ecological disaster. Used wisely, it offers a rapid alleviation of all the purely economic difficulties of mankind. It offers to rich and poor nations alike a rate of growth of economic resources so rapid that economic constraints will no longer be dominant in determining how people are to live. In some sense this technology will constitute a permanent solution of man's economic problems. Just as in the past, when economic problems cease to be pressing, we shall find no lack of fresh problems to take their place.

It may well happen that on Earth, for aesthetic or ecological reasons, the use of self-reproducing machines will be strictly limited and the methods of biological engineering will be used instead wherever this alternative is feasible. For example, self-reproducing machines could proliferate in the ocean and collect minerals for man's use, but we might prefer to have the same job done more quietly by corals and oysters. If economic needs were no longer paramount, we could afford a certain loss of proficiency for the sake of a harmonious environment. Self-reproducing machines may therefore play on Earth a subdued and self-effacing role.

[470]

The true realm of self-reproducing machinery will be in those regions of the Solar System that are inhospitable to man. Machines built of iron, aluminium and silicon have no need of water. They can flourish and proliferate on the Moon or on Mars or among the asteroids, carrying out giant industrial projects with no risk to the Earth's ecology. They will feed upon sunlight and rock, needing no other raw material for their construction. They will build in space the freely floating cities that Bernal imagined for human habitation. They will bring oceans of water from the satellites of the outer planets, where it is to be had in abundance, to the inner parts of the Solar System where it is needed. Ultimately this water will make even the deserts of Mars bloom, and men will walk there under the open sky breathing air like the air of Earth.

Taking a long view into the future, I foresee a division of the Solar System into two domains. The inner domain, where sunlight is abundant and water scarce, will be the domain of great machines and governmental enterprises. Here self-reproducing machines will be obedient slaves, and men will be organized in giant bureaucracies. Outside and beyond the sunlit zone will be the outer domain, where water is abundant and sunlight scarce. In the outer domain lie the comets where trees and men will live in smaller communities, isolated from each other by huge distances. Here men will find once again the wilderness that they have lost on Earth. Groups of people will be free to live as they please, independent of governmental authorities. Outside and away from the Sun, they will be able to wander for ever on the open frontier that this planet no longer possesses.

Source: Freeman J. Dyson, *The World, the Flesh and the Devil. The Third J. D. Bernal Lecture*, delivered at Birkbeck College, London, 1972.

Infertile Solution

English novelist Naomi Mitchison (1897–1999) had no scientific training but grew up in a scientific environment. Her father was a physiologist, her brother the noted biologist and science-writer J. B. S. Haldane. Aldous Huxley was an early friend. In the First World War she served as a VAD nurse, and after the war worked in a London birth-control clinic. Her dystopia *Solution Three* (1975) depicts a world in which biological engineering is used to solve the population problem. The Third World War (known as 'the Aggression') has destroyed many of the world's cities and left large tracts uninhabitable. The survivors, still far more numerous than the planet can easily sustain, are packed into high-rise mega-cities, to leave all available space for food crops. The world is ruled by a benevolent Council, devoted to reducing population and preventing aggression, in conformity with an unquestioned 'Code'. The widespread use of cannabis ('the aggression dispeller') is encouraged. Homosexuality is officially sanctioned as the normal means of sexual expression. Heterosexuals are regarded as deviants, and in some parts of the world whipped or castrated (though the Council frowns on such measures). To regulate reproduction, almost all children are produced from cloned cells, gestated in the wombs of selected mothers, from whom, while still infants, they are separated for rigorous social conditioning.

The novel is dedicated 'To Jim Watson' (i.e., the American geneticist James Watson, co-discoverer of the molecular structure of DNA) 'who first suggested this horrid idea'. Mitchison herself married at nineteen and had six children, and her distaste for the sexual arrangements she describes in the book is unconcealed. The characters in the following excerpt are members of the world's ruling Council. Mutumba, a Negro woman, is its chairperson. The 'Professorials' referred to are intellectuals and scientists – members, that is, of Mitchison's own social group. They are presented as redemptively natural, preserving true human values in the teeth of sexual inversion and political conformity.

'Lovely, lovely technology!' sang out Elissa, coming over to them with a couple of the film capsules she had been demonstrating earlier, and smiling at Jussie, showing off her own debt to technology. She was always happening on a new sprayer; not being one for folds and swirls, she had taken a close off-crimson spray that ended in fine lines whiskering out a few centimetres from her golden ears, the same down toewards from her ankles. This had been topped off with wavy lines reminding the viewer of – what? Ric found her just a little repulsive, as after all, women normally were, though this was easily blotted out with a colleague, Mutumba or Jussie or Shanti. But as she came near, Jussie looked hungrily and simply had to stroke Elissa down, a long shoulder to buttocks, and pull her for a moment into the same chair. Elissa responded with a quick hand between Jussie's legs, but just as a greeting. Really, she had hoped that Mutumba would notice her, but Mutumba was talking to Stig and Andrei and only smiled briefly and in an un-lit-up way at Elissa who was, all the same, one of the brightest of the younger Councillors and had produced some exceedingly good ideas while business was on. And was about to go off on a dangerous mission.

And not so long ago, thought Ric, as history time goes, Elissa would doubtless have thrown herself at me, yes, me! Oh, with legs and arms open, those breasts pointing like greedy animals and I would have responded and scrambled under her – no, over – and got into her, how revolting, and she would have sucked me in and held me – no, I can't think of it! He looked for relief at gentle, slender, narrow-shouldered Hiji all in black but for his silver badge. Yes, it had been like that, and the women giving birth, popping the new lives out, over-populating, until at last it was realized that attraction between the sexes was only a snare and an aggression; the real thing was man to man and woman to woman. There alone was love. Ric believed deeply in love; it was strength; it was part of the Code. But, in the old inter-sex pattern, it had always led to violence and pain. Students of historical literature, as he had been, understood this well. Tragedy, tragedy. Shakespeare, Molière, Tolstoy, the lot, right up to the great break-through.

One saw these tragedies re-enacted among the Professorials and other dissenters. They agreed with the code in principle. How not? In fact the Cloning was due to Professorials. It could never have been done without the work of the biologists Quereshi and the great Sen and, earlier, Watson and Mitchison. But the Professorials had been unwilling to accept the inevitable new morality of Solution Three, essential to human survival, and, according to the Code, force was not to be used on them. Only understanding. Some of them, naturally, had come into a state of agreement and even enthusiasm, but the majority of the non-clone births were among this class. There were still, no doubt, quite a few elsewhere, but the absolute numbers dropped year by year. People do not on the whole break their customs and social morality and face the disapproval of their peer group for something as unimportant as inter-sexual love.

There had of course been some intensive school-age hormone and psychological treatment during the years of population crisis. It could be laid on more subtly now if there seemed to be a relaxing of social imperatives in any group. The children of inter-sex marriages were carefully watched and, if necessary, treated. All this was one of the important monitoring jobs for the members of the Council who were away on their duties all about the world. There might, for instance, be a recrudescence in India, or, more rarely, Africa, usually associated with some religious revival. So far, all had been contained.

And there was Ric's colleague and friend Jussie, approaching Elissa. Really, really! Though of course in a way highly suitable. Nothing to be shocked at, only Ric just couldn't imagine the attraction. After a little they appeared hand in hand and Jussie was gently pulling Elissa towards the sauna room. And they would roll around on the floor no doubt and take the birch twigs to one another and tickle up one another's nipples and those other parts which he had been shown as video-tactiles in his adolescence, made to touch, and found as revolting as half decayed meat. Well, well, if they enjoyed it, perhaps one should think no more about it. It was all right and proper.

Source: Naomi Mitchison, *Solution Three*, Dennis Dobson, 1975.

Mixed Motherhood

Woman on the Edge of Time (1979) by Marge Piercy (b.1937) is typical of modern idealistic feminist utopias in combining peaceful anarchy, ecological reverence, sexual permissiveness, and the elimination of what the West has generally understood as the male. The central character is one of society's victims, Connie Ramos, a thirty-seven-year-old Mexican-American woman with a history of crime and violence, currently detained in a New York mental hospital. By exercising her mediumistic power, she makes contact with a civilization in the year 2137, and learns to live in its space-time.

The dwellers in this utopia bewilderingly unite simple, peasant life-style with advanced technological gadgetry. They live in villages made of recycled junk – scavenged wood, bricks, cement blocks. For air-travel they potter about in what seem to be balloons fitted with small, quiet propellers. They grow vegetables, keep goats and free-range chickens, and have (so far as we can tell) almost no industry. The only factory we see makes pillows and padded jackets, and runs on methane from composting waste. Their other energy sources are sun, wind, waves, rivers and 'wood gas'.

Despite this seeming primitivism, however, they all wear micro-computers ('kenners') on their wrists, which give them instant access to encyclopaedic databases. They also wage constant sci-fi war with the wicked former rulers of the earth, largely composed of androids, robots and cybernauts (partly automated humans), who inhabit Antarctica, the moon and platforms in outer space.

Friendly relations with the natural world are important to them. They sing a song of thanks to every tree and bush they pick fruit from. They have learned to talk to animals by means of sign language, and on the rare occasions when they kill an animal for food (mostly they are vegetarian) they explain to it beforehand what they are going to do. It is not clear whether the animal has any chance of discussing the matter. The natural world is also regarded as a trial and a challenge. At about the age of thirteen every child is taken to a wilderness area, armed with knife, bow and arrows, and left alone for a week. If the child survives this rite of passage it is treated as an adult.

The community is ruled by a council, the members of which are chosen by lot and serve for one year. Selection by lot is favoured because it removes any sense of real superiority from those in authority. Leaders of work projects are also chosen by lot. So are judges and detectives, but these roles seldom need to be filled as there is little crime. Rape has not occurred within living memory, but murder and assault still sometimes happen. If found guilty the perpetrators are tattooed on the hand for identification purposes and sent to work in mines or on space stations. For a second offence they are executed. This severity towards violent criminals contrasts with the treatment of thieves. If you steal, everyone gives you presents, recognizing it as a sign that you feel neglected.

As far as possible, gender has been eliminated. It is hard to tell men and women apart, and language does not distinguish between them. 'Person' is used instead of the pronouns 'he' and 'she', and 'per' instead of 'him' and 'her'. There are no surnames or family names. Names are often chosen from the natural world (Jackrabbit, Peony) and you are free to change your name as often as you like. There are no restrictions whatever on sexual intercourse. Homosexual or heterosexual, promiscuous or otherwise, you are free to follow your inclinations. Children aged six or seven are seen trying to have sex, and no one interferes. There is no mention of birth control, but it must be practised, for natural childbirth is a thing of the past. Arrangements for reproduction and parenting are the most advanced aspects of this utopia. The human hatchery, which in Huxley's *Brave New World* (see p. 447) was dystopian, is here the community's proudest showpiece, and Connie is taken to see it.

The yellow building was odd, like a lemon mushroom pushing out of the ground. Decorated with sculpted tree shapes, it was windowless and faintly hummed. She realized that except for the creaking of windmills, this was the first sound of machinery she had heard here. Indeed, the door sensed them and opened, admitting them to an antechamber, then sliding shut to trap them between inner and outer doors in a blue light.

'What is all this?' She shifted nervously.

'Disinfecting. This is the brooder, where our genetic material is stored. Where the embryos grow.'

The inner doors zipped open, but into space that looked more like a big aquarium than a lab. The floor was carpeted in a blue print and music was playing, strange to her ears but not unpleasant. A big black man leaning comfortably on a tank painted over with eels and water lilies waved to them. 'I'm Bee. Be guest! Be guest to what I comprend [understand] was a nightmare of your age.'

'Bottle babies!'

'No bottles involved. But fasure [certainly] we're all born from here.' . . .

Bee smiled. He was a big-boned, well-muscled man with some fat around his midriff, and he moved more slowly than Luciente [Connie's guide], with the majesty and calm of a big ship. He steered placidly among the strange apparatus, the tanks and machines and closed compartments, something that beat slowly against the wall like a great heart, the padded benches stuck here and there. Either Bee was bald or he shaved his head, and the sleeves of his rose work shirt were rolled up to reveal on each bicep a tattoo – though the colors were more subtle and the drawing finer than any she had seen. On his left arm he had, not the cartoon of a bee, but a Japanese-looking drawing of a honeybee in flight. On his right he wore a shape something like a breaking wave. 'Here embryos are growing almost ready to birth. We do that at ninemonth plus two or three weeks. Sometimes we wait tenmonth. We find that extra time gives us stronger babies.' He pressed a panel and a door slid aside, revealing seven human babies joggling slowly upside down, each in a sac of its own inside a larger fluid receptacle.

Connie gaped, her stomach also turning slowly upside down. All in a sluggish row, babies bobbed. Mother the machine. Like fish in the aquarium at Coney Island. Their eyes were closed. One very dark female was kicking. Another, a pink male, she could see clearly from the oversize penis, was crying. Languidly they drifted in a blind school. Bee pressed something and motioned her to listen near the port. The heartbeat, voices speaking.

'That can't be the babies talking!'

'No!' Bee laughed. 'Though they make noise enough. Music, voices, the heartbeat, all these sounds they can hear.'

'Light, Sacco-Vanzetti. How's it flying?' Luciente said.

The kid was maybe sixteen. Lank brown hair in braids, swarthy skin, the kid wore a yellow uniform much like everybody's work clothes. 'Is this the woman from the past?'

Luciente performed the introductions.

Sacco-Vanzetti, whose sex she could not tell, stared. 'Did you bear alive?'

'Come on Sacco-Vanzetti, don't be narrow!' Luciente made a face.

'If you mean have I had a baby, yes.' She stuck out her chin.

'Was there a lot of blood?'

'I was knocked out, so how do I know?'

'Was it exciting? Did it feel sexual?'

'It hurt like hell,' Connie snapped, turning back to the wall of babies. 'Were you all born from this crazy machine?'

'Almost everybody is now,' the kid said. 'I have to go down to threemonth to check the solutions. I'll be in touch. If you remember more about live bearing, I'd be feathered to hear about it.' The kid went out.

Bee closed the viewing port. 'Wamponaug Indians are the source of our culture. Our past. Every village has a culture.' . . .

Bee beamed, ambling toward another tank where he opened the viewing port. 'I have a street friend living in Cranberry dark as I am and her tribe is Harlem-Black. I could move there anytime. But if you go over, you won't find everybody black-skinned like her and me, any more than they're all tall or all got big feet.' He paused, looking intently at a small embryo, fully formed and floating just at his shoulder level. 'At grandcil – grand council – decisions were made forty years back to breed a high proportion of darker-skinned people and to mix the genes well through the population. At the same time, we decided to hold on to separate cultural identities. But we broke the bond between genes and culture, broke it forever. We want there to be no chance of racism again. But we don't want the melting pot where everybody ends up with thin gruel. We want diversity, for strangeness breeds richness.'

'It's so . . . invented. Artificial. Are there black Irishmen and black Jews and black Italians and black Chinese?'

'Fasure, how not? When you grow up, you can stick to the culture you were raised with or you can fuse into another. But the one we were raised in usually has a . . . sweet meaning to us.' . . .

'I don't think I want to look at any younger . . . babies.' The little third-month child the doctor had shown her in the basin. Her stomach lurched. 'I don't feel too good.'

'We'll leave.' Bee took her arm. 'Maybe it's the filtered air? Grasp, the plasm is precious. Life flows through here for sixteen villages in all, the whole township.'

Outside she took a deep breath of salty air and detached herself from Bee.

'You saying there's no racism left? Paradise on earth, all God's children are equal?'

'Different tribes have different rites, but god is a patriarchal concept.' Luciente took Bee's arm and hers. 'Our mems [family members], our children, our friends include people of differing gene mixes. Our mothers also.'

'But Bee's kids would be black. Yours would be brown.'

'My child Innocente has lighter skin than you do.' Bee stopped to admire a walk lined with rosebushes blooming in yellows and oranges and creamy whites. 'There's no genetic bond – or if there is, we don't keep track of it.'

'Then this kid isn't really your child?'

'I *am* Innocente's mother.'

'How can men be mothers! How can some kid who isn't related to you be your child?' She broke free and twisted away in irritation. The pastoral clutter of the place began to infuriate her, the gardens everyplace, the flowers, the damned sprightly-looking chickens underfoot.

Luciente urged her along. 'We're walking Bee back to the lab. Where I'd be with the rest of our plant genetics base except for you. Bee and I work together. Maybe that's why we've been sweet friends so long, twelve years already.'

'I thought it's cause I'm too lazy to run from you the way any sane lug would. I never noticed other cores who worked in the same base stuck so long.'

'We're so ill suited we can't give up. Connie, apple blossom, listen to me – '

'Be on guard when Luci calls you soft names.' Bee managed to saunter more slowly than they walked and yet keep up.

'It was part of women's long revolution. When we were breaking all the old hierarchies. Finally there was that one thing we had to give up too, the only power we ever had, in return for no more power for anyone. The original production: the power to give birth. Cause as long as we were biologically enchained, we'd never be equal. And males never would be humanized to be loving and tender. So we all became mothers. Every child has three. To break the nuclear bonding.'

[479]

'Three! That makes no sense! Three mothers!'

The system, Connie learns, is that when you feel sufficiently motherly you find two other people (men or women) similarly disposed and apply, with them, to have a child. The brooder then produces one. The old idea of the family, with biological parents and blood relationships, has been entirely displaced, in the interest of ironing out gender differences. Breast-feeding, as Connie observes, is not left to the female mothers only.

The infants lay in low cradles with slatted sides that moved on runners to and fro. Connie counted five babies, including one yelling its lungs out, and then three empty cradles, also rocking.

Barbarossa burst in, out of breath. 'I hear you, I hear you. You almost blew the kenner off my wrist, you rascal! What a pair of lungs.' He picked up the crying baby. 'They can hear you ten miles out on the shelf farm, you hairy little beast!' He sat down with the baby on a soft padded bench by the windows and unbuttoned his shirt. Then she felt sick.

He had breasts. Not large ones. Small breasts, like a flat-chested woman temporarily swollen with milk. Then with his red beard, his face of a sunburnt forty-five-year-old man, stern-visaged, long-nosed, thin-lipped, he began to nurse. The baby stopped wailing and begun to suck greedily. An expression of serene enjoyment spread over Barbarossa's intellectual schoolmaster's face. He let go of the room, of everything, and floated. Her breasts ached with remembrance. She had loved breast-feeding – that deep-down warm milky connection that seemed to start in her womb and spread up through her trunk into her full dark-nippled breasts . . .

She felt angry. Yes, how dare any man share that pleasure. These women thought they had won, but they had abandoned to men the last refuge of women. What was special about being a woman here? They had given it all up, they had let men steal from them the last remnants of ancient power, those sealed in blood and in milk.

'I suppose you do it all with hormones,' she said testily.

'At least two of the three mothers agree to breast-feed. The way we do it, no one has enough alone, but two or three together share breast-feeding.'

'Why bother? Don't tell me you couldn't make formula?'

'But the intimacy of it! We suspect loving and sensual enjoyment are rooted in being held and sucking and cuddling.'

In time Bee and Connie become lovers. However, when she has (or dreams she has) a child, it is not in the old biological way.

She was watching a birth. The three mothers were ritually bathed in a sauna-sweat house and, dressed in red, they were brought in a procession of family and friends to the brooder. One of the mothers was Sojourner, the old person from Luciente's family with eyes of coal chips, one of the mothers was Jackrabbit, and the third was her. They held each other's hands and she walked in the middle. The robes were heavy, encrusted with embroidery. On hers were doves and eggs. Everyone was carrying bouquets of late summer flowers, asters and phlox and white lilies streaked with crimson and wide as plates that lay down a heavy scent, bouquets of marigold and nasturtium.

Some were drumming, and toward the back of the procession a child was playing one of those flutes that sounded poignant and sad to her, although the melody was gay enough. Her heart felt too large under the robe. She gripped the hands of her comothers tight, tight, till Sojourner gently asked her not to squeeze so much, while Jackrabbit gave her grip for grip. Just behind them Luciente beat on her carved drums a syncopated galloping march. Bee nodded to her, carrying a sheaf of yellow and red and bronze bold-faced sunflowers.

As they came to the brooder, everyone fell back except the three of them, who entered. They stood under the sterilizer, helping each other out of the robes and hanging them on hooks to the side. Naked they went into the center chamber, where Barbarossa, the birther, was waiting for them. Dressed in his brooder uniform of yellow and blue, he embraced each. As she looked down at herself, she felt her breasts, swollen from the shots, already dribbling colostrum. She and Jackrabbit were to breast-feed. Sojourner explained she had decided not to try it.

'I didn't have my first child till I was fifty-five,' she said. 'I fought in the battle of Space Platform Alpha. And in the battle of Arlington and Fort Bragg. Long, long before we had brooders, I had myself sterilized so that I wouldn't be tempted to turn aside from the struggle. I thought I had left my sex behind me. Now I am seventy-four and my family does me the honor of believing there's enough life in me to make a mother a second time.'

Now all three knelt, the old woman getting down slowly but stubbornly on her gnarled knees. Barbarossa stood before them like a priest officiating at Mass. 'Do you, Sojourner, desire this baby to be born?'

'I, Sojourner, desire to mother this child.'

'Do you, Jackrabbit, desire this baby to be born?' and then, 'Do you, Connie, desire this baby to be born?'

She said softly, 'I do. I, Connie, desire to mother this child.'

Barbarossa turned. The gawky teenage assistant she had met in the brooder was delivering the baby from the strange contracting canal while Barbarossa stood by to tie the cord and hold it squalling up, screaming and squirming. A small black girl whose skin gleamed waxy and bright.

'Do you, Sojourner, accept this child, Selma, to mother, to love, and then to let go?'

Sojourner held out her old black arms for the baby, nestling it to her. 'I'll mother you, love you, and let you go, Selma.'

'Do you, Jackrabbit, accept this child to mother, to love, and then to let go?'

Jackrabbit received the baby from Sojourner. 'I'll mother you, love you, and let you go, Selma.'

At last Connie held the baby and its small ruby-red mouth closed around her nipple, sucking deep. Black, like Bee: she was sure she was given this baby from her time with Bee, a baby black and velvety with huge eyes to drink in the world.

Source: Marge Piercy, *Woman on the Edge of Time*, Women's Press, 1979.

Having What You Want

The most brilliant and the most profound of modern British utopias is the last chapter of Julian Barnes's *A History of the World in 10½ Chapters* (1989), entitled 'The Dream'.

I dreamt that I woke up. It's the oldest dream of all, and I've just had it. I dreamt that I woke up.

I was in my own bed. That seemed a bit of a surprise, but after a moment's thought it made sense. Who else's bed should I wake up in? I looked around and I said to myself, Well, well, well. Not much of a thought, I admit. Still, do we ever find the right words for the big occasions?

There was a knock on the door and a woman came in, sideways and backwards at the same time. It should have looked awkward but it didn't; no, it was all smooth and stylish. She was carrying a tray, which was why she'd come in like that. As she turned, I saw she was wearing a uniform of sorts. A nurse? No, she looked more like a stewardess on some airline you've never heard of. 'Room service,' she said with a bit of a smile, as if she wasn't used to providing it, or I wasn't used to expecting it; or both.

'Room service?' I repeated. Where I come from something like that only happens in films. I sat up in bed, and found I didn't have any clothes on. Where'd my pyjamas gone? That was a change. It was also a change that when I sat up in bed and realized she could see me bollock-naked to the waist, if you understand me, I didn't feel at all embarrassed. That was good.

'Your clothes are in the cupboard,' she said. 'Take your time. You've got all day. And,' she added with more of a smile, 'all tomorrow as well.'

I looked down at my tray. Let me tell you about that breakfast. It was the breakfast of my life and no mistake. The grapefruit, for a start. Now, you know what a grapefruit's like: the way it spurts juice down your shirt and keeps slipping out of your hand unless you hold it down with a fork or something, the way the flesh always sticks to those opaque membranes and then suddenly comes loose with half the pith attached, the way it always tastes sour yet makes you feel bad about piling sugar on the top of it. That's what a grapefruit's like, right? Now let me tell you about *this* grapefruit. Its flesh was pink for a start, not yellow, and each segment had already been carefully freed from its clinging membrane. The fruit itself was anchored to the dish by some prong or fork through its bottom, so that I didn't need to hold it down or even touch it. I looked around for the sugar, but that was just out of habit. The taste seemed to come in two parts – a sort of awakening sharpness followed quickly by a wash of sweetness; and each of those little globules (which were about the size of tadpoles) seemed to burst separately in my mouth. That was the grapefruit of my dreams, I don't mind telling you.

Like an emperor, I pushed aside the gutted hull and lifted a silver dome from a crested plate. Of course I knew what would be underneath. Three slices of grilled streaky bacon with the gristle and rind removed, the crispy fat all glowing like a bonfire. Two eggs, fried, the yolk looking milky because the fat had been properly spooned over it in the cooking, and the outer edges of the white trailing off into filigree gold braid. A grilled tomato I can only describe in terms of what it wasn't. It wasn't a collapsing cup of stalk, pips, fibre and red water, it was something compact, sliceable, cooked equally all the way through, and tasting – yes, this is the thing I remember – tasting of tomato. The sausage: again, not a tube of lukewarm horse-meat stuffed into a French letter, but dark umber and succulent . . . a . . . a sausage, that's the only word for it. All the others, the ones I'd thought I'd enjoyed in my previous life, were merely practising to be like this; they'd been auditioning – and they wouldn't get the part, either. There was a little crescent-shaped side-plate with a crescent-shaped silver lid. I raised it: yes, there were my bacon rinds, separately grilled, waiting to be nibbled.

The toast, the marmalade – well, you can imagine those, you can dream what they were like for yourselves. But I must tell you about the teapot. The tea, of course, was the real thing, tasting as if it had been picked by some rajah's personal entourage. As for the teapot . . . Once, years ago, I went to Paris on a package holiday. I wandered off from the others and walked around where the smart people live. Where they shop and eat, anyway. On a corner I passed a café. It didn't look particularly grand, and just for a minute I thought of sitting down there. But I didn't, because at one of the tables I saw a man having tea. As he poured himself a fresh cup, I spotted a little gadget which seemed to me almost a definition of luxury: attached to the teapot's spout, and dangling by three delicate silver chains, was a strainer. As the man raised the pot to its pouring angle, this strainer swung outwards to catch the leaves. I couldn't believe that serious thought had once gone into the matter of how to relieve this tea-drinking gentleman of the incredible burden of picking up a normal strainer with his free hand. I walked away from that café feeling a bit self-righteous. Now, on my tray, I had a teapot bearing the insignia of some chic Parisian café. A strainer was attached to its spout by three silver chains. Suddenly, I could see the point of it.

It soon becomes clear that the narrator is in heaven: a heaven where every wish is instantly gratified. He cruises on an electric buggy round heaven's commodity-crammed supermarket, buying up vast cargoes of luxury, with no spending limit. He meets all the famous people he wants. He has sex every night with beautiful women. When he plays golf, he can hole in one every time. The newspapers carry just the news he wants (e.g., that his team, Leicester City, have won the FA Cup; that doctors have found a cure for cancer). And all this can – does – go on for centuries, he is assured. After a time he starts to worry about totally senseless things (his golf, his bank account – though he does not have a bank account). So he consults his carer, Margaret.

'I don't want to sound ungrateful,' I said cautiously, 'but where's God?'

'God. Do you want God? Is that what you want?'

'Is it a question of what I want?'

'That's exactly what it's a question of. Do you want God?'

'I suppose I thought it wasn't that way round. I suppose I thought either there would be one or there wouldn't be one. I'd find out what the case was. I didn't think it depended on me in any way.'

'Of course it does.'

'Oh.'

[485]

'Heaven is democratic these days,' she said. Then added, 'Or at least, it is if you want it to be.'

'What do you mean, democratic?'

'We don't impose Heaven on people any more,' she said. 'We listen to their needs. If they want it, they can have it; if not, not. And then of course they get the sort of Heaven they want.'

'And what sort do they want on the whole?'

'Well, they want a continuation of life, that's what we find. But . . . better, needless to say.'

'Sex, golf, shopping, dinner, meeting famous people and not feeling bad?' I asked, a bit defensively.

'It varies. But if I were being honest, I'd say that it doesn't vary all that much.'

From Margaret he learns, too, that there is death in heaven.

'Everyone has the option to die off if they want to.'

'I never knew that.'

'No. There are bound to be a few surprises. Did you really want to be able to predict it all?'

'And how do they die? Do they kill themselves? Do you kill them?'

Margaret looked a bit shocked at the crassness of my idea. 'Goodness, no. As I said, it's democratic nowadays. If you want to die off, you do. You just have to want to for long enough and that's it, it happens. Death isn't a matter of hazard or gloomy inevitability, the way it is the first time round. We've got free will sorted out here, as you may have noticed.'

I wasn't sure I was taking all this in. I'd have to go away and think about it. 'Tell me,' I said, 'these problems I've been having with the golf and the worrying. Do other people react like that?'

'Oh yes. We often get people asking for bad weather, for instance, or for something to go wrong. They miss things going wrong. Some of them ask for pain.'

'For pain?'

'Certainly. Well, you were complaining the other day about not feeling so tired that – as I think you put it – you just want to die. I thought that was an interesting phrase. People ask for pain, it's not so extraordinary. We've had them requesting operations, as well. I mean, not just cosmetic ones, real ones.'

'Do they get them?'

'Only if they really insist. We try to suggest that wanting an operation is really a sign of something else. Normally they agree with us.'

'And what percentage of people take up the option to die off?'

She looked at me levelly, her glance telling me to be calm. 'Oh, a hundred per cent, of course. Over many thousands of years, calculated by old time, of course. But yes, everyone takes the option, sooner or later.'

'So it's just like the first time round? You always die in the end?'

'Yes, except don't forget the quality of life here is much better. People die when they decide they've had enough, not before. The second time round it's altogether more satisfying because it's willed.' She paused, then added, 'As I say, we cater for what people want.'

I hadn't been blaming her. I'm not that sort. I just wanted to find out how the system worked. 'So . . . even people, religious people, who come here to worship God throughout eternity . . . they end up throwing in the towel after a few years, hundred years, thousand years?'

'Certainly. As I said, there are still a few Old Heaveners around, but their numbers are diminishing all the time.'

'And who asks for death soonest?'

'I think *ask* is the wrong word. It's something you want. There aren't any mistakes here. If you want it enough, you die, that's always been the ruling principle.'

'So?'

'So. Well, I'm afraid – to answer your question – that the people who ask for death earliest are a bit like you. People who want an eternity of sex, beer, drugs, fast cars – that sort of thing. They can't believe their good luck at first, and then, a few hundred years later, they can't believe their bad luck. That's the sort of people they are, they realize. They're stuck with being themselves. Millennia after millennia of being themselves. They tend to die off soonest.'

Source: Julian Barnes, *A History of the World in 10½ Chapters*, Jonathan Cape, 1989.

The Lottery State

Modern political scientists have proposed that choosing representatives by lot might be a fairer way of distributing political power in a democracy than our present methods. In her book *Justice by Lottery* (1992), Barbara Goodwin, Professor of Politics at the University of East Anglia, pursues this idea, pointing out that distribution of land and other privileges by lottery goes back to classical and biblical times. Her first chapter takes the form of a utopia (or dystopia) inspired in part by Jorge Luis Borges's story 'Lottery in Babylon' in his collection *Labyrinths*.

TENDAY, TERTIA, DECADE 8

I, Fortunata Smith (called 'Lucky' by my friends), having drawn a five-year ticket as Public Relations (External) Exec, have been allocated an immense task – no less a task than to prepare the voiceover for the new in-flight videdisk which will be played to visiting foreign dignitaries travelling here on the orbishuttle. My commentary must inform them frankly and honestly of all that is best in our social and political system. My last two allocations, as a plumber and as community relations animator in the Northern sector of the London floodplain, have scarcely fitted me for this ambitious endeavour, but I was lucky enough to draw a polyversity place in my youth, and I hope that my studies of logic and rhetoric will aid me now. But it is with great humility and trepidation that I embark on this enterprise, and I hope that the eminent visitors (and my own superiors!) will look leniently on any shortcomings in my commentary. Forsfortuna help me!

Esteemed visitors, welcome aboard the superspeed orbishuttle flight to Aleatoria. Aleatoria is an island off the west coast of Europe, with a population of 200 million. Most of its inhabitants are devotees of Forsfortuna, but there is a substantial Muslim minority. The Christian and Hindu sects were suppressed long ago because their tenets about reward and reincarnation were incompatible with the prevailing ideology. Aleatoria is a republic. It used to be called the United Kingdom, until the signs of disunity became too pressing to ignore. The social cleavages which abounded under the then system of liberal-democratic capitalism eventually brought about a change of political system, and with it a change in our dear country's name. The Official Chronologers have recorded all these changes and how they came about, and when you disembark you will be presented with a Souvenir Posterity Videdisk which will show you more of our history. But I am going to describe our present state to you. I should say, however, that the Changes involved great disruption. There were periods of dictatorship and oligarchy in the late twentieth century and early this century, interspersed with intervals of complete chaos. After many years of these vicissitudes, a member of the then ruling junta discovered, quite by chance, a revolutionary text in the dusty diskstacks of the National Library – a book called *Justice by Lottery*. At that time, people in general wanted to go back to a democratic form of government, and they favoured some version of neo-socialism which would be more socially just than the crypto-fascism that had oppressed them for some years. In fact, the junta was very happy to abdicate because the housing riots had reached anarchic proportions and the paras were rampaging all over the country, and making the junta very unpopular. When Adolfa Qdfi (as the junta member was called) described the lottery system proposed in the book to her co-juntees, they agreed that it pointed them to an excellent escape route from their unpalatable situation. They immediately announced that there would be a referendum to approve a new constitution which would save the country from ruin. Then they saturated the population with pro-lottery propaganda. For months, the streetscreens and airwaves were monopolized by mathsists, philos and juntees explaining how just and impartial a lottery society would be. When the referendum was finally held, the great majority agreed that the new Constitution should be the Total Social Lottery. (Those who disagreed were given compulsory exit visas.) So that is how the Great Change came about. To celebrate the new Constitution, we renamed our country Aleatoria. You can see, then, that the system that I am about to describe is the direct result of the people's choice.

You would probably like to know about our political system first of all. We call it 'neo-democracy' because it differs in important respects from the representative democracy of earlier, liberal times, and from the one-party democracies which still survive in some backward – I mean, high-potential – parts of the globe. The idea of a representative body chosen by lot came from the book which had started the Change, which now forms the preamble of our revered Constitution, and from another book called *A Citizen Legislature* [by E. Callenbach and M. Phillips, 1985], which was found on the same disk. The authors of that, as every schoolchild knows, proposed that there should be a randomly selected House of Representatives in what was then called the United States of America (now Luckyland). Such a body would – they said – represent all the pressure groups and interest groups which existed in those days. They also said that selection by lot would give fairer representation to women, blacks, Hispanics and other groups which were politically marginalized by their money-dominated political system. The whole book was based on a notion of 'typical representation', rather than representation via electoral choice. Perhaps I should explain what that means, for the benefit of those of you from high-potential countries. If someone were typical of a number of groups in society (for example, if she were a parent, a keen spaceball player, a manual worker, a pro-Earth agitator, and so on) then she would be likely to promote the interests of those sorts of people spontaneously, even though no one had elected her to do that. Most importantly, the authors of the book said, she would not have to spend her time trying to extract money from corporations for her next election campaign, or pandering to voters. She would have more time to spend on thinking and debating, and she could freely promote the policies that she believed in, and be truthful about her views. The juntees found all these arguments so convincing that all the proposals were incorporated into the new Constitution. Aleatoria adopted a neo-democratic system where typical representatives are chosen randomly. These photos of our current Lotreps officiating at the summer Forsfortuna festival show you that we have representatives of every age and race.

The Lotreps serve for a five-year period and cannot be reselected. In the House of Lots, they determine the policies in the context of which the various distributive lotteries will operate. They make decisions on the economy, population levels, pest and dustbowl control, and all the other issues that concern governments – and very little, we hold, is not the concern of government. They can introduce new lotteries for the distribution of scarce luxuries, like the recent one for dog ownership, and eliminate or reconstitute lotteries which are failing to distribute justly.

Every two years the Lotreps choose by lot a new executive committee which is called the government. Lottery-selection eliminates the formation of parties, and encourages genuine debate and voting according to one's conscience. In the House of Lots, difficult issues, where the pros and cons are equally weighted, are decided by a throw of dice.

The Aleatorian system is nothing if not consistent. Just as the task of government is allocated randomly, so are the various public duties which any state requires to be carried out. The bureaucracy, the judiciary, our juries, the police, and our fighting forces are all composed of people chosen by lot for a five-year period. The advantages are similar to those which we enjoy in our Lotrep system. No one holds office long enough to develop a professional ethos, or to invent professional secrets, or to be corrupted. The principle which one of our State Heroes, Aristotle, thought characteristic of democracy – 'rule and be ruled in turn' – makes the individuals who fulfil these functions far more responsive to the needs of the rest of the population, from which they themselves are only temporarily set aside.

I admit that we are not totally innovative in this approach to universal public service. In the past, the United Kingdom and some other countries had jurors chosen at random. This apparently reflected the aspiration that people should be judged by their peers, although it never lived up to this in reality. There was also a small, mountainous country in Central Europe, now part of Lotteria, which had a people's army, in which everyone served annually for a limited period. This and the other conscripted armies of the last century – the Age of Warfare, as we call it – foreshadowed our Lotarmy, although the principle involved in those days was rotation of this disagreeable burden by age rather than by random selection. Luckyland used random selection for the draft during the Vietwar, I believe, but only those who were young were eligible. How superior our system is! Everyone runs an equal risk of the call to service, unless ill-health or good luck disbars her. This film of the great military parade last Septua shows how smart our Lotsoldiers are, even the octogenarians. Of course, the officers in the Lotarmy and the sea, air and space forces are all chosen by lot for a two-year period, which prevents any hierarchy from developing – although some critics allege that our near disaster in the second war against our inveterate enemy Voluntaria was due to incompetent and inexperienced commanders.

Our Lotpolice also consists of people chosen at random. The idea of a people's police force was sometimes advanced by radical critics of the police in the Bad Times; they thought it a preferable alternative to the highly professionalized and unaccountable police force of their time, which acted according to private norms and was suspicious of – and I generally disliked by – the public which it was intended to serve. As we have discovered, policing becomes a very different activity when it is carried out by people who will soon revert to being members of the general public . . .

The major achievement of the Total Social Lottery system (usually called the TSL) is the demystification of all our state institutions, the dispersal of power and the breakdown of elites. An incidental benefit has been the abolition of the old oppressive principle of confidentiality which used to bedevil state institutions, although some intemperate critics would say that this hampers police and military operations and has impeded the Lotpolice's drive to eliminate subversives. However, no one could deny that the executive, judicial and defensive branches of the state are far more 'typically' representative than those of the past, and closer to the people. At the start of the TSL, the public services underwent deprofessionalization on a large scale. (In fact, the word 'professional' is now rather archaic, and usually refers to someone who is very enthusiastic about a hobby, or a hobbyhorse.) To take one example: the selection of judges and advocates by lot produced a radical change in the legal system, since legal principles and arguments had to become comprehensible to people with no training at all. The same was true of the principles of administration, policing and warfare. At the same time, the educational effect of mass participation in the country's vital institutions has been considerable. Most adults now understand how all the organs of state work, through their own experience and the shared experience of friends and relatives who have performed these various public duties. Our citizens are not alienated from any of the state's institutions, although a few mysteriously continue to harbour grudges against its operations . . .

The vast majority of jobs are allocated and regularly reallocated at random by the Joblottery. Once again, each new job includes a training period of something between a few days and six months. The initial introduction of the Joblottery was contentious; it almost produced a counter-revolution because people in those days were convinced that in an advanced industrial economy many jobs, especially high-income ones, required people with credentials, expertise, and a certain level of intelligence. But, to their amazement, many of the jobs which had formerly been considered 'expert' or 'professional' were found to be capable of performance by people of so-called average intelligence and ability, after an intensive training period. We also discovered that people performed better in jobs of limited duration – no one holds a job for more than five years, of course. In fact, they get greater work satisfaction, because they actually enjoy the learning process. So all non-expert jobs are distributed in this way . . .

The Aleatorian system overturns the system of lifetime job allocations which used to be common in industrialized societies, which meant that some people were destined from birth for comfortable and lucrative professions, while others suffered a lifetime of manual drudgery or routine clerical monotony . . .

Some of you will probably be dying to ask the obvious question: 'What about jobs which really require skills and expertise?' I will give you the Aleatorian answer. In the early debates on the Joblottery, many Lotreps said that they did not wish to be examined by Lotdoctors, still less have their teeth filled by Lotdentists. Initially, the need for people with such specialized skills was a problem for the Aleatorian system, given its strong impetus towards equalization of status. People realized early on that even if they could democratize work and put an end to phoney professionalism, some skilled individuals would still have to undertake lengthy training and spend their whole lifetimes in one kind of work, to meet economic and human needs. Medical practitioners and scientists were the examples always given; looking back now, you can see that the argument reflected contemporary obsessions about the importance of health and scientific innovation. We now regard those obsessions as outdated because of our self-help and self-heal mode of living. But initially the Lotreps decided that some occupations would be treated as specialist, *pro tem*, and that their practitioners should be able to practise them for life.

The best compromise they could devise between this necessity and the lottery principle was that those in the so-called expert professions should spend one year in five or two months in every year doing some randomly assigned, non-expert work. Videdisks of the House of Lots debates on this vexing topic contain many references to a great Chinese guru called Mowzedoong, who believed that doctors and teachers should spend some time doing agricultural work. Apparently this belief made him unpopular, but it seems clear to me that this Mowzedoong hit on a very obvious antidote to professional elitism – as you can see from the fact that the early Aleatorians came to an identical conclusion.

We find that the time spent in non-expert work does not really disrupt the experts' activities, and it prevents them from becoming too proud or – as I said – elitist. It is healthy for an astro-neurologist to rub shoulders with ordinary people, we maintain. In fact, some experts actually volunteer for one or two five-year spells outside their profession to stop themselves becoming stale. This sort of opportunity was never available in pre-Change times because career specialization was reinforced by ambition and competition for success – more outdated ideas! The Mobility Draw for experts means that they are obliged to move geographically from time to time. Scientists have to change their polyversity every five or ten years, and doctors must go and practise in a new area. This prevents the development of favoured institutions and locales . . .

By now you will all be wondering about how people are paid for their work. The most contentious and vitriolic debates about the TSL centred on the constitutional principle that resources should be allocated to people randomly, regardless of contribution. The Founding Lotreps agreed that all work was of equal value to society, and that people – except experts – must be treated as fungible – that is, as interchangeable between occupations. One faction in the House of Lots, the Lotlabs, drew the logical conclusion that everyone should receive equal payment. Another group, the Lotanarchs, said that this covertly retained the discredited concept of reward for contribution, whereas the philosophy of the TSL excluded any such notion.

The two factions eventually agreed that there would be economic and social advantages in retaining a range of incomes which would be distributed randomly and reallocated every five years. One advantage was that this would maintain and boost the luxury sector of the economy and also promote the production of an interesting range of goods, thus giving individuals a variety of experiences. In short, their solution was aimed at retaining the 'rich tapestry of life', while ensuring that everyone spent some time enjoying the richer parts. The objection to luxury goods, palatial houses and expensive cars was not simply that they existed, but that they had always been the prerogative of the few. The farseeing Lotreps of the second decade came up with the revolutionary idea of the 'lifestyle package'. The lifestyle package links housing with income and preserves variety through differential allocations which are justly distributed by lottery.

Inclusion of housing, as well as income, in the lottery, was an important step, since inequalities in housing, ranging from luxury to hovel to homelessness, were among the most glaring in the old dispensation. Co-ordination of the Lifestyle Package Lottery with the Joblottery ensures that the best houses go with the least pleasant jobs, by way of compensation. So everyone changes job, income and house every five years on a random basis. Just as there is no longer any correlation between job and income, so there is none between job and lifestyle. Even if you win a Luxury Lifestyle Package, enabling you to run a yacht for five years, you still have to work.

In firms and corporations managers, and duties, are allocated by lot, reducing the gulf between managers and workers. It was feared at first that the absence of any correlation between productivity and reward (all incomes being random, and unrelated to the job) would reduce incentive. However, the planners of Aleatoria took a more optimistic view of human nature, and have been proved right. Aleatorians all regard themselves as workers contributing to the social whole.

The Aleatorian idealists argue that human nature is not competitive, possessive and self-interested, and that new circumstances will produce a new, social and cooperative kind of human being. The Founder of what is now Commielotland, Lenin, chastised utopians for putting off the revolution until human nature had changed – that is, for ever. He misunderstood the utopian way of thinking. We utopians believe that the revolution is itself a process of changing human nature. As the TSL improves in its operations, so will people's motivation, and then no more will be heard of self-interest or the profit motive. On a related issue, it may interest you to know that the Aleatorian economy is tax-evasion-proof. The needs of the state and the cost of all the services are calculated annually, and this sum is deducted from the state's expected income for the year: the remainder is then available for distribution in lifestyle packages. People pay no separate taxes. The prior deduction method means that when the economy is in a downturn everyone suffers fairly and equally. But, as you have seen from the film sequence of our busy factories and well-filled shop windows, our economy is far from depressed. The recent adoption of the TSL by those three great countries Commielotland, Lotteria and Luckyland has improved our economy greatly, because now our competing industries have the same efficiency coefficient. The more the lottery principle pervades the international community, the better it is for Aleatoria . . .

Soon after the Change, when the enthusiasm for the TSL was almost fanatical, a group of Lotreps advanced the proposition that sexual partners should be allocated by lot. The idea titillated their co-legislators and they introduced a twice-yearly Sexlot for partner allocation. I am too young to remember that time, but my mother participated in the Sexlot and she told me that at first they all found the sexual novelty and erotic possibilities it opened up very exciting. For a time, family life almost ceased and children were brought up haphazardly or in state institutions. But after a few years, random promiscuity – as its opponents called it – began to fall out of favour. People started to long for emotional stability, and they would sneak away from home to spend time with some former Lotpartner with whom they had fallen in love. The Lotpolice's enforcement of the decrees of the Sexlot became half-hearted. Two years later, there was a huge demonstration in Lot Square, where over a million people tore up their Sexlot tickets and ritually burned them. My mother was there, and she says that a number of Lotreps came out and joined the crowd. After that, people just ignored the Sexlot – they started living with their chosen partners, and reclaimed their children from the Childzoos, boarding schools and twenty-hour crèches. The new Lotreps quietly annulled the Sexlot decree, and that was the end of our sexual revolution!

But family life has not remained unchanged. When our population reached saturation point a few years ago, the Lotreps decided that population control was necessary and that any hardship this might involve should be fairly distributed. They introduced the Maternity

Lottery (which most people call the Poplot). This allocates the right to have a child to women at random, and the number of 'winning' tickets (or losing tickets, as some women regard them) is altered annually according to population needs. Not every woman of child-bearing age who draws a ticket wants to have a child, but most of them do so, out of a sense of duty to the state. The Lotpolice have been diligent to the point of oppressiveness in preventing any grey market developing for maternity tickets, and the system seems to work and to be accepted as the most just solution to our problems. We actually implement the Maternity Lottery in the following way: all our water supplies are impregnated with contraceptive drugs, and the women who draw a maternity ticket are given an antidote for a one-year period. This prevents anyone from trying to break the law by claiming that she became pregnant by accident. I think that the overpopulated high-potential countries might learn a lot from our system.

Aleatoria's economic success rests on its fine education system. Individuals take on multiple roles during their lives, which means that education must be universal, high-level and effective. We cannot, as previous societies did, sub-educate large numbers of people on the supposition that they are destined for dead-end jobs. We endorse the liberal John Stuart Mill's analysis of the close link between education, participation and good citizenship. We also argue that if people are going to be fungible in adult life with respect to occupation, it is illogical to give them differential degrees of knowledge. It is also true that education is seen as a social and personal good, and the people and their Lotreps want the best of it for themselves and their children. They would not tolerate scarce polyversity places being allocated by lot if we could instead make tertiary education universal. In the old neo-fascist United Kingdom and other elitist societies, the children of politicians were, magically, highly successful in gaining university places, so that the struggles and disappointments of those who failed were not insistently present in the minds of the policy-makers. Now they are: the Lotreps know that to draw a losing education ticket would blight the life of any child – including their own child. So their aim is universal education to the highest level.

The Founders of Aleatoria encountered a motley education system with a mixture of state schools and private schools; the teaching and conditions at the latter were usually far superior. The Lotreps decided that since it was impossible to transform the system overnight, the proper interim measure was to make the exclusive 'public school' education (as private education was called) available to everyone through a special rarity lottery. That used to be called the Pink Tie Lottery, and all sorts of children benefited from an education which had formerly been the exclusive province of the wealthy and the upper classes. After Decade 1, the state had poured so much money into all the other schools that they could offer equivalent facilities. At that point the Pink Tie Lottery was abolished, and the wearing of pink ties was made illegal.

Our current education system works like this: at secondary schools there is minimum differentiation between pupils, and we educate everyone to the same level. We have shown that people's innate abilities are approximately equal, and they can all reach a similar level of achievement if the teaching and learning facilities are good and there are no environmental factors such as deprivation to hold them back. Initially, people thought that universal tertiary education would be too expensive, so polyversity places were allocated by lot. But the Lotreps were worried that this would replicate the old elitist university system. They also worried that their own children might not draw winning tickets. So later, spurred on by enlightened self-interest, they rapidly took steps to introduce tertiary education for all. Our polyversities currently favour high-level generalist learning in the humanities and pure sciences, on the assumption that intensive in-job training will fill any gaps when someone draws a job ticket requiring special skills or knowledge.

In schools and colleges, competition and rivalry have died out, because students realize that their talents are not deserved, and that their successes are chance events. In keeping with this educational philosophy, the giving of grades and marks has ceased.

You will be interested to hear that criminal behaviour has largely been eradicated by our sane and fair system. The Lotpolice have good relations with the community, and criminals find it hard to escape the scrutiny of their neighbours (some of whom will be Lotpol-icepersons themselves), who will certainly inform the authorities about any antisocial behaviour. Detection rates are therefore very high. If someone is found guilty by the jury, she can opt to be sentenced by the Judgeperson, or she can ask for a Lot Penalty. In that case, her number is entered in the Penal Lot, which delivers 'losing tickets' with varying punitive values. She might draw five years in an open prison, or two years' hard labour in a penal factory, for example. Most people opt for a Lot Penalty . . .

Our crime rate is small compared with that of the Bad Times. Most crimes motivated by greed for property have disappeared, and people are no longer driven to crime by deprivation. People know that if they are relatively unlucky in the current draw, they may be luckier next time. They also know that those who have drawn the Luxury Package this time will not be privileged indefinitely. Where nothing is fixed and permanent, there is no cause for envy . . .

The effect of the TSL is to make people think: 'There but for the grace of the draw go I. And in the next lottery, I may well draw that unfortunate ticket myself.' This insight makes people more humble and more sympathetic to each other's problems. The Lotreps therefore make every endeavour to solve social problems such as bad housing and, if there are evils endemic to our society which cannot be eradicated, they make sure that these are suffered equally and randomly by everyone and do not always afflict the same unfortunate people, as they did in the past. The cycle of deprivation has been broken.

In a single generation, the TSL destroyed such ideas as status based on birth, breeding, occupation or other accidental qualities. The logic of the lottery is an egalitarian logic. It is blind to attributes such as gender and race, as well as class, and it has eliminated many invidious forms of discrimination which permeated the former system. The TSL has engendered a truly classless society. In Aleatoria, people see their temporary roles as a necessary part of the social whole, rather than regarding their jobs and houses as permanent, private territory, created or staked out by their personal efforts.

Source: Barbara Goodwin, *Justice by Lottery*, Harvester, 1992.

What Women Want

In 1995 the largest social audit of women's opinions ever conducted in the United Kingdom was undertaken by the Women's Communications Centre. Four million green and mauve postcards and forms were distributed around the country by hundreds of women's groups, trades unions, religious organizations, banks and shops. Ten thousand women replied in time for the United Nations Fourth World Conference on Women, held in Beijing. The question asked was simply 'What do you want?' These are some of the replies.

Clean air to breathe. Smiling faces in the street. The sea to be clean enough to swim in. Freedom to roam. Peace. Respect for the earth. A clean and happy world for my daughter to grow up in. Global love. Aah (what a beautiful dream). – *Sarah, Kent*

Less bare breasts for no good reason and much more male nudity, full frontal, to redress the to-date imbalance and exploitation of the female body. Also erections – women and girls should see/know these, often! Women's all is frequently seen in childbirth. – *Jenny, Chichester*

Contraceptive pills for men. – *Tina, London*

Freedom from the tyranny of thinness which is ever present all around us – in attitudes and all visual representations of the female form. – *H. D-L., Reading*

The freedom to enjoy pornography without being labelled by feminists as anti-feminist, which I am not. End to war, better education, freedom of speech, legalize drugs, no censorship, toleration between people, an end to sizeism, ageism, racism, and all other isms, an end to homelessness, an end to starvation, an end to poverty, a more equitable society, better working conditions for people, happiness, more green spaces – better public transport, more money, less pollution, better NHS, better and more human system of justice, freedom of sexuality, the right to be who and where you want to be. – *Rosanne, London*

I want love and peace and happiness, my dream to come true and to have people smile back at me as they ride on bikes and run through fields. I want sunshine and flowers, blue skies and survival. I want a relaxed body and calming sleep. I want sweet dreams and harmony. – *Anna, York*

Heard on radio – man who rapes man gets life, a man who rapes a woman gets, what? five to ten years max. What the hell is going on? Women judges for women rape victims. Life and castration for all rapists. – *Penny, Cirencester*

Boys brought up so they do not feel superior to girls or wish to be violent/aggressive towards them. Girls free and loving their physical and emotional strength and intelligence, knowing they are extraordinary for who they are. Then, they can make the rest happen! – *Fiona, London*

Good health. Space. Freedom to breast feed my daughter without criticism. Peace of mind. A garden. Cheap public transport. An end to exploitation. Decent housing for all. Jeremy Paxman, giftwrapped! – *Allie, Swindon*

Mental health. I want a ban on all media stories that cause distress and anguish unless
   (a) they give equal air time or column space to the women and children involved and
   (b) they tell me, the listener, what I can do about it. – *Linda, London*

To be free of what society expects. I would love to be married for only six months of the year and be by myself for the other six!! I would like men to be stronger than they appear to be nowadays. – *J. T., Coventry*

Obliteration of prejudice against sexuality, colour, gender and belief, and a world with reduced testosterone levels in men. – *Sarah, Portsmouth*

Women's biggest enemies are themselves. I have noticed my friends putting on the 'little girl' act in the company of men, goggling their eyes at them in a stupid way and pretending that they don't know anything, e.g. like spelling words wrong deliberately. Until this idiotic attitude stops, men are still going to treat women as morons. – *Sheila, Chelmsford*

Women-friendly restaurants; restaurants where one can buy a light meal after 5 p.m. or 5.30 p.m. Our cities and suburbs are filling up with pubs and boozers: what we need is more tea-houses. They would help civilize our society. – *M. D., London*

Compulsory community work for all of us. – *T. B-B., London NW3*

I want a change in the collective consciousness so that those with excessive greed or desire for power over others are recognized as 'sick' and in need of therapy. I want all babies and children to be seen as possible messiahs by the adults in their lives. I want more public celebration with dance, music, theatre etc. – *Madeline, Diss*

I want to feel secure when I walk the streets at night and know that my daughter can do the same. I want action not talk from the police and courts when thugs go around destroying private property and having sex in my garden (leaving the evidence behind!). I want my eldest girl not to be intimidated by being one of two females doing A-level computers at school. Finally, I want my wheelchair-bound daughter to have free access to buildings and not to have to ask for help all the time because of the steps. – *Evelyn, Rugby*

No pornography – no Page 3, even. – *Emily, London EC4*

It should be compulsory for local authorities to provide adequate numbers of public lavatories. Travelling in Britain is very difficult for women alone. There are fewer and fewer public loos; those that do exist close around 5 p.m. It's not easy for a woman alone to go into a pub – which is the only alternative. Sorry – this is a mundane 'wish' but one that would make a big difference to my freedom and confidence! – *Bronwen, Sale*

Each and every person should be educated from earliest childhood to be imaginative. Each person should be different from every other person. Each person should be interested in every other person (not just tolerant!) – *J. L. C., Sussex*

How is it that men get the world and I get this poxy little postcard? I want more power, more recognition that women are not a minority group, equal access. Equal pay, equal opportunities; to be patronized less. – *Sally, Bristol*

Less noise (roads, pop music). Less speed obsession. Less sport. Less 'news' dominance. More tranquillity. Women having female fun with other women. – *Sandra, Netherlands*

I want the right to decide whether I shall be kept alive or not – in consultation with doctors: if I should suffer a dense stroke I would rather they used their efforts to save someone else. – *Olive Jahn, researcher*

For machismo to wither and die. – *Lynette, Leeds*

More courtesy/consideration by, particularly male, drivers. Girls in senior schools shouldn't have to wear gym knickers – skirts would be preferable. My daughter is in lower school and feels very strongly. More and easier support from courts re divorce – so much red tape is costly. – *H. F., Solihull*

More trees for our future – we need to breathe, and we need forests and green places to put us in touch with the earth again. – *S. N., St Andrews*

An election where all the parties' candidates must be female to redress the balance of the last eighty years' male domination. – *Louise, London SW14*

I don't want equality – I want women replacing men in all the power positions in the world and a total ban on arms and related equipment manufacture throughout the world. That is the only way we are ever going to create peace and save the planet. – *Marion, Essex*

A world with far fewer humans, consuming far less, destroying other species and habitats less. A society in which kids can walk to school. All of which may mean more restraints on our activities and some of our 'freedoms'. – *Mrs V., Loughborough*

A return to a place where the feminine was revered and the universal worship of the goddess. – *Claire, Northern Ireland*

I want to ban the pictorial prostitution of women in advertising,

selling anything from newspapers to hub caps. It demeans all of us.
– *Patricia, Nottingham*

Silence. Space. Self-possession. A society that can no longer take
shopping seriously. – *Gillian, Durham*

Equality, fair pay and for men to have babies and periods. – *Marian,
Sutton Coldfield*

Source: *What Women Want*, edited by Bernadette Vallely, Virago, 1996.

Utopian Coursework

Many utopian writers would have benefited from training of the kind offered by Professor Jim Dator of the Department of Political Science, University of Hawaii.

Every semester for the past 12 years I have been asking students in my introductory futuristics classes to undertake something like the following assignment:

In 15 to 25 typewritten pages, indicate your design of the best, possible, real society you can imagine for some real place. In so doing, undertake the following:

1. State the goals of your society – what behaviours or conditions do you want to facilitate? Which do you want to discourage or prevent? Why?

2. Operationalize those goals. For example, if you say you want a society where everyone is equal, what do you mean by 'equal?' Everyone five feet tall? Everyone black? Everyone having the same, or a range of, income or political power (if the latter, how is that operationalized?) or what?

3. Devise alternate institutions that will help you achieve your goals. Remember to consider all forms of technology. While you may of course adapt an existing institution or technology, try instead to invent something 'new'. For example, assuming that you mean by equal, 'everyone five feet tall by age 21', there are a number of ways you might seek to have this achieved:

- Everyone over or under a certain height (or height range) could be killed.
- People over a certain height could be forced to crouch, or be bound and clothed so as to be reduced appropriately, or live

and move in special grooves, or live in height-group communities, or . . .

- People under a certain height could be required to wear high heels, or high hats, or ride horses, or bicycles, or use stilts, or be stretched, or . . .
- Groups of people who 'normally' deviate from the required height – for example, Japanese and Watusis – could be required to intermarry.
- Height-enhancing or inhibiting foods and/or drugs could be prescribed.
- People could undergo lengthening or shortening operations.
- Medical service could be encouraged to discover the 'height genes', and to manipulate them accordingly.
- Educational institutions could develop growth-oriented curricula, and grade people according to their limits to growth.
- Religious organizations could exhort people to 'grow right with God' and threaten hellfire to those who disobeyed.
- The national and/or artificial environment could be controlled so that people would be conditioned to 'grow right' without freedom and dignity, according to a schedule of reinforcements which would reward activity conductive to achieving and maintaining a proper height, and punish deviance.

4. Since you certainly will have more than one goal for your preferred society, see that they are mutually compatible. For example, many Americans say they want a society where everyone is 'free and equal'. On the face of it, that seems to be impossible. If everyone is free, they are not likely to be the same. If they must be equal, how can they be free – and different? By defining 'free' and 'equal' appropriately, you may be able to design such a society, but it will take care. Similarly, other goals must be operationalized so as to lessen incompatibility – or else the resulting dynamic tension must somehow be recognized and managed.

5. Since you presumably are designing a world that is not the world of today, what are you doing in your design to assure that it will stay as you want it to be, and not permit it to alter in undesirable ways? Note that I do not intend to imply here that you should prefer a stable world. You may prefer one in considerable flux. But how, then, can you prevent that world from stabilizing in un-

desired ways? In any event, how will you monitor the future of your world?

Source: *Visions of Desirable Societies*, edited by Eleanora Masini, Pergamon Press, 1996.

The Intelligent Planet

Michio Kaku, Professor of Theoretical Physics at the City University of New York, gives an upbeat overview of the twenty-first century in *Visions* (1998). By 2020, he calculates, microprocessors may be as cheap as scrap paper, scattered everywhere in the environment, giving us 'smart' homes, cars and jewellery that respond to us when we speak, and sense our presence and mood. They will be flattened into wall-screens or miniaturized to fit on to a wristwatch, spectacles or key chain. Since they will be linked to the Internet, we shall simply have to talk to them to access the entire planet's body of knowledge. The surface of the earth will become a 'living membrane' endowed with 'planetary intelligence'. It will be rather like living inside a Disney movie, where inanimate objects offer advice and crack jokes. The 'smart bathroom' may serve as a computerized nurse, discreetly analysing our urine, taking our pulse via the toilet seat, and sending the information silently to our doctor. By 2020, too, it may be possible to have access to our personal DNA code, showing our individual risk to future diseases, based on our inherited genes. A new generation of imaging machines, improving on current MRI scanning, may make it possible for doctors to detect potential problems decades before they develop. At the same time, new technologies such as 'smart molecules' may be used to attack diseases such as cancer. On a more mundane level, traffic jams will be cured by 'mass transit' – cars bunched six feet apart, travelling in unison, controlled by computer (a trial system is currently being installed on Interstate 15 north of San Diego). All these improvements and more are included in Kaku's 'Week in the Life' scenario of what life may be like in the year 2020 if you are an executive dealing with the latest technology (and, of course, rich and American).

6.30 a.m. June 1, 2020

A gentle ring wakes you up in the morning. A wall-sized picture of the seashore hanging silently on the wall suddenly springs to life, replaced by a warm, friendly face you have named Molly, who cheerily announces: 'It's time to wake up!'

As you walk into the kitchen, the appliances sense your presence. The coffeepot turns itself on. Bread is toasted to the setting you prefer. Your favorite music gently fills the air. The intelligent house is coming to life.

On the coffee table, Molly has printed out a personalized edition of the newspaper by scanning the Net. As you leave the kitchen, the refrigerator scans its contents and announces: 'You're out of milk. And the yogurt is sour.' Molly adds: 'We're low on computers. Pick up a dozen more at the market while you're at it.'

Most of your friends have bought 'intelligent agent' programs without faces or personalities. Some claim they get in the way; others prefer not to speak to their appliances. But you like the convenience of voice commands.

Before you leave, you instruct the robot vacuum cleaner to vacuum the carpet. It springs to life and, sensing the wire tracks hidden beneath the carpet, begins its job.

As you drive off to work in your electric/hybrid car, Molly has tapped into the Global Positioning System satellite orbiting overhead. 'There is a major delay due to construction on Highway 1,' she informs you. 'Here is an alternate route.' A map appears ghostlike on the windshield.

As you start driving along the smart highway, the traffic lights, sensing no other cars on this highway, all turn green. You whiz by the toll booths, which register your vehicle PIN number with their laser sensors and electronically charge your account. Molly's radar quietly monitors the cars around you. Her computer, suddenly detecting danger, blurts out, 'Watch out! There's a car behind you!' You narrowly miss a car in your blind spot. Once again, Molly may have saved your life. (Next time, you remind yourself, you will consider taking mass transit.)

At your office at Computer Genetics, a giant firm specializing in personalized DNA sequencing, you scan some video mail. A few bills. You insert your smart wallet card into the computer in the wall. A laser beam checks the iris of your eye for identification, and the transaction is done. Then at ten o'clock two staff members 'meet' with you via the wall screen.

4 p.m.

Molly informs you that it is time for your doctor's appointment. As Molly makes the connection, your virtual doctor appears on the wall screen. 'We picked up trace amounts of a certain protein in your urine. There is a microscopic cancer colony growing in your colon,' he says.

'Is that serious?' you ask anxiously.

'Probably not. No more than a few hundred cancer cells. We'll zap them with a few smart molecules.'

'And just out of curiosity, what would have happened before protein testing and smart molecules?' you ask.

'Well, in ten years, you would have developed a small tumor; at that point there would have been several billion cancer cells growing in your body, and your chances of survival would be about five percent.'

The virtual doctor frowns and says, 'We also used the new MRI machine to take a peek inside your arteries. At the present rate of plaque buildup, the computer calculates that within eight years, you will have an eighty percent increased risk of a heart attack. I'm video-mailing a strict program of exercise, relaxation, meditation, and yoga.'

Oh great, Molly will have one more function: that of your personal trainer.

Evening

That evening, you attend a company cocktail party. As you wander among the guests, the video camera in your glasses scans the faces in the crowd and Molly matches the faces with the computer profiles in her memory.

Molly whispers in your ear who each person is from a special miniature transmitter in your glasses.

By the end of the party, you've drunk a bit too much. Molly whispers, 'If you drink any more, the breath analyzer in the dashboard won't allow you to start the car.'

Midnight, Wednesday

You decide to do some last-minute shopping. 'Molly, put the virtual mall on the screen; I need to buy a new sweater.'

The wall screen flashes an image of a town mall. You wave your hands above the coffee table, and the video image changes, as if you are walking through the mall.

You pick out the sweater you want from the racks. You like the design, but the size is wrong. Fortunately, Molly maintains your precise 3-D measurements.

'Molly, I want a red sweater, not a blue one, but without those frills. Send the order, and put it on my smart card.'

Then you decide to house-hunt some apartments in the city and several beach houses in Europe. Pictures of apartments and beach houses in the price range you specified appear on the wall screen. You walk through them with your fingers.

Thursday night

You have no date for that weekend. On a whim, you tell Molly to scan the names of all the eligible single people in the area, matching them to your tastes and hobbies.

A list of faces appears on the screen, with a brief description beneath each picture.

'Well, Molly, whom do you think I should contact?'

'Well, I think numbers three and five look rather promising. They're an eighty-five percent match to your interests.' Molly then scans the facial features of each person and performs some computations on their facial measurements. 'Plus, I think numbers three and six are rather attractive, don't you?' Molly says. 'And don't forget number ten. Good parents.'

Molly has picked out the most austere, conservative-looking people in the group. Molly is beginning to sound just like your mother!

Saturday night

One of the people you picked from the list has agreed to go out with you.

You and your date go to a romantic restaurant, but just as you are about to eat, Molly scans your meal for its nutritional content. 'There's too much cholesterol in that food.'

You suddenly wonder if you can turn off Molly.

Afterward, the two of you decide to go back to your apartment to watch an old movie.

'Molly, I'd like to see *Casablanca*. But this time, could you replace Ingrid Bergman's and Humphrey Bogart's faces with ours?'

Molly downloads the movie off the Net and begins to reprogram all the faces in the movie.

Soon you see yourselves transported on the screen back to war-torn Morocco. You can't help but smile at the end of the movie as you see yourselves in the final scene at the airport, staring into each other's eyes.

'Here's looking at you, kid.'

Source: Michio Kaku, *Visions*, Oxford University Press, 1998.

Designer Children

On 23 February 1997, British scientists cloned a lamb (Dolly) from a single cell taken from an adult sheep. Cloning – a means of reproduction that has been compared to taking cuttings from plants – greatly facilitates genetic engineering. This is the process whereby scientists can alter or add specific genes to the genetic material present in the embryo, so that an individual will be born with characteristics he or she would not otherwise have had.

The long-term social consequences are predicted by Professor Lee M. Silver of Princeton University in his book *Remaking Eden* (1998). Human cloning, and the opportunities for genetic choice that it opens up, will, Silver estimates, have become practical possibilities by the middle of the twenty-first century. They will eventually enable affluent parents to have children who are immune to many physiological and mental diseases, among them breast cancer, AIDS, schizophrenia, manic depression, alcoholism, and obesity. These will become 'lower-class' disorders, and interest in finding methods of treatment for them will wane. Those without genetic exemption from them are likely to be considered unacceptable for life-insurance.

Governments and the Roman Catholic church have already expressed their hostility. The reaction of the British government to Dolly was to withdraw all research funding from her creator Ian Wilmut. When, in 1993, it was reported that two American scientists had cloned human embryos, the Vatican condemned it as a 'venture into the tunnel of madness', and the European Parliament voted unanimously to ban human cloning as 'unethical and morally repugnant'.

Silver argues plausibly, however, that governments will be powerless to check human cloning. In America, he points out, surrogate parenthood is widely practised even in states where it is outlawed. The indication is that no laws or regulations will prevent parents achieving their reproductive goals. The ready market for private education in Europe and America points to the same conclusion. Considerations of 'unfairness' will not prevent parents securing the best for their children. Many doctors and laboratories have already indicated that they will be willing to help parents have designer children. Even supposing such practitioners could be excluded from Europe and America, underdeveloped countries would, Silver points out, be happy to welcome them and reap the tax income.

Since with human cloning male sperm is not involved in the process of reproduction, men will, genetically speaking, become redundant. The feminists' dream of a man-free world will become a possibility. More seriously, humans will for the first time have the power to control the very nature of their species. The ideals of Francis Galton and the eugenics movement (see p. 393) will be realized, not by state-imposed eugenicist aims, as in Nazi Germany, but by the unconquerable power of parental love and ambition.

The results are worked out in Silver's account of American society in the year 2350.

The United States of America still exists, but it is a different place from the one familiar to you. The most striking difference is that the extreme polarization of society that began during the 1980s has now reached its logical conclusion, with all people belonging to one of two classes. The people of one class are referred to as *Naturals*, while those in the second class are called the *Gene-enriched* or simply the *GenRich*.

These new classes of society cut across what used to be traditional racial and ethnic lines. In fact, so much mixing has occurred during the last three hundred years that sharp divisions according to race – black versus white versus Asian – no longer exist. Instead, the American populace has finally become the racial melting pot that earlier leaders had long hoped for. The skin color of Americans comes in all shades from African brown to Scandinavian pink, and traditional Asian facial features are present to a greater or lesser extent in a large percentage of Americans as well.

But while racial differences have mostly disappeared, another difference has emerged that is sharp and easily defined. It is the difference between those who are genetically enhanced and those who are not. The GenRich – who account for 10 percent of the American population – all carry synthetic genes. Genes that were created in the laboratory and did not exist within the human species until twenty-first-century reproductive geneticists began to put them there. The GenRich are a modern-day hereditary class of genetic aristocrats.

Some of the synthetic genes carried by present-day members of the

GenRich class were already carried by their parents. These genes were transmitted to today's GenRich the old-fashioned way, from parent to child through sperm or egg. But other synthetic genes are new to the present generation. These were placed into GenRich embryos through the application of genetic engineering techniques shortly after conception.

The GenRich class is anything but homogeneous. There are many types of GenRich families, and many subtypes within each type. For example, there are GenRich athletes who can trace their descent back to professional sports players from the twenty-first century. One subtype of GenRich athlete is the GenRich football player, and a sub-subtype is the GenRich running back. Embryo selection techniques have been used to make sure that a GenRich running back has received all of the natural genes that made his unenhanced foundation ancestor excel at the position. But in addition, at each generation beyond the foundation ancestor, sophisticated genetic enhancements have accumulated so that the modern-day GenRich running back can perform in a way not conceivable for any unenhanced Natural. Of course, all professional baseball, football, and basketball players are special GenRich subtypes. After three hundred years of selection and enhancement, these GenRich individuals all have athletic skills that are clearly 'nonhuman' in the traditional sense. It would be impossible for any Natural to compete.

Another GenRich type is the GenRich scientist. Many of the synthetic genes carried by the GenRich scientist are the same as those carried by all other members of the GenRich class, including some that enhance a variety of physical and mental attributes, as well as others that provide resistance to all known forms of human disease. But in addition, the present-day GenRich scientist has accumulated a set of particular synthetic genes that work together with his 'natural' heritage to produce an enhanced scientific mind. Although the GenRich scientist may appear to be different from the GenRich athlete, both GenRich types have evolved by a similar process. The foundation ancestor for the modern GenRich scientist was a bright twenty-first-century scientist whose children were the first to be selected and enhanced to increase their chances of becoming even brighter scientists who could produce even more brilliant children. There are numerous other GenRich types including GenRich businessmen, GenRich musicians, GenRich artists, and even GenRich intellectual generalists who all evolved in the same way.

Not all present-day GenRich individuals can trace their foundation ancestors back to the twenty-first century, when genetic enhancement was first perfected. During the twenty-second and even the twenty-third centuries, some Natural families garnered the financial wherewithal required to place their children into the GenRich class. But with the passage of time, the genetic distance between Naturals and the GenRich has become greater and greater, and now there is little movement up from the Natural to GenRich class. It seems fair to say that society is on the verge of reaching the final point of complete polarization.

All aspects of the economy, the media, the entertainment industry, and the knowledge industry are controlled by members of the GenRich class. GenRich parents can afford to send their children to private schools rich in the resources required for them to take advantage of their enhanced genetic potential. In contrast, Naturals work as low-paid service providers or as laborers, and their children go to public schools. But twenty-fourth-century public schools have little in common with their predecessors from the twentieth century. Funds for public education have declined steadily since the beginning of the twenty-first century, and now Natural children are only taught the basic skills they need to perform the kinds of tasks they'll encounter in the jobs available to members of their class.

There is still some intermarriage as well as sexual intermingling between a few GenRich individuals and Naturals. But, as one might imagine, GenRich parents put intense pressure on their children not to dilute their expensive genetic endowment in this way. And as time passes, the mixing of the classes will become less and less frequent for reasons of both environment and genetics.

The environmental reason is clear enough: GenRich and Natural children grow up and live in segregated social worlds where there is little chance for contact between them. The genetic reason, however, was unanticipated.

It is obvious to everyone that with each generation of enhancement, the genetic distance separating the GenRich and Naturals is growing larger and larger. But a startling consequence of the expanding genetic distance has just come to light. In a nationwide survey of the few interclass GenRich–Natural couples that could be identified, sociologists have discovered an astounding 90 percent level of infertility. Reproductive geneticists have examined these couples and come to the conclusion that the infertility is caused primarily by an incompatibility between the genetic makeup of each member.

Evolutionary biologists have long observed instances in which otherwise fertile individuals taken from two separate populations prove infertile when mated to each other. And they tell the sociologists and the reproductive geneticists what is going on: the process of species separation between the GenRich and Naturals has already begun. Together, the sociologists, the reproductive geneticists, and the evolutionary biologists are willing to make the following prediction: If the accumulation of genetic knowledge and advances in genetic enhancement technology continue at the present rate, then by the end of the third millennium, the GenRich class and the Natural class will become the GenRich humans and the Natural humans – entirely separate species with no ability to cross-breed, and with as much romantic interest in each other as a current human would have for a chimpanzee.

Source: Lee M. Silver, *Remaking Eden: Cloning and Beyond in a Brave New World*, Weidenfeld and Nicolson, 1998.

Acknowledgements

I have been greatly helped by discussions with and suggestions from a number of people in the generation of this book. In particular I should like to express my gratitude to Dinah Birch, David Bradshaw, Angelique Corthals, Maggie Gee, Barbara Goodwin, David Leopold, Julian Loose, Richard McCabe, Nick Rankin and Jessica Rawson. Readers of Frank E. and Fritzie P. Manuel's *Utopian Thought in the Western World* (Blackwell, 1979) will understand how much I have profited from their formidable learning, and I should like to place my debt to them on record.

J.C.

For permission to publish copyright material in this book grateful acknowledgement is made to the following:

ANONYMOUS: 'The Tale of the Shipwrecked Sailor' from *The Tale of Sinuhe and Other Ancient Egyptian Poems, 1940–1640 BC*, translated by R. B. Parkinson (Oxford University Press, 1997), by permission of the publisher; GRACCHUS BABEUF: from *The Defense of Gracchus Babeuf before the High Court of Vendome*, translated by John Anthony Scott, with an Essay by Herbert Marcuse and Illustrations by Thomas Cornell (University of Massachusetts Press, 1967; originally published by Leonard Baskin's Gehenna Press, Northampton, Massachusetts, 1964), by kind permission of John Anthony Scott; JULIAN BARNES: from *A History of the World in 10½ Chapters* (Jonathan Cape, 1989), by permission of the Peters Fraser & Dunlop Group Ltd and Random House UK Ltd; KATHARINE BURDEKIN: from *Swastika Night* (Victor Gollancz, 1937), © Katharine Burdekin 1937, by permission of A. M. Heath & Co Ltd on behalf of the Estate of the Late Katharine Burdekin; ETIENNE CABET: from *Journey through Utopia*, translated by Marie Louise

ACKNOWLEDGEMENTS

Bernini (Freedom Press, 1982), by permission of the publisher; ITALO CALVINO: from *Invisible Cities*, translated by William Weaver (Secker & Warburg, 1974), by permission of Random House UK Ltd; TOMMASO CAMPANELLA: from *The City of the Sun: A Poetical Dialogue*, translated with an Introduction and Notes by Daniel J. Donno (University of California Press, 1981), © 1981 The Regents of the University of California, by permission of the publisher; JIM DATOR: from *Visions of Desirable Societies*, edited by Eleanora Masini (Pergamon Press, 1996), by permission of the author; ANTOINE NICOLAS DE CONDORCET: from *Sketch for a Historical Picture of the Progress of the Human Mind*, translated by June Barraclough (Weidenfeld & Nicolson, 1955), by permission of The Orion Publishing Group; MARQUIS DE SADE: from *Justine, Philosophy in the Bedroom, Eugenie de Franval and Other Writings*, translated by Richard Seaver and Austryn Wainhouse (Arrow Books, 1991), by permission of Random House UK Ltd; FREEMAN J. DYSON: 'The World, the Flesh and the Devil', The Third J. D. Bernal Lecture Delivered at Birkbeck College, 1972, by kind permission of the author; MICHIO KAKU: from *Visions: How Science Will Revolutionize the 21st Century and Beyond* (Oxford University Press, 1998), © 1997 by Michio Kaku, by permission of Doubleday, a division of Random House, Inc.; JAMES HILTON: from *Lost Horizon* (Macmillan, 1933), © the Estate of James Hilton, by permission of Curtis Brown Ltd, London, on behalf of the Estate of James Hilton; ADOLF HITLER: from *Hitler's Table Talk, 1941–1944*, translated by Norman Cameron and R. H. Stevens (Weidenfeld & Nicolson, 1953), by permission of The Orion Publishing Group; ALDOUS HUXLEY: from *The Doors of Perception* (Chatto & Windus, 1954) and *Island* (Chatto & Windus, 1962), by permission of Mrs Laura Huxley and Random House UK Ltd; RUDYARD KIPLING: from *The Jungle Book* (1894), by permission of A. P. Watt Ltd on behalf of The Natural Trust for Places of Historic Interest or Natural Beauty; D. H. LAWRENCE: from *Etruscan Places* (Martin Secker, 1932), by permission of Laurence Pollinger Ltd and the Estate of Frieda Lawrence Ravagli; EDWARD LEAR: from *Edward Lear* by Vivien Noakes (William Collins, 1968), by kind permission of Vivien Noakes; KARL MARX: from *Critique of the Gotha Programme, with Appendices by Marx, Engels, and Lenin* (Lawrence & Wishart, 1938), by permission of the publisher; NAOMI MITCHISON: from *Solution Three* (Dennis

Dobson, 1975), by permission of David Higham Associates Ltd;
GEORGE ORWELL: from *Nineteen Eighty-Four* (Secker & Warburg,
1949), © George Orwell, 1949, by permission of A. M. Heath &
Co Ltd on behalf of Martin Secker & Warburg Ltd and Mark
Hamilton as the Literary Executor of the Estate of the Late Sonia
Brownell Orwell; MARGE PIERCY: from *Woman on the Edge of Time*,
first published in Great Britain by The Women's Press Ltd, 1979, 34
Great Sutton Street, London EC1V OLQ, by permission of Sheil Land
Associates; PLATO: from *The Republic of Plato*, translated with an
Introduction and Notes by Francis MacDonald Cornford (Oxford
University Press, 1941), by permission of the publisher; TAO QIAN:
from 'Account of Peach Blossom' in *An Anthology of Chinese Litera-
ture: Beginnings to 1911*, edited and translated by Stephen Owen
(Norton, 1996), © 1996 by Stephen Owen and The Council for
Cultural Planning and Development of the Executive Yuan of the
Republic of China, by permission of W. W. Norton & Company,
Inc.; JEAN-JACQUES ROUSSEAU: from *The Social Contract: Discourses*.
Introduction by G. D. H. Cole (J. M. Dent & Sons, 1913), by
permission of Everyman's Library, David Campbell Publishers Ltd;
ST IRENAEUS: from *The Ante-Nicene Fathers: Translations of the
Fathers down to AD 325*, edited by Rev. Alexander Roberts, DD, and
James Donaldson, LL. D (T. & T. Clark, 1989), by kind permission of
the publisher; HENRI SAINT-SIMON: from *Selected Writings on Science,
Industry and Social Organisation*, translated with an Introduction
and Notes by Keith Taylor (Croom Helm, 1975), by permission of
Routledge Ltd; LEE M. SILVER: from *Remaking Eden: Cloning and
Beyond in a Brave New World* (Weidenfeld & Nicolson, 1998),
by permission of The Orion Publishing Group; H. G. WELLS: from
*Anticipations of the Reaction of Mechanical and Scientific Progress
upon Human Life and Thought* (Chapman & Hall, 1901), by permission of A. P. Watt Ltd on behalf of The Literary Executors of the
Estate of H. G. Wells; W. B. YEATS: from *A Vision* (Macmillan, 1981)
and 'The Lake Isle of Innisfree' from *Collected Poems* (Picador,
1990), by permission of A. P. Watt Ltd and Michael B. Yeats.

Every effort has been made to trace or contact all copyright holders.
The publishers would be pleased to rectify any omissions brought to
their notice at the earliest opportunity.

Index of Authors

Index